Studies in Economic History

Aims and Scope

This series from Springer provides a platform for works in economic history that truly integrate economics and history. Books on a wide range of related topics are welcomed and encouraged, including those in macro-economic history, financial history, labor history, industrial history, agricultural history, the history of institutions and organizations, spatial economic history, law and economic history, political economic history, historical demography, and environmental history.

Economic history studies have greatly developed over the past several decades through application of economics and econometrics. Particularly in recent years, a variety of new economic theories and sophisticated econometric techniques—including game theory, spatial economics, and generalized method of moment (GMM)—have been introduced for the great benefit of economic historians and the research community.

At the same time, a good economic history study should contribute more than just an application of economics and econometrics to past data. It raises novel research questions, proposes a new view of history, and/or provides rich documentation. This series is intended to integrate data analysis, close examination of archival works, and application of theoretical frameworks to offer new insights and even provide opportunities to rethink theories.

The purview of this new Springer series is truly global, encompassing all nations and areas of the world as well as all eras from ancient times to the present. The editorial board, who are internationally renowned leaders among economic historians, carefully evaluate and judge each manuscript, referring to reports from expert reviewers. The series publishes contributions by university professors and others well established in the academic community, as well as work deemed to be of equivalent merit.

All books and chapters in the Studies in Economic History book series are indexed in Scopus.

Hikaru Tanaka

Micro-Credit in Modern Japan

An Alternative Financial System for Sustainable Development

Springer

Hikaru Tanaka
Chuo University
Tokyo, Japan

ISSN 2364-1797 ISSN 2364-1800 (electronic)
Studies in Economic History
ISBN 978-981-97-6939-1 ISBN 978-981-97-6940-7 (eBook)
https://doi.org/10.1007/978-981-97-6940-7

Translation from the Japanese language edition: "Mouhitotsuno Kinyu Shisutemu—Kindai Nihon to Maikuro Kurejitto (Another financial system: Modern Japan and Micro-credit)" by Hikaru Tanaka,

This Springer imprint is published by the registered company Springer Nature Singapore Pte Ltd.
The registered company address is: 152 Beach Road, #21-01/04 Gateway East, Singapore 189721, Singapore

Preface to the English Version

This book consists of a detailed exploration of the micro-credit that supported the development of regional economies and stability of rural livelihoods and communities in modern Japan. As it covers small-lot financing, this is classified as research in the field of financial history. For that reason, as I proceeded with the research, I often faced uncourteous questions that I was dealing with insignificant case examples, such as "Did such small-amount loans helped to raise national productivity?" and "Can you say that the presence of such small-sized management entities was able to promote regional economies?" I used to be told to research about much more "significant" financial cases, such as mega banks or big companies' financial management.

The Novel Prize by Grameen Bank's micro-credit case may perhaps attribute global acknowledgement of the new knowledge in economics. Though the fact that micro-credit contributes to the prevention and alleviation of poverty was not recognized as seriously compelling in Japanese society. Micro-credit and its resource in Japan, the subject of the analysis in this book, was supported by postal savings and agricultural cooperatives, and as these financial institutions were such everyday matters for men and women of all ages living in Japan, and therefore they were not recognized as something important. In most of Japanese minds, these organizations are far distant from hard stories about big banks and stock markets that make up the financial news. These Japanese atmosphere made the questions and criticism to this book's research at the beginning. Nobody in Japan believed that 10-yen coins lying around in the kitchen were going to have an impact that significantly swayed the Japanese economy.

The aggregation of savings that ordinary people accumulated in nonprofit financial institutions closely attached to their everyday life, or what this book describes as popular funds, has occupied an important position that could never be ignored in the Japanese economy since its formation at the beginning of the 20th century and up to the present time. Japan's postal savings, while they followed a path toward privatization in the 2000s, still boast of one of the largest concentrations of savings in the world as a single financial institution, and Norinchukin Bank, the central organization of Japanese agricultural cooperatives, is functioning as one of the largest financial funds in the world.

However, when I pointed out the sheer size of funds held by these nonprofit financial institutions and the importance of analyzing their management, my research invited another round of criticism. The critics included those who said that "we now understand the presence of massive funds, but of what use were such funds? There is nothing remarkable or famous about them. We suspect that the presence of such small-amount financing rather prolonged inefficient sectors and that such unnecessary loans helped preserve Japan's inefficient business management and feudalistic customary practices."

It is true that most of the cases of micro-credit in this book include the provision of loans to small-scale management entities, for instance, self-employed businesses such as agriculture and small- and medium-sized enterprises, as well as funds for supporting the livelihoods of rural households. There is no direct evidence that the management of these borrowers spectacularly contributed to Japan's industrial revolution or technological innovation. At the same time, however, such small-scale management entities were indeed the economic entities that accounted for the main part of the Japanese economy from the modern period and up to the present. The farming population that accounted for half of the country's total population around World War II did decrease significantly later, but at the present time in the 2020s, 99% of Japanese companies are still small- and medium-sized firms that employ 70% of all domestic workers. Disregarding these small-scale management entities that comprise the greater part of Japanese society would be tantamount to neglecting the very foundations of the Japanese economy itself.

To begin with, the role that the "other financial system" created by the popular funds covered by this book played in the Japanese economy was not "leading Japan's economic growth by investing such funds in sectors with the best production efficiency or in cutting-edge sectors." This role was to be played by large corporations supported by the ordinary financial system backed up by big banks and stock markets. The financial system supported by popular funds examined in this book functioned instead to "create and maintain economic foundations that may have a relatively low efficiency but were broadly necessary for the stability and development of society."

Furthermore, these popular funds were used not only for micro-credit in rural communities but also for investment in rural infrastructure and as funds for measures to counter unemployment. Popular funds formed in modern Japan were managed by placing emphasis on reproduction in rural communities to help those areas and households to survive and develop, if possible, instead of giving importance to efficiency in production and investment. The maintenance of a broad-based stable society through this safety-net financial function supported the development of diverse regional economies in Japan.

This "alternative financial system" has played the role of "shadow work," so to speak, in the financial sector. In that sense, this book aims not only to verify the economic importance of micro-credit based on case examples of modern Japan but also points out the social and economic importance of the function of nonprofit financial institutions, often overlooked from the existing viewpoint of financial history.

I have examined unsorted historical documents at actual rural sites, not only in museums or archives for years to collect resources for this research. When I first visited Seinaiji Village as part of a practical intensive course of historical research led by Prof. Yoshida Nobuyuki of the Department of Japanese History, Faculty of Letters, University of Tokyo, I was just an undergraduate student in Faculty of Economics. The JA [Japan Agricultural Cooperative] Kanō branch generously welcomed an unknown young girl who claimed to be a graduate student from Tokyo and requested for access to the Coop's historical old documents. And they also helpfully introduced me to the home of descendants of the founder of the Kanō industrial cooperative, the roots of the agricultural cooperative. A Staff of JA took me to the founder's house by car, which passed by apple orchards and vineyards on a rolling hill. The founder, the Fukai family's house, is shaded by tall, bright green pine trees. The Fukai family also generously allowed the outsider who claimed to be a researcher from Tokyo without any guaranteed name card, to use a private Japanese-style *zashiki* hall room for viewing the old documents and treated with their fresh fruits from the family garden.

While a local railway station was located nearby, people from the Fukai family and the JA Kanō branch barely move around without automobiles these days. In modern era, the time before the spread of automobiles, it was far more difficult for local residents than present business trips to collect information of the demand in the global markets and urban areas, or to go to Nagano City and Tokyo to gather information. However, there were people who continued to make such actions for their rural communities. I believe that some of individuals in this book's cases, they found it possible and easy to choose the option of moving to the more prosperous urban areas rather than live in their rural communities. In reality, however, many people stayed in rural communities in modern Japan and wished to develop the rural areas where they were born and brought up.

At present in the 21st century, the overconcentration of people and wealth in the capital is turning into a political issue in Japan. The decline of regional economies and depopulation of rural areas have been considered serious social problems from the millennium began. This indicates that the structure of social reproduction in rural communities that supports regional economies is beginning to crumble. By examining the types of financial systems that underpinned the development of regional economies in Japan since the latter half of the 19th century to 20th century, this book aims to consider anew what kind of economic system is needed to maintain economic development and social stability in rural areas.

In carrying out the research for this book and translating it, I received assistance from a large number of people and organizations.

I am much obliged to everyone in the Kanō branch of JA Shinshū Ueda and Mr. Hotta Yūji of the Tōmi City Office for their assistance in finding materials about the Kanō industrial cooperative and Kanō Village Office. I am extremely grateful to Mr. and Mrs. Fukai, who readily accepted the outsider who suddenly appeared. It was a particularly extraordinary experience to have the opportunity to read the documents in the space where the late Mr. Fukai Isao, the founder and the first president of the Kanō industrial cooperative, himself actually lived and managed the cooperative.

I was greatly helped by the people of the former Seinaiji Village. I learned a great deal not only from the materials but also by listening to Mr. and Mrs. Hara of the post office and other villagers about the present ways of life in Seinaiji Village. With respect to the Deposit Bureau of the Ministry of Finance, I was much obliged to Mr. Yamamoto Junsei, formerly with the ministry's Financial Bureau, to whom I was introduced by Wakayama Tarō, for the information provided by him.

The National Archives of Japan, the Postal and Telecommunication Museum of Japan, the Nagano Prefectural Museum of History, the Numazu City Archives of Meiji History, the Hiroshima Prefectural Library, the Matsudo City Museum, the Mishima City Local Museum, the Mishima Municipal Higashi Elementary School and Minami Elementary School, the Shizuoka Prefectural Central Library, and the Hiroshima City Museum of History and Traditional Crafts also provided me with great assistance. I also wish to express my gratitude to the University of Tokyo Library System, and the Library for Social Sciences at Kobe University.

I would also like to express my deepest gratitude to those who shared their opinions with me at workshops, etc. In particular, I owe much to members of the study group on "Seinaiji history and culture" for long years of assistance and particularly to Kojima Yōhei and Chiba Takuma for their help with research related to Kanō Village. In addition, it would not have been possible to access materials on Kanō Village without an introduction by Prof. Kase Kazutoshi of the Institute of Social Science, the University of Tokyo. Prof. Ueda Kenji of Soka University was of great assistance in helping me to access informational documents related to the former Nihon Kangyō Bank. I also greatly appreciate the numerous opinions and advice offered by Prof. Saitō Osamu, Prof. Takeda Haruhito, and Prof. Tanimoto Masayuki.

Furthermore, I owe much to the guidance provided by Prof. Yoshida Nobuyuki and Prof Suzuki Jun, who taught me, since the days when I was still literally uncertain of reading historical materials, how to read through written and unwritten portions of historical materials and ways to look for historical materials. Prof. Nakamura Naofumi patiently looked after me over many years, and I am grateful to Prof. Okazaki Tetsuji, my supervising professor, who went to a great deal of trouble to assist my research. I am deeply obliged to them all.

I was greatly assisted by Lingua Guild, Inc. in Tokyo, and Steven Ivings of Kyoto University for the translation of this book. I am profoundly grateful for their services.

Finally, I am sincerely thankful to my parents.

Tokyo, Japan Hikaru Tanaka

Contents

About the Author

Dr. Hikaru Tanaka received her undergraduate, master's, and Ph.D. degrees in Economics from the University of Tokyo. Her research focuses on Japanese socio-economic history, with a particular emphasis on the impact of economic systems on the lives of ordinary individuals during the industrialization process. By traveling to various local areas, she is able to identify both universal and unique aspects of history. In 2018, the Business History Society of Japan awarded her an encouragement award in recognition of her contributions to the field. Following a period of service for several years at Kobe University, the author is currently employed as an associate professor at Chuo University.

List of Figures

List of Tables

Chapter 1
Personal Small Savings and Japan's Economic Development

1.1 Network of Popular Funds that Underpinned Japan's Modernization

It is beyond reasonable doubt that the financial system is essential for the economy. The circulation of funds, "the blood of the economy," is indispensable for smooth daily economic activities, playing a critical role in a nation's economic growth, in the daily operations of corporations, and in the daily lives of individuals. Therefore, countries that have up to now developed into advanced or industrial nations have a well-developed financial system of one form or another, be it the banking system or the stock market. Japan is no exception.

In Japan, the banking system is attached the highest value among the national financial system. Japanese modern banking system was established since the legislation of the National Bank Act in 1872, after the Meiji Restoration had triggered the modernization process. As the Bank of Japan, the central bank of Japan was established in 1882, many private banks' activity supported nation-wide vigorous entrepreneurships. Japanese private banks developed pyramid-shaped financial relationships between the BOJ in proportion to the scale of each capital that this system set the BOJ on the top and enabled big private banks to supply sufficient loans to their affiliated companies smoothly. This financial structure is known as "multi-layered financial structure",[1] inherited in the post WWII Japanese economy and took a main role in the postwar financial protection policy known as "convoy system" which lasted until 1990s.

In the other hand, highlighting this Japanese financial main stream may risk ignoring huge part of Japanese economy around twentieth century. Because the most of Japanese households were small-size farmers or self-employed people. They were

[1] Tsurumi Masayoshi, "*Nihon Shinyō Kikō no Kakuritsu—Nihon Ginkō to Kinyū Shijō (The Establishment of Japanese Banking System—The Bank of Japan and Financial Markets)*," Yūhikaku Publishing, 1991.

H. Tanaka, *Micro-Credit in Modern Japan*, Studies in Economic History,
https://doi.org/10.1007/978-981-97-6940-7_1

not affluent enough to obtain credit from private banks, but their economic growth was not negligible in modern Japanese economy.

In twenty-first century, to prevent poverty and support these kind of small-size self-employed business, we consider to use power of micro-finance. The economic effects of small-amount finance, or loans for ordinary people, mainly middle- and low-income earners in rural regions, also called micro-credit and micro-finance, has drawn keen attention in recent years, particularly after Muhammad Yunus was awarded the Nobel Peace Prize in 2006 for pioneering the concepts of micro-credit and micro-credit through the Grameen Bank.

The Grameen Bank provided low-income populations in the rural areas of Bangladesh, one of the world's poorest countries, with financial opportunities, albeit in small amounts. Such small-amount finance, generally supplied at interest rates lower than loans provided by private financial institutions, has been credited with paving the way for poor farmers to rise out of poverty. Following in the footsteps of the Grameen Bank's achievements, a large number of non-governmental organizations (NGOs) have also undertaken similar initiatives in many parts of the world.[2]

However, if it was asked whether the Grameen Bank was the first to take the initiative for small-amount finance for middle- and low-income individuals at such low interest rates, the answer is no. Cooperative movements in multiple countries and regions have been providing small-amount finance opportunities in regional economies since the nineteenth century. Moreover, while small-lot finance by NGOs in the twenty-first century, including the Grameen Bank, often depended on foreign capital rather than the local regions for their foundational funding, cooperative movements are characterized by their basic dependence on funds contributed by local individuals. Cooperative small-lot financial institutions, including those in Japan, are also characterized by democratic management within cooperatives based on cooperative unionism.

Japanese financial system includes these cooperative small-lot financial institutions. And there are also state-owned financial institutions for non-profit purpose loans. The Postal Savings and the Ministry of Finance Deposit Bureau which managed the Postal Savings deposits were the biggest financial institution in such non-profit public financial organizations in Japan. The Postal Savings Bank, which was privatized in 2007 is still the most common depository institution in Japanese society. This book calls this financial system as the "alternative financial system" consisting of non-profit financial organizations and their network, which was developed along with the "multi-layered financial structure" expansion and Japanese economic development.

And there is another feature in Japanese financial system in macroeconomic perspective. That is, the scale of households savings. The Japanese are often referred to as keen savers.[3] In fact, there are perhaps few Japanese at present who do not

---

[2] Muhammad Yunus, *Creating a World without Poverty: Social Business and the Future of Capitalism*, Public Affairs, 2008.

[3] Karel Van Wolferen, "*Ningen wo Kōfuku ni Shinai Nippon to Iu Shisutemu (The False Realities of a Politicized Society)*," The Mainichi Newspapers, 1994, p. 59.

have a bank account. If postal savings accounts, on top of bank deposit accounts, are included, it is not uncommon that adolescents have an account. Indeed, it is quite common in contemporary Japanese society for individuals to open accounts at multiple financial institutions.

This indicates that it has become a social norm in Japan for individuals to routinely create deposits and savings, and deposit them in banks, post offices and various other financial institutions. The fact that deposits and savings have been accumulated at financial institutions indicates that they are being managed in the financial system as funds for investment. In Japan, the basic macroeconomic model that regards deposits and savings as investment has been realized through domestic financial institutions.

When did this oft-mentioned tradition of savings become habitual in Japan? What position have personal savings occupied or what role have they played in the Japanese economy? In particular, what impact have the personal small savings of the general public, that is, middle or low-income earners, or by women and children, who are not the main income earners in most households, had on the Japanese economy?

Generally speaking, or as economists tend to suggest, what is assumed by the term 'financial system' is, in many cases, the private banking system or the securities market, including the stock market. Here the behavior of financial institutions, most of all megabanks, how they behave on the capital market and how they provide funds to other industries, has been the focus of attention.

However, little consideration has been paid to how deposits and savings, the resources for funding investment and management actions of financial institutions, were collected and with what intentions such household funds found their way to financial institutions. Additionally, how these funds contributed to households, the original suppliers of the funds, is often overlooked. The economic impact of routine savings by people on a nation's economy has almost never been the direct subject of academic research.

When retracing the growth of the Japanese economy, in particular the history of industrialization in modern times, it is clear that there was a nationwide growth which included the development of regional economies and small businesses, instead of a centralized pattern of growth concentrated only on the capital city and large corporations. This is in contrast to the pattern of economic growth seen in developing countries in recent years. Japan in the Meiji period, for example, was a country where "the national economy was formed with few regional disparities," as Ishii Kanji pointed out, and marked it "one of the limited eras which could fittingly be termed as 'an era of regions'".[4] Nakamura Naofumi also argued for the significance of the growth of regional economies, describing the period from the latter half of the nineteenth century to the early twentieth century as "'the era of regions', a rarity in Japanese history, which witnessed the emergence of an economic structure displaying few regional disparities as a result of the regional dispersion of industries." He wrote that "regions at the time and the various economic entities or organizations in them assumed the task of developing the basic infrastructure that served as the foundation

[4] Ishii Kanji, "*Taikei Nihon no Rekishi 12—Kaikoku to Ishin (Compendium of Japanese History 12—The Opening of Japan and the Meiji Restoration)*," Shogakukan, 1989, p. 56.

of the industrial revolution [in Japan] and in so doing played a significant role in this process".[5]

Statistics indicate that national economic development at the time was achieved with the simultaneous development of the industrial sector and the agricultural sector, with rural regions the suppliers of labor and raw materials to the industrial sector.[6] In other words, the success of Japan as an industrial nation was achieved not only thanks to the success of a limited number of large corporations in urban areas but also on the basis of the success of a broad range of industries, including agriculture, in rural regions.

This raises the question of what were the conditions that underpinned the pattern of economic growth in modern Japan in which growth was supported by the development of small and medium-sized self-employed individuals, including those in the agricultural sector, and the growth of small and medium-sized companies across Japan? What sort of systems supported Japan's economic growth in which regular people all over the country played an important role, rather than government and large corporations dominating?

With the awareness of such issues, this book provides a new focus to the role of the financial system in modern Japan. Finance by the so-called big banks, or, Japan's "multi-layered financial structure",[7] which incorporates big banks with the Bank of Japan at the summit, as described by Ishii Kanji, is not, however, the financial network that this book sets out to analyze. The financial system this book takes up and focuses on concerns the functions of various financial institutions managed with massive funds created by the aforementioned accumulation of savings by the general public in Japan. Since modern times, the bulk of savings, which should be called popular funds, formed by the personal small savings of people, were accumulated not only at banks but also at post offices for savings, and cooperative financial institutions (industrial cooperatives in prewar Japan). These financial institutions operated by management entities differing from private companies, such as local governments and cooperatives, played important roles in regional economies in modern Japan. One of these roles, and the function to which this book gives most attention, is the supply of small-amount credit, or micro-finance to local sites in regional economies.

As is well known, Amartya Sen attempted to capture the essence of such measures by "human development," or the concept of capability to measure indicators such as improvements in the health and education levels of individuals, political freedom, as well as the presence or absence of financial opportunities.[8] The affluence by region

---

[5] Nakamura Naofumi, "*Chihō Kara no Sangyō Kakumei (The Industrial Revolution from the Countryside)*," The University of Nagoya Press, 2010, p. ii.

[6] Nakamura Takafusa, "*Senzenki Nihon Keizai Seichō no Bunseki (An Analysis of Economic Growth in Prewar Japan)*," Iwanami Shoten, 1971.

[7] Ishii Kanji, "*Nihon Keizaishi Dai 2han (Japanese Economic History Second Edition)*," The University of Tokyo Press, 1991, Chap. 4.

[8] Amartya Sen, *Development as Freedom*, Alfred A. Knopf, 1999.

Based on this theory, beginning in 1990, the United Nations has also utilized the Human Development Index (HDI), which incorporates the average life expectancy and the idea of educational levels such as school attendance rate and literacy rate in assessing the development level of a nation.

and social bracket in a given country and their differences cannot be captured by measuring them in terms of economic growth alone, in particular by using such indicators as the growth of gross domestic product (GDP).

In other words, the presence or absence of economic support for regional economies and middle- and low-income people through micro-credit itself is starting to become an indicator of the equitable development of a national economy. While the provision of opportunities by small-amount finance in a regional economy is a means of promoting a regional economy, it also represents the reallocation of funds by a financial method and is consciously intended to be a means of correcting disparities.

However, little attention has been given to this function of reallocation by finance in the context of the reallocation of funds under fiscal-based social security policy and the welfare state. For example, Gøsta Esping-Andersen classified welfare states into three types—liberal, corporatist and social democratic regimes. He pointed out that in liberal states, such as the United States, the reallocation of income and assets is held to the minimum, and thus disparities arise in the markets between the working class and the higher class to create "the hierarchy-based political double structure." On the other hand, he argues, in social democratic welfare states in Scandinavia, the powerful reallocation function through state finance holds back such class differentiation and realizes a society with higher equality.

In this classification, postwar Japanese society is positioned as a corporatist welfare state supported by both the government and corporate sector, close to the continental European model. Though described as corporatist, when compared with Germany and other continental European countries, security provided by the state is relatively weak and left to the market in Japan, with stronger liberal aspects.[9]

The welfare state model by Esping-Andersen gives weight to the labor market as a factor conducive to class disparities and primarily assumes that the disparities are to be eliminated by full employment and reallocation under pension and social insurance policies. In this context, the reallocation of financial funds is not necessarily considered as a positive way to correct disparities, since it is not direct reallocation of income and assets such as pensions and various benefits funded by taxation and intra-corporate reserves.

However, as suggested earlier by Sen, who regards the presence or absence of financial opportunities itself as an indicator of free and fair allocation, small-amount finance indicates a reallocation method on a track differing from the method through social welfare and social policies financed by fiscal funds.

It is generally acknowledged that the deepening of industrialization not only stimulates a nation's economic growth, it also widens the gap between the rich and the poor.[10] However, popular funds and the small-amount finance that is supported by them are believed to have successfully corrected social disequalization from the

---

In addition, democracy in management, which is embraced by the system of cooperatives, is often counted as one of the indicators of political freedom.

[9] Gøsta Esping-Andersen, "*Fukushi Shihonshugi no Mittsu no Sekai (The Three Worlds of Welfare Capitalism)*," Minerva Shobo, 2001.

[10] Karl Marx, "*Shihonron (The Capital)*," Vol. 1, Otsuki Shoten, 1968 (The original work, Vol. 1, 1867); Simon Kuznets, "Economic Growth and Income Inequality", *American Economic Review*,

financial side. This book is designed to clarify in concrete detail the financial system backed by popular funds, which in modern Japan played the role of providing small-amount finance as a means of promoting regional economies and, at the same time, a means of mitigating widening of disparities.

1.2 Subject of Analysis and Positioning in History of Study

The subject of this book is the process of accumulating savings, including how savings were formed by people and the financial institutions or organizations that accumulated and handled such personal small savings. Hence, this book addresses principally postal savings and funds amassed at industrial cooperatives, as well as their management.[11] While these organizations are financial institutions, the postal savings system is operated by the state and does not itself engage in the lending business. While industrial cooperatives are private organizations, they are not banks, and as cooperatives they are managed as not-for-profit organizations. They are also characterized by a democratic form of management under the one-member-one-vote principle, which is different from the joint-stock company system.

There is no doubt that the subject covered by this book indeed constitutes a major part of Japan's financial system. It can also be described as a kind of "intermediary-type subsystem where a savings surplus entity and a savings shortage entity raise funds and invest assets in negotiation transactions via a financial intermediary organization like a bank," an expression used by Teranishi Jurō when describing the banking system.[12]

However, though postal savings and industrial cooperatives, just as private banks, are organizations that collect deposits and savings and manage such funds, they were largely left out of the scope of analysis in previous studies of Japanese financial history. This has come despite the scale of their funds ranking alongside private banks in the modern age, let alone in the postwar period.

Research into the history of finance in Japan has progressed mainly several studies that analyzed the flows of loans to companies by large private banks, as represented by an analysis of the "multi-layered financial structure," with the Bank of Japan

---

vol. 45, no. 1, 1955; Robert Solow, translated by Fukuoka Masao, "*Seichō Riron (Theory of Economic Growth)*," Iwanami Shoten, 1971; Thomas Piketty, translated by Hiroo Yamagata et al., "*21 Seiki no Shihon (Capital in the Twenty-First Century)*," Misuzu Shobo, 2014, pp. 13–17.

[11] Needless to say, apart from postal savings and industrial cooperatives, there are also many institutions that handled personal small savings by ordinary people among regional banks, particularly savings banks. In terms of statistical data, however, it is difficult to pick out from private banks only those regional banks that handled such personal small savings. It can be judged that these banks collected not only small savings from ordinary people but also large-lot deposits from high-income individuals who are often business owners and corporations. These banks were therefore excluded from the subject of the primary analysis in this book.

[12] Teranishi Jurō, "*Senzenki Nihon no Kinyū Sisutemu (Financial System in Prewar Japan)*," Iwanami Shoten, 2011, p. 4.

at the summit.[13] This was because the development of the banking system and its smooth supply of funds to companies, or so-called 'industrial finance', has been viewed as the major factor behind the successful modernization of Japan. Therefore, the study of the history of finance was undertaken in a form that could be termed 'an accumulated history of banks'.[14] On the other hand, Okazaki Tetsuji and others argued that the financial system in prewar Japan was not principally led by banks, and that importance was found in the market-oriented system that leveraged the capital market and money market closer to Anglo-American types.[15]

Discussions on whether Japan's financial system in the prewar period was driven by banks or the capital market, or whether it can be argued that contributions by both helped to facilitate a relatively smooth industrialization, have yet to be settled. However, at least through these discussions and a new study that provides an overview of the relationship between the banking system and the financial market,[16] the study of the history of the capital market[17] and the study of the history of banks, which had, in practice, previously been undertaken separately, have now converged into a single domain as the study of the history of finance. The study of the financial system in Japan therefore has recently entered a new stage. On that basis, however, this book argues that any claim that the combination of these two systems—i.e. large private banks with the Bank of Japan at the summit, and the capital market—has provided researchers with a comprehensive overview of Japan's financial system in the prewar period is false. This is because such a view would still overlook another significant flow of funds within the Japanese economy.

Needless to say, the sheer size of postal savings, as well as the spread of industrial cooperatives and the importance of their financial operations within regions, had already been recognized since prewar years,[18] and researchers were well aware of their existence when studying special banks closely related to these activities, such

---

[13] Sugiyama Kazuo, "Bōseki Gaisha no Tegata Hakkō to Shichū Ginko (Bill Issuance by Cotton Spinning Companies and Commercial Banks)," Yamaguchi Kazuo, ed., "*Nihon Sangyō Kin-yushi Kenkyu—Bōseki Kin-yu Hen (Studies on the History of Industrial Finance in Japan-The Textile Industry)*," University of Tokyo Press, 1970.

Ishii Kanji, "*Kindai Nihon Kinyūshi Josetu (The Financial History of Modern Japan)*," University of Tokyo Press, 1999.

[14] Kato Toshihiko, "*Honpō Ginkoshi Ron (History of Banks in Japan)*," University of Tokyo Press, 1957.

[15] Okazaki Tetsuji, Hamao Yasushi and Hoshi Takeo, "Senzen Nihon ni Okeru Shihon Shijō no Seisei to Hatten—Tokyo Kabushiki Torihikijo heno Kabushiki Jōjō wo Chūshin toshite (The Genesis and Development of the Capital Market in Pre-War Japan—Listing Policy and Development of the Tokyo Stock Exchange in the Pre-War Period)," "*Keizai Kenkyu (The Economic Review)*" (Hitotsubashi University), Vol. 6, No. 1 (2005), pp. 15–29.

[16] Tsurumi Masayoshi, "*Nihon Shinyō Kikō no Kakuritsu—Nihon Ginkō to Kinyū Shijō (The Establishment of Japanese Banking System—The Bank of Japan and Financial Markets)*," Yūhikaku Publishing, 1991.

[17] Shimura Kaichi, "*Nihon Shihon Shijō Bunseki (An Analysis of the Japanese Capital Market)*," University of Tokyo Press, 1969.

[18] Takahashi Kamekichi, "*Nihon Kinyū Ron (Treatise on Japanese Finance)*," Toyo Keizai Press, 1931.

as the Nihon Kangyō Bank and prefectural Agricultural and Industrial banks, as well as in the study of the history of finance.[19]

However, these were categorized into the history of special banks or the history of agricultural finance and were only recognized within the area of the history of agriculture and the history of policymaking. Furthermore, since the management of postal savings as funds was institutionally undertaken by the Ministry of Finance, it was often covered from the aspect of the history of public finance. For this reason, postal savings, while representing massive amounts of financial funds, were rarely seen as being on the same level as the general financial system.[20] Small-amount finance by industrial cooperatives were also viewed in the same light as traditional finance, such as "*mujin*" mutual loans and "*shichiya*" pawn shop financing, or often seen as part of the policies for the relief of the poor, with the importance of their financial status seldom considered in the history of studies on finance.[21]

As seen above, the financial roles of postal savings and industrial cooperatives have not attracted significant interest thus far in financial history, perhaps because the sources of funds were small-amount savings of ordinary individuals. It is also possible that such savings were overlooked because they were regarded as "people's financing" in that they were provided to recipients considered totally unrelated to modernization or economic growth, or perhaps because their management entities were not-for-profit organizations. Neither has the importance of small-amount finance opportunities in regions come into focus in broader historical research thus far, at least in terms of its relevance to economic development. This book argues, however, that under the Japanese financial system, postal savings and industrial cooperatives are indeed a "popular funds network" that complements to the multi-layered network of banks.

This alternative financial system emerged in modern times with institutional improvements. It grew together with the Japanese economy, and supported the postwar Japanese economy for a long period, as symbolized, still in the twenty-first century, by the gigantic size of postal savings and the high organization rate and financial muscle of agricultural cooperatives.

---

[19] Saeki Naomi, "*Nihon Nogyō Kinyūshi Ron (Treatise on the History of Agricultural Finance in Japan),*" Ochanomizu Shobo, 1963.

Saito Jin, "Tokushu Ginko (Special Banks)," Watanabe Sahei et all, ed., "*Gendai Nihon Sangyō Hattatsu Shi (The History of Industrial Development in Modern Japan),*" Vol. 26 Banks, Kojunsha Publishing Department, 1966.

Shibuya Ryuichi, "*Meijiki Nihon Tokushu Kin-yu Rippo Shi (The History of the Legislation of the Special Finance in Meiji Era),*" Waseda University Press, 1977.

[20] Denda Isao, "Yūbin Chokin Seido no Rekishiteki Igi—Okurasho Yokinbu Shikin no Keisei Katei (A Historical Analysis of the Postal Savings Bank System in Japan: The Establishment of the Deposit Bureau Fund of the Ministry of Finance)," "*Kenkyu Kiyo (Bulletin of Research),*" (Library of Archives Attached to the Faculty of Economics, Shiga University), No. 5 (1972).

Kanazawa Fumio, "*Kindai Nihon Chiho Zaisei Shi Kenkyu (The History of Local Public Finance in Modern Japan),*" Nihon Keizai Hyouronsha, 2010.

Kamiyama Tsuneo, "*Meiji Keizai Seisakushi no Kenkyu (Studies in the History of Economic Policymaking in Meiji Japan),*" Hanawashobo, 1995.

[21] Shibuya Ryuichi, "*Shomin Kinyū no Tenkai to Seisaku Taio (Development of People's Finance and Policy Response),*" Nihon Tosho Center, 2001.

In order to shed light on the formation of this system and to ascertain its role, this book attempts to confirm the process of the accumulation of personal small savings into modern financial institutions and the management of accumulated popular funds from the Meiji period until World War II. In other words, this book attempts to analyze the movement of funds in postal savings and in their management entity, the Deposit Bureau Fund of the Ministry of Finance, along with the activities of industrial cooperatives in regional economies, and confirm their financial cooperation.

1.3 Structure and Methodology

In addressing the subjects above, this book is organized into two parts comprising eight chapters and an addendum.

Part I, entitled "Collect/Manage", traces the process of accumulation of small savings by ordinary people and corroborates the process of the formation of that system by looking into how popular funds accumulated in that manner came to be managed within regions. It examines how personal small savings came to be accumulated in massive amounts at modern financial institutions in modern Japan. It also examines the significance of these saving, in the early stages, for both individuals and their wider regional economies. These points are examined from the perspective of socioeconomic history.

Chapter 2 utilizes statistics from the Meiji period to the early Showa era in order to confirm the presence and scale of personal small savings in the Japanese economy at the time. This chapter also seeks to corroborate the fact that Japan's modernization was underpinned not only by urban areas and the industrial sector but also by rural areas and the agricultural sector, and to examine statistically where investment funds for modernization were procured.

Chapter 3 looks at how popular small savings, the existence of which was confirmed in the previous chapter, were formed and collected nationally, and analyzes the institutional picture and actual social conditions. The process of the spread of postal savings is analyzed to verify specifically how the spread of saving behavior to modern financial institutions was achieved. The postal savings system was established ahead of other private financial institutions with branches deployed across the country, and postal savings were popularized just as a change in the propensity to save emerged at the beginning of the twentieth century. Thus, the case of postal savings is both symbolic and representative for considering the process of the national spread of saving behavior in modern Japan.

In Chap. 4 I analyze how popular funds were managed in regional communities and contributed to the development of regional economies by looking at the early development of industrial cooperatives that accumulated popular funds within their region. Industrial cooperatives played a significant role as organizations accumulating deposits in the years prior to World War II. The case of Kanō Village (now part of Tōmi City) in Nagano Prefecture is taken up to demonstrate how industrial cooperatives used accumulated funds to provide micro-finance to local residents. Based on this case, the economic and social roles of industrial cooperatives, which had already spread across the country in the prewar period, are examined to provide the basis for understanding industrial cooperatives as marginal on-site organizations of the financial network in this chapter and thereafter.

Chapter 5 then covers the process of institutional formation for the management of postal savings and the actual conditions of the early operation of the system of returning postal savings funds to regions. Postal savings were managed under the system called the Deposit Bureau Fund of the Ministry of Finance. In this chapter, the condition of the system of returning postal savings funds to regions, created in 1909, and the path it built to supply these funds to local sites in regional economies are examined on the basis of the 1914 case of relief financing.

At the end of Part I, an addendum as Chap. 6 looks at how the government recognized the Ministry of Finance Deposit Bureau system, formed between the Meiji period and World War I, as an institution and how the government attempted to reform it during the interwar period. The Ministry of Finance Deposit Bureau reform in 1925 was intended to reform the management system of the Ministry of Finance Deposit Bureau Fund, which was plagued with ambiguous legal grounds as well as arbitrary and opaque management. The development of the legal system following this reform led to the establishment of the Steering Committee of the Deposit Bureau Funds, an advisory committee, which also included members from outside the Ministry of Finance and the government. Based on the minutes of the first committee meeting, the addendum looks into the nature and role of the advisory committee, which was able to influence the management of the Deposit Bureau Fund during the interwar period after 1925. With this addendum, Part I thus shows that the system to "Collect/Manage" small savings had been largely completed by the interwar period, the discussion then proceeds to Part II, which mainly covers the interwar period itself.

Part II, entitled "Share," examines how the popular funds-driven financial system supported the lives of people in difficulties by reallocating such funds to regional economies. Part II articulates how the financial system built on popular funds during the interwar period, when the Japanese economy remained mired in the doldrums, supported regional communities in the face of economic crises, strengthening its networks for that purpose, and how regional organizations, such as industrial cooperatives, expanded their functions.

Chapter 7 looks at how the system of returning Ministry of Finance Deposit Bureau Funds to regions were instrumental in mitigating the difficulties of regional economies during recessions in the interwar period. Following the Deposit Bureau reform in 1925, covered in the addendum, the Deposit Bureau Fund gave greater weight to transparency in the fund's management and the idea that fund management would involve returning more funds to regions. In 1923, the Central Bank for Industrial Cooperatives was established. In the interwar period, the financial networks driven by popular funds were called upon to demonstrate their functions more rapidly and to engage in closer cooperation between the two different financial networks of industrial cooperatives and the Deposit Bureau, in order to cope with both persistent depressions and natural disasters. Chapter 7 examines the case of relief financing in response to damage caused by natural disasters centering on Nagano Prefecture, which occurred in the midst of the 1927 Showa financial crisis, marking the beginning of the aforementioned cooperation. Through this case, I examine the two types of popular funds, which showed different modes of operation due to institutional differences, and their significance to regional economies.

Chapter 8 once again returns to the case of Kanō Village in Nagano Prefecture to verify the socioeconomic impact on the region of the local industrial cooperative which had a record of excellent management and a close relationship with the central national organization. The case of Kanō Village also sheds light on the impact of the cooperation between the two different lines of popular funds of the Ministry of Finance Deposit Bureau Fund and industrial cooperatives (also covered in Chapter 7). This is because exemplary industrial cooperatives both accumulated savings independently within regional communities and maintained links with networks for external funds.

Whilst Chap. 8 examines cases of regions that had local industrial cooperatives, Chap. 9, on the other hand, examines an entirely different case so as to draw comparisons with regions without local industrial cooperatives in order to see how such regions dealt with economic difficulties during the interwar period. No industrial cooperative was established in Seinaiji Village (now part of Achi Village), Nagano Prefecture, until the latter half of the 1930s, a rare development within Nagano Prefecture. In Chap. 9, I examine the mechanism by which Seinaiji Village responded to a crisis without the use of a modern cooperative system. This chapter shows that while the Ministry of Finance Deposit Bureau Fund was able to provide funds to communities without an industrial cooperative, Seinaiji Village could not connect itself to the network of popular funds in the system-based financing of industrial cooperatives as it did not have its own industrial cooperative which could act as a contact point.

Chapter 10 provides a general examination of how the Deposit Bureau system and the industrial cooperative system in postwar Japan, after institutional reorganizations into the Trust Fund Bureau and agricultural cooperatives, respectively, managed to sustain their organizations and functions in Japan up to the present. The principal theme of this book is to trace the process of the formation of the financial system driven by popular funds in prewar Japan and clarify how the micro-credit provided by that system supported regional communities. However, much of the financial system driven by the popular funds that are the subject of analysis in this book continued to function in the Japanese economy into the postwar period.

The Final Chap. 11 summarizes the book and attempts to show how the financial network of popular funds, the alternative financial system formed in prewar Japan, is positioned in modern Japanese history as well as in the international community.

Whilst incorporating statistical information, this book mainly uses the approach of historical science and adopts the methodology of concretely and empirically analyzing systems and actual conditions. Quantitative analysis is excellent for gaining an overview and identifying problems and major changes. However, examining numbers alone may result in a failure to notice the actual changes that occurred in public consciousness and problems that simply cannot be captured in statistics. Thus, this book first provides a quantitative overview, then conducts a historical analysis and attempts to capture the actual conditions of the "alternative financial system" that developed, albeit somewhat regulated and constrained by institutions and convention.

The attempt to understand what functions savings in Japan, particularly savings by ordinary citizens, performed is also an attempt to analyze what factors supported Japan's modernization and Japan's long sustained economic growth which began in the late nineteenth century. The existence of savings as well as the financial system that appropriately managed such funds are already understood to be essential factors for economic development from the standpoint of economic theory. The accumulation and reallocation of social capital, an essential factor for eliminating disparities associated with economic development, in contrast, deserves far greater attention from the financial perspective.

Small savings, which individuals casually and routinely make for themselves, or their families and communities, grow into an extensive financial system that can be described as an important social foundation as they are returned again to regional economies to contribute to economic development and people's livelihoods in the regions. Modern Japan achieved the building of such a popular funds-driven financial system, along with industrialization, and maintained that system within society through the later period of high-speed economic growth. This book is designed to shed light on part of that dynamism.

1.4 Summary

The financial system is essential for the economy. In Japan, the banking system is attached the highest value among the national financial system. And there is another feature in Japanese financial system in macroeconomic perspective, the scale of household's savings. The Japanese are often referred to as keen savers. When did this oft-mentioned tradition of savings become habitual in Japan? What position have personal savings occupied or what role have they played in the Japanese economy?

The most of Japanese households were poor small-size farmers or self-employed people.in the beginning of 20th century. In 21st century, to prevent poverty and support these kind of small-size self-employed business, we consider to use power of micro-finance after Muhammad Yunus was awarded the Nobel Peace Prize in 2006 for pioneering the concepts of micro-finance through the Grameen Bank. In modern Japan, cooperative movements supplied the micro-finance in local area and they accumulated their funds by their savings.

Since modern times, the bulk of savings, which should be called popular funds, formed by the personal small savings of people, were accumulated not only at banks but also at post offices for savings, and cooperative financial institutions. The financial system this book takes up and focuses on concerns the functions of various financial institutions managed with massive funds created by the accumulation of savings by the general public in Japan, not megabanks.

Part I
Collect/Manage

Chapter 2
What Supported the Development of Traditional Rural Economies? The Forgotten Financial Infrastructure

2.1 Introduction

This chapter elucidates the macroeconomic position of funds accumulated from personal small-amount savings, and seeks to ascertain the relationship of these funds with economic growth. Before conducting a historical analysis of this topic utilizing specific examples, this chapter outlines the aforementioned *popular funds* and through relevant statistics confirms their position in the Japanese economy. First of all, the chapter charts Japan's modernization and economic development. In doing so, particular attention is given to the development of light industry, as it is often referred to, and the growth of regional economies (including the agricultural sector) from a macroeconomic viewpoint, in an effort to determine the extent to which they have contributed to the Japanese economy. It also seeks to determine how savings and the financial system have supported their modernization and development. Throughout, a focus is maintained on the accumulation of personal savings and the resulting formation of massive funds that have often been overlooked in analyses of the above process.

2.2 Japan's Modernization and Its Foundation

What are the necessary conditions for successful modernization, the fostering and maintenance of economic growth? These are fundamental questions in economics and have generated an extensive literature with varied arguments. As pointed out in the introductory chapter, the growth of a country's economy and the improvement of the living standards of its people are not necessarily positively correlated. The trickle-down hypothesis, which states that if the rich get richer along with the advancement of a country's economy, their wealth will trickle down uniformly to lower-income segments of the population, is incongruous theoretically, historically and empirically,

H. Tanaka, *Micro-Credit in Modern Japan*, Studies in Economic History,
https://doi.org/10.1007/978-981-97-6940-7_2

as indicated by numerous economists, including the Nobel prizewinner in Economics Joseph E. Stiglitz.[1]

Was economic growth and modernization in modern Japan achieved in ways that improved and secured the daily lives of the general public? This chapter begins the consideration of this issue by confirming what growth was like in rural areas, where the majority of Japan's prewar population resided. It then explores changes in the living standards of the general public by looking at the trends in the propensities to consume and save as well as the financial opportunities individuals were able to access. Classical studies have focused on the growth of the modern industrial sector, centering on heavy manufacturing industries, symbolized by military-related industries and the industries in which giant *zaibatsu* conglomerates were active.[2] In prewar Japan, however, powerful heavy industries, such as present-day automobile and precision equipment manufacturing, were virtually non-existent. Instead, it was light industries, such as raw silk, spinning and the production of sundry goods that developed and had international competitiveness, as shown by Nakamura Takafusa and others. Moreover, statistical data shows that the development of miscellaneous manufacturing industries made up primarily of small businesses and the agricultural sector supported Japan's economic growth in the modern era.[3]

In fact, as seen in Fig. 2.1, the Japanese economy between the Meiji period and the interwar period continued to grow at an almost constant pace. The number of those employed in agriculture, while gradually decreasing, largely remained at a level of around 14 million. In addition, in the same period, the number of farming households slightly rose from 54.9 million in 1885 to 55. 6 million in 1920, signifying that the number of independent self-employed farmers increased. Thus, until the interwar period, agriculture maintained a degree of economic vibrancy, enough at least to warrant the establishment of new some new operations (Fig. 2.1).

One major factor that supported the growth of the Japanese economy at the time was an expansion of exports. As seen in Table 2.1, the expansion of exports was of greater importance in terms of contribution to economic growth in the modern era than increases in fixed capital formation. This shows that the development of small- to medium-scale industries, which typically required limited fixed capital, rather than large-scale capital-intensive industries was an important factor in economic growth. Among the major export items at the time were silk—and cotton-related products as well as miscellaneous light industry-produced sundry goods whose production did not require massive capital investment (Table 2.2).

Straw braids were a notable example among sundry good exports, accounting for as much as 2% of total exports in 1900 and 1.3% in 1910. The production of straw braids was established as an industry in the United Kingdom in the seventeenth

---

[1] Joseph E. Stiglitz, "*Sekai ni Kakusa wo Baramaita Gurobarizumu wo Tadasu (Making Globalization Work)*", Tokuma Shoten, 2006, p. 168.

[2] Moritarō Yamada, "*Nihon Shihonshugi Bunseki (Analysis of Japanese Capitalism)*", Iwanami Bunko, 1977, First Edition, 1934.

[3] Takafusa Nakamura, "*Senzenki Nihon Keizai Seichō no Bunseki (An Analysis of Economic Growth in Prewar Japan)*", Iwanami Shoten, 1971.

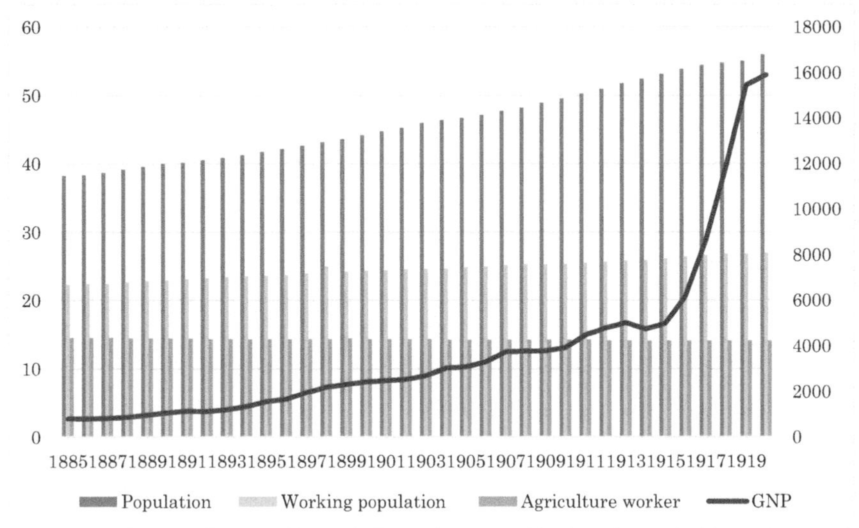

Fig. 2.1 Japan's economic growth and population growth in the early modern period. LHS: population; Unit: million; RHS: GNP, Unit: million yen. *Sources* Compiled from Tables 8 and 8-A of Ohkawa Kazushi et al., "*Chōki Keizai Tōkei 1 Kokumin Shotoku (Long-Term Economic Statistics 1, National Income),*" Toyo Keizai Shinpōsha, 1974, and Tables 1, 2, 10 and 11 of Umemoto Mataji et al., "*Chōki Keizai Tōkei 2 Rōdōryoku (Long-Term Economic Statistics 2, Labor Force),*" Toyo Keizai Shinpōsha, 1988

Table 2.1 Contribution of investment and exports to economic growth in modern Japan

	GNE	Private-sector fixed capital formation		Government fixed capital formation		Exports	
1890–1894	1276	72	5.6%	39	3.1%	86	6.7%
1895–1899	2056	62	3.0%	102	5.0%	163	7.9%
1900–1904	2844	97	3.4%	130	4.6%	322	11.3%
1905–1909	3668	157	4.3%	244	6.7%	534	14.6%
1910–1914	4785	262	5.5%	290	6.1%	692	14.5%
1915–1919	9047	529	5.8%	452	5.0%	2172	24.0%
1920–1924	15,577	1148	7.4%	1139	7.3%	2247	14.4%
1925–1929	16,485	1016	6.2%	1248	7.6%	2716	16.5%
1930–1934	15,236	858	5.6%	1161	7.6%	2273	14.9%
1935–1939	25,651	2496	9.7%	3054	11.9%	4129	16.1%

Unit of amounts in the table = One million yen, 5-year average in nominal terms
Source Prepared based on Table 0·3 in Nakamura Takafusa, "*Senzenki Nihon Keizai Seichō no Bunseki (An Analysis of Economic Growth in Prewar Japan)*", Iwanami Shoten, 1971

Table 2.2 Share of major exports items (%)

FY	1880	1890	1900	1910	1920
Raw silk	30.8	24.8	22.3	28.6	18.5
Cotton yarn		0.0	10.2	10.0	7.4
Coal	3.9	8.6	10.0	3.6	2.2
Tea	26.2	10.9	4.0	2.9	0.8
Copper	1.5	9.6	6.4	4.6	0.2
Silk products	0.1	6.6	11.5	8.3	8.1
Cotton products	0.1	0.3	3.1	4.9	16.4
Sundry goods	6.5	10.2	12.5	9.8	7.9

Silk products: silk fabrics, silk handkerchiefs; Cotton products: cotton fabrics, cotton towels; Sundry goods: matches, straw braids, electrical light bulbs, flower straw mats, glass products, pottery, lacquerware, umbrellas, brushes, buttons

Source Prepared based on Table 0·15 in Nakamura Takafusa, "*Senzenki Nihon Keizai Seichō no Bunseki (An Analysis of Economic Growth in Prewar Japan)*," Iwanami Shoten, 1971

century, as it could be used as raw material for making straw hats. In Japan, British merchants started purchasing Japanese straw braids in 1870. The principal places of production in Japan were rural areas in places such as Okayama Prefecture, where production flourished as a side occupation of farmers.[4]

Japanese exports were not limited to raw silk, though this product certainly accounted for a large share of Japanese exports in the prewar period. The procurement of raw materials for straw products such as straw braids and flower straw mats were among a multitude of exported sundry goods. Though technically such items were manufactured products, their production took place in the countryside and thus they were part of the rural economy. As Nakamura Takafusa has pointed up, in the period up to World War I the Japanese economy achieved a kind of equilibrium growth encompassing both urban and rural areas.[5] In rural areas growth came not only from the development of the agricultural sector in terms of expanding the food supply, as previously understood, but also from the expansion of the production of various raw materials and inputs for new manufactured products.

The role of rural areas was not limited to supplying the raw materials for the production of light industrial products, rural areas also provided labor and served as the location for production facilities. In this way, it can be said that Japan's modernization was not limited to the development of large-scale industries by the government

---

[4] Okayama-ken Nōkai (Okayama Prefecture Agricultural Association), "*Okayama-ken no Tokushu Sakumotsu to Sono Kakō (Okayama Prefecture's Special Crops and Their Processing)*," 1926, pp. 188–189. In 1926, "straw braid was manufactured actively as a side job for female workers. Annual output amounted to over 2 million yen, becoming one of the prefecture's important products." Okayama Prefecture, "*Okayama-ken Annai Shashincho (The Photo Album Guide for Okayama Prefecture)*," 1926.

[5] Nakamura Takafusa, "*Senzenki Nihon Keizai Seichō no Bunseki Daiichibu 'Kinko Seichō—Daiichiji Taisen Made' (An Analysis of Economic Growth in Prewar Japan Part I 'Equilibrium Growth—Up to the First World War')*."

and *zaibatsu,* it also included the growth of regional economies which provided a source of raw materials and labor, hosted industrial clusters and various industries characterized by small- and medium-sized businesses, besides their agricultural production. At the same time, this also signifies that modern Japan achieved relatively balanced development, inclusive of regional economies, unlike patterns seen in the modernization of other developing countries during the modern period, which often saw growth concentrated in a small number of urban areas.

What were the financial foundations underlying the development of such regional economies and smaller industries? Even though the large-scale fixed capital investment required for heavy manufacturing industries was not required in these regional economies, access to small-scale capital and revolving funds are essential for any industry. As noted in the introductory chapter, financial history research in Japan has already produced several studies on financial flows such as the accumulation of funds within *zaibatsu* and their investment, the provision of funds under the multi-layered financial structure with the Bank of Japan at the top and ordinary commercial banks under it, and the flows of fund procurement via the stock markets.[6] These funding routes, however, were essentially those accessible to *zaibatsu*, heavy industries and light industries such as the cotton spinning sector that required relatively large-scale capital investment. They were not designed to provide the required funds of smaller industries, or the agricultural sector, which is the focus of this study. As such, there must have been another system of finance available in modern Japan through routes other than those above.

2.3 Overview of Capital Formation by Personal Savings

At the macroeconomic level, domestic savings, that were to serve as investment funds in the Japanese economy, almost constantly maintained a relatively high level of around 10% of gross national product (GNP) from the beginning of the twentieth century onwards (see Fig. 2.2). Figure 2.2 also shows that there was a certain degree of linkage between the rate of GNP growth and the savings rate. Moreover, it also suggests that instead of bringing in investment funds from overseas, Japan was able to raise the funds for its modernization effort from within the country and to revolve them domestically.

A high level of investment is considered one of the necessary conditions for modernization. Therefore, in the absence of investment funds from overseas, a high level of national savings is viewed as a necessary component of generating modern economic growth. The general validity of this line of thinking itself, as represented by Rostow's take-off theory that the savings rate would surge simultaneously with the industrialization of a national economy, is now being called into question because it does not match the economic development pattern of recent years, which is based

[6] Kanji Ishii, "*Nihon Keizaishi Dainiban (Socio-Economic History of Modern Japan Second Edition)*," University of Tokyo Press, 1991, Chap. 5.

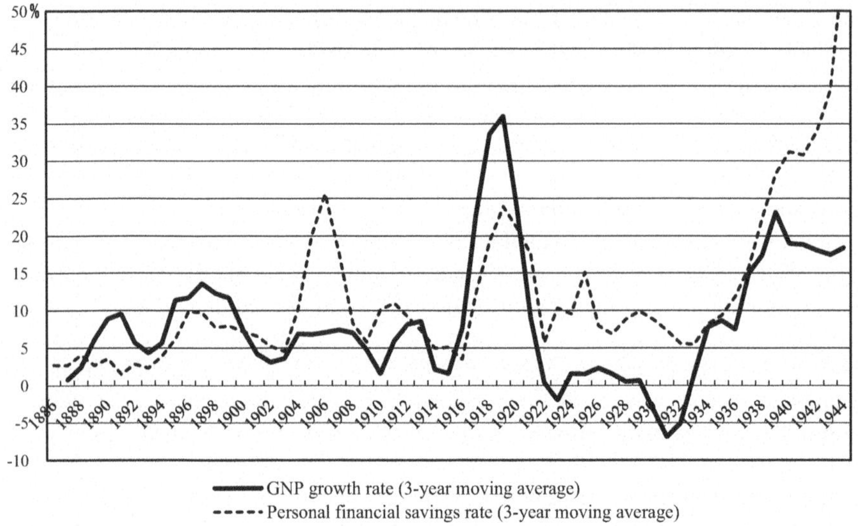

Fig. 2.2 GNP growth rate and savings rate. Personal financial savings rate = {Private-sector financial savings (deposits + insurance + currency and deposit currency + securities) − tained earnings}/ GNP. *Sources* Prepared based on Table 2 of Emi Kōichi et al., "*Chōki Keizai Tokei 5 Chochiku to Tsūka (Long-Term Economic Statistics 5, Savings and Currency)*," Toyo Keizai Shinpōsha, 1988, and Table 1 of Ohkawa Kazushi et al., "*Chōki Keizai Tokei 1 Kokumin Shotoku (Long-Term Economic Statistics 1, National Income)*," Toyo Keizai Shinpōsha, 1974

on attracting overseas capital. However, as previous studies have pointed out, it corresponds well to the experience of modern Japan. Rather, the Japanese case is often cited as an example which supports Rostow's theory.[7]

The high level of savings in modern Japan had certain notable characteristics some of which are observable in Table 2.3. Especially notable is that a large portion of domestic savings came from the private sector rather than the government, and the bulk of private-sector savings were formed by households rather than by corporations. Thus, the source of investment funds that supported the continuous economic growth of modern Japan through a high savings rate were derived from domestic household savings. What, then, were the characteristics that led to the high propensity to save among Japanese households during the modern period?

The high degree of consciousness regarding savings among the Japanese population drew attention internationally after World War II, particularly as the country passed through an era of high economic growth in the 1960s. Given Japan's remarkable economic growth, the Japanese themselves and others have often described Japanese people as "striving to save in accordance with the tradition of frugality".[8] However, we have to verify whether this was really a "tradition" of the Japanese

---

[7] Hayami Yujirō, "*Kaihatsu Keizaigaku (Development Economics)*," Sōbunsha, 2000, p. 163.

[8] Karel van Wolferen, "*Ningen wo Kofuku ni Shinai Nihon Toiu Sisutemu (The Japanese System That Does Not Make Humans Happy)*," Mainichi Newspapers, 1994, p. 59.

Table 2.3 Government/private-sector ratio in domestic savings

Fiscal year	Domestic savings			Component ratio in domestic savings		Component ratio in private-sector savings	
	Private-sector savings	Government savings		Private sector (%)	Government (%)	Individuals (%)	Corporations (%)
1883–1887	15.8	26.8	42.6	37	63		
1888–1892	29.2	26.9	56.1	52	48		
1893–1897	123.9	−23.2	100.7	123	−23		
1898–1902	155	20	175	89	11		
1903–1907	501	170	671	75	25	*95	*5
1908–1912	416	150	566	73	27	96	4
1913–1917	777	258	1035	75	25	86	14
1918–1922	1910	411	2321	82	18	101	−1
1923–1927	1951	784	2735	71	29	102	−1

Monetary unit: One million yen Figures show 5-year averages. *Indicates the figure for FY1906-1907
Private-sector savings = Deposits + insurance + currency and deposit currency + securities + retained earnings
Source Tables 3.1a and 3.2 of Emi Kōichi et al., "*Chōki Keizai Tōkei 5 (Long-Term Economic Statistics 5)*"

people that existed before the early modern period and whether it was a habit or custom that had already taken hold prior to industrialization. At least from the early-to-mid Meiji period (1868–1890s), or during the nineteenth century, despite the establishment of modern financial institutions, the amounts of deposits and savings could not be viewed as huge and the savings rate could not be described as high, as can readily be ascertained from Fig. 2.2 and Table 2.3. The savings rate in modern Japan, more or less in line with Rostow's hypothesis, rose from around 5% (a rate considered to have been consistent with rates in the early modern period) to approximately 10% at around the turn of the twentieth century as industrialization progressed. The principal constituent entities of these savings were, as explained above, not the government but the private sector, and in the private sector, individuals rather than corporations. The "tradition of frugality" of the Japanese public, which was later often pointed out by journalists and sometimes scholars, is thus most likely to have been a new habit formed in the modern period.

Below I verify whether this great change in consciousness was a result of an intrinsic link between the increase in the savings rate and the growth of gross national product (GNP). I posited the dummy variable (D), assuming that the household propensity to save changed during this period, and conducted a regression analysis on the assumption that the savings rate changes in tandem with the growth of GNP.

$$\text{Household savings rate S} = \beta_0 + \beta_1 y + \beta_2 D, \ \ y = \text{GNP growth rate}$$

Table 2.4 Outcome of regression analysis of the household savings rate (3-year moving average) concerning the presence of a change in the propensity to save

Multiple correlation R		0.772824	
Heavy decision R^2		0.597257	
Correction R^2		0.582612	
	Coefficient	T	*P*-value
Intercept	−3.30598	−1.8482	0.069952783
GNP growth rate (3-year moving average)	0.799256	8.502575	0.00000000001
Dummy variable (Presence of any change in the propensity to save)	5.223	2.800091	0.007034714

Sources Emi Kōichi et al., "*Chōki Keizai Tōkei 5 (Long-Term Economic Statistics 5)*," and Ohkawa Kazushi et al., "*Chōki Keizai Tōkei 1 (Long-Term Economic Statistics 1)*"

It was found that, with 1900 as the boundary, a statistically significant change took place at the 1% level[9] (Table 2.4). In other words, it can be said that the relative stability and high level of the savings rate after Japan entered the twentieth century resulted from the change in the household savings rate itself. Household savings in Japan became the source of funds supportive of growth in the national economy for the first time as Japan entered the twentieth century. After this, household savings were constantly accumulated and in combination formed massive sums.

Japan's industrial revolution was well underway by the beginning of the twentieth century and savings were formed by high-income individuals who accumulated wealth during the course of industrialization. The change in the propensity to save was a phenomenon that occurred among a part of this bracket of people, and it is possible that the change had not spread to the Japanese people as a whole, including the low- and medium-income classes. However, looking at Table 2.5, we can see that there was a change in the propensity of individuals to save; savings were held in various types of deposits and savings, instead of in securities whose units were in relatively large amounts likely out of reach for most excepting high-income groups. Bank deposits were not the only forms of deposits and savings that were common, deposits and savings placed with small savings institutions for everyone, including people with low- or medium-incomes, such as postal savings and industrial cooperative deposits, also had a considerable presence.

With financial assets, the orientation toward the formation of savings by securities was stronger in the early modern period, but did not undergo much change around the turn of the century. On the other hand, the formation of savings by deposits

[9] A 3-year moving average was used for both the household savings rate and the GNP growth rate. The dummy variable was set at 0 up until 1900 and at 1 from 1901 onward and was examined over a period of 58 years from 1887 and 1944. I examined the assumption that the change did not take place or the assumption that the change in the propensity to save occurred after the 1897 depression following the Sino-Japanese War for each fiscal year up to 1910, including the Russo-Japanese War period. In all 14 years examined, we could not obtain test results that surpassed the determination function in the case of a change that arose in 1900.

Table 2.5 Breakdown of forms of personal financial assets held

	Personal investment in securities	Total balance of domestic deposits and savings	% of postal savings in total deposits and savings (%)	% of postal savings + industrial cooperative deposits in total deposits and savings (%)
1891	305	80	27	27
1896	585	250	11	11
1901	1057	590	5	5
1906	2858	1454	6	6
1911	3821	1937	10	11
1916	3637	3638	9	10
1921	9706	10,159	9	12
1926	13,392	13,481	9	16
1931	16,061	16,284	17	25
1936	17,673	21,527	16	25
1941	28,636	61,731	16	30

Monetary units: 1 million yen

Sources Prepared based on Table 5 of "*Yūsei Tōkei Shiryō; Ekitei Kyoku Tōkeisho Yūsei Hyakunenshi Shiryō Somokuji (Postal Service Statistical Data; Central Post Office Statistical Report Tables of the Contents Data Set of the Centennial History of Postal Services)*," Yoshikawa Kobundo, 1971, and Tables 4, 14, 18 and 22, "*Chōki Keizai Tōkei 5 (Long-Term Economic Statistics 5)*"

and savings increased in weight in domestic savings around the turn of the century (Table 2.6). It can be said that the change in the propensity to save since the beginning of the twentieth century was closely linked to the new formation of savings, including small-amount savings such as postal savings, other deposits and savings, not the formation of savings by high-denomination savings such as securities.

In this book, funds based on such personal small-amount savings are referred to as *popular funds*. They are distinct from the general financial system where sources

Table 2.6 Specific weight by element of personal financial savings

Fiscal year	1885 (%)	1890 (%)	1895 (%)	1900 (%)	1905 (%)	1910 (%)	1915 (%)	1920 (%)	1925 (%)	1930 (%)	1935 (%)	1940 (%)	1945 (%)
Deposits and savings	−9	20	49	40	31	49	52	202	39	47	52	69	80
Securities	71	90	40	64	67	60	70	−124	56	45	25	12	71

Personal financial savings = Private-sector financial savings (deposits + insurance + currency and deposit currency + securities) − retained earnings

Deposits and savings = Time deposits + year-on-year increases of demand deposits (including postal savings)

The sum of the component ratios of deposits and savings and securities surpasses 100% because other elements of personal financial savings are negative. The 5-year moving average was used

Source Prepared based on Tables 2 and 18 of Emi Kōichi et al., "*Chōki Keizai Tōkei 5 (Long-Term Economic Statistics 5)*"

of funds circulate through banks and financial markets. In the next section, the scale of these funds in comparison with general industrial funds, the funds the government or corporations could manage in the general financial system, are examined.

2.4 The Size of Popular Funds in the Japanese Economy

What was the position of the funds accumulated by the personal small-amount savings of individuals nationwide in the modern Japanese economy?

Postal savings had neither a lending function, nor, from the beginning, capital for business operations. With respect to industrial cooperatives, due to a lack of basic data on capital, deposits and savings, or lending, the overall picture of their operations is not available for a long period after the establishment of the industrial cooperative system in 1900. Based on the data that is available, I have compiled a simple fund size comparison between banks, industrial cooperatives and postal savings (Table 2.7). This comparison shows that popular funds, which were small in scale around the turn of the twentieth century, grew to one-tenth the size of deposits at private-sector banks, which included deposits by corporations, after the end of World War I, and increased further to the scale of over one-fifth of these deposits by the interwar period. Popular funds expanded not only in terms of the absolute size of these funds but also in terms of their relative share.

It is important to compare the scale of state-operated postal savings with central government finances. This is covered in detail in Chap. 5, but within the government, the Ministry of Finance was designated as the organization charged with the management and operation of personal savings accumulated as postal savings. These funds were called Deposit Bureau funds of the Ministry of Finance, and were mostly composed of postal savings. Though Deposit Bureau funds of the Ministry of Finance were treated as a type of special account within central government finances after 1925, they were independent funds in that they were unrelated to tax revenue. Thus, the Deposit Bureau of the Ministry of Finance functioned as a state-owned financial institution with the sole function of fund management. Table 2.8 shows that Deposit Bureau funds increased to sizable amounts prior to World War I, and then continued to expand consistently. This trend stemmed chiefly from the increase in postal savings. The Deposit Bureau eventually came to manage funds twice as large as the government's general finance derived from tax revenue thanks to a further expansion of postal savings in the depression period in the 1930s. The situation in postal savings alone shows that popular funds in Japan reached a scale that even matched state finance.

As Japan entered the twentieth century, the sources of finance in the Japanese economy diversified. Besides the funds of the general financial market owned by corporations and the wealthy, massive funds were accumulated by low- and middle-income people. These funds were not accumulated in ordinary commercial banks or the capital market but in non-profit organizations such as cooperative organizations, including postal savings and industrial cooperatives.

Table 2.7 Size of funds of banks, industrial cooperatives and postal savings

Fiscal year	Banks			Industrial cooperatives (note: this number only includes unions that reported operations)				Postal savings
	Capital	Deposits	Loans	Capital	Savings	Loans	Report rate (%)	
1903	334	758	923	1		1	46	22
1906	359	1395	1419	2	1	3	39	113
1909	438	1506	1527	4	4	8	46	105
1912	534	1941	2304	–	18	29	73	162
1915	622	2569	2872	28	30	52	79	207
1918	888	7236	6819	30	122	84	46	589
1921	1747	9494	10,239	61	285	247	39	783
1924	1953	10,232	11,568	112	525	467	46	935
1927	1886	11,247	11,801	–	886	756	73	1566
1930	2489	11,332	10,030	184	921	840	79	1809
1933	2312	11,651	9138	204	982	845	–	1968
1936	2142	14,093	9509	221	1262	879	–	2493
1939	2112	26,307	15,363	249	2524	855	–	4922
1942	1938	50,041	26,710	306	5750	935	–	9004

Monetary unit: million yen

Sources Prepared based on Tables 11.9a, 11.12 and 11.15 of statistics bureau, management and coordination agency, "*Nihon Chōki Tōkei Sōran (comprehensive list of Japanese long-term statistics),*" Vol. 3, 1988, and ministry of agriculture and commerce, "*Sangyō Kumiai Yōran (Industrial cooperative Directory)*" for each fiscal year

2.5 Summary

The statistics shows that Japan's modernization and economic growth were not confined to urban areas. They were achieved through a close relationship between growth and development in both industry and agriculture, and as such incorporated regional economies in rural areas.

And there was the high rate of savings in modern Japan, often cited as evidence of Rostow's take-off hypothesis, which has long been considered by researchers as the main source of investment funds that supported Japan's modernization and sustained economic development. This chapter has added to this understanding and confirmed that such domestic savings began to be formed as individuals' propensity to save changed at the beginning of the 20th century, after which Japan continued to see high and stable rates of saving.

The high rate of savings was not only underpinned by securities and other savings by corporations and the wealthy; it included the deposits and savings of ordinary households. In particular households increasing placed deposits and savings with

Table 2.8 Scale of postal savings and central government general finance

Fiscal year	Postal savings	Ministry of finance deposit bureau funds	Ratio of postal savings to deposit bureau funds (%)	Central government general account	Deposit bureau funds/general finance (%)
1885	9	17	53	62	27
1890	20	21	95	106	20
1895	29	51	57	187	27
1900	25	60	42	274	22
1905	56	76	74	530	14
1910	170	270	63	657	41
1915	241	307	79	813	38
1920	885	1005	88	2001	50
1925	1167	1683	69	2071	81
1930	2497	3122	80	1597	195
1935	3233	4471	72	2259	198
1940	7915	11,545	69	6445	179
1945	47,152	65,757	72	23,487	280

Monetary unit: 1 million yen
Source Prepared based on Tables 11.5, 11.13abc and 12.1a of statistics bureau, management and coordination agency, "*Nihon Chōki Tōkei Sōran (Comprehensive List of Japanese Long-Term Statistics)*," Vol. 3

cooperative organizations such as postal savings and industrial cooperatives. This accumulation of massive funds consisting of small-amount savings in such non-profit organizations, referred to as popular funds in this book, has been acknowledged at least statistically, but its function within the financial system has failed to come under the spotlight.

Chapter 3
The Birth of Postal Savings: The Formation of the Personal Small Savings Collection System

3.1 Introduction

As described in the previous chapter, early in the twentieth century, Japan's savings rate rose in parallel with the country's industrialization, reaching around 10% of gross national product (GNP) and then stabilizing. This is viewed as an indicator of Japan's successful industrialization and takeoff growth.[1] The rise in the savings rate came about mainly as a result of a change in the propensity to save among households, supported by the stable growth of relatively small deposits and savings by a large number of individuals, rather than through the savings and security holdings of corporations and the wealthy.[2] What was the nature of these popular savings and the behavior that aided their formation? Why did such a change come about precisely at the turn of the twentieth century? The main task of this chapter is to examine these specific questions. In so doing, it focuses on the development of savings institutions for individuals, in particular the postal savings system.

For a wide range of ordinary people in Japan the option of saving at modern financial institutions can be said to have started with the establishment of postal savings. Postal savings were established before the spread of the modern banking system and emerged as the de facto first modern deposit-taking institution for personal savings in the Japanese economy, ahead of all other financial institutions. As shown in Fig. 3.1, the share of postal savings in the total amount of deposits and savings declined late in the nineteenth century when private-sector financial institutions developed, but maintained a share of around 10% as a single financial institution after entering the twentieth century. Subsequently, the total amount of postal savings followed an increasing trend in tandem with the trend of the total amount of deposits and savings. Indeed, postal savings maintained an important position as a popular savings institution throughout the prewar period, and continued to attract massive savings after

---

[1] HayamiYujirō, "*Kaihatsu Keizaigaku (Development Economics)*," Sobunsha, 2000, p. 163.

[2] Koichi Emi et al., "*Chōki Keizai Tōkei 5 Chochiku to Tsūka (Long-Term Economic Statistics, 5 Savings and Currency)*," Toyo Keizai Shimpōsha, 1988.

H. Tanaka, *Micro-Credit in Modern Japan*, Studies in Economic History,
https://doi.org/10.1007/978-981-97-6940-7_3

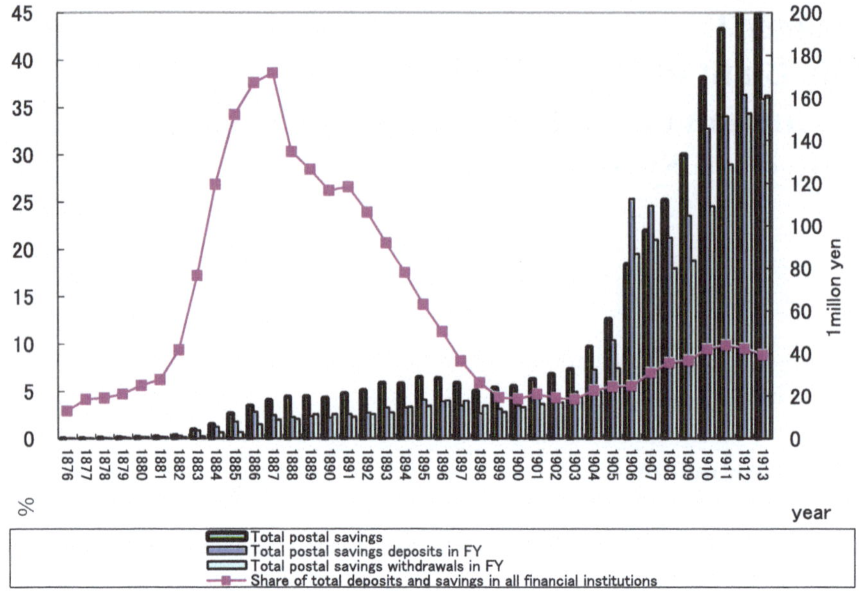

Fig. 3.1 Changes in the size of postal savings. Total deposits and savings = the balance of time deposits + demand deposits (including postal savings). *Source* Ministry of posts and telecommunications, "*Yūsei Hyakunenshi Shiryō 30-Kan (history of the 100 years of postal services materials, Volume 30)*", Yoshikawa Kobundo, 1971, Cho-Table 5; Emi Kōichi et al., "*Chōki Keizai Tōkei 5 Chochiku to Tsūka (long-term economic statistics, 5)*", Toyo Keizai Shimpōsha, 1988, Table 4

the Second World War and well into the twenty-first century. As such, an analysis of the growth of postal savings provides the most suitable example for understanding trends in national popular savings behavior in Japan.

How have previous studies appraised the role of postal savings? Even prior to the Second World War, researchers paid attention to the post office as a financial institution for individuals and the growth of postal savings. The pioneering research on postal savings by Ōuchi Hyoe, "Yūbin Chokin ni okeru Shoshiminsei to Shakaisei no Mujun (The Contradiction between the Petit-Bourgeois Nature and the Social Nature of Postal Savings)" (1931)[3] asserted that postal savings were "temporary surplus funds from the living expenses of the petit-bourgeois and small farmers" and pointed out that they were used for "school expenses to succeed in life, funds for independent and self-employed life, and purchases of equipment and machinery necessary for their occupations." However, Ōuchi's article was essentially an analysis of contemporary (interwar) postal savings rather than an investigation into the

[3] Ōuchi Hyoe, "Yūbin Chokin ni okeru Shoshiminsei to Shakaisei no Mujun (The Contradiction between the Petit Bourgeois Nature and the Social Nature of Postal Savings)," *Ōuchi Hyoe Chosakushū Dai-Yonkan (Collection of Writings by Ōuchi Hyoe, Volume 4)*, Iwanami Shoten, 1975. The research paper was first published in 1931.

characteristics and nature of postal savings, nor the conditions under which they were established.

In the 1970s, Teranishi Jurō pointed out that during the 1927 financial crisis, "a considerable volume of large-amount savings were shifted from banks to postal savings," casting doubt on the then prevailing view that postal savings were primarily composed of individual savings in small amounts.[4] However, Teranishi did acknowledge that the amounts of individual postal savings "gradually became smaller and smaller." Meanwhile, Mukai Yurio examined whether postal savings had been composed of such petty funds since their establishment, and showed that initially, or prior to the twentieth century, many users of postal savings were in fact government officials and operators of commercial business. The postal savings system thus also accepted large-amount savings from wealthy classes. At the same time, however, Mukai noted that postal savings after the turn of the twentieth century "accommodated the petty savings of small farmers and small commercial business operators, or in other words, people based on small commodity markets." Teranishi and Mukai's research has demonstrated that postal savings, hitherto viewed as the accumulation of popular petty savings, were in fact used by the rich in the initial phase after the system's establishment and again during the financial crisis of the 1920s.[5]

A series of research papers by Sugiura Seishi[6] focused on the dissociation between the government's policy goals and the realities during the expansion of postal savings from their initial establishment into the early twentieth century. Sugiura examined the relationship between the network of third-class post office postmasters and large depositors, then discussed the positioning of postal savings in the government's policy system for encouraging savings, showing that the popularization of postal savings became a definite trend around the time of the Russo-Japanese War. In addition, he pointed out that the growth of postal savings in that period, when viewed in terms of flows, was not at all monotonous but relied on policy support from the transfer of "wartime rewards" in the form of pensions for injured soldiers or compensation paid to families for deaths while on active service. In other words, while postal savings were recognized as a popular savings institution by Ōuchi and other researchers, reassessments by Teranishi, Sugiura and others from the 1970s onwards showed that postal savings temporarily became a savings accumulation institution primarily for

---

[4] Teranishi Jurō, "Kinyūteki Hatten no Ichi Sokumen: Anzen Shisan no Riyō Kanōsei to Ginkōgyō no Shūchū Katei (One Aspect of Financial Development: Availability of Safe Assets and the Process of Concentration of the Banking Business)," Minami Ryoshin et al. ed., *Kindai Nihon no Keizai Hatten (the Economic Development of Modern Japan)*, Toyo Keizai Shimpōsha, 1975.

[5] Mukai Yurio, "*Yūbin Chokin no Hatten to Sono Shoyouin (The Development of Postal Savings and It's Contributing Factors)*," United Nations University, 1981.

[6] Sugiura Seishi, "Taishuteki Reisai Chochiku Kikan Toshiteno Yūbin Chokin no Seiritsu—Nisshiin Sen Go no Tenkai to Sono Seikaku (The Establishment of Postal Savings as a Popular Small Financial Institution: The Development and Nature of Postal Savings after the Sino-Japanese War)," *Socio-Economic History*, Volume 52, No. 4 (1986); Sugiura Seishi, "Nichiro Sen Go no Yūbin Chokin no Tenkai to Chochiku Shōrei Seisaku (the Development of Postal Savings after the Russo-Japanese War and Savings Incentive Policy)," *Socio-Economic History*, Volume 56, No. 1 (1990).

the wealthy both immediately after the establishment of the postal savings system, and after the Showa financial crisis.

These revisions should not be taken to as a denial that, after the turn of the twentieth century, the postal savings system primarily functioned as an institution that collected personal small savings. Rather, previous research[7] showed that the early twentieth century, the main period analyzed in this chapter, was an epochal period that saw the popularization of postal savings during which postal savings became in name and in fact an institution for the collection of personal small savings. Moreover, this achievement, as stated earlier, was paralleled by a rise in the savings rate in the Japanese economy and changes in the household propensity to save. How did these changes in people's savings behavior occur and on what were they based? In previous research references to this question have been limited to mentions of temporary events such as the transfer of "wartime reward payments" as pointed out by Sugiura. Compared with the accumulation of research on the history of the postal savings system, specific empirical research on the savings behavior of ordinary people is almost nonexistent.

The establishment of the postal savings system alone would not change the savings behavior of people. A variety of mediating policies and mechanisms, as well as social matters, were at work in encouraging a broad range of people to place their small-amount funds with post offices as savings. In this chapter, I discuss the central government's policies and institutional design, and then clarify how savings behavior operated in regional communities at the time, examining various examples across Japan, and providing a detailed review of the example of the town of Mishima in Shizuoka Prefecture.

---

[7] Other research that addresses the development of postal savings in the period covered by this chapter include Kato Toshihiko, "Yūbin Chokin no Hatten—Meiji-ki yori Shōwa Shoki Made (The Development of Postal Savings—From the Meiji Period to the Early Showa Period)," *Senshū Daigaku Shōgaku Kenkyū Nempo (The Senshū University Annual Bulletin of Commercial Sciences)*, No. 10 (1985); Denda Isao, "Yūbin Chokin Seido no Rekishiteki Igi—Okurasho Yokinbu Shikin no Keisei Katei (The Historical Significance of the Postal Savings System: The Process of Formation of Funds of the Deposit Department of the Ministry of Finance)," *Kenkyū Kiyō (Research Bulletin)*, (The Archival Museum Attached to the Faculty of Economics, Shiga University) No. 5 (1972).

3.2 The Emergence of a Savings Institution for Individuals: The Establishment of the Postal Savings System

3.2.1 The Purpose of the Establishment of Postal Savings and the Initial Situation

In 1874, the "Chokin Azukari Kisoku (Regulations for the Acceptance of Savings)," which later developed into the postal savings system, were enacted.[8] Postal savings were established with the aim of creating an institution for the petty savings of the "masses," or people among the lower classes. Only 2 years after the enactment of the National Bank Act, the introduction of a state-run savings institution for individuals at a time when there were still few private-sector banks[9] and the financial system could hardly be described as 'developed' was an outcome of the efforts and influence of Maejima Hisoka, Minister of Posts and Telecommunications, who had just returned from the United Kingdom.

After several years of heated deliberations, the postal savings system was established in the United Kingdom in 1861 as the world's first. The holding of small-amount savings among the working classes was thought to contribute to the stability of their lives. Furthermore, the small savings made by the working poor, it was hoped, could effectively substitute for the government's social policies under the Poor Laws. As such, it was concluded that a stable state-run savings institution was necessary in order to take the place of unstable private-sector financial institutions.[10] A state-run savings institution was viewed as beneficial in that it "not only improves the economy and public morals, it also is a favorable and beneficial way to relieve and provide assistance to the poor."[11] It was not expected to play any role in improving the financial resources of the state as a state-run enterprise. Instead, the prevailing view in the United Kingdom was that the flows of fragile deposits to the government as surplus funds through this enterprise would rather be inconvenient.

---

[8] "Chokin Azukari Kisoku (Regulations for the Acceptance of Savings)" were enacted on August 31, 1874 (*"Yūsei Hyakunen-shi Shiryō Ikkan Yūbin Chokin/Kawase Dajo Ruiten Kobunroku (Centennial History of Postal Services Materials, Volume 1: Postal Savings/Postal Order Dajo Ruiten Official Document Records),"* Yoshikawa Kobundo, 1971, p. 127. Prior to this, the Savings Regulations were put into place within the Central Post Office, but the postal savings system was enforced publicly only from 1875.

[9] The establishment of the Bank of Japan came in 1882. After the 1872 enactment of the National Bank Act, only four private-sector banks were initially established. The rush in establishing private-sector banks came only after a revision of the National Bank Act in 1876. Nakamura Takafusa, "*Meiji Taishō Ki no Keizai (The Economy during the Meiji and Taisho Periods)*," University of Tokyo Press, 1985, p. 36; Kamiyama Tsuneo, "*Meiji Keizaiseisakushi no Kenkyū* (*Research on the History of Economic Policy during the Meiji Period*)," Hanawashobo, 1995, p. 14.

[10] William Lewins, *A History of Banks for Savings in Great Britain and Ireland*, S. Low, son and Marston, London, 1866. Since the eighteenth century, people such as D. Defoe and J. Bentham underscored the necessity for a stable institution for collecting individual petty savings.

[11] Maejima Hisoka, "*Yūbin Sogyō Dan (The Story of the Establishment of Postal Services)*," Communications Association, 1936, p. 144.

Japan followed the example of the UK and postal savings were from the outset intended to function for the benefit of social security. From public announcements published in newspapers and other media, it could be seen that the government at the time regarded the formation of petty savings for "ordinary common people living in dire poverty" as something that "keeps them healthy and prevents them from falling ill, enables them to sustain their livelihoods in the prime of life with a view to their old age, and preserves their right of independence".[12] However, postal savings did not fare well in this regard immediately after their establishment.[13] When the postal savings system was put into place in 1875, the number of post offices handling postal savings stood at only 19 in the Tokyo and Yokohama areas. In addition to the small number of post offices handling savings, another basic reason for the postal savings system's failure to spread far and wide was that its offered interest rates below market rates.[14]

3.2.2 *The Expansion of Postal Savings as a Large-Sum Financial Institution*

From the latter half of the 1870s, measures were taken to remove obstacles to the popularization of postal savings. With the introduction of the local specified third-class post office system, under which relatively wealthy civilians[15] managed post offices, the total number of post offices increased across Japan (see Table 3.1). Growth in the total number of post offices also meant an increase in the number of those handling postal savings. Even in comparison to the increase in the number of national banks and private banks which were also being established and spreading across Japan, the growth in the number of post offices handling postal savings was particularly noteworthy.

---

[12] "Chokin Azukari Kisoku (Regulations for the Acceptance of Savings)," 1874, "*Yūsei Hyakunenshi Shiryō Ikkan (Centennial History of Postal Services Materials, Volume 1),*" pp. 127–128.

[13] In the United Kingdom, in contrast, postal savings achieved considerable growth immediately after they were launched, particularly among the working class in urban areas. Hiroshi Shimomura, "*Chochiku Kikan Ron (Comments on Savings Institutions),*" Hobunkan, 1911. Maejima Hisoka once gave out coins to ordinary people to have them open postal savings accounts. Maejima Hisoka, "Jijoden (Autobiography)," Ichino Yasaburō ed., *Kosokon*, 1920, p. 123.

[14] Interest rates on postal savings soon after the system's establishment were relatively low. "When we inquired at the post office about interest on postal savings, they said the interest rate is 3%... we thought that nobody would deposit their money with the post office at such a low interest rate." "Yūbin Chokin Azukari no Koyo (Tosho) [the Utility of Receipts of Postal Savings (Letter)]" *Tokyo Nichinichi Shimbun*, June 4, 1874 "*Yūsei Hyakunenshi Shiryō 21-Kan Shinbun Zasshi Kiji Shū (The History of 100 Years of Postal Services Materials, Volume 21: Collection of Newspaper and Magazine Articles*" Yoshikawa Kobunkan, 1971, pp. 25–26).

[15] In 1882, *Udaijin* (Minister of the Right) Iwakura Tomomi said: "Farmers and merchants with assets and reputation who stand out in their communities are usually heads of towns/villages or Health Committee members, or if not, post office chiefs." (Kōmon Tada ed., "*Iwakura-ko Jitsuki Gekan (the True Account of Duke Iwakura, Final Volume),*"1906, p. 934).

Table 3.1 Expansion of financial institutions handling personal savings

	Total number of post offices	No. of third-class post offices	Post offices handling postal savings	National banks	Private banks
1875	3815	3612	22	4	0
1880	5036	4733	810	151	38
1885	4795	N.A	4338	139	217
1890	4134	3540	2804	134	272
1895	4240	3626	3030	133	908
1900	4798	3782	4930	–	2289

Sources Mukai Yurio, "*Yūbin Chokin no Hatten to Sono Shoyouin (the Development of Postal Savings and its Contributing Factors)*," United Nations University, 1981, Table 17; TeranishiJurō, "*Nihon no Keizai Hatten to Kinyū (Japan's Economic Development and Finance)*," Iwanami Shoten, 1982, p. 36

Interest rates on postal savings were revised almost every year and rose to 7.2% in 1881.[16] As a result, however, a situation arose that was utterly different from that what the government had intended. As a result of the series of measures described above and the economic slump of the Matsukata Deflation from 1881, postal savings established for "the purpose of encouraging poor people to save and thereby protect themselves," came to be used in the 1880s "not infrequently by wealthy people". In "extreme cases" this included "temporarily accumulated large-scale commercial funds for financial reasons".[17] This is reflected in statistics on postal savings in the 1880s, as shown in Fig. 3.2. The government viewed this situation as both contrary to the purpose of the postal savings system and also disadvantageous for government finances as a whole. It was argued that "it would not be advisable for the state to take deposits of large-scale funds for which the redemptions time remains uncertain in terms of finance policy".[18]

Right after their establishment in the nineteenth century, postal savings were functioning contrary to the government's policy goal. They were not serving as a savings institution for middle- and low-income earners. As indicated by the fact that deposits of postal savings and talented human resources of third-class post offices flowed out to private-sector banks amid the rapid increase in the number of banks

[16] Ministry of Posts and Telecommunications, "*Yūsei Hyakunenshi Shiryō 29-Kan (The History of 100 Years of Postal Services Materials, Volume 29)*", Yoshikawa Kobundo, 1972, pp. 17–25.

[17] Sugiura, "Taishuteki Reisai Chochiku Kikan Toshiteno Yūbin Chokin no Seiritsu (The Establishment of Postal Savings as a Popular Small Financial Institution)," p. 523.

[18] "Yūbin Chokin Jōsei wo Sadamu (the Postal Savings Ordinance Enacted)," 1890, ("*Yūsei Hyakunenshi Shiryō 1-Kan (The History of 100 Years of Postal Services Materials, Volume 1)*," pp. 47–48).

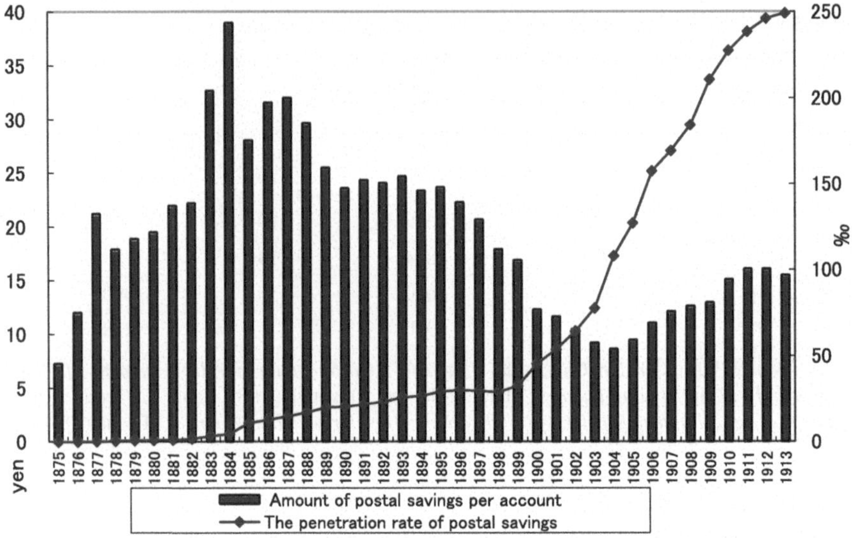

Fig. 3.2 The trend of the popularization of postal savings. The postal savings penetration rate (‰) = The number of postal savings accounts per 1000 people. *Sources* Ministry of posts and telecommunications, "*Yūsei Hyakunenshi Shiryō 30-Kan (The history of 100 years of postal services materials, Volume 30)*", Yoshikawa Kobundo, 1971, Cho-Table 5; Ohkawa Kazushi et al., "*Chōki Keizai Tōkei 1 (long-term economic statistics 1)*", Table 1

in the 1890s,[19] the principal users of the postal savings system were the relatively affluent, including "local leaders of high repute".[20]

The government had a dim view of the savings behavior of middle- and low-income earners. It assumed that they "do not plan for the evening in the morning, immediately spend whatever they gain, and in extreme cases, seem to regard frugality and savings as a shame".[21] Intellectuals viewed people "below the middle class" as "devoid of diligence and thrift" with a "habit of spending what they earn within the same day". They were seen as "extremely weak-minded about savings", and even "people above the middle class" were seen as "given to speculate in pursuit of a

[19] Sugiura, "Taishuteki Reisai Chochiku Kikan Toshiteno Yūbin Chokin no Seiritsu (The Establishment of Postal Savings as a Popular Small Financial Institution)," pp. 524–525.

[20] The definition of local leaders of good repute follows Einosuke Yamanaka, "*Kindai Nihon no Chihō Seido to Meiboka (The Local Government System in Modern Japan and Local Leaders of Good Repute)*" (Kobundo, 1990), and the term is used to mean "people who, based on rich assets and economic power within specific communities, enjoy the trust and support of residents in their communities for some reasons, including family lineage, heroic behaviors, acts of benefaction, leadership, vitality and so on, and thereby have qualities and abilities to act as representatives of community residents, and also people who have the honor and popularity of earning the high esteem of community residents in the sense that they are expected to have qualities, abilities and the potentiality to engage in administration in their communities".

[21] "Chokin Azukari Kisoku (Regulations for the Acceptance of Savings)," 1874.

shortcut to getting rich quickly, rather than pursue steady and sound enterprises".[22] During the nineteenth century, much of the Japanese population had not acquired an orientation toward savings, nor towards taking advantage of modern financial institutions.

3.2.3 The Broadening of Policy Intentions and the Improvement of Institutional Infrastructure

Though the habit of making personal petty savings at modern financial institutions had yet to take firm root among Japanese people, the government went ahead and expanded the economic functions of individual savings. Faced with the challenges of an expanding demand for funds among businesses and the need to maintain Japan's place on the gold standard after the Sino-Japanese War, the government's intentions regarding the use of postal savings shifted. In effect, postal savings began to be seen as one of the state's fiscal resources, a departure from the aims set out in the Postal Savings Ordinance of 1890.[23] In addition, an expansion of demand for funds from the private sector following the sudden rise of corporations led to a financial market crunch and resulted in a depression in 1898, following the Sino-Japanese War. This downturn drove home to the government the necessity of forming investment funds by accumulating domestic savings, as well as the necessity of encouraging savings, and the need for the government to raise industry relief funds whilst maintaining the currency system.

Under these circumstances, "*Chochiku Shōrei ni Kansuru Yutatsu* (*Official Instructions on Encouragement of Savings*)," issued to local government officials by Minister of Finance Inoue Kaoru in 1898, came to be often referred to as the point of departure for a subsequent series of measures for encouraging savings.[24] These instructions set forth a groundbreaking savings policy by stating that "having people desist from unnecessary consumption to prepare for their future would be in their own great interest, and in the interest of the national economy".[25]

An address on "Chochiku Shōrei Ron (Call for the Encouragement of Savings)," made by Minister of Finance Matsukata Masayoshi at a meeting of local government officials in 1890 indicated that the government regarded individual savings as having both a social security function and a function as a source of funding for industry, or as Matsukata put it: "savings are the way to have people desist from unproductive

---

[22] Amano Tameyuki, "Tobakuteki Kokumin ha Gaishi Yunyū wo Kataru Bekarazu (People Who Like Gambling Should Not Talk about Imports of Foreign Capital)," *Toyo Keizai Shimpo* No. 155 (1900), p. 392.

[23] Kamiyama Tsuneo, "*Meiji Keizaiseisakushi no Kenkyū (Research on the History of Economic Policies during the Meiji Period)*," Hanawashobo, 1995, Chap. 4.

[24] "*Ginkō Tsūshinroku (Bankers' Magazine)*," No. 175 (June 1900), p. 926.

[25] Minister of Finance Inoue Kaoru, "Chochiku Shōrei ni Kansuru Yutatsu (Official Instructions on Encouragement of Savings)," published in *Tokyo Keizai Zasshi (Tokyo Economics Magazine)*, No. 931 (1898).

consumption and generate productive capital".[26] Matsukata also thought that individual savings would help make it possible for Japan to curb imports and maintain its foreign currency reserves by acting as a restraint on extravagant consumption.

The policy intention of curbing consumption through the encouragement of savings has drawn attention among financial history researchers in both the pre- and post-Second World War periods,[27] What the government at the time actually sought was only to restrain "unnecessary consumption," and it should be noted that extreme cases of consumption restraint such as cutting back on meal expenses were subjected to criticism.[28] Though the government set forth the policy of constraining consumption in the private sector, that policy, unlike official slogans during the Second World War, cautioned against a large increase in imports, calling on people to specifically refrain from purchasing luxury goods such as imported watches. The government policy was not designed to lower the standard of living, it did not seek to reduce the consumption of food, for example, much of which was domestically produced.

Because these official instructions and addresses were also published in private-sector magazines, the concept of turning petty savings into a funding resource for government finances and industry is believed to have spread to private-sector businesspeople and the intellectual class.[29] In the late nineteenth century, with the Japanese economy standing on the threshold of industrialization after experiencing the development of the financial system and currency system and the rise of companies, individual savings came to be regarded as funding resources in the face of the shortage of funds as the demand for funds expanded. Since an increase in private-sector funds was an important issue for the government, it placed no limits on where to deposit savings. After recognizing postal savings as a de facto funding resource of the state, the government was particularly sensitive to any decline in postal savings, as it regarded "an increase in postal savings as an increase in capital of the state".[30]

[26] Minister of Finance Matsukata Masayoshi, "Chochiku Shōrei Ron (Call for Encouragement of Savings)," shorthand records of the April 1900 meeting of local government officials, published in "*Ginkō Tsūshinroku (Bankers' Magazine)*," No. 175 (June 1900), p. 926.

[27] The encouragement of savings also represented a comprehensive price policy, designed to control an outflow of specie and keep prices from rising through declines in demand and the volume of currency in circulation. "Japanese people… are hooked on consumption. One of its harmful effects is…sharp rises in prices." Cabinet Office, "Yūbin Chokin Rishi Wariai Keisei Su (Postal Savings Interest Rates Revised)," *Kobun Ruiju (Collection of Official Documents)*, 1898, Volume 25. References to the theory of consumption restrictions in research on financial history include Takizawa Naoshichi, "*Kohon Nihon Kinyūshi Ron (Manuscript on the Theory of Japanese Financial History)*" (Yuhikaku Shobo, 1912, p. 603); Ohshima Kiyoshi, "*Nihon Kyoko Shiron Jo (the Theory of Japanese Depression History Part 1)*" (University of Tokyo Press, 1952, p. 173).

[28] Shimomura Hiroshi (Director-General of the Savings Bureau, Ministry of Posts and Telecommunications), "*Tomi to Chochiku (Wealth and Savings)*," Dobunkan, 1911.

[29] "Count Inoue Kaoru advocated the encouragement of savings…Bank of Japan Governor Yamamoto…made speeches about this at various places…and are at the moment, speaking about how to encouraging savings…" "*Ginkō Tsūshinroku (Bankers' Magazine)*," No. 175 (June 1900), p. 926.

[30] Ministry of Posts and Telecommunications, "*Yūbin Chokin Annai (Guide to Postal Savings)*," 1905, p. 26.

"The remarkable spread of diligence, thrift and savings from the government in the face of the currency and fiscal system crisis"[31] indicated expectations for individual savings by the government and the business community. The slogan of "diligence, thrift and savings" did not simply represent idealism but had a practical importance, or as it was put "a necessity in terms of the national economy" and "a necessity in terms of social policy".[32] In order to promote the slogan further, the government proceeded with the development of the financial system and other relevant organizations. This included banks, with the easing of fund management conditions under the revised National Bank Act and the rise of companies, regional banks (including savings banks) were established across Japan in the latter half of the 1890s,[33] as shown in Table 3.1. The number of post offices handling postal savings also rose during this time, and in 1900, the Industrial Cooperative Act was enacted and enforced. From the late nineteenth century and early twentieth century, the formation of individual savings with modern financial institutions by ordinary people was no longer impossible in Japan.

3.2.4 Popularization of Individual Savings

Following the broadening of the government's policy intentions and the improvement of the institutional infrastructure of the financial system, the savings rate in the Japanese economy stabilized at the relatively high level of around 10% in the early twentieth century. From this point forward, the total amount of deposits and savings at a variety of financial institutions, including banks, industrial cooperatives and postal savings, followed an increasing trend, with funding resources being formed in various sectors. Among them, postal savings grew in scale and by around 1910 accounted for over 10% of government finance. A breakdown of the size of postal savings accounts shows that accounts with savings of less than 5 yen, which had accounted for just over 50% of the total number of postal savings accounts at the end of the nineteenth century, increased to over 80% as of 1904 (Table 3.2). This indicates that by this time postal savings had come to serve as a system that collected small-amount savings instead of high-amount savings. Though the share of accounts with savings of less than 5 yen marginally decreased between 1904 and 1909, the total number of accounts doubled and the total amount of postal savings more than tripled. Small-amount savings maintained a high share among postal savings in terms of number of accounts.

---

[31] Shirai, Kikuwaka "*Nihon no Kinyū Kikan (Japanese Financial Institutions),*" Moriyama Shoten, 1939, pp. 142–143.

[32] Aoki Daizaburō (Head of the Osaka Telegraph and Post Office), "*Gakudo Chokin Dan (The Story of Schoolchild Savings),*" 1898, p. 1.

[33] Kyowa Bank History Editing Office, "*Honpo Chochiku Ginkōshi (History of Savings Banks in Japan),*" Kyowa Bank, 1969; Asai Yoshio, "Chochiku Ginkō Ho to Dokusenteki Chochiku Seido no Keisei (Jo) (Enactment of the Savings Bank Act and the Formation of the Monopolistic Savings System (Part 1)),'' *The Economic Review*, No. 64 (1979).

Table 3.2 The scale of use of postal savings

Amount of postal savings per account	1893		1904				1909			
	No. of accounts		No. of accounts		Amount		No. of accounts		Amount	
Total of accounts with less than 5 yen	595	56.1%	4034	80.6%	4462	10.3%	7909	76.7%	10,939	8.2%
Accounts with 5 yen to less than 100 yen	398	37.6%	881	17.6%	18,715	43.4%	2147	20.8%	48,104	36.1%
100 yen or more	67	6.4%	91	1.8%	19,975	46.3%	251	2.4%	74,358	55.7%

Unit: 1000 accounts, 1000 yen
Source Shimomura Hiroshi (Director-General of the Savings Bureau, Ministry of Posts and Telecommunications), "*Chochiku Kikan Ron (Comments on Savings Institutions)*" (Hobunkan, 1911)

Small-amount savings were not huge quantitatively in comparison to their size in later years. Nevertheless, the steady accumulation of small-amount savings in postal savings accounts after the turn of the twentieth century can be described as supportive of the subsequent smooth growth of overall deposits and savings in Japan. The habituation of popular savings behavior nationally, starting from the national popularization of postal savings for the formation of small-amount savings, was an important foundation for the structure of mobilizing the small-amount funds of individuals.

The question is how such savings behavior arose and took root in Japanese society. While the central government established various systems to cultivate and promote new sources of funds, whether to take advantage of such systems to form savings was entirely dependent on the behavior of individuals. In fact, even before the turn of the twentieth century, the encouragement of savings itself was conducted by various entities. For example, already during the Matsukata Deflation period in the latter half of the 1880s, local governments across Japan issued official instructions concerning diligence, thrift and savings mainly by way of famine countermeasures.[34] However, such developments fell short of influencing the trends of deposits and savings at financial institutions or causing a major change in the propensity to save in the whole Japanese economy.

[34] For example, such instructions were issued in Shizuoka Prefecture in 1885. "There is nothing more horrible in the world than famine...people in all towns and villages should be diligent in their work, stay thrifty and prepare for famine in advance...," "Meiji 18-nen 6-gatsu 27-nichi Yutasu (Official Instructions Issued on June 27, 1885), Shizuoka Prefecture, *(Genkō Shizuoka-ken Reitatsu Ruisan 1899-nendo 1-kan (Collection of Current Orders and Instructions of Shizuoka Prefecture FY1899, Volume 1).*

The central government's savings promotion policy launched at the end of the nineteenth century continued as part of local community improvement movement after the Russo-Japanese War.[35] The central government encouraged the realignment, or creation, of various organizations within regional communities. Though this movement represented state policy, it could only materialize with the participation of private-sector entities and local actors.[36] In 1908, after the launch of the movement for local community improvement, the Minister of the Interior, Hirata Tōsuke, said that "cooperative-activity is most necessary for the convenience of local industry... industrial cooperatives, saving associations or mutual aid associations... are the most appropriate methods for promoting industry." In its industrial promotion policy, the central government recognized the importance of generating funding resources through the accumulation of small-amount savings which could be used for the invigoration of regional economies. It also recognized that appropriate organizations were necessary to promote the formation of such savings.[37] Though an individual's savings ultimately belonged to that individual, at the same time they were regarded as a funding resource for the state and industry, as well as an important element in the structure and activities of regional communities.

Why did the government's savings promotion policy begin to exhibit effects at the beginning of the twentieth century? What were the receptions and responses to it in regional communities? In the following sections I examine the impact that government policy and organizations had on the formation of individual small-amount savings and consider the situation of people in the background.

---

[35] Research providing an overview of the movement for local community improvement includes that of Miyachi Masato, "*Nichiro Sengo Seijishi no Kenkyū—Teikokushugi Keiseiki no Toshi to Nōson (Research on Political History after the Russo-Japanese War—Cities and Farming Villages in the Formation Period of Imperialism)*," (University of Tokyo Press, 1973). The Boshin Shosho (Boshin Imperial Rescript) of 1908 is often considered to mark the start of the movement for local community improvement.

[36] The policy developments of these state approaches to the Japanese people's sense of values and everyday behavior and voluntary responses by private-sector organizations appear to be different from the U.S. experiences. Sheldon Garon, *Molding Japanese Minds: The State in Everyday Life*, Princeton University Press, Princeton, 1998, p.xiv. While Garon mainly covered developments after the interwar period, Okada Kazunobu, "Chochiku Shōrei Undō no Shiteki Tenkai: Shōgaku Chochiku Hikazei Seido no Genryū (Historical Development of the Savings Encouragement Movement: The Headwater of the Small Amount-Savings Tax Exemption System)," (Doubunkan Shuppan, 1996) elaborates on the relationship between private-sector banks and savings associations.

[37] A summary of the instructions by Minister of the Interior Hirata Tōsuke at a meeting of prefectural governors in October 1908. Taikakai ed., "Naimusho-shi Dai 4-kan (History of the Ministry of the Interior, Volume 4)," 1971, reprinted edition, 1980, p. 358.

3.3 The Spread of the Habit of Savings: The Process of the Popularization of Postal Savings

3.3.1 *Systems for the Popularization of Postal Savings*

Table 3.3 shows the occupational breakdown of postal savings users between 1893 and 1909. The data show a noticeable increase in the number of farmers and students (including all ages from elementary schools to universities) among savers. As Sugiura pointed out, the payment method of "wartime reward payments" for those who fought in the Russo-Japanese War led to a temporary but remarkable rise in the number of soldiers,[38] but the ratio of soldiers was not so high compared with the two categories of farmers and students. Therefore, this section focuses on farmers and students in its examination of the national popularization of postal savings. Though the amounts of savings were not large at this point of time, the participation of these social groups in postal savings signifies that savings behavior had penetrated deeply into the social strata raising the propensity to save of the entire nation. Farmers accounted for a majority of those employed in Japan at the time and were present throughout the nation.[39] Students were young and represented the next generation.

How did postal savings draw out the savings behavior of these two major and important social groups? In order to assess this, we first have to consider the sluggish growth of postal savings during the nineteenth century and the government's response to this. In particular, the fact that the amounts and the number of accounts of postal savings both declined sharply during the Sino-Japanese War depression deeply shocked the government and was considered "a big stain in the history of postal savings." This experience of a sharp fall in savings steeled the government's determination to promote savings, and overcome any barriers to that effect among government ministries and agencies.[40] With consensus and cooperation within the government, various institutional revisions were implemented and new systems were introduced with respect to postal savings. Firstly, in 1898, as trumpeted by the instructions from the Minister of Finance cited earlier, the interest rate was raised from 4.2 to 4.8%. Furthermore, following the criticism of a group of large bank capitalists

[38] Because of the handling of postal savings at battlefields and the payments of most of postwar allowances as "award postal savings" of soldier users and the amounts of their savings showed a sharp temporary increase in statistics of postal savings during and after the Russo-Japanese War. Bureau of Postal Savings, Ministry of Communications, "Yūbin Chokin Kyoku Yūbin Chokin Jimusho Dai I-pen (History of Administration of Postal Savings, Bureau of Postal Savings, Part 1)," 1910.

[39] Statistics Bureau, Management and Coordination Agency, "Nihon Chōki Tōkei Sōran Dai 1-kan (Compendium of Japanese Long-Term Statistics, Volume 1)," Japanese Statistical Association, 1987, Table 2.18; Umemura Mataji, "*Chōki Keizai Tōkei 2 Rōdōryoku (Long-Term Economic Statistics, 2, Labor Force)*," Toyo Keizai Shimpo, 1988, Tables 1, 5 and 10.

[40] "*Yūbin Chokin Kyoku Yūbin Chokin Jimushi Dai I-pen (History of Administration of Postal Savings, Bureau of Postal Savings, Part 1)*," p. 36.

Table 3.3 The breakdown of occupations of postal savings users

	1893	1897		1902		1906		1909	
	No. of users	No. of users	Amount	No. of users	Amount	No. of users	Amount	No. of users	Amount
Agriculture	87	485	842	799	772	2145	2060	3036	3453
	27%	38%	32%	27%	25%	29%	26%	29%	31%
Commerce	71	206	537	331	547	746	1278	1157	2574
	22%	16%	21%	11%	18%	10%	16%	11%	23%
Industry	34	92	220	143	205	362	500	620	1103
	11%	7%	8%	5%	7%	5%	6%	6%	10%
Miscellaneous	29	74	185	140	236	337	581	526	944
	9%	6%	7%	5%	8%	5%	7%	5%	8%
Hired craftsmen and ordinary employees	32	59	120	141	151	400	438	782	894
	10%	5%	5%	5%	5%	5%	5%	8%	8%
Government officials and soldiers	33	80	203	186	288	726	1159	790	1508
	10%	6%	8%	6%	9%	10%	14%	8%	13%
Students	18	68	36	577	153	1843	691	2501	1091
	6%	5%	1%	20%	5%	25%	9%	24%	10%
Fishermen and sailors	4	15	30	41	50	109	139	198	265
	1%	1%	1%	1%	2%	1%	2%	2%	2%
No occupation	3	17	39	64	90	184	309	269	483
	1%	1%	1%	2%	3%	2%	4%	3%	4%
Shrines, temples and other organizations	7	24	83	13	37	29	111	57	412
	2%	2%	3%	0%	1%	0%	1%	1%	4%
Occupation unknown	N.A	144	320	473	515	536	731	371	582
		11%	12%	16%	17%	7%	9%	4%	5%
Total	319	1265	2616	2907	3046	7414	7996	10,307	11,211

Unit: 1000 persons, 10,000 yen

Sources Bureau of postal savings, ministry of communications, "Yūbin Chokin Kyoku Yūbin Chokiin Jimushi Dai I-pen (history of administration of postal savings, bureau of postal savings, Part 1)," 1910, table on p. 238

Ministry of communications, "Yūbin Kawase Chokin Jigyō Gaiyō Dai 19-kai Meiji 42-nendo (Overview of the postal money order savings businesses, 19, FY1909)

who argued that "the rate is still much too low", the interest rate was raised again to 5.0% in 1904.

At the time, private-sector banks tended not to be very proactive about postal savings as they thought the acceptance of popular small-amount savings did not justify their costs. After several rounds of interest rate increases, the interest rate on postal savings was still lower than market interest rates at the time. Private-sector banks did not therefore regard postal savings as a competitor in acquiring deposits and viewed developments with postal savings only as a policy of support for medium- and low-income earners.[41]

In order to stimulate the formation of small deposits that generate little interest, opportunities and convenience of using deposits were more important, and revisions to this system were more dramatic.[42] The promotional brochure distributed across the country, "Yūbin Chokin Annai (Guide to Postal Savings)," issued by the Ministry of Communications in 1905, was itself part of the proactive savings promotion policy. It was also indicative of how the introduction of various systems contributed to the popularization of postal savings and how the Ministry of Communications encouraged individual savings.[43] The brochure preached at the outset that "now is the age of diligence and savings for the entire nation," and presented thrift as the secret method of "earning money to be saved", together with checkoff from revenue and engaging in side jobs. After explaining these methods, the brochure pointed out that holding onto savings generated in households ran the risk that "the savings would be taken by thieves, burned in fires or swept away in flooding." The brochure stated that if people used postal savings, they would not see their money disappear in such a way and "they would generate interest upon interest" which was likened to "savings breeding like rabbits [*nezumizan*]." Furthermore, the brochure pitched postal savings as "the safest vehicle, as the government oversees them" and "the most convenient, as they are handled by over 6200 post offices in cities, towns and country areas across Japan."

Regarding the ample opportunities to handle postal savings, the introduction in 1899 of the system for post office officials to handle them out of office on a dispatching "*shucchō*" basis, cannot be overlooked.[44] As a result of the introduction of this

[41] "Chochiku Shōrei ni Kansuru Yurakukai Chōsa Iin no Iken (the Opinion of an Investigation Member of the Yurakukai Concerning the Encouragement of Savings)," *Ginkō Tsūshinroku (Bankers' Magazine)*," Volume 30, No. 180 (1900), p. 926. Regarding interest rates, the opinion stated, "while some people voiced criticisms when the interest rate on postal savings was raised, the average interest rate at savings banks today stands at around 6.5%...postal savings should not be seen as competition."

[42] Sugiura, "Taishuteki Reisai Chochiku Kikan Toshiteno Yūbin Chokin no Seiritsu (the Establishment of Postal Savings as a Popular Small Financial Institution)," p. 536. As Sugiura pointed out in "Nichiro Sen Go no Yūbin Chokin no Tenkai to Chochiku Shōrei Seisaku (the Development of Postal Savings after the Russo-Japanese War and Savings Incentive Policy) (p. 44), the interest-rate sensitivity of small-amount savings, including postal savings, is believed to have increased only in periods after the popularization of these savings had been achieved.

[43] "Yūbin Chokin Annai (Guide to Postal Savings)," 1905. Hereinafter, quotations in this sector below are from pp. 4–19 of the brochure, unless otherwise specified.

[44] Ministry of Posts and Telecommunications, "*Yūsei Hyakunenshi Shiryō 29-Kan (The History of 100 Years of Postal Services Materials, Volume 29)*," pp. 52–53.

system, under which the post office would go to "government offices, barracks, factories and other places where a large number of people place savings simultaneously and handle postal savings on predetermined days," postal savings provided a large number of opportunities for use that could never be offered by other financial institutions at the time. Postal savings were handled at some 6000 post offices as well as 2966 "*shucchō*" postal savings handling temporary offices and 10,151 post collection points as of 1905. "In rural communities where no post offices exist, this method was created for postmen to collect postal savings at predetermined local government offices, schools, shrines or temples," and it became unnecessary for people "to take the trouble of going to post offices when they are busy."

The brochure also explained other characteristics of postal savings. The permitted savings amounts per account at the time started from 10 sen, rising up to 1000 yen, but no upper limits were imposed on savings by public entities, shrines, temples, schools, non-profit corporations, groups, cooperative savings or industrial cooperatives. Fractions of less than 10 sen could also be placed in savings with the use of postage stamps, a method described as "very convenient for school children and women saving tiny amounts like 5 rin or one sen." This method was called stamp savings,[45] which raised strong expectations, even prior to its launch, for the encouragement of savings among young people, including students. Paul Mayet pointed to the advantages of stamp savings within the government in 1890,[46] and the private sector also talked them up.[47] As a result, a survey was conducted in 1898,[48] and the postage stamp savings were enforced in March 1900. The regulation on the method of using the postage stamp savings was simple. "In order to make postal savings using stamps...all you have to do is to purchase 'the postage stamp savings mount'...paste postage stamps on the entire inner surface of the mount...and submit it to a post office with a savings passbook" (Fig. 3.3).

Partly because the stamp mount was free of charge initially, the wasteful use of mounts became an issue,[49] since "at the start of the stamp savings system, curious students tended to seek a large amount of stamp mounts, but those who actually placed savings with the use of stamp mounts failed to reach even 50% of the number of mounts given out." Looking at this from another perspective, however, it showed that a number of people equal to nearly 50% of the total number of stamp

---

[45] This system originated in postal savings enforced in the United Kingdom in 1880. Aoki, "*Gakudo Chokin Dan (The Story of Schoolchild Savings)*," p. 14.

[46] Paul Mayet, "Nōgyō Hoken Ron (Agricultural Insurance in Organic Connection with Savings-Banks, Land-Credit, and the Commutation of Debts)," Nihon Shoseki, 1890.

[47] Tokura Yoshikazu, "*Ikanishite Yokin wo Kyūshū Subekiya (Zoku) (How Should Deposits Be Absorbed? (Sequel)*," Toyo Keizai Shimpo, No. 95 (1898).

[48] "Kitte Chokin Jikkō no Gi (About the Enforcement of Stamp Savings)," *Tokyo Keizai Zasshi (Tokyo Economics Magazine)*, No. 931 (1898), pp. 1269–1270.

[49] Bureau of Postal Savings, Ministry of Communications, "*Yūbin Chokin Kyoku Yūbin Chokiin Jimushi Dai I-pen (History of Administration of Postal Savings, Bureau of Postal Savings, Part 1)*," p. 103. In order to solve this problem, the method for stamp savings was changed in October 1900 to the use of mounts on which stamps were printed, sold for the actual prices of the postage stamps.

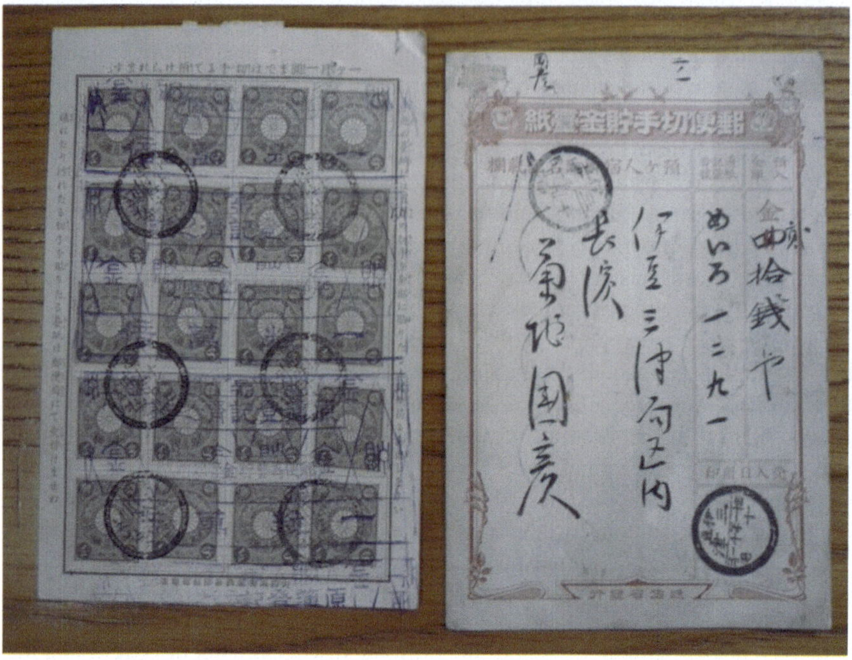

Fig. 3.3 Stamp savings mount. *Source* Ministry of communications, "postage stamp savings mount" 1908 (in the possession of the Numazu City Meiji Historical Museum)

mounts distributed placed their money in postal savings accounts as savings from immediately after the start of the stamp savings system.

As can be seen in Table 3.3, the number of students using postal savings increased dramatically after 1900. Sugiura has already pointed out this fact, noting that the introduction of postage stamp savings led to an increase in small-amount savings accounts by students and this was a major factor behind the trend toward smaller lots of postal savings at the beginning of the twentieth century.[50] As a result of this system, a bureaucrat at the Ministry of Communications proudly stated as follows in 1910:

> It is difficult to acquire the traits of diligence, thrift and savings in the prime of manhood…the training of self-control and restraint should absolutely be conducted during boyhood. Particularly in Japan, given the evil practice of despising money-making, it is all the more urgent…savings by students have rapidly increased since the start of the postage stamp savings system…its impact on society and public feelings in Japan has been great…and it should

[50] Sugiura, "*Taishuteki Reisai Chochiku Kikan Toshiteno Yūbin Chokin no Seiritsu (the Establishment of Postal Savings as a Popular Small Financial Institution)*," p. 520. However, while Sugiura viewed the expansion of postal savings and their decline as just disruptive developments caused by the increase in the number of student users, he also said they had "an important significance in nurturing savers in the future under the government policy" and "a starting point in the policy history of a series of policy evolutions to broadly capture 'lower-class people in society' as savers".

> lead to a major renovation in the psychology of the Japanese people in less than a decade or so down the road.[51]

As seen above, the introduction of the postage stamp savings system was one of the major factors for the popularization of postal savings. It is thought to have played a significant role in educating the young about savings, preparing the next generation to become savers and thus raising the propensity to save. During this period postal savings also introduced a unique system not seen at other financial institutions. The system was the so-called "special savings" system,[52] including covenant savings, deferred savings and cooperative savings. Covenant savings were defined as "making deposits of savings under an arrangement among a large number of people with pledges not to withdraw the money without good reason." This method was recommended as "the most suitable system for a large number of people who agree to strictly enforce savings." Covenant savings were "handled in a special manner, and even when savers apply for withdrawals, unless applications for withdrawals are approved in accordance with pledges set out in covenants, withdrawals would not to be permitted." Deferred savings were a system where "post offices do not allow withdrawals unless the initially set period of deferment has lapsed." The period of deferment could be set between 3 and 10 years at the discretion of users. For cooperative savings, a general representative of a saving cooperative was appointed, and the members of the cooperative would make savings in the name of the general representative.

The special savings (covenant savings) system was a system under which voluntary groups that agreed on private savings covenants saved money as postal savings. As Table 3.4 shows, after the introduction of the system in 1903, the number of users of special savings rose to account for nearly 10% of all users of postal savings in 1908.[53] This showed that individual savings made as groups were conducted by social groups other than students mobilized by schools. The remainder of this chapter, examines the circumstances behind the use of postal savings at the time.

---

[51] *"Yūbin Chokin Kyoku Yūbin Chokiin Jimushi Dai I-pen (History of Administration of Postal Savings, Bureau of Postal Savings, Part 1),"* pp. 103–104.

[52] Ministry of Posts and Telecommunications, (*"Yūsei Hyakunenshi Shiryō 29-Kan (The History of 100 Years of Postal Services Materials, Volume 29)"*), p. 21. The covenant savings system itself existed from 1876 in the early years of the postal savings system as "a system for a small number of people to make savings in the name of a general representative." By adding other systems, such as deferred savings and cooperative savings, in 1903, it was launched anew as part of the "special savings" system.

[53] The number of cooperative accounts stood at 197 at the end of FY1904 and at 1141 as of the end of FY1908, which may seem small, but as savings under this system were used by two or more people together, the actual number of users of cooperative savings is believed to have been at least a few times larger.

Table 3.4 The share of covenant savings within postal savings (FY1908)

	Users (No. of accounts)	Balance (1000yen)
Deferred savings	177,319	934
Covenant savings	417,653	2853
Cooperative savings	1141	85
Total Postal savings	8,557,077	105,330
The ratio of specially handled savings to total postal savings	7.0%	3.7%

The numbers for deferred savings are gross totals regardless of years of deferment
Source Ministry of communications, "*Kawase Chokin Kyoku Tōkei Nenpō Meiji 41-nen Dai 18-kai (18th Statistical Annual Report of the Money Order Savings Bureau, FY1908),*" 1908

3.3.2 The Process of Phased Popularization: From the Central Part of Japan to the Regions

The formation of individual small-amount savings and the popularization of postal savings was a multi-layered process. Through this process the central government, which was not directly involved in the daily lives of people, intended to influence the day-to-day activities of people through improvements in the postal savings systems and via speeches and instructions. How were the various systems for the use of postal savings, developed and improved by the central government, and how were they used in people's everyday lives? These questions are taken up in this section and below through specific examples.

Wherever the central government was able to have direct contact with people's daily lives, direct measures for encouraging savings were implemented. At the Yokosuka Navy Arsenal, for example, "Shokkō Yūbin Chokin Toriatsukai Tetsuzuki (Procedures for Handling the Postal Savings of Mechanics)" were enacted on April 30, 1901. These procedures provided that "hereafter savings by mechanics shall be made with an amount of money checked off from each mechanic's monthly salary which officials of the accounting section shall handle." More specifically it explained that "mechanics making savings on their pay day shall bring their savings passbooks to the savings handling temporary office and hand them over to the accounting section officials there".[54] It was not only employees of state-run enterprises like this who were under the direct supervision of the central government. Local administrative officials such as *gunchō* (county mayors) also encouraged savings and made savings themselves. For example, in Ibo County, Hyogo Prefecture, it was reported in 1909 that since the new county mayor took office, "the county secretary, the county school inspector and the county engineer as well as all clerical staff were asked to save at least 10% of monthly salaries," and formed savings worth 2750 yen, including hypothec

[54] Yokosuka Navy Arsenal, "Yokosuka Kaigun Kosho Shi Dai 4-kan (History of the Yokosuka Navy Arsenal, Volume 4)," Yokohama Prison, 1935, pp. 142–143.

debentures. The county also implemented other ways of generating savings by "creating what was called bicycle savings ... in order to promote alacrity in routine office work."

Ibo County also "implemented '*tanomoshiko*' mutual financing ... for purchasing Western clothes." While the amount of savings made within the county office were only marginal, they served as a motivation to save and a model for others to follow. The formation of savings in such a way soon "spread to schools." The habituation of group savings implemented at local governments thus spread to other modern organizations. These efforts in Ibo County produced results. The county's "flourishing savings," included nearly 40,000 yen in student savings, "over 17,000 yen in youth association savings, over 44,800 yen in cooperative savings, over 56,600 yen in postal savings, and two million yen in bank deposits." The practical encouragement for individual savings within government offices had an impact on various regional organizations, spurring the formation of savings with a broad range of financial institutions besides postal savings.[55]

As the above cases suggest, the education sector responded to government policy. For example, in response to Minister of Finance Matsukata's address on the promotion of savings at a meeting of local government officials in 1900, "Kyōiku Jiron (the Educational Review)," a major education-related magazine at the time, immediately published a favorable article, which read: "Even a mere child knows that diligence, thrift and savings are virtues and that indulgence and luxury are bad habits... it is also apparent that these bad habits have infiltrated both the upper and lower classes in Japan... it may be a bit too late, but the fact that society is gradually moving toward an awakening should be welcomed and congratulated."[56]

Among the main articles in that issue of the magazine, titled "Shōgakkō ni Okeru Kunrenteki Seikatsu no Keito (The System of Training Life at Elementary Schools)", discussed some of the goals of educational training: "a lack of sense of public morality, time wasting, lies, luxury, a lack of fortitude and being unable to keep one's head, etc. must be unfailingly corrected... a thrifty mind must be nurtured, and [thus] students should record their consumption of school supplies."[57] Teachers and school principals who unlike the government were actually in everyday contact with elementary school students across Japan took note of the above goals, and as a result, the savings systems for school children, such as postage stamp savings, were implemented at school with the full cooperation of elementary schools. For example, Fukuoka Village in Atsumi County, Aichi Prefecture, had the following experiences:

> ▲ *Diligence, thrift and savings as well as the charity alms box*...Despite possessing land with great value for agriculture and sericulture as well as vegetable growing, the people are not striving to improve and advance this land. Rather they despise enterprise and spend money wastefully. The evils of these behaviors are having no small impact on the young and

---

[55] Ministry of the Interior, "*Jikken Dan Dai 2-kai Chihō Kairyo Jigyō Koshūkai (Story of Experiments: The Second Workshop on Local Community Improvement Projects)*," 1909, pp. 102–103.

[56] "Kingen Chochiku wo Shōrei Suru no Gi (About the Encouragement of Diligence, Thrift and Savings,)," *Kyōiku Jiron (the Educational Review)*, No. 541 (1900), p. 23.

[57] Tai Katōji, "Shōgakkō ni Okeru Kunrenteki Seikatsu no Keitō (the System of Training Life at Elementary Schools), *Kyōiku Jiron (the Educational Review)*, No. 541 (1900).

> elementary school children… As measures to correct such evils, firstly, we *impressed upon elementary school students the importance of diligence, thrift and savings.* More specifically, savings by students at school are now made with postage stamps. Schools purchase the stamps in advance, and hand over the purchased stamps to students as necessary. Subsequently, with respect to sources of money for purchasing postage stamps, we set four types: (1) *those specifically provided by fathers and/or mothers*, (2) those received as prizes, (3) *those obtained by one's own labor*, and (4) *those obtained by saving money on students' school supplies.* We restrict other sources of money for fear of giving rise to adverse effects.[58]

After elementary school education became free of charge following the 1900 third revision to the *Shōgakkō Rei (Elementary School Order)* (Imperial Edict No.344 of the 33rd year of the Meiji era), the enrollment rate for elementary education in Japan rose rapidly from a little over 60% in 1898, to over 80% in 1900, and to 97% in 1907.[59] The influence that elementary school education had over regional communities grew much stronger as a result. The magazine article cited above continued by saying, "the outcome of the encouragement of savings enforced in this way extended to homes," and emphasized that between 1903 and 1905 the number of savers grew to 200 and the amount saved exceeding 600 yen. This outcome stemmed from the saving of revenues from side jobs such as sericulture and poultry raising by students' fathers, elder brothers, mothers and elder sisters, or from any surplus money each month. There were over 50 savers for "savings handled by schools" alone and "over 100 other households that directly made postal savings", which meant these systems "reached a majority of the households across the village." In this way, elementary school education influenced not only students themselves but also their families.

These activities at schools often involved cooperation with local governments and contributed to regional industries. In Kōga County, Shiga Prefecture, "teachers led elementary school children from third graders and above… to collect the eggs of rice stem borer moths." In this practice, "the agricultural association gave rewards to students at the rate of 2 sen 5 rin per 100 eggs" with the rewarded students encouraged to "save rewards as postal savings."

In Minamoto Village, Chiba Prefecture, as well, there existed a system of cooperation between the elementary school and the village office. In the village, along with an arable land redevelopment project, a savings project was implemented across the whole village with "the village headman's assistant responsible for savings." It was said that "the collection of savings was made almost in the same manner as in other regions," but in reality, "on the 15th of each month, a student made the rounds of savers in his class to collect savings in a bag." From 1908, postage stamps were used for these savings. The village office that obtained revenues from fees for the purchase of stamps after negotiations "appropriated the revenue for savings incentives… rewards for students collecting savings… and rewards for people who diligently made savings." Rewards were given not in cash but in the form of goods

---

[58] Ōhashi Shigesei, "Shakaika Shitaru Shōgakkō (Socialized Elementary Schools)," *Shimin*, Part 1, No. 9 (1906), p. 10.

[59] Nakagawa Kiyoshi, "*Nihon no Toshi Kasō (The Urban Lower Class in Japan,)*, Keiso Shobo, 1985, p. 155.

or postage stamps.[60] As seen above, educators, who were relatively sensitive to the intentions of the central government through education administration and magazines, as well as county mayors, town mayors, and village headmen, who were in a position to receive instructions directly from central government bureaucrats, in collaboration with people with the power to mobilize people in their regions, carried out a variety of plans for the formation of savings.

Furthermore, personal connections and networks such as "*mujin*" mutual financing that had traditionally existed in village societies were reorganized to help encourage modern savings. For example, in Kamiminochi County, Nagano Prefecture in 1897, the county mayor, an official appointed by the central government, issued an official notice on the encouragement of savings for distribution to villages, preparing the format of the articles of association for savings cooperatives that used postal savings covenant savings accounts.[61]

In Tokiwa Village, Kita-Azumi County, Nagano Prefecture, at the initiative of a large "*shoya*" village headman in the early modern period, who became a postmaster of a third-class post office, a diligence, thrift and savings cooperative was established in 1909, and postal savings were promoted among the village residents. The "Tokiwamura Ippongi Honku Nanbu Kinken Chochiku Kumiai Kiyaku (the Code of the Diligence, Thrift and Savings Association of the Southern Main District of Ippongi, Tokiwa Village) stated that "the purpose of the association is to nurture a sound spirit by diligently attending to usual business, living simply and implementing savings in order to increase the financial resources of association members and enhance their welfare." It stipulated that association members "shall make covenant savings pursuant to the diligence, thrift and savings regulations" in minimum units of 10 sen each month. The cooperative also provided that when a member dies, a successor "shall naturally become a cooperative member… and succeed to his rights and obligations."[62] The family of the village headman created an association of relatives alone and created the "Kamikaze Kō (Divine Wind Association)" savings[63] by putting their money in postal savings.

In the case of a young men's association in Seinaiji Village, Shimo-Ina County, Nagano Prefecture, the continuity from the early modern period "Wakashu Gumi (Young Men's Group)" was even clearer.[64] This group, which inherited the customs

[60] Ministry of the Interior, "Jikken Dan (Story of Experiments)," the example of Koka County, p. 120, the example of Minamoto Village, p. 110.

[61] Documents of the Hara Family, Kamiminochi County Office, "*Kokuyu Dai 1-gou (Official Notice No. 1)*," 1897, in the possession of the Nagano Prefectural Museum of History.

[62] Documents of the Shimizu Family, "*Tokiwamura Ippongi Honku Nanbu Kinken Chochiku Kumiai Shorui (Documents of the Dilligence, Thrift Savings Cooperative of the Southern Main District of Ippongi, Tokiwa Village)*,"1909, in the possession of the Nagano Prefectural Museum of History.

[63] Documents of the Shimizu Family, Suehirosha, "Kamikaze Kō Chokin no Ken (the Case of the Divine Wind Savings)," 1891.

[64] Documents possessed by Shimo District, Seinaiji Village, Nagano Prefecture, Shimo-Seinaiji Young Men's Association, "*Shokurin Bo (Afforestation List)*," 1910. For details of the continuity and change in character of various communities in Seinaiji Village from the early modern period to the modern period, see Tanaka Hikaru, "Kinsei kara Kindai Shoki ni Okeru Kyōdōtai Kino no

and rules of the early modern period as they were, such as joint afforestation, village rituals and drinking parties after wedding ceremonies, placed some of its collective property in postal savings.[65] Changes in the rules of the young men's association shows well the growing orientation toward modern education and savings and how it shaped people's awareness. The code book of 1893 contained only clauses similar to the prohibitions of the early modern period such as prohibitions on gambling and weekday drinking parties,[66] but in the 1912 version phrases such as diligence, thrift and the improvement of customs and manners were incorporated. This was the type of language often used in the movement for local community improvement, the code book explained that "the association's purpose shall be to seek the cultivation of knowledge and virtue, the fine customs of diligence and thrift, the development of the forestry industry, and the nurture of sound and moderate thought".[67]

At "Sekizen Savings Society," launched in 1906 in Mabashi Village, Chiba Prefecture, the number of society members came to 36, with a monthly amount of savings per member ranging widely from 3 sen to 5 yen at the discretion of each member. The savings collected were "deposited with secure banks," and the society was to be dissolved after a 3-year maturity of the deposits.[68] The format of the collection book was almost identical with that of *mujinko* (mutual financing association), involving lot drawing and what, in practice, was the lending of money around the same time.[69] This case indicates the adoption of a savings method that simultaneously made use of the "*mujin*" format and the depositing of money with modern financial institutions such as banks and postal savings.

The community functioned in a way that encouraged the participation of individuals in savings initiatives. This was also true of cases where modern organizations, such as local governments, led the savings initiative, and in many cases savings coalitions were made up of complex groups from a variety of social classes. In Tokura Village, Nishi-Tama County, Tokyo, a savings cooperative was formed within the village and savings of at least 5 rin (0.005 yen) a day were encouraged and collected in savings boxes. A women's group, named "Tokura Village Saturday Ladies' Association," called for "making postal savings (or other savings) of at least 10 sen every

---

Hensen—Seinenkai to Kukai ni Chūmoku Shite (Transition in Community Functions from the Early Modern Period to the Modern Period—Focusing on the Young Men's Association and the District Association)" (Nobuyuki Yoshida ed., "*Yamasato Seinaiji no Shakai Kōzō (Social Structure of the Mountain Village Seinaiji)*," Yamakawa Shuppansha, 2018). Hereinafter, documents and materials related to Seinaiji Village are in the possession of former Seinaiji Junior High School in Seinaiji, present-day Achi Village.

65 Shimo-Seinaiji Young Men's Association, "*Kihon Zaisanbo (Basic Property List)*," 1923.

66 Shimo-Seinaiji Village Elderly, "Sashiage Mosu—Fuda no Koto (We Present Our Opinion in This Document)," 1811: Shimo-Seinaiji Young Men's Association, "*Kiyakusho (Code Book)*," 1893.

67 Shimo-Seinaiji Young Men's Association, "Seiyenkai Kisoku (Rules of the Young Men's Association," 1901: Shimo-Seinaiji Young Men's Association, "*Seiyenkai Kiyaku (Code of the Young Men's Association)*," 1912.

68 Ohkawa Gohee and Onda Mangoro, "*Kyōdō Chokin Shukinbo (the Cooperative Savings Collection Book)*," 1906, in the possession of the Matsudo Museum.

69 Documents of the Hara Family, "Jintokuko Cash Receipt Book, 1904.

month" in its regulations.[70] In the case of Minamoto Village, Chiba Prefecture, cited above, funds "saved through the village office" became postal savings, and individuals could put "funds for savings either in a credit cooperative or a joint-stock bank in the village."[71] In Yodo Village, Ehime Prefecture, "the village headman himself distributed passbooks to solicit savings," and implemented "Sunday savings" from 1901. Elementary school students were mobilized to collect savings and out of a total of 486 households in the village, 630 residents participated initially, an indication of a village-wide savings campaign.

> "...One woman says that she would rather have monthly savings because making savings every week are too bothersome. She says she will put 2 yen or even 3 yen in a lump sum in savings each month. Another woman says that just as she was doing her hair the other day, a school kid came up to ask her to put up her savings money. She told the kid that she cannot do that now as she was doing her hair and that she would do so next time around. But the school kid would not listen and told her that he would wait until she finished doing her hair and did not go away... In the case of monthly savings, there is no opportunity to be reminded of the need of savings for the remaining 29 days, but for Sunday savings, there is no time for not thinking about savings. Indeed, the reason for the need of weekly savings lies here. A petty amount of 1 sen is very precious. If you can think of savings of 1 sen, you can save much larger amounts. When women handle consumable items in their kitchens every day, they can also pick up around 1 sen..."[72]

In Yodo Village, the savings campaign initially started in a semi-coercive manner from the perspective of participants. If the campaign leader was a positive and influential person in the region, there was practically no option for households but to participate even if they were skeptical about the formation of savings. However, when the accumulated funds grew to huge amounts over time, village people grew conscious of the unity within the village and also of the importance of savings, changing their previously-held negative perception. Consequently, an industrial cooperative was established in Yodo Village in 1908, with Sunday savings used as capital contributions by the individuals involved.

As seen above, in various areas across Japan in and around this period, the collective formation of individual small-amount savings had commenced. Many initiatives had a sense of "jumping on the bandwagon" about them, though there was diversity in the savings entities and methods employed locally in creating making postal savings. The pattern of actions for the formation of savings taken by individuals were in step with the government's policy goals and defined by the structure of regional society. In such a way they began to spread across Japan as can be observed in a myriad of specific examples recorded across the country, including those cited above.

---

[70] Tokyo Agricultural Association, "*Tokyo Nishi-Tamagun Tokura-mura Nōji Chōsa Fu Sonze (Agricultural Survey and Villege code of Tokura Village, Nishi-Tama County, Tokyo)*," 1907, pp. 102–103, p. 132.

[71] Ministry of the Interior, "*Jikken Dan (Story of Experiments)*," p. 110.

[72] Murata Uichirō, "*Chihō Kairyo no Jirei (Examples of the Improvement of Regions)*, Chūō Hōtokukai, 1926, pp. 95–96.

3.3.3 *The Real Picture of Savings Behavior: The Case of Mishima Town, Shizuoka Prefecture*

As seen in the preceding sub-section, the government's savings encouragement policy penetrated into regional communities through various organizations and schools, with the activities of those various organizations impacting people's behavior. In order to gain a closer understanding of this process in a regional community, this section examines the example of Mishima Town, Tagata County, Shizuoka Prefecture. Mishima Town was located along the former Tokaidō Road, and as of the end of FY1908, had a population of 10,654 who made up 1949 households. Approximately 20% of the employed population worked as farmers, 40% in commerce and 30% in miscellaneous businesses.[73] Mishima Town's financial institutions consisted of five banks, including branches, and one third-class post office by 1890.[74] As seen in Table 3.5, Tagata County, where Mishima Town was located, did not stand out in terms of its financial position. Shizuoka Prefecture as a whole had a relatively large number of banks at the time. In terms of the shares of the number of accounts and amounts, however, both bank deposits and postal savings were commensurate with the prefecture's population. The status of the collection of deposits of private-sector banks in Tagata County was not noteworthy either, and the ability to mobilize people to take out new postal savings may be described as approximately equal to the national average. How were savings encouraged and promoted in Mishima Town and what kind of savings behavior could be observed as a result?

Around 1893 Mishima Elementary School set "regulations for student savings" to encourage savings by its students. The regulations explained the purpose of saving as a way to "develop the habit of doing away with lavish spending and to enjoy seeing small amounts accumulate and grow larger." The regulations further stated that in soliciting savings, "teachers, in lecturing on morals, should advise students on the virtues of diligence and thrift ahead of any other matters and together strive to implement savings." Savings were made twice a week, and "students willing to make savings shall bring their funds to a teacher responsible for handling the savings along with their passbooks before the start of classes." In addition, the regulations noted that "amounts of less than 10 sen shall be combined and temporarily deposited at the post office".[75]

As the regulations suggested, Mishima Elementary School and Mishima Post Office had close cooperative ties. Watanabe Jutarō, postmaster of the third-class post office in Mishima at the time, ranked in the 10th grade (out of 28 grades in all) in the prefectural tax household levy (*kosuwari*), which positioned him in the top 25%

[73] Mishima Town Office, confirmed by survey slips included in "*Meiji Yonjūni-nen Gengisho Tsuzurikomi (File of Official Documents for 1909).*

[74] Mishima Town, "*Mishima Machi Shi (Mishima Town Magazine),*" 1912, p. 30.

[75] Mishima Municipal East Elementary School, "*Kaikō Hachiju-nen Shi (The History of 80 Years since the Opening of the School),*" (Manuscript), 1947, pp. 699–702.

Table 3.5 Relative positions of postal savings in Japan, Shizuoka prefecture and Tagata County

	Population		Banks				Postal savings						
			No. of outlets		Amount of deposits	No. of accounts	No. of post offices handling savings	Amounts of postal savings		No. of accounts		No. of new accounts	
	Pref./Japan	County/Pref	Pref./Japan	County/Pref	Pref./Japan	County/Pref	County/Pref	Pref./Japan	County/Pref	Pref./Japan	County/Pref	Pref./Japan	County/Pref
1898	3	9	4	9	1	3	8	–	–	–	–	3	1
1900	3	9	7	11	0	4	7	–	–	–	–	2	30
1901	3	9	7	11	1	5	6	–	–	–	–	1	23
1903	3	9	6	–	1	3	2	–	–	–	–	2	14
1906	3	9	6	–	1	–	–	1	12	2	13	1	8
1909	3	9	6	–	1	–	13	1	9	2	12	2	13

Unit: %

Sources Shizuoka Prefecture, "*Shizuoka-ken Tōkeisho (Shizuoka Prefecture Statistical Report)*" for each fiscal year; Ministry of Finance, "*Ginkō Eigyō Hokoku (Bank Business Reports)*," "*Ginkō Oyobi Tanpo-tsuki Shasai Shintaku Jigyō Hokoku (Bank and Secured Bond Trust Business Reports)*" for each fiscal year; Ministry of Communications, "*Kawase Chokin Kyoku Tōkei Nenpō (Statistical Annual Report of the Money Order Savings Bureau)*" for each fiscal year; Ministry of Posts and Telecommunications, "*Yūsei Hyakunenshi Shiryō 30-Kan (The History of 100 Years of Postal Services Materials, Volume 30)*," Cho-Table 5; Japanese Statistical Association, "*Nihon Chōki Tōkei Sōran (Compendium of Japanese Long-Term Statistics)*," Volume 1, 1987, Volume 3, 1988.

income group.[76] He donated 20 yen to the school endowment of Mishima Elementary School in 1906.[77] In May 1900, when the postage stamp savings system was launched, he sent a letter of complaint to the Ministry of Communications. Watanabe explained that "currently, postage stamp savings are prospering enormously, and schools and others are requesting stamp savings every day," and as a result, the Mishima post office "is running out of stamp mounts and the post office has found itself without even one mount." Postmaster Watanabe decried the situation as damaging to his personal reputation and also as undermining the sense of trust in the government. In his complaint he underscored the importance of urging students to save money through the stamp savings, warning that "the lack of stamp mounts will damage trust in me and compromise the post office in encouraging and inducing students to make savings". He worried that "it would be very difficult for students to catch up with savings" which though he acknowledged "might seem trifling," nevertheless left him with "a deep sense of regret".[78]

As seen above, the postage stamp savings system was well received across Japan in its first two months,[79] so well received in fact that the Ministry of Communications ran out of stamp mounts. In this sense Mishima Town was no exception. While the implementation of stamp savings in Mishima caused initial confusion, we can get some idea of the detailed status of the use of the stamp savings from the remaining books covering eight months from August 1900 through to March 1901. As can be seen from Table 3.6, which was derived from the records contained in these books, over 60% of the number of uses of the stamp savings system were made by elementary school children.

The eventual acquisitions of new savings passbooks by stamp savings during this period came to just around 20%, the number of new users was greater as the system commenced in March 1900, and this trend was not limited to student users. This tells us that the stamp savings indeed had the effect of encouraging people to whom savings passbooks were hitherto a novelty to hold postal savings. In Tagata County, the number of new postal savings savers stood at over 3000 in FY1900, nearly 80% of whom were postage stamp savers.[80]

---

[76] The estimate is based on the breakdown of the per household levy of the prefectural tax. Nearly 40% of all the income in Mishima Town was earned by some 5% of the town's households (up to the 10th grade). The Gini coefficient stood at 0.55. The town mayor ranked 9th grade. Mishima Town Office, calculated from the "*Meiji Sanjuni-nen Kenzei Zenhanki Kosu Wari Tokyu Hyō (Table of the Grades for the Per Household Levy of the Prefectural Tax for the First Half of 1899)*," included in "*Meiji Sanjuni-nen Genan Tsuzurikomi (File of Draft Proposals of 1899)*".

[77] Mishima Town Office, "*Dai Juni-go Gian (Draft Proposal No. 12)*," included in "*Meiji Sanjūkyū-nendo Genan Tsuzurikomi (File of Draft Proposals of 1906)*".

[78] The manuscript of the letter written by Mishima Third-Class Post Office Postmaster Watanabe Jutarō and addressed to Supervisor Aoki in the Ministry of Communications (dated May 19, 1900), is included in Mishima Third-Class Post Office, "*Chokin Shōreisho (Savings Encouragement Book)*".

[79] "*Yūbin Chokin Kyoku Yūbin Chokiin Jimushi Dai 1-pen (History of Administration of Postal Savings, Bureau of Postal Savings Part 1)*," p. 103.

[80] Shizuoka Prefecture, "*Shizuoka Ken Tōkeisho (Shizuoka Prefecture Statistical Report)*" FY1900.

Table 3.6 Actual situation of the use of stamp savings at Mishima Third-Class Post Office (August 1900 to March 1901)

Total amount of savings during the period (yen)	859.915
Total no. of deposits	2527
No. of new savings accounts	474
Average amount of savings	34.0 sen
Most frequent amount	20 sen
Median	27.5 sen
Ratio of use by students	64%
Largest group of student users	84 students
Ratio of new accounts	19%
Daily average no. of deposits	10 persons

Source Mishima town post office, "*Kitte Chokin Yobo (Stamp Savings Account Book),*" for August–November 1900 and December 1900–March 1901

Particularly noteworthy was the collective use of this system by elementary school children. They appeared as a group carrying the same school name in the book and made savings at an average of 11 students and a maximum of 84 students (Fig. 3.4). On November 10, 1900, there were 53 users from Mishima Elementary School, made up of third and fourth graders and an accompanying teacher. Given that a total number of 410 students graduated from these grades, these 52 students, under the direction of the teacher and led by him in classes, are believed to have gone to the post office to save their money in the form of stamp savings[81] Some of these student users began to put their money in postal savings individually or in small groups of two to three students about 1 year after the postage stamp savings system had commenced. Individual elementary school students had by this point become oriented toward saving and were in the habit of making savings even without the direct instruction of their teachers.

The case of stamp savings users in Mishima Town demonstrates clearly how an orientation toward forming savings was generated among children and others in local communities in line with what the Ministry of Communications official Hiroshi Shimomura had envisioned in the document cited earlier. The encouragement of savings at elementary schools was practiced, it is believed, regardless of whether the school was located in a town or village. In Nishiura Village, a village in the same county as Mishima Town, for example, the elementary school report card also had a column for "savings amount" besides the spaces devoted to school grades and attendance record.[82]

[81] East Elementary School, "*Kaikō Hachijū-ne Shi (The History of 80 Years since the Opening of the School),*"pp. 295–298; Mishima Post Office, "*Kitte Chokin Yobo (Stamp Savings Account Book),*" 1900.

[82] Kou Elementary School, "Katei Tsūchi You (Take-Home Report Card)" (1904), Numazu City, "*Numazu Shi Shi Shiryō Hen Kindai 1 (History of Numazu City, Historical Records, Modern Period 1),*" 1997, p. 762.

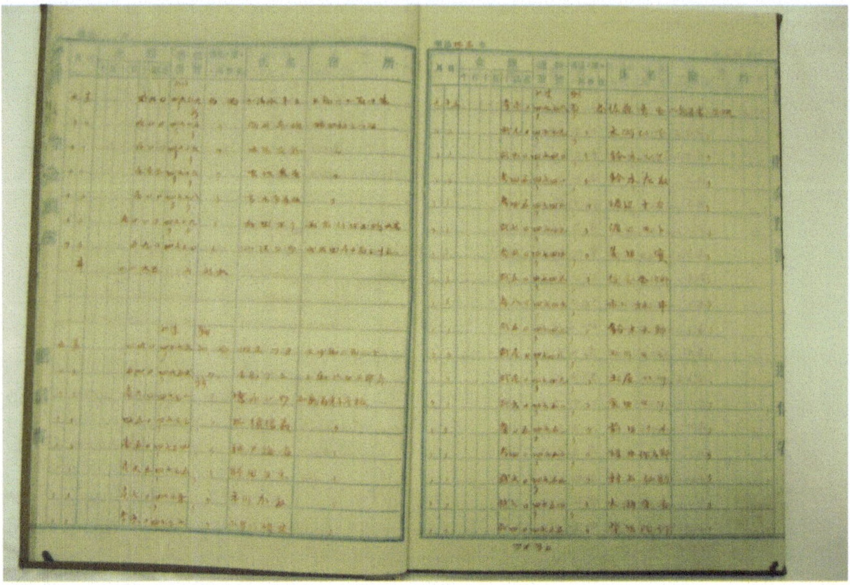

Fig. 3.4 The stamp savings account book kept at Mishima post office. *Source* Mishima post office, "*Kitte Chokin Yobo (stamp savings account book)*," the pages show entries for September 13–15 in the ledger for August-November 1900

Furthermore, postmaster Watanabe of Mishima Third-Class Post Office undertook activities to encourage savings besides those aimed at elementary schools. Already from 1887, the postmaster prepared and distributed "Chokin no Shushu (The Main Purpose of Savings)," an advertising brochure with a table of postal savings interest rates by the number of years of savings. The brochure praised savings by pointing out that "the main purpose of savings is to create assets, have stability of mind and living, and enhance welfare." It made bolder assertions that despite changing times savings will bring "financial muscle and will give you supreme power." The brochure warned non-savers that "if you stick to old customs, you will find yourself kneeling before others for money and suffering the unhappiness of being despised by other people."[83]

In 1891, postmaster Watanabe formed a group, called the "Eiseikai"(co-prosperity society), and became its general representative for the promotion of covenant postal savings. The group's savings amounted to over 100 yen in 1899, which were used to purchase government bonds. The group was created with "the purpose of providing relief from misfortunes through incessant diligence and savings." It formed its savings by "saving at least 10 yen each month with the Ministry of Communications… sending the money on the 20th of the month to a designated agent." The group was designed for collective savings led by the postmaster, but "while savings

83 Mishima Post Office, "Chokin no Shūshū (The Main Purpose of Postal Savings," 1887.

are supposed to be made with the Ministry of Communications, depending on circumstances… savings may be placed with other institutions." Though the specific circumstances are unclear, this explanation in the group's book suggests that the group used other financial institutions according to their own convenience.[84]

Postmaster Watanabe also initiated a covenant savings scheme within the post office itself in 1892, by which post office employees made savings.[85] He also prepared covenant savings regulations, "Kōjō Tsumitatekin Kitei (Regulations for Installment Savings by Female Factory Workers) for a handkerchief factory nearby."[86] In addition, the postmaster worked out separate savings regulations with the Mishima Town Inheritance (*Kō*) Mutual Financing Association," in which he himself participated. Its regulations called for "the association to save 30 sen every month until the balance reaches one million yen so as to ensure the permanent survival of the participants' family names," and said that "the manager shall collect savings by the 22nd of each month and deposit them with postal savings as deferred savings in the name of each member." The regulations set out that the savings shall be renewed successively upon the expiration of the determent period.[87] This savings association, carrying the name of "*ko*" or traditional mutual financing group, was launched with 21 members, and was covered in "Jiji Shimpo," a major Japanese language newspaper at the time.[88] The "Chokin Shōreisho (Savings Encouragement Book)" prepared by the postmaster included a template for anonymous covenant savings that did not state any specific amount of savings. This is another indicator of the postmaster's eagerness for the encouragement of savings actions in his region.

Players who strove for the encouragement of savings in Mishima Town, who recognized the formation of savings as "part of the contribution to the state through the collection of savings as fiscal resources for the state,"[89] were not limited to elementary schools and post offices. In 1909, in response to an inquiry from Tagata County, Mishima Town conducted a survey on cooperative savings in the town. Table 3.7 is derived from the surviving survey returns and gives an indication of the savings situation at the time of the survey. The table shows that at least ten groups were implementing savings in the town. All of these groups were included in the materials of Mishima Third-Class Post Office, and many of them were conventional organizations based on territorial connections from sub-districts of the town.

---

[84] Included in Mishima Post Office, "*Chokin Shōreisho (Savings Encouragement Book)*".

[85] Mishima Post Office, "*Kyokunai Chokin Kiyaku Sho (Post Office Savings Code Book),*" 1892.

[86] Mishima Post Office, "Kojo Tsumitatekin Kitei (Regulations for Installment Savings by Female Factory Workers)," included in "*Chokin Shōreisho (Savings Encouragement Book),*" presumably prepared in 1899–1900.

[87] Mishima Post Office, "*Mishima Machi Sozoku Ko Kumiai Kankei (Related to the Mishima Town Inheritance Mutual Financing Association Cooperative (Ko)),*" 1917.

[88] "Savings of One Million Yen for the Survival of Family Names," *Jiji Shimpo*, No. 12214 (August 12, 1917).

[89] Mishima Post Office, "Kiyaku Chokin Tokubetsu Toriatsukai Ninka Shinseisho (the Application for Approval of the Special Handling of Covenant Savings)," included in "*Chochiku Shōreisho (Savings Encouragement Book)*".

Table 3.7 Joint savings survey in Mishima Town in 1909

Document No	Number of savers (persons)	Current balance (yen)	Founding date (year, month, day)	Amount per saver (yen)	Financial institutions used	Remarks
①	18	86.446 260.467 75	1900.1 1906 1907	23.44	Banks	Groups based in village districts, savings in multiple installments
②	34	53.28	1904 1909 5.20	1.57	Banks	Groups based in village districts, emergency reserves, distributed once in March 1909 upon maturity
③	N.A	55.20	1905.7		Postal savings	Groups based in village districts
④	9	55.86	1905.7.27	6.21	Postal savings	Reporting via a village district headman
⑤	7	50.00	1905.7	7.14	Unknown	Reporting via a village district headman
⑥	30	90.00	1908.11	3.00	Mixture of bank and postal savings	Groups based in village districts, monthly savings (minimum 30 sen, maximum 50 sen)
⑦	11	151.20	1909.6.2	13.75	Banks	Groups based in village districts, daily savings
⑧	6	52.00	1908.6	8.67	Postal savings	Groups based in village districts, Great Exhibition savings
⑨	93	892.75	1908.9	9.60	Banks	Individual representative, daily savings, for tax payments
⑩	35	207.60	1906.1	5.93	Postal savings	Individual representative, daily savings, for tax payments
Average	27	202.98		7.52		

Source Survey returns included in Mishima Town Office, "*Meiji Yonjuni-nen Gengisho Tsuzurikomi (File of Official Documents for 1909)*"

At the time Mishima Town had twenty autonomous organizations that had existed since the early modern period.[90] Many of these organizations served as entities for implementing festivals and rites in local districts, and at least six districts directly implemented savings actions, as far as can be confirmed by their names appearing on survey slips. This means that at least 30% of districts in the town were engaged in collective savings, led by district headmen. The average number of savers in these organizations was 27 and the average total amount of savings was approximately 200 yen. Regarding the financial institutions they used for their savings, half appear to have been postal savings and the other half banks.[91] These districts had been autonomous units since the early modern period and at the same time were subject to the influence of the town office through meetings of the district headmen. Reports prepared by the town office stated that, since the selection of district headmen in 1905, "Mishima Town has taken measures to constantly encourage diligence, thrift and savings." The town office "convened meetings of district headmen several times each year and at each of those meetings, the office encouraged the creation of cooperatives for diligence, thrift, savings and tax payments." The result of the detailed instructions on how to establish such cooperatives was that more than ten were established, as found in the survey, and that "other organizations came into being successively."[92]

Indeed, in Miya District, Mishima Town, ordinary citizens formed a savings cooperative independently of the district headman. Given that the cooperative submitted its reports to the town office via the district headman, it can be assumed that the savings cooperative had relations with the district's activities.

In Hase District, the method adopted was to "divide Hase town into four groups, and in each group, one household, taking turns, is to collect certain stamps twice, on the 20th day and the final day of each month, to submit them to the representative, who is to put them together for the four groups to deposit at a bank." The amount of savings on each occasion was set in accordance with the income of savers. "Poorer people below the middle class, who recognize the need for savings by practicing thrift in their daily expenditure, endeavor to make 80 sen of savings, whilst other people deposit one yen each time." The purpose of savings was to make "appropriations for emergency reserves," and this group, which had been implementing savings since 1904, before the town office instructed district headmen to encourage savings, made

[90] "Mishima Machi Shi (Mishima Town Magazine), p. 1; Heibonsha Center for Regional Materials "*Nihon Rekishi Chimei Taikei 22 Shizuoka-ken no Chimei (System of Japanese Historical Names, 22 Names of Places in Shizuoka Prefecture),*" Heibonsha, 2000.

[91] As for bank interest rates in Shizuoka Prefecture, time and savings deposit interest rates exceeded 7.2% and long-term deposit interest rates were over 8.77% at Shisan Bank in 1901, and current deposit interest rates were lower than 4% at Shunto Jitsugyō Bank in 1908. In Mishima Town, it is possible that the relationships of interest rates were bank time deposit rates > postal savings rates (5.04%) > bank current account deposit rates. Suruga Bank, " < *Suruga* > *Hachiju-nen no Ayumi (The History of 80 Years of* < *Suruga* > *),*" 1975; Shizuoka Bank, "*Shizuoka Ginkō Shi (History of Shizuoka Bank),*" 1993.

[92] "Ko Sho Dai Hyakukyūjūroku-go (Ko Sho No. 196) included in "Meiji Yonjūni-nen Gengisho Tsuzurikomi (the File of Official Documents of 1909)."

one "refund" when the savings account matured in 1909.[93] The group's activities were very similar to the "*mujin*" savings-oriented mutual financing association.[94]

At other organizations as well, a similar system of setting savings amounts in accordance with income could be found. The confirmed purposes of savings were varied, ranging from tourism to tax payments, and they also had the aspect that resembled a "*kō*" mutual assistance association, referring to their representatives as "parents." Rather, these savings organizations may have inherited their behavioral habits from the forms of previous "*mujin*" and "*kō*," but using modern financial institutions.

As seen above, savings groups that appeared in large numbers in Mishima Town during this period included not only groups organized according to modern systems and organizations, such as elementary schools, the town office, and factories in the area, but also organizations that had organizational and personal continuity from the early modern period which came to utilize postal savings and banks. The case of Mishima Town indicates the way in which the formation of individual small-amount savings spread through a combination of the systems and organizations of the modern period and the customs and organizations of the early modern period. The formation of such individual and collective savings was not limited to Mishima Town or Shizuoka Prefecture. It spread widely across Japan region's in the early twentieth century.

3.4 Summary

This chapter shows how Postal savings prevailed in modern Japan. Postal savings were established before the spread of the modern banking system and emerged as the de facto first modern deposit-taking institution for personal savings in the Japanese economy, ahead of all other financial institutions. However, postal savings did not fare well immediately after their establishment. Though the habit of making personal petty savings at modern financial institutions had yet to take firm root among Japanese people, the government went ahead and expanded the economic functions of individual savings. Following the broadening of the government's policy for individual savings, the central government's savings promotion policy launched at the end of the 19th century continued as part of local community improvement movement.

[93] Table 3.7, document numbers 430, 431 and 427. The numbers were allotted in "*Meiji Yonjūni-nen Gengisho Tsuzurikomi (File of Official Documents of 1909)*".

[94] Tsukagoshi Otaro, "*Mujin to Chochiku Ginkō* (*Mujin Mutual Financing Associations and Savings Banks*)," Horitsu Shimbunsha, 1916, pp. 17–20. It was not unusual since the early modern period that people participated in "*mujin*" mutual financing associations for the main purpose of savings.

Postal savings, as previous research has indicated, were heavily influenced by government policy, especially its efforts to promote savings. However, the popularization of postal savings in the early 20th century was also impacted greatly by the formation of various local organizations by local people themselves and their active participation in the communities.

Chapter 4
Formation and Development of Industrial Cooperatives—Self-Circulating Micro-Credit

4.1 Introduction

As discussed in the preceding chapter, a myriad of local organizations with various functions had been established or reorganized in local societies in Japan by the early twentieth century both by adopting modern systems and new policy initiatives on the one hand, and building on the existing traditional networks on the other. Many of these local organizations encouraged their members to save money, and sometimes they themselves, as organizations, saved money and accumulated funds for business activities.

Industrial cooperatives were one type of these newly established organizations. Industrial cooperatives in Japan were modeled on the cooperative movement that had arisen in Europe. They were voluntary organizations of local community residents which organized under the cooperative system as established under the Japanese legal system. Many industrial cooperatives were established in rural regions and later developed into agricultural cooperatives. Industrial cooperatives emerged in modern Japanese society as not-for-profit organizations and as such they differed from banks, though they also acted as familiar financial organizations where people could deposit their day-to-day savings. This chapter considers how industrial cooperatives, which spread across Japan by the time of the interwar period, were able to penetrate Japan's regions and achieve growth. It also examines the wider impact they had. While industrial cooperatives, many of which were established in rural regions, were legally able to perform non-financial functions as their main function, in practice most were created as credit cooperatives handling small-amount financing.

In modern Japan, the ability of cooperatives to provide residents in the country's regions with opportunities to access small-amount financing is believed to have contributed to the development of regional economies and the agricultural sector. However, previous studies on industrial cooperatives have seldom critically examined the growth and proliferation of industrial cooperatives, nor have they addressed questions such as why regional societies sought small-amount financing and how

H. Tanaka, *Micro-Credit in Modern Japan*, Studies in Economic History,
https://doi.org/10.1007/978-981-97-6940-7_4

industrial cooperatives responded to such funding needs. In this chapter, I consider industrial cooperatives as financial institutions based in particular local areas that rely on people's funds as their principal source of finance, and I examine the scale and scope of their financial function and the socioeconomic role they played in regional economies. However, in order to consider why the small-amount financing opportunities provided by cooperatives were in such demand, it is first necessary to consider the economic conditions prevalent in Japan at the time.

In the latter half of the nineteenth century, the Japanese economy became linked to world markets as Japan opened up a number of its ports to foreign trade in the last days of the Edo period.[1] Less than a century later, by World War II, Japan had progressed through an industrial revolution and had achieved industrialization. As pointed out in Chap. 2, this growth in the Japanese economy was achieved not solely by the modern industrial sector, such as the cotton spinning industry and the steel industry. It also owed much to the growth of traditional industries, including agriculture.

Above all, the silk-reeling industry, as the biggest foreign currency earning industry in the prewar period, was one of the first industries to introduce modern technology. Moreover, it was deeply linked to the agricultural sector via the supply of silkworm cocoons.[2] In the development of regional economies in modern Japan, as symbolized by the growth of the sericulture industry, a major role was played by individual small businesses, including farming households. They responded to expanding markets by applying traditional technologies so as to expand production and market their produce.[3] After the 1890s, Japan expanded silk production in response to the demand from the mechanized U.S. silk fabrics industry. This was only possible because both Japanese companies in urban regions and production systems in Japan's rural regions were able to respond to the increased demand from global markets. This is seen in the fact that the range of functions of silk farming,

---

[1] Sugihara Kaoru, "*Ajia-kan Boeki no Keisei to Kozo (Patterns and Development of Intra-Asian Trade)*," Minerva Shobo, 1996, pp. 32–38.

[2] Nakamura Takafusa, "*Senzenki Nihon Keizai Seicho no Bunseki* (*The Analysis of Japan's Economic Growth in the Prewar Period*)," Iwanami Shoten, 1971, p. 38.

[3] In recent years, in the field of economic theory, economic analysis by the unit of one particular region or even a broader area has been gaining recognition. The recession in the north of England, the birthplace of the industrial revolution, in contrast to the booming state of the national economy of the United Kingdom as a whole, and the emergence of units covering a broad area, such as the European Union (EU), cannot be explained only by the concept and analytical framework of a national economy, making people strongly aware of a region-based analysis (H. Armstrong and J. Taylor, translated by Sasaki Komei, "*Chiiki Keizaigaku to Chiiki Seisaku* (*Regional Economics and Policy*)," revised edition, Ryutsu Keizai University Press, 2005, pp. 327–339). Nonetheless, this theoretical analysis basically represents a method of analysis of a national economy on a reduced scale by region in traditional economics, and, as such, does not provide direct answers to such issues as the relationship between a regional economy and a regional society and what economic effect it would have on the functions of organizations that make up that society. In fact, however, developments in a regional economy, as recognized by an analysis of regional economics itself, have an inseparable relationship with the way that regional society should be. This chapter, as a whole, is designed to explore how to capture the substance of the growth of a regional economy in an empirical field on the basis of a case example of one region.

silk reeling and exports were sometimes termed the sericulture industry as a single industry.[4]

With respect to farming villages in modern Japan, previous studies focused on the parasitic landlord system as a social problem. Given the areas of lands owned, however, the greater part of agriculture in modern Japan was carried out by local farmers who might be described as small farmers operating varying plot sizes, rather than an agricultural sector characterized by the dominance of absentee landlords who owned large tracts of lands worked by agricultural laborers.[5] In other words, agricultural production in Japan, including sericulture, was carried out to a large extent by small-scale, self-employed farmers, including land-owning farmers and tenant farmers.

For such small businesses to achieve development by responding to the opportunities and risks brought about by links to the global marketplace, the role of small-amount financing is thought to have been of great significance, as illustrated by the example of the Grameen Bank in Bangladesh in recent times.[6] It is well known, however, that in contemporary developing countries, there is not necessarily a sufficient supply of small credit in rural areas. For ordinary urban companies, such as banks, it is difficult to develop and maintain a credit market in rural regions due to an asymmetry of information, higher transaction costs and greater default risk.[7] In prewar Japan, a developing country at the time, how then were the small-scale yet essential funding needs of small business entities in regional economies satisfied? As already discussed, the voracious demand for funds in regional economies was met by cooperative-style financial institutions, rather than by banks or corporate financial institutions.

This raises several questions: How then were industrial cooperatives established in regional societies? How were they managed in order to achieve growth? How did they satisfy the demand for funds in regional economies? Previous studies on industrial

---

[4] The U.S. silk market prominently expanded from around the 1890s as a result of the mechanization and technological innovation of the silk fabrics industry, and much of the expanding demand was covered by imports of Japanese silk. In 1912, exports of silk by Japan exceeded 40% of global silk production, accounting for 70% of the U.S. silk market. Ueyama Kazuo, *"Nihon Kindai Sanshigyo no Tenkai (The Development of Japan's Modern Sericulture Industry),"* Nihon Keizai Hyouronsha, 2016, pp. 8–9, p. 55.

[5] Even as of 1941, land owned by absentee landowners accounted for 41% of tenanted land in six prefectures in the Tohoku region, 28% in six prefectures in Kinki region, and 37.5% in the sericulture areas, including Nagano Prefecture, covered in this chapter (Gunma, Saitama, Yamanashi, Nagano, Gifu and Aichi prefectures). Mori Takemaro, *"Senkanki no Nihon Noson Shakai—Nomin Undo to Sangyo Kumiai (Japan's Agricultural Communities in the Interwar Period—Farmers' Movement and Industrial Cooperatives),"* 2005, p. 38.

[6] Mahabub Hossain, *Credit for Alleviation of Rural Poverty: The Grameen Bank in Bangladesh*, Int Food Policy Res Inst. 1988, p. 20.

[7] Kojima Yohei and Takahashi Kazushi, "Senzen Nihon no Sangyo Kumiai ni Okeru Shinyo Shinsa no Jittai to Kaihatsu Tojokoku heno Gan'i: Nagano-ken Chiisagata Coungy Kano Sangyo Kumiai wo Jirei to Shite (Historical Credit Assessment in Pre-War Japan and Its Implications in Contemporary Developing Countries: A Case Study of Kano Credit cooperative, Nagano Prefecture)," *Ajia Keizai (Asian Economy)*, Volume 58, No. 2, June 2017, p. 14.

cooperatives have shed light on their institutional development and growth at the national level, but it cannot be said that these studies were able to fully clarify the relationship between industrial cooperatives and the regional societies in which they operated, nor the actual business conditions they faced in their formative years.[8] In this chapter, therefore, to specifically verify the actual situation, I take up the case of the management of one industrial cooperative, which was created relatively soon after the establishment of the industrial cooperative system and expanded into a business entity that effectively satisfied local financing needs. The period of analysis extends from the period of the industrial cooperative's foundation to the time when it became more firmly established, or in this case the period from 1900, when the Industrial Cooperative Act was enacted, to the end of World War I, by which time industrial cooperatives had spread across Japan. The case examined here is the Kanō Industrial Cooperative which was established in Kanō Village, Chiisagata County, Nagano Prefecture, in 1903, and subsequently grew steadily in the following decades. This chapter seeks to understand the interrelationship between industrial cooperatives and regional economies/societies through an analysis of the background in which industrial cooperatives were established as well as their early operations.

4.2 The Industrial Cooperative System as Regional Small-Amount Financial Institutions

4.2.1 Policy Design of the Cooperative System: Organization for Safeguarding People's Daily Lives and Economic Development

Increased global contacts and the development of transport networks saw the spread of export-related side businesses, including sericulture, among farming households. In turn, this saw a surge in demand for small-amount financing in Japan's regional economies, including in Nagano Prefecture. Under such circumstances, the central government enacted the Industrial Cooperative Act in 1900, based on its recognition that "many of the agricultural, commercial and industrial businesses that occupy an essential source of national wealth belong to the category of small businesses and usually have few assets." As such the Industrial Cooperative Act was established in order to "contribute to the financing of agricultural and industrial business operators

[8] Shibuya Ryuichi ed., "*Meijiki Nihon Tokushu Kinyu Rippo Shi* (*The History of Special Finance Legislation in Japan in the Meiji Period*)," Waseda University Press, 1977; Hikaru Shinoura, "*Noson Kyodo Kumiai no Tenkai Katei* (*The Development Process of Cooperatives in Farming Villages*)," Akishobo, 1972; Shibuya Ryuichi, "*Shomin Kinyu no Tenkai to Seisaku Taio* (*The Development of People's Finance and Policy Responses*)," Nihon Tosho Center, 2001.

in the middle and lower classes, the core of Japan's industry."[9] The aim of this system can be readily seen in a speech made by Minister of Home Affairs Hirata Tōsuke at a meeting of the Gubernatorial Council in 1908:

> In a country like Japan, where small-scale farmers and industrial and commercial operators are the driving force of national industry, what is most important for the promotion of industry in the regions is to collaborate in helping operators access capital... Industrial cooperatives, savings unions or mutual aid associations are the most suitable method to achieve that objective…[10]

In Europe since the mid-nineteenth century, the cooperative system was advocated as a means to promote the improvement of the situation of middle- and low-income earners. Japanese government officials who visited Europe to inspect the development of credit cooperatives in Germany, consumer cooperatives in the United Kingdom and producer cooperatives in France,[11] designed and enacted the Industrial Cooperative Act by integrating the systems operating in these countries. The original cooperative movement in Europe was primarily designed to protect small producers against market turmoil and impoverishment through people's solidarity. The Industrial Cooperative Act of Japan was designed not only with such a defensive objective in mind but also with the positive, industrial policy-like intention of building a foundation for economic development driven by small producers.[12]

> Developments of social trends are like the swift flow of a large river…the struggle for survival is becoming increasingly fierce, the fact of the survival of the fittest is becoming increasingly prominent and the power of the strong to pressure the weak is becoming mightier…the industrial cooperative is the fittest organization to mitigate this irresistible momentum and prevent its outburst. The industrial cooperative is designed to unite the weak majority and leverage this united force to confront the strong and protect the weak, while recognizing the force of the strong, so as to mutually strive to boost their respective interests and thereby promoting the good fortune of the country. In other words, the industrial cooperative may be termed a panacea for social improvement, which is designed to collect small capital and turn it into big capital, to gather the weak to face the strong, to relieve and protect the poor and improve their living conditions, while, on the other hand, it is intended to promote industry, support autonomy, activate national customs and also enhance the moral character.[13]

---

[9] Ministry of Agriculture and Commerce, "Sangyo Kumiai Hoan Riyusho (The Statement of Reasons for the Industrial Cooperative Bill)," 1899, submitted to the 11th Diet, included in Imperial Agricultural Association, "*Chūshono to Sangyō Kumiai* (*Small/Midsize Farmers and Industrial cooperatives*)," 1913.

[10] Summary of Instructions of Minister of Home Affairs Hirata Tōsuke at a meeting of the Gubernatorial Council in October 1908 (Taikakai ed., "*Naimushoshi* (*The History of the Ministry of Home Affairs*)," Volume 4, 1971, reprinted edition, 1980, p. 358).

[11] Imperial Agricultural Association, "*Chūshono to Sangyō Kumiai (Small/Midsize Farmers and Industrial cooperatives)*," pp. 44–69; Friedrich Wilhelm Raiffeisen, "*Shinyo Kumiai (Credit Cooperative)*" (Original Work: Darlehnskassen-Vereine, Neuwied, 1866), translation supervised by Hon-iden Yoshio, Ie-No-Hikari Association, 1971, pp. 1–3.

[12] Shinoura Hikaru, "*Noson Kyodo Kumiai no Tenkai Katei* (*The Development Process of Cooperatives in Farming Villages*)," p. 13; Tosuke Hirata, "*Sangyo Kumiai Ho Yogi* (*The Essence of the Industrial Cooperative Act*)," 1900, pp. 4–5; Shibuya Ryuichi, "*Shomin Kin-yu no Tenkai to Seisaku Taio* (*The Development of People's Finance and Policy Response*)," pp. 162–164.

[13] Imperial Local Improvement Association, "Chiho no Kairyo (Improvement of Rural Areas)," 1913, pp. 2–3 (The Bureau of Areas, the Ministry of Home Affairs ed., "Chiho Kairyo Kankei

As described above, at the outset of the 1910s the importance of industrial cooperatives was recognized and they were introduced by the government as a multi-functional system, simultaneously representing social and industrial policy, as well as a policy for promoting local stability. The Industrial Cooperative Act established a new organizational framework in the Japanese economy, a non-profit management entity that uses capital collected from members to operate a variety of businesses and which is democratically governed by members with equity interests. The initial scope of business that industrial cooperatives were allowed to engage in consisted of five categories: (1) credit cooperatives that undertake financial services; (2) purchasing cooperatives through which members make joint purchases of necessary goods; (3) marketing cooperatives through which members make bulk sales of their products; (4) producer cooperatives for joint production; and (5) user cooperatives through which members use facilities jointly. From 1906 onward, it became possible for industrial cooperatives to operate credit cooperative business concurrently with other businesses.

Compared with corporate organizations, including for-profit *kabushiki kaisha*, or incorporated companies, industrial cooperatives, established as non-profit organizations, were provided with tax breaks. The Industrial Cooperative Act provided for lighter business taxes on industrial cooperatives than those imposed on corporations undertaking similar business operations. Though the industrial cooperative system ultimately came under the jurisdiction of the Ministry of Agriculture and Commerce, in practice the Ministry of Home Affairs was a major force behind it,[14] as it also related to the local improvement movement policies of the Ministry of Home Affairs.[15] Under the industrial cooperative system, which had the promotion of regional economies as one of its objectives, encouragement was given to the creation of an industrial cooperative in each municipality. The number of industrial cooperatives, mainly credit cooperatives, increased across Japan into the 1910s. Indeed, the "dissemination rate" of industrial cooperatives, calculated by dividing the total number of unions by the number of municipalities in Japan, reached a striking 98% by 1917.[16]

The fact that industrial cooperatives spread rapidly in a short period of less than 20 years and that nearly 90% of them were either credit cooperatives or industrial

---

Shiryoshu 2 (The Second Collection of Documents Related to Improvement of Rural Areas)," reprinted edition, Hobunkaku, 1987).

[14] Ryuichi Shibuya ed., "*Meijiki Nihon Tokushu Kinyu Rippo Shi* (*The History of Legislation for Special Finance in Japan in the Meiji Period*)," p. 435. The introduction of the industrial cooperative system itself began with what Hirata Tōsuke and Shinagawa Yajiro saw and experienced when they were studying in Germany. Both of them held various posts successively as officials of the Ministry of Home Affairs and the Ministry of Agriculture and Commerce, respectively. Okutani Matsuji, "*Shinagawa Yajiro Den* (*The Life History of Shinagawa Yajiro*)," Koyo Shoin, 1940, pp. 264–276.

[15] Ioka Yasutoki, "Sangyo Kumiai to Buraku Kaizen Undo ni Kansuru Oboegaki—Nara-ken no Jirei kara (A Memorandum on Industrial cooperatives and the Buraku Improvement Movement—The Case of Nara Prefecture)," *Buraku Kaiho Kenkyu* (*Buraku Liberation Research*), No. 159, 2004, p. 5.

[16] This value was used after that time as a criterion to measure the extent of the dissemination of industrial cooperatives.

cooperatives concurrently operating a credit cooperative showed that demand for small credit, "provided based on personal credit, in principle...unlike ordinary banks and lending by loan sharks," was widespread across Japan.[17] As seen from Fig. 2.2 in Chap. 2, the size of funds, both in terms of capital as well as deposits and savings, grew steadily in tandem with the spread of industrial cooperatives nationally, though it was relatively small in comparison to banks or postal savings.[18]

4.2.2 Background to Demand for Small Credit Opportunities in Chiisagata County, Nagano Prefecture

As evident from the discussion above, industrial cooperatives were firmly established throughout Japan and had grown greatly by World War 1. Nevertheless, there were gaps between and within regions in the dissemination and growth of industrial cooperatives. Nagano Prefecture and Gunma Prefecture were among the regions that stood out in terms of the establishment and development of industrial cooperatives.[19] The principal subject of analysis in this chapter, Kanō Village, was located in Nagano Prefecture. Why then was the establishment of industrial cooperatives particularly vibrant in Nagano Prefecture? The expansion in the production of silk exports is likely the most important factor in answering this question.

Nagano Prefecture occupied a prominent position in the modern Japanese economy in terms of both the scale and growth of its silk production. This is evident by the fact that "by the end of the second decade of the Meiji period [i.e. the decade from 1877], when the value of cocoon production by prefecture was known, Nagano Prefecture came out on top, and while second-ranking Gunma Prefecture and third-ranking Fukushima Prefecture showed little increase during the third decade of the Meiji period [from 1887], Nagano Prefecture alone achieved rapid growth." Furthermore, the prefecture's Chiisagata County, where Kanō Village was located, was renowned since the Tokugawa period as a region engaging in sericulture. It remained a dominant sericulture area of Nagano Prefecture and accounted for about 20% of

[17] Ministry of Agriculture and Commerce, "*Sangyo Kumiai Yoran (The Directory of Industrial cooperatives)*," annual issues; Imperial Agricultural Association, "*Chūshono to Sangyō Kumiai (Small/Midsize Farmers and Industrial cooperatives)*," pp. 38–41, p. 78.

[18] Statistics Bureau, Management and Coordination Agency, "*Nihon Choki Tokei Soran (Historical Statistics of Japan)*," Volume 3, Japan Statistical Association, 1988, Figure 11.12; Ministry of Posts and Telecommunications, "*Yusei Hyakunenshi Shiryo 30-kan, Yusei Tokei Shiryo; Eiteikyoku Tokeisho Yusei Hyakunenshi Shiryo Somokuji (Materials on a Century in the History of Postal Services Volume 30, Postal Services Statistical Materials; Post Office Statistical Report, Total Contents of Materials on a Century in the History of Postal Services)*," Yoshikawa Kobunkan, 1971, Savings Figure 5; Emi Koichi et al., "*Choki Keizai Tokei 5 Chochiku to Tsuka (Long-Term Economic Statistics 5 Savings and Currency)*," Toyo Keizai Inc., 1988, Figure 4.

[19] Ministry of Agriculture and Commerce, "*Sangyo Kumiai Yoran (The Directory of Industrial cooperatives)*," annual issues.

the prefecture's total cocoon output as of 1889.[20] Furthermore, it was recognized then by the government as well as by prefectural agricultural associations and other regional officials that "sericulture is generally engaged in as a small-scale business." It was thought that "for them [small-scale businesses] to achieve development" the way forward was to "encourage a large number of small operators to get together to jointly establish a union".[21]

Kanō Village was located midway between Ueda and Komoro in the northern part of Nagano Prefecture. This region was covered by the government's plan to construct a railroad linking Tokyo to the Hokuriku region, with a route from Naoetsu, Niigata Prefecture, to Karuizawa via Ueda opening in 1888. A link to a government-run railroad to Yokokawa, Gunma Prefecture, had already been opened in 1885, and transport to and from Karuizawa Depot was temporarily provided for by a horse-drawn carriage railroad, the full railroad route was due to open in 1893. This shortened the time required for travel between Tokyo and Nagano from six days on foot to 11 h and 20 min.[22]

The upgrading of the transportation infrastructure reduced the cost of distribution and also deepened connections between regional economies along the railroad and wider markets, including the global market. By the mid-1900s, the cocoon markets in eastern Japan were all but integrated. In the U.S. market, to which a greater part of Japanese silk was exported after 1883, Japanese silk had a market share of 50% by the late 1880s. Despite a further expansion of market demand, the market share of Japanese silk in the U.S. almost constantly increased in the Meiji and Taisho periods.[23] In order to meet the expanding demand for silk cocoons from markets at home and overseas, the Japanese sericulture industry more intensively applied fertilizer to mulberry cultivation so as to expand production of mulberry leaves to feed silkworms. According to a survey of mulberry field fertilization in Japan in 1920, the usage of chemical fertilizers was twice that of self-supplied organic fertilizers

[20] Nagano Prefecture, "*Nagano Kenshi Tsushi Hen Dai 7-kan Kindai Ichi* (*Comprehensive History of Nagano Prefecture Volume 7, Modern Period 1*)," 1988, pp. 262–264.

[21] Ministry of Agriculture and Commerce, "*Kunrei Dai 43-go* (*Instructions No. 43*)," 1906. The central government encouraged regions to establish industrial cooperatives by issuing these instructions or by sending officials on tours to regions to speak on industrial cooperatives. In Nagano Prefecture as well, agricultural associations and the prefectural government, while keeping contacts with the central government on the matter, engaged in activities to push for the establishment of industrial cooperatives by sponsoring lectures and briefing sessions. Nagano Prefectural Agricultural Association, "*Nagano-ken Sangyō Kumiai Shi* (*The History of Industrial cooperatives in Nagano Prefecture*)," 1944, pp. 83–106.

[22] In 1895, the railroad was renamed the Shinetsu Line. "*Nagano Kenshi Tsushi Hen Dai 7-kan* (*Comprehensive History of Nagano Prefecture Volume 7*)," pp. 337–338.

[23] Nakabayashi Masaki, "Kindai Shihon Shugi no Soshiki—Seishigyo no Hatten ni Okeru Torihiki no Tochi to Seisan no Kozo (Organizations of Modern Capitalism—Governance of Transactions and Structure of Production in the Development of the Silk-Reeling Industry)," University of Tokyo Press, 2003, p. 136, p. 170, p. 214.

and the value of chemical fertilizers used in Nagano Prefecture marginally exceeded the national average.[24]

At the time, sericulture was an easily accessible economic opportunity for farmers in Nagano Prefecture and elsewhere to expand their income. Though wealthier farmers played an important role in the industry, the expansion of sericulture production was not limited to them. A large number of farmers, including middle- and lower-level farmers, were also engaged in sericulture.[25] However, among the numerous sericultural farmers were farmers of limited means who could not afford to pay for fertilizers with their own funds, because of the seasonal characteristics of the sericulture industry, and its final product, silk, was vulnerable to price fluctuation risk on overseas export markets. As such, many farmers required external financial support. Already in the second decade of the Meiji period (from 1877) in Nagano Prefecture, a number of financial institutions had been established for this purpose. These included banks such as the 19th Bank that played a central role in financing the silk-reeling industry, with support from the Bank of Japan and the Yokohama Specie Bank, in order to meet the demand for funds from the sericulture industry.[26]

Quasi-banking companies, financial institutions of smaller size that failed to obtain banking licenses, were also established in large numbers during the same period. Nagano Prefecture had the highest number of quasi-banking companies in Japan, and Chiisagata County n accounted for nearly 70% of the prefectural total. Many of them are thought to have been "financial institutions providing funds for agricultural village communities".[27] The fact that the said region was one of the major sericultural regions in the prefecture led to the establishment of a large number of such small-scale financial institutions, along with the subsequent spread of industrial cooperatives. Among these new financial institutions were those created as a direct lineage of the organizations of the Tokugawa period. For instance, Eizokusha [a union for eternity], established in Kami-Shiojiri Village in Chiisagata County, was a permanent *kō* organization, a long-term financial structure for economic mutual aid, created in 1813 and reorganized in 1882 into a quasi-banking company, the Nagano prefectural government being notified of its existence in 1889. The stated objective of Eizokusha was that "should any household among *kō* members face ruin, to endeavor to prevent

[24] Ikawa Katsuhiko, "Kindai Nihon Seishigyo to Manu Seisan (The Modern Japanese Silk-Reeling Industry and Cocoon Production)," Tokyo Keizai Joho Shuppan, 1998, p. 69.

[25] Nagano Prefecture, "Nagano-ken ni Okeru Nosangyo to Jikyoku no Kankei (The Relationship between Agriculture/Sericulture in Nagano Prefecture and the Current Situation)," included in *Kobun Hensatsu Taisho 3-nen Dai 3-ka Sangyō Kumiai* (*Jikyoku Kyusai ni Kansuru Shorui*), *Bound Book of Official Documents 1914 The Third Section Industrial Cooperative* (*Documents Concerning Economic Stimulus Public Works*), 1914.

[26] Ishii Kanji, "*Nihon Sanshigyo Shi Bunseki* (*An Analysis of the History of the Japanese Sericulture Industry*)," University of Tokyo Press, 1974, p. 206.

[27] Nagano Prefecture, "*Nagano Kenshi Tsushi Hen Dai 7-kan* (*Comprehensive History of Nagano Prefecture Volume 7*)," p. 324.

this from happening…and strive to assist the household".[28] It is presumed that there was a fairly large number of cases where *mujin* mutual loan organs and *kō* that existed since the Tokugawa period were also reorganized as financial institutions in the modern era in other parts of Japan. These small-scale financial institutions, by the nature of their predecessors, are believed to have inherited and maintained the various traditional community-based or personal connections-based networks.

A large number of quasi-banking companies were also established in Kanō Village in Chiisagata County. However, many private-sector banks lent funds only to wealthier farmers, and there was a sense that the management of quasi-banking companies was unstable. Therefore, demand for microcredit from local farmers amid an overall expansion of the sericulture industry could not be easily satisfied by the numerous pre-existing financial institutions. Thus, in 1900, the industrial cooperative system was launched across Japan.

4.3 The Establishment of the Kanō Industrial Cooperative

As discussed above, after the enactment of the Industrial Cooperative Act in 1900, industrial cooperatives rapidly spread across Japan. By the late 1910s they provided convenient microcredit to each regional economy. In Kanō Village, Chiisagata County, Nagano Prefecture, the industrial cooperative was established in 1903. Here the post office had only offered savings services, without a lending function, before being abolished in 1880, and it was revived only in 1921.[29] Thus, prior to the establishment of the industrial cooperative in Kanō Village, it is likely that there were extremely limited opportunities to access the financial amenities of small-amount savings and lending. The Kanō Industrial Cooperative was launched as a credit cooperative that undertook financial services, and it was one of the earliest industrial cooperatives established in the region, obtaining the No. 2 in the registration jurisdiction of Ueda. On what foundations was the industrial cooperative, with the objective of mutual aid for members and autonomy of local industries, established in the village? In order to answer this question, it is first necessary to consider the social conditions in Kanō Village at the time.

The administrative unit of Kanō Village was created in 1876. The village, formed through a merger of seven villages, was composed of six wards: Higashi Ueda, Tazawa, Kuribayashi, Sone, Higashi Fukai and Nishi Fukai. By absorbing Kaizenji Village in 1889, it comprised seven wards, and then in 1917, came to have eight wards, as Ōkawa Ward was established by separating from Kuribayashi Ward. Of these eight

---

[28] Eizokusha, "Eizokusha Moshiawase Kisoku (Concerted Rules of Eizokusha)"; Nagano Prefecture, included in *Kobun Hensatsu Sho Kaisha Teikan* (*Bound Book of Official Documents Articles of Incorporation of Various Companies*), 1889.

[29] The Society for Publication of the 60-year History of Communications, "Teishin 60-Yen Shi (Sixty-year History of Post and Communications)," supervised by Yamaguchi Osamu, "*Zenkoku Yubin Kyoku Enkaku Roku—Meiji Hen* (*The Record of Development of Post Offices across Japan—Meiji Edition*)," Nihon Yushu Shuppan, 1980.

wards, Higashi Ueda, Kuribayashi, Sone, Higashi Fukai and Tazawa became part of the same school district by donating funds for construction when local communities petitioned for the construction of Kanō Elementary School in 1897, integrating the school districts of Kyōritsu, Higashi Ueda and Higashi Tazawa. Subsequently, Nishi Fukai was also integrated into the same school district in 1886. Kanō Elementary School was located almost in the center of Kanō Village and the school building still exists at the time of writing. Its construction played an important role in integrating the regional unit of Kanō Village.[30]

Postwar statistics by ward indicate that each ward in Kanō Village was of approximately the same size.[31] The total population of the village had increased steadily from the Meiji period until the end of World War I. As of 1922, for which adequate data is available, 609 out of 690 households were farmers, and of a population of 4115, as many as 3622 people, or nearly 90%, belonged to farming households. The average paddy field area per farming household was 4 *tan* and 6 *se*(approximately 4600 m^2) and average dry field area was 8 *tan* and 2 *se* (approximately 8200 m^2).[32] With regard to dry fields, "mulberry fields expanded sharply from the end of the Meiji period to the last years of the Taisho period, with mulberry planted in all dry fields except for a small tract of land kept as a vegetable garden for private use," while "around the end of the Russo-Japanese War of 1905 village farmers began to convert their paddy fields to mulberry gardens".[33] In 1922, of about 495 *chō* (about 490 ha) of dry fields in Kanō Village, over 70%, or 359 *chō* (about 356 ha), were planted with mulberry,[34] indicating that many farmers based their farming operations on sericulture. Although the exact year is unknown, "*Kanō Mura Shi—Gendai Hen (Kanō Village History—Modern Era Edition)*" stated that "mulberry fields covered an area of 500 *chō* (about 500 ha) (the number of sericultural households standing at 600) and the quantity of cocoon produced in three crops a year reached about 60,000 *kan* (roughly 225 tons) in the heyday of sericulture in Kanō Village (in the Taisho period).[35]" During the period prior to the end of World War I, the economy of Kanō Village depended on sericulture and grew through an expansion of its cultivation.

Describing the overall situation in the village as of 1921, the Kanō Industrial Cooperative stated that "the overall economic conditions are generally good and the gap between the rich and the poor is not particularly conspicuous. This means there are few needy people. In the village of 687 households, the number of farmers cultivating land of one *chō* (roughly 1 ha) or larger is a little over 430 and only three persons own

---

[30] The Society for Publication of the Kanō Village History, "*Kanō Son Shi Gendai Hen (Kanō Village History—Modern Times Edition)*," 1963, pp. 4–20, pp. 202–211.

[31] "*Kanō Son Shi—Gendai Hen (Kanō Village History—Modern Era Edition)*," p. 64, Fig. 3.2.

[32] "*Kanō Son Shi—Gendai Hen (Kano Village History—Modern Era Edition)*," p. 66.

[33] "*Kanō Son Shi—Gendai Hen (Kano Village History—Modern Era Edition)*," p. 78.

[34] This figure does not include paddy fields planted with mulberry.

[35] "*Kanō Son Shi—Gendai Hen (Kano Village History—Modern Era Edition)*," p. 81.

land exceeding 10 *chō* (roughly 10 ha)... the economic conditions are generally favorable as a farming village.[36]" Clearly this was a positive assessment of the village's level of equality and ability to maintain small-scale producers. The Gini coefficient in 1901, estimated by the household tax data, stood at 0.46,[37] when the national average is estimated to have been between 0.43 and 0.52. Income disparity in Kanō Village, therefore, was essentially equivalent to the national average.[38] (Fig. 4.1) In 1891, the central government recognized that Japanese society was formed of relatively households operating medium- and small-sized businesses, and noted that, as they saw it, "the disparity between rich and the poor is not yet as striking as in foreign countries."[39] At the same time, Kanō Village, located on the Shinetsu railway line, was being greatly affected by the changing distribution of commodities and was on a path towards economic development centered on sericulture. It too was a relatively equal society comprised of medium- and small-scale farm households. The Kanō Industrial Cooperative was established to provide financial support for the development of such a regional economy.

On March 18, 1903, the Kanō Industrial Cooperative obtained the Nagano prefectural government's permission to establish itself as a credit cooperative for financial operations. The cooperative commenced business operations on April 1, 1903, with an initial union membership of 179. The village's population stood at 4056 in 1903, with 675 households, and thus it is fair to say that about one-quarter of the village's households joined the cooperative. 20 yen was the minimum required payment for participation in the cooperative, and it was stipulated that the full amount should be paid in within 2 years, with the first installment set at 2 yen. The initial number of capital contributions was 309, and thus, the Kanō Industrial Cooperative was

[36] Kanō Industrial Cooperative, "*Yugen Sekinin Kanō Shinyo Hanbai Kobai Kumiai Gyosekisho* (*Financial Results of Limited Liability Kanō Credit, Marketing and Purchasing Cooperative*)," (Manuscript), 1921.

[37] Estimated on the basis of the formula: Gini coefficient = 1 − the sum of (the relative frequency of the number of households by grade in the total number of households × the cumulative relative frequency of an amount of tax by grade in the total amount of the household tax) × 2.

The household tax is an important local tax that accounts for the bulk of revenues of towns and villages for much of the period covered by this chapter. Except for a small number of households acknowledged by the tax authorities as unable to pay, all households were liable to pay the tax. The tax authorities in this case were local municipalities, such as village offices, and household grades and tax amounts were assessed by them without the involvement of any other examining authorities. For this reason, in the imposition of the household tax, more often than not "the tax authorities were arbitrary in their assessments, overestimating revenues, underestimating liabilities and overestimating the tax imposed." Because of this, if we estimate the income distribution by using the above, it is possible that the income of higher-level grades is assessed excessively higher than their actual income. Mizumoto Tadatake, "*Kosuwari Zei no Seiritsu to Tenkai* (*The Establishment and Development of the Household Tax*)," Ochanomizu Shobo, 1998, p. 258.

[38] Minami Ryoshin, "Nihon no Keizai Hatten to Shotoku Bunpu (Economic Development and Income Distribution in Japan)," Iwanami Shoten, 1996, p. 30–108.

[39] Based on an address by Minister of Home Affairs Shinagawa Yajirō at the House of Peers of the First Parliament in 1891, included in Imperial Agricultural Association, "*Chūshono to Sangyō Kumiai* (*Medium- and Small-Sized Farmers and Industrial cooperatives*)," 1913.

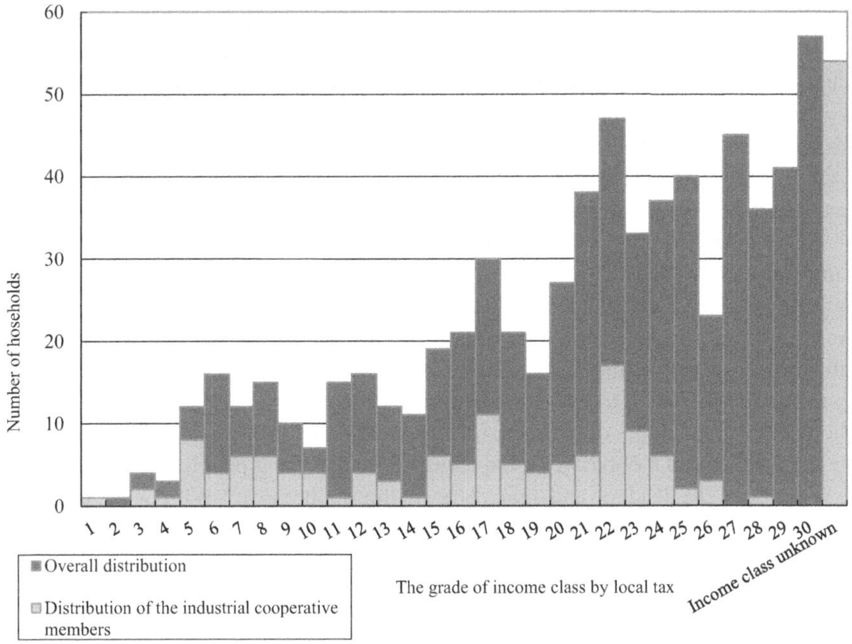

Fig. 4.1 Income class distribution and distribution of industrial cooperative members in Kanō Village. *Source* Kanō Villege "*Meiji 34-nendo Kenzei Kosuwari Fukagaku Tokyu Ketsugi An (A Draft Resolution for Grades of Prefectural Household Tax Rate Assessed Amount in FY1901)*," (included in Kanō Village Office, "Gijiroku Meiji 33-nen kara Meiji 34-nen (Minutes from 1900 to 1901)," Kanō Industrial Cooperative, "*Shusshikin Haraikomi Bo (Book of Investments in Capital Paid In)*," 1904

launched with an initial capital of 3090 yen.[40] *Mujin* or *kō* traditional mutual financing associations existing in Kanō Village at the time required payments per unit ranging between 100 and 300 yen in total, with initial installments set at 10 yen in many cases. Participation in the cooperative was thus well within the range of amounts contributed to traditional financial organizations.[41]

The "*Shusshikin Haraikomi Bo (Account Book for Investment Capital Paid In)*," prepared in 1904, shows an exhaustive list of the names of cooperative members at its inception. A comparison between this name list and the name list for the collection of prefectural tax rates by household in 1901 indicates the income class of cooperative members in the village (as long as the members were also household heads). As indicated by Fig. 4.1, the Kanō Industrial Cooperative was established with participation from a broad range of villagers with the exception of the lowest social stratum. Until 1918, the cooperative was run at the cooperative head's own

[40] Kanō Credit Cooperative, "*Jigyō Gaiyō Hōkokusho* (*Report on an Overview of Business*)," included in Zatsu Shorui Tojikomi (File of Miscellaneous Documents), 1903–1916.

[41] "*Kanō Son Shi—Gendai Hen* (*Kano Village History—Modern Era Edition*)," p. 64, p. 165, p. 168, p. 170, p. 172. In 190, one *kan* of cocoon was priced at 4.96 yen in Nagano Prefecture.

house with the clerical labor of his wife and thus the cooperative office was located in Higashi Fukai at the western edge of the village. Cooperative members were said to have walked all the way there to make use of the cooperative, an indication that the cooperative was formed across the whole village, i.e. not only in terms of income class but also geographically.[42]

As can be seen in Fig. 4.1, there are also cooperative members whose income class could not be determined. This may be because these members were younger members and were thus not household heads at the time. General meetings of the Kanō Industrial Cooperative were often held at Kanō Elementary School and the cooperative's head also headed the Kanō Young Men's Association, formed around the same time as the cooperative. This indicates a close relationship between the industrial cooperative, the Young Men's Association and the elementary school in Kanō Village. As such, there were members of the Kanō Young Men's Association who were also members of the industrial cooperative,[43] and thus the membership of the Kanō Industrial Cooperative also included many young people.[44]

Who were the leaders and managers of the cooperative? With what sense of purpose did they establish the cooperative? In 1921, two decades after its establishment, the Kanō Industrial Cooperative summarized the initial conditions it faced and its objectives at the time of establishment as follows:

> The background to the establishment of the Kanō Industrial Cooperative: Considering that the absence of smooth financing and sharp rises in interest rates in general threaten to undermine the foundation of the farm household economy, and considering that no optimism is warranted for the farm household economy given the prospects of sericulture developing further in the future, those holding prestigious village positions or organization heads participating in the village administration, including the current cooperative leader, directors and auditors, consulted with each other regarding the village's mission. They deciding to first establish a credit cooperative within the industrial cooperative in order to facilitate the provision of funds, enhance the village's production capacity, and cultivate the beneficial practices of hard work and savings, thereby achieving the full development of autonomy. After consultations with influential people in the village, the cooperative secured the consent of 179 residents across its hamlets, solicited funds for a total of 309 units of capital contributions, at 20 yen per unit, and obtained the permission for the establishment of the credit cooperative on March 18, 1903, which commenced operations in April 1903.[45]

As shown in the summarized statement above, at its inception the Kanō Industrial Cooperative had six directors and three auditors, all of whom had strong cooperative ties with other organizations in the village. The cooperative leader Fukai Isao, a leading person in the establishment of the cooperative, was recommended to assume the post of president of the newly-created Young Men's Association in the village

---

[42] Kanō Industrial Cooperative, "*Yugen Sekinin Kanō Shinyo Hanbai Kobai Kumiai Gyosekisho* (*Financial Results of Limited Liability Kanō Credit, Marketing and Purchasing Cooperative*)," (Manuscript), 1921.

[43] Kanō Young Men's Association, "*Kanō*," No. 1, 1906, the membership list at the end.

[44] Members of the Kanō Young Men's Association were men between 15 and 40 in Kanō Village. "*Kanō Son Shi—Gendai Hen* (*Kano Village History—Modern Times Edition*)," p. 249.

[45] "*Yugen Sekinin Kanō Shinyo Hanbai Kobai Kumiai Gyosekisho* (*Financial Results of Limited Liability Kanō Credit, Marketing and Purchasing Cooperative*)," (Manuscript).

in October 1903. After graduating from the department of law at Tokyo Senmon Gakkō (now Waseda University) in 1894, he returned to Kanō Village at the age of 29. Among eight other directors and auditors, there were five people who had the experience of serving in official positions in the village (village mayor, deputy mayor and treasurer) up to 1903.[46] This fact is indicative of strong ties between the Kanō Industrial Cooperative and the village's municipal authorities. Many of the cooperative's senior officials were counted among people with relatively high income in the village (Fig. 4.1, Table 4.1).

Prior to the establishment of the Kanō Industrial Cooperative, the financial situation in the village was as follows: "A great number of business corporations or *mujin-kō* mutual financing associations created in the first year of Meiji were in bad shape and not a few of them failed ... [To secure] funds necessary for industry many relied on banks in the neighboring town or on rich men in the village, and savings had to be placed solely in post offices".[47] In other words, not everyone in the village could borrow funds from banks, but, on the other hand, senior officials of the Kanō Industrial Cooperative included those who themselves had firsthand experience of directly operating a moneylending business, could borrow funds from banks. In fact, when the cooperative leader sought loans from a bank for cooperative management in the early years after the establishment of the cooperative, he was told that the bank could lend funds to him as an individual but not as the cooperative leader. This indicates that there were people of high creditworthiness among the cooperative's senior officials.[48] The industrial cooperative's directors were not, however, elected only on the basis of their monetary wealth. One of the directors, when the quasi-banking companies that previously existed in large numbers were dissolved, was involved in the disposal of their remaining affairs on several occasions.[49] He appears to have been a trusted person in the local community at large, but his household income class grade was not among the wealthy. He had also previously served as village mayor, and thus his case shows that a person's influence in the village was dependent on other social factors rather than pure monetary wealth.

As described above, the Kanō Industrial Cooperative rallied the entire community of Kanō Village both economically and socially. It was a modern cooperative organization and also had a strong relationship with other organizations and educational institutions in the village. The Kanō Industrial Cooperative was a modern institution but it also made use of personal connections and credit networks that had existed in

---

[46] None of them were incumbent village officials at the time of the establishment of the industrial cooperative. There were many who held official village posts after the cooperative's establishment. "*Kanō Son Shi—Gendai Hen* (*Kano Village History—Modern Times Edition*), pp. 31–32, p. 170.

[47] "*Yugen Sekinin Kanō Shinyo Hanbai Kobai Kumiai Gyosekisho* (*Financial Results of Limited Liability Kanō Credit, Marketing and Purchasing Cooperative*)," (Manuscript).

[48] "*Kanō Son Shi—Gendai Hen* (*Kano Village History—Modern Times Edition*)," p. 171.

[49] Kyōzensha of Kanō Village, Chiisagata County, Nagano Prefecture, "*Meiji 21-Nen Kohanki Kokajo* (*The Performance Report for the Second Half of 1888*)," Kōshōsha, "*Meiji 21-Nen Kohanki Kokajo* (*The Performance Report for the Second Half of 1888*)," (included in Nagano Prefecture, "*Kōbun Hensatsu—Ginkō Kōkajo—Nōshomu-Ka—Meiji 22-nendo* (*Bound Book of Official Documents—Bank Performance Report—Agriculture and Commerce Division—FY1889*). ".

Table 4.1 Senior members of the Kanō industrial cooperative at its Inception in 1903

Name	Official village posts held up to 1920	Income class*	Other remarks
Fukai Isao	1901–1913: assembly member; 1903: president of the Kanō Young Men's Association (created in 1903); 1914: mayor	Grade 3	Kanō Industrial Cooperative leader; his own house was used as the cooperative's office; graduate of Tokyo Senmon Gakkō (Waseda University)
Fukushima Manbei	1892–1896: treasurer; 1897–1898: deputy mayor 1898–1902: mayor 1907–1913: assembly member	Grade 5	
Tanaka Shintarō	1894–1895: deputy mayor 1897–1898: mayor 1901–1913: assembly member 1905–1906: mayor	Grade 2	*Sake* brewer
Tsuchiya Wasaku	1889–1895: assembly member 1899–1900: deputy mayor 1902: mayor	Grade 15	A member of the committee that handled residual work at quasi-banking companies Kyōzensha and Kōshōsha established in 1888 (both were dissolved in the following year)
Seki Rinosuke	1896–1910: assembly member 1917–1920: deputy member	Grade 8	
Tomioka Jukichi	1898–1910: assembly member	Grade 15	
Kodama Hikosuke	1889–1896: treasurer 1895–1901: assembly member 1896–1897: deputy mayor	Grade 1	Cooperative auditor, soy sauce producer, managed Kodama Gōmei Kaisha (Kodama general partnership company) (financial business)
Iijima Rinsaku	1895–1907: assembly member	Grade 5	Cooperative auditor
Seki Manabu	1902–1905: treasurer 1910–1925: assembly member	Grade 3	Cooperative auditor

Sources Kanō Village magazine editorial committee, "*Kanō Son Shi—Gendai Hen (Kanō Village Magazine—Modern Times Edition),*"1963, pp. 31–36, pp. 369–373; "*Meiji 34-nendo Kenzei Kosuwari Fukagaku Tokyu Ketsugi An (A Draft Resolution for Grades of Prefectural Household Tax Rate Assessed Amount in FY1901),*" (included in Kanō Village Office, "Gijiroku Meiji 33-nen kara Meiji 34-nen (Minutes from 1900 to 1901)"

*Based on FY1901 prefectural household tax rate grades. The number of households assessed for taxation was 666 with a total of 30 income class grades. Households assessed up to Grade 15 (one-quarter of the number of households in the village) accounted for a little less than 60% of the village's total income

the previous Tokugawa period. The context and ideas behind it were expressed in the cooperative's prospectus of establishment:

> The Intent of the Establishment of the Kanō Industrial Cooperative Limited Liability
>
> The Founder
>
> In getting on in the world, there is nothing more enjoyable than to have sufficient clothing, food and housing, to live within our means, to complete the path of loyalty and filial piety, and to tend to and foster descendants, thereby promoting the country's future prosperity... However, the country imposes taxes, households have to meet food and clothing expenses, the companionship or association with our relatives and friends also requires expense... In this ever-evolving world, those who take advantage of new opportunities and methods become increasingly affluent and prosper, and those who are not able to fall behind and could ultimately sink to the extreme of poverty in the end. All of this depends entirely on the presence or absence of capital. This is inevitable in a world where everyone must come under the control of capital... The best way to obtain capital is to establish a law for credit cooperatives. A credit cooperative is formed by a large number of people who each invest a small amount of capital which is then pooled to allow each member to borrow or lend. Though the contribution from each member is extremely small, when put together, it results in a large pool of capital, and a member who is able to borrow money from it can buy fertilizers for cultivation or mulberries for raising silkworms. In this way, even poor people can easily find a means of obtaining capital and can have their share of fair living and follow the path of human righteousness. This is why this credit cooperative is most necessary for industry... As the Japanese government also sees it this way, it promulgated the Industrial Cooperative Act the year before last. Thus, we have decided to organize this cooperative under the Act to find a way to encourage new industry. We hope a large number of people in Kanō Village will support this initiative.[50]

As can be gleaned from the prospectus above, the primary purpose of the cooperative's establishment was to prevent ordinary households in Kanō Village from falling into destitution. This was to be achieved by autonomously creating opportunities to access small-amount finance locally based on the funds collected from ordinary households themselves. In turn, this would also "encourage new industry," in the area. The prospectus also indicated that these goals were very much inline with those of the central government in enacting the Industrial Cooperative Act, as shown below:

> If people below the middle class are to hope to maintain independence in an economy of free competition and look forward to personal industrial development... there should exist appropriate financial institutions to that end. In other words, since a credit cooperative is a cooperative financial institution around which people below the middle class can unite, get closer to each other, and establish, operate and conduct themselves by their own exertions without relying on other external assistance, ... there is no need for concern that it would become overwhelmed by major capitalists even in the strong tides of free competition... [and] its other indirect benefits... should limit the gap between the rich and the poor.[51]

The policy of the central government and the direction sought by local communities at this point of time almost entirely overlapped in Kanō Village. This overlap

---

[50] "*Kanō Son Shi—Gendai Hen* (*Kano Village History—Modern Edition*)," pp. 168–169.

[51] Hirata Tōsuke, "*Sangyō Kumiai Ho Yogi* (*The Essence of the Industrial Cooperative Act*)," p. 22.

took shape in the form of the establishment of an industrial cooperative in 1903. For people who lived in local communities, this was a reaction to the opportunities and the risks brought about by increasing links to wider markets with the development of transportation and telecommunications networks. For the central government, it was an important means through which to promote the development of the national economy whilst maintaining social stability.

4.4 The Development of the Management of the Kanō Industrial Cooperative

4.4.1 The Operational Scale and Seasonality of the Kanō Industrial Cooperative

How did the Kanō Industrial Cooperative develop over time? The cooperative's membership rose steadily, almost equaling the total number of households in the village by 1922, almost 20 years after it was first established. And it continued to increase thereafter.[52] Behind this steady development was the cooperative's stable management and the growth in its capital (Table 4.2). Capital contributions, the very foundation of the cooperative, already exceeded 10,000 yen going into the 1910s. In addition, the Kanō Industrial Cooperative accumulated deposits and reserves from its profits each fiscal year. Partly because the cooperative recorded profits each fiscal year, the amount of deposits and reserves exceeded 10,000 yen by 1917, an amount equivalent to more than half its capital (contributions). With respect to external borrowing, annual borrowing from banks increased in the 1900s in tandem with an expansion of lending operations, but decreased again during the 1910s. It can be said that during its growth phase, the Kanō Industrial Cooperative was able to achieve the self-circulating financing of its regional economy throughout the course of a given year, the policy objective of the cooperative, despite maintaining a short-term dependence on external funds.

Underpinning the sound management of the cooperative were the expansion of both the number and total amount of small-amount loans, the core business of the credit cooperative's operations, and their trouble-free repayment. The amount of lending by the Kanō Industrial Cooperative to members increased healthily, but the amount per loan, in contrast, declined prior to the outbreak of World War I. In other words, the Kanō Industrial Cooperative concentrated its efforts on financing a large number of small-scale enterprises in the village.

The lending business brought steady profits to the Kanō Industrial Cooperative. The revenue of the Kanō Industrial Cooperative in its founding period came exclusively from interest on loans (Table 4.3). As it became more established thanks to

[52] "*Kanō Son Shi—Gendai Hen* (*Kano Village History—Modern Edition*)," p. 172.

Table 4.2 Kanō cooperative's business management

	Total assets	Population	No. of house-holds	No. of members	Capital paid in		Deposits+reserves		Year-end balance of cooperative savings			Balance of bank borrowings	
											No. of units		
1903	7632	4056	675	179	3090	40%	0	0%	821	11%	–	500	7%
1904	7719	–	–	183	4695	61%	133	2%	869	11%	27	0	0%
1905	8423	–	–	183	6340	75%	374	4%	958	11%	30	0	0%
1906	13,013	–	–	197	7436	57%	800	6%	1107	9%	–	0	0%
1907	15,172	–	–	208	8809	58%	1401	9%	1710	11%	–	0	0%
1908	19,418	–	–	211	10,423	54%	1977	10%	629	3%	–	4500	23%
1909	19,299	4268	696	212	11,010	57%	2616	14%	1100	6%	–	3000	16%
1910	20,416	–	–	213	11,190	55%	3482	17%	4037	20%	123	0	0%
1911	25,930	–	–	221	11,430	44%	4414	17%	8584	33%	153	0	0%
1912	29,268	–	–	223	11,460	39%	5149	18%	11,093	38%	173	0	0%
1913	37,215	–	–	225	11,580	31%	5990	16%	17,923	48%	196	0	0%
1914	43,224	–	–	226	11,700	27%	6989	16%	22,660	52%	224	0	0%
1915	44,365	–	–	223	11,670	26%	8081	18%	22,580	51%	220	0	0%
1916	60,991	4545	693	247	12,591	21%	9317	15%	36,333	60%	244	0	0%
1917	102,726	–	–	325	18,924	18%	10,658	10%	70,761	69%	281	0	0%
1918	156,444	–	–	425	24,874	16%	10,842	7%	117,400	75%	544	0	0%

(continued)

Table 4.2 (continued)

	Year-end balance of lending				Balance of bank deposits		Land/securities assets		Total profit		Total annual lending	Total annual borrowings
			No. of loans	Avg.								
1903	4525	59%		–	0	0%	0	0%	131	2%	7601	2700
1904	5417	70%	83	65	600	8%	0	0%	456	6%	5558	2055
1905	7228	86%	85	85	1000	12%	0	0%	750	9%	8488	6350
1906	8974	69%	98	92	1150	9%	0	0%	965	7%	12,804	7210
1907	8766	58%	110	80	4200	28%	0	0%	1120	7%	11,178	6300
1908	18,356	95%		–	2000	10%	0	0%	1301	7%	24,867	14,200
1909	16,710	87%	149	112	2400	12%	0	0%	1572	8%	18,753	12,950
1910	17,433	85%	110	158	2800	14%	0	0%	1615	8%	17,304	7100
1911	18,866	73%	105	180	5900	23%	870	3%	1502	6%	18,977	7500
1912	21,282	73%	104	204	5900	20%	870	3%	1570	5%	19,383	6000
1913	24,842	67%	110	225	10,000	27%	1110	3%	1721	5%	27,756	12,500
1914	31,853	74%	131	244	8800	20%	1700	4%	1873	4%	31,501	10,800
1915	34,614	78%	125	278	6100	14%	2261	5%	2033	5%	27,262	12,950
1916	31,772	52%	133	238	24,500	40%	2441	4%	2050	3%	23,949	11,000
1917	35,007	34%	175	200	60,022	58%	5575	5%	1926	2%	50,249	0
1918	51,665	33%	202	256	90,058	58%	10,355	7%	2638	2%	62,863	0

Shown in yen, discarding *sen* (1/10 yen) and below. The number of units and loans are as shown in the original data. % indicates the ratio to total assets.
Source Kanō Industrial Cooperative, "*Jigyō Hōkokusho (Business Report)*" 1903–1918.

profits gained from interest and the high rate of repayment, the Kanō Industrial Cooperative, in addition to lending, began to deposit its funds with the 19th Bank and the Nihon Kangyō Bank. It also invested in government bonds and other securities. The cooperative also purchased land to use as experimental farms.[53] After World War I, revenue from other areas of business came to take on a greater importance, but interest on loans still accounted for the bulk of its revenue.

Behind the stable growth of its small-amount financing operations was the sericulture boom and a resultant expansion of demand for funds. The "*Yūgen Sekinin Kanō Shinyo Hanbai Kōbai Kumiai Jisekisho (Performance Report of the Limited Liability Kanō Credit, Marketing and Purchasing Cooperative)*" states as follows:

> Over the past 10 years [the 1880s, author's note], the sericulture industry has become extremely buoyant and mulberry fields have been expanded so sharply that the amount of manure applied could only cover a portion of that required for fertilization. As an increasingly large amount of chemical fertilizers are required each year, farming households have not found it easy to procure funds for purchasing fertilizer. Thus, in a large number of cases, they were compelled to borrow money at high interest rates or to make disadvantageous purchases under deferred payment contracts. The absence of smooth financing and sharp rises in interest rates threaten to undermine the foundation of the farm household economy, and concerned that no optimism is warranted for the farming household economy amid the prospect of the sericulture developing further in the future... the cooperative decided to launch its operations.[54]

For farmers, the expansion of sericulture either meant an extensive expansion of the area of mulberry under cultivation using existing dry fields, or a more intensive use of fertilizers. Both stimulated individual farmers' demand for cash to pay for fertilizers or the purchase/development of land. Data indicates that over 60% of loans to cooperative members by the Kanō Industrial Cooperative were used to pay for fertilizers (Table 4.4). Compared with the ratio of approximately 30% of loans provided by ordinary industrial cooperatives used for fertilizers,[55] it can be seen that the specific characteristics of the regional economy in Kanō Village enhanced demand for fertilizers. It can also be said that the Kanō Industrial Cooperative accurately responded to the demand for funds brought about by the structure of the regional economy.[56]

The fact that payments for fertilizers accounted for the bulk of demand for funds meant that financing needs showed a significant seasonal fluctuation, and the Kanō

---

[53] Source: Kanō Industrial Cooperative, "*Jigyō Hōkokusho* (*Business Report*)" for each fiscal year.

[54] "*Yugen Sekinin Kanō Shinyo Hanbai Kobai Kumiai Jisekisho* (*Performance Report of the Limited Liability Kanō Credit, Marketing and Purchasing Cooperative*)," (Manuscript).

[55] Ministry of Agriculture and Commerce, "*Yūryō Sangyō Kumiai Jirei* (*Cases of Excellent Industrial Cooperatives*)," 1920; Shinoura Hikaru, "*Nōson Kyodo Kumiai no Tenkai Katei* (*The Development Process of Rural Cooperatives*)," p. 37.

[56] In providing unsecured loans to cooperative members, the Kanō Industrial Cooperative prepared a "Table of Credit Ratings" each year after the year of its establishment. Items on the ratings table included assets, equity, commitments and diligence, rating hard information and soft information on individual members with the same weight. For more details on the credit assessment by the Kanō Industrial Cooperative, see Kojima Yohei and Takahashi Kazushi, "Senzen Nihon no Sangyo Kumiai ni Okeru Shinyo Shinsa no Jittai to Kaihatsu Tojokoku heno Gani (Historical Credit Assessment in Pre-War Japan and Its Implications in Contemporary Developing Countries).".

Table 4.3 The structure of revenue and expenditure of the Kanō industrial cooperative

	Total assets	Total profit (% of total assets)		Revenue								
				Total		Interest on loans		Interest on bank deposits		Land	Mulberry-fields	Securities
1903	7632	131	2%	250	3%	251	100%	–	–	0	0	0
1904	7719	456	6%	638	8%	638	100%	–	–	0	0	0
1905	8423	750	9%	1041	12%	1041	100%	–	–	0	0	0
1906	13,013	965	7%	1327	10%	1328	100%	–	–	0	0	0
1907	15,172	1120	7%	1449	10%	1449	100%	–	–	0	0	0
1908	19,418	1301	7%	1696	9%	1696	100%	–	–	0	0	0
1909	19,299	1572	8%	2356	12%	2329	99%	27	1%	0	0	0
1910	20,416	1615	8%	2422	12%	2334	96%	89	4%	0	0	0
1911	25,930	1502	6%	2201	8%	1989	90%	178	8%	34	0	0
1912	29,268	1570	5%	2409	8%	2186	91%	187	8%	35	0	0
1913	37,215	1721	5%	3162	8%	2446	77%	681	22%	35	0	0
1914	43,224	1873	4%	3491	8%	2922	84%	531	15%	35	0	0
1915	44,365	2033	5%	4292	10%	3591	84%	636	15%	57	0	6
1916	60,991	2050	3%	4321	7%	3787	88%	473	11%	36	0	24
1917	10,2726	1926	2%	5103	5%	3172	62%	1356	27%	23	0	24
1918	156,444	2638	2%	9622	6%	3430	36%	2512	26%	270	135	24

(continued)

Table 4.3 (continued)

	Expenditure						Interest rate on loans (%)	Interest rate on savings (%)
	Total	Interest on deposits	Interest on borrowings	Dividends (% of gross revenue)		Directors' remuneration, etc		
1903	119	*86	–	0	0%	–	10–12	5
1904	182	–	–	219	34%	–	12	6
1905	291	–	–	317	30%	30	12	7.2
1906	362	–	–	450	34%	50	13	6
1907	329	–	–	509	35%	50	10–12	6
1908	395	–	–	587	35%	75	10–12	6
1909	784	61	657	660	28%	10	10–13	6–8
1910	807	238	400	671	28%	0	11	7
1911	699	445	138	685	31%	110	9–10.8	5.4
1912	839	384	377	687	29%	107	8–10	5.4
1913	1441	952	336	694	22%	100	8–10	6
1914	1618	1312	172	702	20%	100	8–10	6–7
1915	2259	1562	560	700	16%	100	8–10	6–7
1916	2271	1876	219	712	16%	100	8–10	6–7
1917	3177	2799	0	945	19%	100	8	5.4–6
1918	6984	4574	0	1352	14%	130	6–8	4.38–6

*Original data shows a total of interest on savings and interest on borrowings. (–) indicates that no data is available
Source Kanō industrial cooperative, "*Jigyō Hōkokusho (Business Report)*" 1903–1918

Table 4.4 Breakdown of the use of loans by the Kanō industrial cooperative

Year	1907	1909
Fertilizers	64%	68%
Sericulture-related	7%	9%
Estate/mountain forests (land-related)	6%	6%
Other/unknown	22%	17%
Number of loans	98 cases	208 cases
Average loan amount	113.14 yen	84.18 yen
Loan median	100 yen	50 yen
Loan mode value	100 yen	30 yen

Sources Kanō industrial cooperative, "*Kashitukekin Daicho Meiji 40 nendo (Loan Ledger for Fiscal Year Meiji 40)*," 1907; Kanō Industrial Cooperative, "*Kashitukekin Daicho Meiji 42 nendo (Loan Ledger for Fiscal Year Meiji 42)*," 1909

Industrial Cooperative was required to respond to this changing demand. The monthly business conditions of the Kanō Industrial Cooperative in 1907 (Fig. 4.2), show that loans by the Kanō Industrial Cooperative and loan repayments clearly peaked when fertilizer was applied to mulberry fields and when cocoon were sold. More specifically, the cooperative provided loans to members from winter to spring, when fertilization took place, and collected loaned funds mainly during the summer, coinciding with the sale of spring cocoons. The funding cycle in the households of farmers who used the cooperative is demonstrated by the increase in the cooperative's deposits in the summer. The farming households in Kanō Village placed much weight on their sericulture activities which required funds for purchasing fertilizers in early spring and provided them with cash income during the summer months.

In order to respond to changes in the demand for funds by cooperative members in accordance with the seasonal cycle of sericulture, the Kanō Industrial Cooperative was temporarily required to secure a large amount of funds. As discussed earlier, the capital and deposits of the Kanō Industrial Cooperative increased steadily after its founding. As of 1907, for example, the total amount of loans in the year was almost equal to the sum of equity capital and the year-end balance of deposits. In that sense, the management of the Kanō Industrial Cooperative corresponded to the size of its funds, but this was only the case when the cooperative's operations were viewed from a yearly perspective. For the period from spring to early summer in any given year, the Kanō Industrial Cooperative faced a level of demand for funds that it could not cover solely from its own internal cash flow.

In order to deal with this seasonal surge in demand for funds, the Kanō Industrial Cooperative procured funds from external financial institutions such as the 19th Bank (Table 4.5), while also relying on the personal funds of Fukai Isao, the cooperative's head, on a temporary basis. Borrowings from banks were made from February onwards, during the period when members' demand for loans from the cooperative increased. This meant that the Kanō Industrial Cooperative functioned as a window for fund procurement from outside the village in response to the seasonal demand

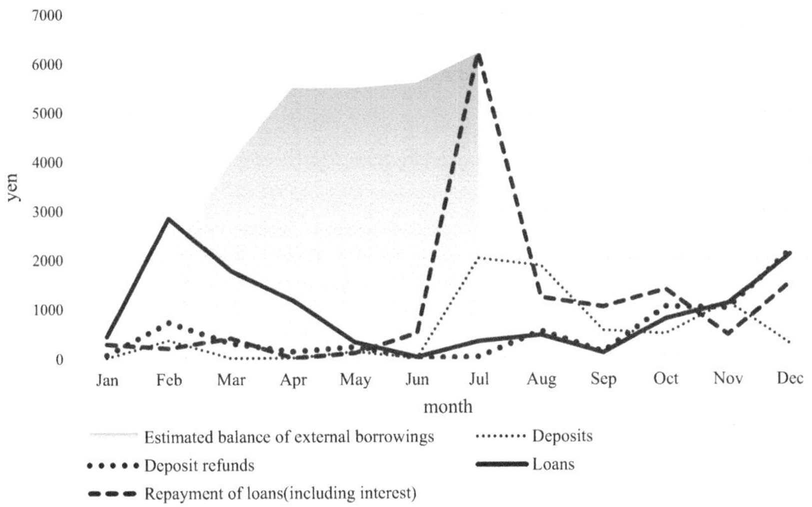

Fig. 4.2 Seasonal business trends of the Kanō industrial cooperative in 1907. Unit for the vertical axis is 1 yen. Values for curves show the monthly total of transactions, not the balances or cumulative values. *Sources* Kanō industrial cooperative, "*Dai Goki Suitocho (Financial Records for the Fifth Period)*," "*Dai Goki Suito Uchiwakecho (Breakdown of Receipts and Disbursements for the Fifth Period)*," 1907

for funds among its members. In 1907, the interest rate levied by the Kanō Industrial Cooperative on loans provided to cooperative members was a uniform 12%, while interest rates on external funds borrowed by the cooperative were around 10%.[57] In 1909, interest rates on small-amount loans to cooperative members ranged from 12.5 to 13%, while most external funds were borrowed at an interest rate of 12.4%. Compared with interest rates on external funds, funds provided within the industrial cooperative were not excessive, and these interest rates indicated that funds were sometimes provided to members with only a very narrow margin by the cooperative. The bulk of these external funds were short-term operating funds, rather than long-term funds, and were repaid within a period of less than six months after borrowing.[58]

[57] Kanō Industrial Cooperative, "*Kashitsukekin Daicho (Loan Ledger)*," FY1907 and FY1909.

[58] Long-term borrowings, which may be described as exceptional, were low-interest funds from the Nagano Agricultural and Industrial Bank.

Table 4.5 Kanō industrial cooperative and external financial institutions

Year	Month	Loan amount	Lender	Annual interest rate	Month set for full repayment	Month of actual full repayment	Borrowing period	Remarks
1906	February	2500	Komoro bank	12%	7	6–7	4–5 mos	Final repayment past the scheduled date by a few days
	February	500	Komoro bank	12.4%		3–7	1–5 mos	
	April	3000	19th Bank	12.4%	7	6–7	2–3 mos	The first repayment of 200 yen covered "the borrowing by Director Tanaka" Final repayment past the scheduled date by a few days
	May	400	19th Bank	12.4%		6–7	1–2 mons	
	May	250	Cooperative leader	12.8%	6	6–7	1–2 mos	Final repayment past the scheduled date by a few days
	April	560	Cooperative leader	Virtually free of interest		5–7	2–3 mos	0.50 yen paid in interest
Annual total borrowings			7210					
1907	February	2000	Komoro bank	10.2%	7	6–7	4–5 mos	Dates entered by the month only
	March	2000	19th Bank	9.9%	7	6–7	3–4 mos	
	April	1500	19th Bank	9.9%	7	6–7	2–3 mos	
	June	100	Cooperative leader	Free of interest		7	3 days	Possibly temporary funds to cover repayments of bank borrowings (borrowed on the dates for interest payments to the 19th Bank and Komoro Bank)
	July	700	Cooperative leader	9.1%		7	8 days	

(continued)

Table 4.5 (continued)

Year	Month	Loan amount	Lender	Annual interest rate	Month set for full repayment	Month of actual full repayment	Borrowing period	Remarks
Annual total borrowings			6300					
1908	March	1500	Komoro bank	12.4%	7	4	1 month	Refinancing (repaid immediately after borrowings from Nagano Agricultural and Industrial Bank)
	April	3500	Nagano Agricultural and Industrial Bank	9%	7	7	3 mos	
	May	1500	Nagano agricultural and industrial Bank	9%	8	8	3 mos	
	May	800	Komoro bank	12.8%	5	5	10 days	
	May	600	19th Bank	12.4%	7	7	1 month	Borrowed at the end of May, repaid at the beginning of July
	December	4500	Nagano agricultural and industrial bank	9%	Aug 1909	Aug 1909	7–8 mos	
Annual total borrowings			12,400					
Year-end balance of borrowings			4500					
1909	January	1500	19th Bank	12.4%	7	6	5 mos	
	February	1500	Komoro bank	13.3%	6	7	4 mos	Repayment planned for the end of June, but actually repaid at the beginning of July
	February	1500	19th Bank	12.4%	7	7	5 mos	
	February	1000	19th Bank	12.4%	6	7	5 mos	Fully repaid, 2 weeks past the scheduled repayment date
	March	1500	Komoro bank	12.4%	7	7	4 mos	
	Arpil	1000	19th Bank	12.4%	7	7	3 mos	
	May	350	Komoro bank	12.8%	7	7	2 mos	

(continued)

Table 4.5 (continued)

Year	Month	Loan amount	Lender	Annual interest rate	Month set for full repayment	Month of actual full repayment	Borrowing period	Remarks
	December	3000	Nagano agricultural and industrial bank	9%	Aug 1910	Aug 1910	8 mos	
Annual total borrowings			11,350					
Year-end balance of borrowings			3000					
1910	February	2800	19th Bank	9.9%	7	7	5 mos	
	March	2800	19th Bank	10.2%	7	6–7	3–4 mos	
	April	500	19th Bank	9.9%	7	6	2 mos	
	May	1000	Komoro bank	11.3%	6	6	1 month	
Annual total borrowings			7100					
1911	February	2500	Komoro bank	9.1%	7	3	1 month	Refinancing (repaid simultaneously with borrowings from the 19th Bank)
	March	2500	19th Bank	8.4%	7	6–7	3–4 mos	
	March	2000	19th Bank	8.4%	7	7	4 mos	
	May	500	19th Bank	8.4%	7	6	1 month	
Annual total borrowings			7500					

Source Kanō industrial cooperative, "*Kariirekin Daicho (Borrowing Ledger)*," 1906–1911. Interest rates are converted into annual rates from per-diem rates

4.4.2 Centricity as Regional Organization

As shown above, for most of the year the Kanō Industrial Cooperative operated without relying on external funds, though it did require a short term injection of them. The stability of its management, it is believed, was premised on the growth of the cooperative's savings business (Table 4.2). The savings business, which was initially used very sparingly by cooperative members, grew with the emergence of new organizations in various sectors within village society and the reorganization of the networks of the Tokugawa period.

As members could now secure a stable source of cash because of the existence of microcredit, they were also encouraged to save using financial institutions. For example, the *Higashi Fukai Jūssenkai* (Higashi Fukai 10-sen Association) was formed in 1904, in order to "encourage [local people] to act upon our principles by ourselves, without any assistance from others, and to accumulate 10 sen (0.1 yen) without fail on a certain date every month." Its 104 members managed to "save up 992 yen" which was then deposited in the Kanō Industrial Cooperative. This was not the only example. The *Kanō Kinken Kumiai* (Kanō Hard Work and Frugality Union), which counted all residents of Kanō Village as members, was "intended to cultivate the laudable custom of hard work and frugality and build the foundation of joint autonomy." It "required union members to save at least one unit [one unit was equal to 5 sen] on the 20th day of each month." Other groups "such as the *Jūssenkai* (10-sen Association), *Gosenkai* (5-sen Association), *Kaikon Chokin* (Land-developing Savings) *and Chokoku Tsumitatekin* (Grain Storage Reserve Fund), adopted similar methods as credit cooperatives" to make deposits. Since savings formed through these savings groups were directly set aside, the balance of deposits placed with the Kanō Industrial Cooperative grew as the years passed.[59]

In the case of the Kanō Industrial Cooperative, as indicated by the personal histories of the cooperative's senior officials and the personal connections between the Kanō Young Men's Association and the cooperative, "the connections between the cooperative, the village office and the school were always close" from the time of the cooperative's establishment. The cooperative's launch into the credit business provided an opportunity to form a large number of savings groups in the village. In addition to the newly formed savings groups, systems and networks existing since the Tokugawa period, such as *mujin-kō* mutual financing associations and organizations of *ujiko*, shrine parishioners, also made use of savings accounts at the Kanō Industrial Cooperative.

The ownership of group savings handled by the Kanō Industrial Cooperative in 1919 showed that the cooperative had ties with a large number and variety of groups that existed in the village (Table 4.6). Savings groups and alumni associations set up at the elementary school, the young men's association and the women's association were organizations created in the modern period and were born out of the reorganization of networks that existed in the village hamlets since the Tokugawa period. These

[59] National Federation of Industrial Cooperatives, "*Dainiji Hyosho Sangyo Kumiai* (*The Second Commended Industrial cooperatives*)," 1911, p. 108.

groups, fusing the traditional and modern, were made up of the various age groups and income classes in Kanō Village society, and they were brought together by the Kanō Industrial Cooperative which handled the receipts and disbursal of their funds on an exclusive basis.

Kanō Village society as a whole came to revolve around the Kanō Industrial Cooperative at its core. This can be seen in the way that in 1910 the Kanō Industrial Cooperative established a deposit system that maintained strong ties with external organizations. The system provided services such as "tax savings," with an incidental special overdraft contract system, and "family savings" that encouraged savings by family members other than household heads. In the process of expanding its savings business, the Kanō Industrial Cooperative was not only able to obtain the funds that provided a strong basis for its management, but it also came to occupy an important position within village society.[60] Leveraging this internal accumulation of funds, the Kanō Industrial Cooperative conducted its credit business, and was also able to construct an office building and agricultural warehouses which were used to handle the sales of rice produced by cooperative members. It expanded the scope of its operations to respond to the demands of cooperative members. In 1919, it established a purchasing department and set up stores with display racks, initiating sales of food, agricultural equipment, fertilizers, school supplies and clothing. Subsequently in 1927, it created a user department to initiate a scheme for the common use of agricultural equipment, such as rice milling machines, flour mill machines and grain threshing machines.[61] With its financing role as its core business, the Kanō Industrial Cooperative came to occupy an important social position in the wider region by bringing the vast majority of village residents into some form of relationship with the cooperative, often in a way that was important in enhancing the convenience of everyday life in the village.

4.5 Subsequent Developments and a Brief Summary

In 1910, the Kanō Industrial Cooperative was commended for its "excellent performance" by the National Federation of Industrial Cooperatives, headed by Minister of Home Affairs, Hirata Tōsuke. The Kanō Industrial Cooperative immediately expressed its intention to participate in the National Federation of Industrial Cooperatives, a national organization of industrial cooperatives created in 1906, and helped establish association branches in Chiisagata County. Evaluation items by the Central Association included an increase in membership and businesses, management with surplus funds and reserves, "progress in businesses by union members

[60] Nagano Branch of the National Federation of Industrial Cooperatives, Miyao Takekazu ed., "*Nagano-ken Sangyo Kumiai Enkakushi* (*The History of Industrial cooperatives in Nagano Prefecture*)," Kyoeisha, 1927, p. 51.

[61] "*Yugen Sekinin Kano Shinyo Hanbai Kobai Kumiai Jisekisho* (*Performance Report of the Limited Liability Kano Credit, Marketing and Purchasing Cooperative*)," (Manuscript), "*Kanō Son Shi—Gendai Hen* (*Kano Village History—Modern Times Edition*)," p. 181.

Table 4.6 Ownership of group savings accounts at Kanō Industrial Cooperative (1919)

East Fukai ladies' association	Long life Koshin consortium
East Fukai youth society	Kanō elementary school's savings union (Matsui)
Sone agricultural union	Kanō elementary school's savings union (T. Miyazaki)
East Fukai division representative	Kanō elementary school's savings union (Kubota)
Tatarado division	Kanō elementary school's savings union (Kobayashi)
Kanō Village youth society	Ōkawa self-training society
Kaizenji-ue Mulberry improvement association	*Kō* for Hurumine Shrine pilgrim
Tazawa club	Accomplishment leading society
Oya group	Kuribayashi division representative
Kuribayashi working and practicing consortium	Tazawa joint purchase union
Encourage agricultural club	Kanō elementary school's savings union (Y. Miyazaki)
Kanō elementary school	Kuribayashi youth society
Kanō Shrine	Imperial ex-military veterans' organization of Kanō division
Kanō Ladies' association	Kanō alumni union
Tatarado youth society	Sone youth society
Mibushiro Shrine	Kaizenji [Temple] youth society
Sone youth society	Endowment funds for Kanō elementary school
Kamamurata youth society	Endowment funds for Kanō village
East Ueda agricultural development consortium	Accomplishment leading society *Mujin* division
Tazawa volunteer bamboo forest union	Kanō industrial savings society
Shimo-Kuribayashi Mulberry improvement association	Alumni association of the 5th grade
East Hukai side-well representative	Alumni association of 1916 graduates
West Tazawa union	Tazawa pig farming association
Jukichi Tomioka union	*Ko* for Ise Shrine pilgrim
Donation for teacher Miyashita's memorial monument	The alumni
Kaizenji agricultural union	Sone division representative
Chikuma alumni association	Kanō true rewarding association
Kaizenji fireguard unit	Kaizenji ladies' association
Kanō village military treatment society	*Kō*for empowerment
East Ueda youth society	Koyuji temple
Village master	*Kō* for prosperity
East Ueda sericulture association	Kuribayashi ladies' association

(continued)

Table 4.6 (continued)

East Fukai ladies' association	Long life Koshin consortium
East Ueda better-produce consortium	*Kō* for Akiba mountain picnic
Tazawa union accounting division	East Ueda encourage agricultural club
Tazawa Ladies' Association	Kanō village agricultural conference
Sone Ladies' Association	Tazawa savings union
Leading Development Consortium	S. Tsuchiya (representative)
The number of groups = the number of accounts (excluding overlapping) = 74	

Source Kanō Industrial Cooperative, "*Dantai Chokin Daicho Taisho Hachi Nendo (Group Savings Ledger, FY1919)*," 1919
Note Fukai, Sone, Tatarado, Tazawa, Oya, Kuribayashi, Kaizenji, Ueda, Okawa are local place names in Kanō village

and regional improvements of industry," "increased wealth of union members" and the "enhancement of morals." The Kanō Industrial Cooperative was assessed highly for providing cooperative members "with the availability and convenience of direct industrial funding,… cultivating the laudable custom of hard work and savings." It also encouraged tax payments and the formation of a large number of savings groups within the village.[62] This commendation simultaneously valued the economic and social contribution of the operations of the Kanō Industrial Cooperative and it subsequently enabled the cooperative to access low-interest loans from government-affiliated financial institutions, including the Nagano Agricultural and Industrial Bank and the Nihon Kangyō Bank.[63]

The Kanō Industrial Cooperative, whilst building on the networks inherited from the Tokugawa period, brought into Kanō Village modern systems and education. Despite its modernity it played an important role in maintaining and enhancing the nature of the community rather than undermining it. Its role in providing access to small-amount credit to cooperative members is one example of that. The Kanō Industrial Cooperative used economic indicators such as members' assets and their equity stake in the cooperative in determining their access to credit. It also considered the moral qualities of individual members in its decision making, paying attention to members' diligence and commitment to contracts which were quantified so as to provide an equal assessment.[64] Among the senior officials of the Kanō Industrial Cooperative were those who had previously been involved in traditional financial

[62] National Federation of Industrial cooperatives, "*Dainiji Hyosho Sangyo Kumiai* (*The Second Commended Industrial cooperatives*)," 1911, pp. 1–5, p. 110.

[63] "*Nagano-ken Sangyo Kumiai Enkakushi* (*The History of Industrial cooperatives in Nagano Prefecture*)," p. 2, p. 17.

[64] Kanō Industrial Cooperative, "*Shinyo Teido Hyo* (*Table of Credit Ratings*)," each fiscal year version.

businesses and this kind of credit assessment presumably was based on their accumulated experiences.[65] In other words, it can be said that the credit rating process at the Kanō Industrial Cooperative successfully incorporated the more subjective credit assessment common in the individual-to-individual granting of credit that had previously existed in the regional economy, turning it into a seemingly objective numerical evaluation used in parallel with the monetary evaluation of assets.

The social functions of reorganized traditional social networks reinforced the economic functions of the Kanō Industrial Cooperative as an economic organization providing microcredit. In the process of its growth, the cooperative responded to the funding needs of individual member farmers with its internal funds, and played the role of procuring funds from external sources which were otherwise unavailable to the individual members of the cooperative. This was especially important when in the regional economy there was a seasonal shortage of funds. The Kanō Industrial Cooperative did not limit the use of its services to the wealthy and those with strong personal standing, i.e. those who enjoyed strong creditworthiness. Instead it built up a system that provided microcredit opportunities to all residents in the village. Moreover, the Kanō Industrial Cooperative developed as a management entity through the process of granting the external creditworthiness of its individual senior officials to the cooperative itself.

The development of financial organizations in the village encouraged a stable expansion of its main industry, sericulture. The broad-based integration of cash crop markets, prompted by the development of modern transportation networks, provided sellers with both risks and opportunities, but Kanō Village overcame the risks that tended to confront small-scale producers through the establishment of the industrial cooperative. The Kanō Industrial Cooperative thus continued to develop throughout the prewar period together with the economy of Kanō Village even amid subsequent periods of economic fluctuation.

Indeed, Kanō Village was not an isolated case. In many regions across Japan localities responded to the impact of greater integration with external markets by establishing industrial cooperatives as microcredit financial organizations. Industrial cooperatives inherited the personal connections that had existed since the Tokugawa period but also emerged as new organizations linked to the modern banking and education systems. In this way they were important parts of the restructuring of local communities.[66] The establishment of industrial cooperatives made it possible for people in local communities to proactively seek economic security as agents

---

[65] These credit ratings were conducted by some 10 full-time evaluation committee members elected each year. In Kano Village, about 70% of the committee members elected from hamlets continuously served in that capacity from 1906 through 1919, carrying the personal trust on their backs.

Kojima Yohei and Takahashi Kazushi, "*Senzen Nihon no Sangyo Kumiai ni Okeru Shinyo Shinsa no Jittai to Kaihatsu Tojokoku heno Gan'i* (*Historical Credit Assessment in Pre-War Japan and Its Implications in Contemporary Developing Countries*)," pp. 23–24.

[66] The case of Yodo Village in Aichi Prefecture provides an example where an industrial cooperative was formed on the basis of "Sunday savings" with a village major leading the way by mobilizing elementary school students to collect savings. (Murata Uichiro, "*Chiho Kairyo no Jirei* (*Cases of Local Improvements*)," Chuo Hotokukai, 1926, pp. 95–96.) Such cases were recorded in large

with significant bargaining power, rather than remaining passive and weak agents vulnerable to external markets.

Industrial cooperatives functioned as a window for securing external funds for growing regional industries, and, in the long term, provided microcredit financial opportunities through the self-circulation of funds within regions. After World War I, many of the industrial cooperatives spread across Japan embarked on non-financial operations, such as warehousing, sales of agricultural products and the cooperative-organized purchasing of fertilizers. In other words, when viewed as management entities, industrial cooperatives stabilized their financing functions between 1900 and the end of World War I, and then grew further by diversifying their functions.

Industrial cooperatives themselves were organizations for the accumulation of personal small savings and for the investment of those savings. However, the functions of industrial cooperatives were not limited to simply a revitalization of local economies by using their equity capital, deposits and savings. They were not only able to supply the necessary funds to regional economies in a self-circulatory manner, but also became able to supply funds on a larger scale to contribute to the stability of regional economies by strengthening their ties to networks that supplied external funds. As the Japanese economy went through structural changes after World War I, established industrial cooperatives came to perform an increasingly larger role in regional societies and the Japanese economy as a whole by connecting themselves to other networks of popular funds such as postal savings. In the following chapters, I look more specifically into the formation of these networks and the design process of such systems.

4.6 Summary

Japanese government enacted the Industrial Cooperative Act in 1900. Cooperative institutions in Japan were modeled on the cooperative movement that had arisen in Europe. In modern Japan, cooperatives' financial function was most selected and the ability of cooperatives to provide residents in the country's regions with opportunities to access small-amount financing is believed to have contributed to the development of regional economies and the agricultural sector.

However, that in contemporary developing countries, there is not necessarily a sufficient supply of small credit in rural areas. For ordinary urban companies, such as banks, it is difficult to develop and maintain a credit market in rural regions due to an asymmetry of information, higher transaction costs and greater default risk. In prewar Japan, a developing country at the time, how then were the small-scale yet essential funding needs of small business entities in regional economies satisfied?

How then were industrial cooperatives established in regional societies? How were they managed in order to achieve growth? How did they satisfy the demand for

numbers in various surveys conducted by both the public and private sectors in local improvement policies early in the twentieth century and in subsequent policy processes.

funds in regional economies? This chapter examines these questions by checking a case of a local industrial cooperative, in Kanō village, which was established in 1903 and succeed to develop their financial power.

Chapter 5
The Return of Postal Savings to the Regions: The Ministry of Finance Deposit Bureau as a Reallocation Mechanism

5.1 Introduction

In preceding chapters, I examined the emergence, up to the beginning of the twentieth century, of a system whereby small-amount savings were accumulated as popular funds in Japan, as well as the process by which these funds were returned to regional economies. But this did not shed light on how the mass funds accumulated via postal savings were managed and how they affected the Japanese economy. In this chapter, therefore, I seek to clarify the function of the return of the Deposit Bureau Fund of the Ministry of Finance to the regions based on specific examples of where such funds were injected.

Following the opening of ports to the subjects of foreign treaty powers in the last days of the Edo period, the Japanese economy, now connected to the global market, underwent significant changes. The impact on regional economies can be observed in cases such as the individual industrial cooperatives in Chiisagata County, Nagano Prefecture, covered in the preceding chapter. Amid the major changes in the economic environment, household savings, that presumably existed in various forms prior to the early modern period, were transformed into savings and deposits at modern financial institutions following the establishment of systems and institutions such as banks and postal savings. Once deposited, they became the funds that provided an important foundation for the growth of the Japanese economy.

Furthermore, in the early modern period, aside from individual savings, villages or feudal domains made savings in the form of collective social relief funds such as "*gisō*" grain-stockpiling warehouses which served as countermeasures against natural disasters. As discussed in Chaps. 2 and 3, some of these social funds and their collective savings systems, including "*mujin*" mutual financing associations

H. Tanaka, *Micro-Credit in Modern Japan*, Studies in Economic History,
https://doi.org/10.1007/978-981-97-6940-7_5

and "*kō*" mutual assistance associations, were, in the Meiji period, absorbed into modern financial institutions such as postal savings and industrial cooperatives.[1]

For households, savings act as a safeguard against future expenditures or risks. In macroeconomic terms, however, savings serve as a source of investment funds. How these accumulated household savings are allocated for investment depends on the actions of financial institutions as intermediaries.

In this chapter, I analyze the investment and functions of postal savings which grew to become the single largest deposit-taking institution, having established a popular base at the beginning of the twentieth century. In particular, I focus on postal savings' function of returning the funds deposited to the regions.[2] Unlike private-sector banks operated with the aim of obtaining profits from the investment of funds, postal savings were a state-run financial institution and cannot be described as entirely operated with the goal of maximizing commercial gain.

The investment of postal savings was managed by the government, more specifically by the Ministry of Finance via the Deposit Bureau of the Ministry of Finance. The system established was not only based on the new, modern system of postal savings, it also inherited, to a certain extent, the systems of the early modern period, such as "*gisō*" grain-stockpiling warehouses. The system was designed to provide relief funds in times of famine or major natural disasters, providing a type of social security. What was significance the significance of this background on the investment of Deposit Bureau funds? How was the flow of these funds related to the flow of funds from the Bank of Japan (BOJ) and private-sector financial institutions supervised by the BOJ, and to relevant economic policies? These are important issues to consider when examining the nature and functions of the Deposit Bureau.

How have preceding studies viewed the Deposit Bureau? Research on the Deposit Bureau can be traced back to around 1925, when the Deposit Bureau system was reformed. "*Ōkurashō Yokinbu Ron (A Discussion on the Deposit Bureau of the Ministry of Finance)*" (1925) by Yamada Kotarō and "*Yokinbu Hishi (The Hidden History of the Deposit Bureau)*" (1928) by Nakatsumi Tomokata were the first works and covered Deposit Bureau funds before the reform of the Deposit Bureau. These works characterized the system as slipshod and pointed to the abuse of the Deposit Bureau when left entirely to the discretion of the Minister of Finance.

As previously discussed in this study, research on Japan's financial history in the postwar period was conducted mainly through an analysis of the "multi-layered financial structure," with the BOJ at its top, together with research on the procurement of funds by large corporations.[3] At the same time however, there has been research

[1] Kikuchi Isao, "*Kinsei no Kikin (Famine in the Early Modern Period)*," Yoshikwa Kobunkan, 1997; Yoshida Nobuyuki, "*Kinsei Kyodai Toshi no Shakai Kozo (The Social Structure of Huge Cities in the Early Modern Period)*," University of Tokyo Press, 1991.

[2] Sugiura Seishi, "Taishuteki Reisai Chochiku Kikan Toshiteno Yūbin Chokin no Seiritsu—Nisshin Sengo no Yūbin Chokiin no Tenkai to Sono Seikaku (The Establishment of Postal Savings as a Popular Small Savings Institution—The Development of Postal Savings after the Sino-Japanese War and Its Nature)," *Shakai Keizai Shigaku (Socio-Economic History)*, Volume 52, No. 4 (1986).

[3] Ishii Kanji, "*Kindai Nihon Kinyūshi Josetsu (The Financial History of Modern Japan)*," University of Tokyo Press, 1999.

on special banks, including Nihon Kangyō Bank and prefectural agricultural and industrial banks, which has highlighted the important role of the Deposit Bureau in the Japanese financial system,[4] as, for example, indicated by Saitō Hitoshi in "*Gendai Nihon Sangyō Hattatsu Shi 26 Kan Ginkō (The History of Industrial Development in Modern Japan, Volume 26, Banks)*." When the Deposit Bureau lent out a portion of its funds to the regions, these funds were provided through various special banks, a flow of funds that differed from ordinary financial routes via private-sector financial institutions or the BOJ.

Kamiyama Tsuneyo,[5] writing from the perspective of fiscal history, pointed out that the importance of Deposit Bureau funds increased following changes in management in the period between and after the Sino-Japanese and Russo-Japanese Wars. During this period, Deposit Bureau funds came to take on the function of a supplementary fiscal resource for the government. Research work on the Deposit Bureau's complementary role as a source of government finance, supplementary to central fiscal resources, was conducted by Denda Isao,[6] Mukai Yurio[7] and Kanazawa Fumio.[8]

Denda shed light on the history of the nascent Deposit Bureau system from the late nineteenth century to the early twentieth century and pointed out the importance of investment in government bonds by the Deposit Bureau at the time. He also analyzed the impact of the 1925 Deposit Bureau reform and its relationship with the idea of policy finance at the time. Mukai's research examined the Deposit Bureau

---

[4] Watanabe Sahei et al., ed., "*Gendai Nihon Sangyō Hattatsu Shi 26 Kan Ginkō (The History of Industrial Development in Modern Japan, Volume 26, Banks)*," Kojunsha Publishing Department, 1966.

[5] Kamiyama Tsuneo, "*Meiji Keizai Seisaku Shi no Kenkyu (Research on the History of Meiji Economic Policies)*," Hanawashobo, 1995.

[6] Denda Isao, "Yūbin Chokin Seido no Rekishiteki Igi—Ōkurashō Yokinbu Shikin no Keisei Katei (A Historical Analysis of the Postal Savings Bank System in Japan: The Establishment of the Deposit Bureau Fund of the Ministry of Finance)," "*Kenkyu Kiyo (Bulletin of Research)*" (Library of Archives Attached to the Faculty of Economics, Shiga University), No. 5 (1972); "Ōkurashō Yokinbu no Kaikaku—Seisaku Kinyū no Tenkai to Kino—(The Reform of the Deposit Bureau of the Ministry of Finance—The Development and Function of Policy Finance)," "*Hikone Ronso (The Hikone Ronso)*," No. 156 (1972).

[7] Mukai Yurio, "Ōkurashō Yokinbu no Seiritsu to Sono Igi (The Establishment of the Deposit Bureau of the Ministry of Finance and Its Significance)" *Nihonshi Kenkyu (Journal of Japanese History)*, No. 149 (1975), "1900 Nendai ni Okeru Ōkurashō Yokinbu no Kino to Seikaku (The Function and Nature of the Deposit Bureau of the Ministry of Finance in the 1900s)," *Kinyū Keizai (The Journal of Financial Economics)*, No. 17 (1979); Ryuichi Shibuya ed., "Meijiki Nihon Tokushu Kinyū Ripposhi Dai Sanbu Dai Nisho (The History of Special Financial Legislation in Japan in the Meiji Period, Part 3, Chap. 3)," Waseda University Press, 1977.

[8] Kanazawa Fumio, "Yokin Bu Chiho Shikin to Chiho Zaisei (Ichi)—1920–1930 Nendai ni Okeru Kuni to Chiho no Zaisei Kinyū Kankei (The Deposit Bureau Local Funds and Local Public Finance (1)—Fiscal and Financial Relations between the Central Government and Local Governments in the 1920s–1930s)," *Journal of Social Science*, Volume 37, No. 3 (1985); "Yokin Bu Chiho Shikin to Chiho Zaisei (Ni) (The Deposit Bureau Local Funds and Local Public Finance (2)," *Journal of Social Science*, Volume 37, No. 6 (1986); "*Kindai Nihon Chiho Zaisei Shi Kenkyu (A Study on the History of Local Public Finance in Modern Japan)*," Nihon Keizai Hyouronsha, 2010.

system from its establishment to the 1910s, focusing on the evolving relationship of the system with government finance over time. While research by Denda and Mukai acknowledged the institutional aspects of the Deposit Bureau, Kanazawa provided a statistical overview of Deposit Bureau funds and clarified the actual situation with regards to the return of Deposit Bureau funds to the regions, utilizing materials produced by the Steering Committee of the Deposit Bureau Funds which was established in 1925.

Before the Deposit Bureau reform of 1925, the system was characterized by a lack of written investment rules, and the investment of Deposit Bureau funds was left to the discretion of the Ministry of Finance. Indeed, while the use of the name "Deposit Bureau" was commonplace throughout the prewar period, a specific bureau by that name did not always exist within the Ministry of Finance. Thus, the actual situation pertaining the investment of Deposit Bureau funds was not entirely clear, especially prior to the reform of the Deposit Bureau, and the actual situation regarding the return of Deposit Bureau funds to the regions remains unclear, a blank for historical researchers.

Nevertheless, as preceding studies have shown, the system for returning Deposit Bureau funds to the regions was an important part of Japan's financial system. Building on the work of Kanazawa and others on the investment methods of the Deposit Bureau, this chapter examines the Deposit Bureau's function of returning funds to the regions through lending. In doing so, I focus on the emergency lending made by the Deposit Bureau in 1914 as this marked the first time that Deposit Bureau funds were used systematically to cope with an economic crisis rather than a natural disaster. This, it is believed, was an important point of departure for the system of returning Deposit Bureau funds to the regions which gained momentum and got into full swing during the interwar period. After the 1925 reform to the system, it was used as a fiscal resource for what could be characterized as Keynesian policies, such as spending on measures to deal with unemployment and funds for rural rehabilitation, particularly in the 1930s. The reformed system further developed into the fiscal investment and loan system in the postwar period, but its roots can be traced to before the interwar period as this chapter will show. Through an analysis of cases Nagano Prefecture this chapter clarifies the manner in which Deposit Bureau funds were used as funds to respond to the crisis in 1914 and their significance to regional economies.

5.2 What Was the Deposit Bureau? Institutional Origins and Management Policy

Before examining the actual situation regarding the investment of its funds, it makes sense to first outline the general structure of the institutional design of the Deposit Bureau of the Ministry of Finance prior to the 1925 reform. Postal savings, which later came to account for the bulk of Deposit Bureau funds, were launched in 1875 as part of the measures to deal with poverty for people in what were considered to be the low- and middle-classes. Decisions on the investment of postal savings was left entirely up to the Ministry of Finance according to Proclamation No. 13 of May 1885 on "Rules for Deposits."

A bureau under the name "Deposit Bureau" was established within the Ministry of Finance on a permanent basis only after the Deposit Bureau reform in 1925. Yet prior to that, even though there was no official Deposit Bureau by name, the name "Deposit Bureau of the Ministry of Finance" was already in common use as an account title since the system's inception.[9] In order to comprehend the nature of the Deposit Bureau, it is necessary to recognize that the Deposit Bureau system was required to accept both postal savings and other miscellaneous funds such as reserve funds controlled by government ministries and agencies. For example, a notification issued by the Ministry of Finance a few months after the enactment of the Rules for Deposits stated that, "following the recent issuance of the Rules for Deposits...all reserve funds of government ministries and agencies are to be deposited with the Savings Bureau of the Ministry of Finance."[10] This meant that all branches of government were urged to concentrate surplus funds, hitherto separately invested, at the Deposit Bureau. The introduction of the Deposit Bureau system was designed in part to concentrate at the Ministry of Finance the authority to manage miscellaneous government funds, other than taxes, which had until then had been autonomously handled by government ministries and agencies. The measure was also intended to strengthen the position of the Ministry of Finance, itself relatively recently established.

Looking at the breakdown of funds collected by the Deposit Bureau, however, except for a period during which reparations were transferred after the Sino-Japanese War, postal savings accounted for over two-thirds of the funds during most periods (Table 5.1).

Furthermore, with regard to the acceptance of postal savings, "Profit and loss of post office savings and responsibility for these savings shall of course pertain to none other than the coffers of the state...The Postal Savings Act is designed to relieve and benefit the poor, and its main idea is not to protect the savings of the general public at all, because postal savings are chiefly in small amounts left only after thrifty and diligent endeavors." Underpinning postal savings, as such statements make clear, was

---

[9] At the same time as the establishment of the system in 1885, the bureau by the name of "*Yokin Kyoku* (Savings Bureau)" was created to handle the Deposit Bureau funds as a split-off bureau of the Government Bond Bureau, but it was abolished in 1893 as a result of the rationalization of administration at government ministries and agencies. After the abolition of the Savings Bureau, the Budget Bureau handled the task until the Financial Bureau took over after 1897. The Fund Planning and Operation Division, Financial Bureau, Ministry of Finance, "*Ōkurashō Yokinbu Shi—Soso Jidai yori Showa Juroku Nen ni Itaru (The History of the Deposit Bureau of the Ministry of Finance—From the Beginning through the 16th Year of the Showa Period)*," first edition, 1941 mimeographed edition, 1964 reprint edition, p. 6.

[10] Dated October 15, 1885, "Ōkurashō Kancho Tsumitatekin Azukeire Kigen wo Yurumeru no Yoshi wo Rinkoku su (The Ministry of Finance Notifies the Relaxing of the Deposit Period of Reserve Funds of Government Ministries and Agencies)," *Kōbun Ruiju (Collection of Official Documents)*, 1885, Part 9, Volume 21.

Table 5.1 Breakdown of sources of funds held by the ministry of finance deposit bureau

	Deposit Bureau current balance	Postal savings current balance at end of FY	Ratio of postal savings (%)	Increase in postal savings	Central famine-relief funds*		3 funds created after the Sino-Japanese War**		Deposit bureau/ central government finances (%)	Deposit bureau/ central + local government finances (%)
1885	18,636	10,620	57		2712	15%			31	20
1886	25,299	15,476	61	4856	3062	12%			30	21
1887	25,724	17,393	68	1917	3418	13%			33	23
1888	28,037	19,425	69	2032	3823	14%			34	24
1889	25,664	19,255	75	−170	4091	16%			31	22
1890	20,652	18,322	89	−933	3453	17%			27	17
1891	22,709	20,162	89	1840	2108	9%			27	20
1892	23,619	21,497	91	1335	2096	9%			14	20
1893	27,218	24,660	91	3163	1838	7%			12	22
1894	26,956	24,438	91	−222	1828	7%			16	12
1895	50,671	27,278	54	2840	1748	3%			22	18
1896	53,380	26,684	50	−594	383	1%			32	25
1897	28,353	24,303	86	−2381	9	0%			11	9
1898	23,838	20,719	87	−3584	46	0%			8	6
1899	77,940	22,098	28	1379	50	0%	50,559	65%	20	16
1900	60,242	22,121	37	23			21,978	36%	17	13
1901	68,734	26,776	39	4655			31,606	46%	23	15

(continued)

Table 5.1 (continued)

	Deposit Bureau current balance	Postal savings current balance at end of FY	Ratio of postal savings (%)	Increase in postal savings	Central famine-relief funds*		3 funds created after the Sino-Japanese War**		Deposit bureau/ central government finances (%)	Deposit bureau/ central + local government finances (%)
1902	90,689	29,210	32	2434			53,527	59%	27	18
1903	96,235	31,668	33	2458			54,914	57%	28	19
1904	81,709	42,101	52	10,433			63,002	77%	11	9
1905	75,910	55,586	73	13,485			9100	12%	8	7
1906	99,756	67,931	68	12,345			397	0%	10	9
1907	144,931	96,135	66	28,204			415		14	12
1908	185,857	112,453	61	16,318			475		22	17
1909	202,232	138,703	69	26,250			498		25	19
1910	275,048	172,694	63	33,991			521		22	18
1911	248,156	194,374	78	21,680			337		27	21
1912	269,677	204,765	76	10,391			351		29	21
1913	248,479	202,010	81	−2755			352		24	18
1914	262,845	214,193	81	12,183			368		27	21
1915	307,329	246,965	80	32,772			384		34	26
1916	382,702	333,100	87	86,135			273		40	30
1917	526,451	462,904	88	129,804			286		45	34

(continued)

Table 5.1 (continued)

	Deposit Bureau current balance	Postal savings current balance at end of FY	Ratio of postal savings (%)	Increase in postal savings	Central famine-relief funds*		3 funds created after the Sino-Japanese War**		Deposit bureau/ central government finances (%)	Deposit bureau/ central + local government finances (%)
1918	692,265	613,345	89	150,441			298		43	33
1919	870,580	748,731	86	135,386			312		33	27

Unit = ¥1000. *As the central famine-relief funds were not deposited in whole and the actual amount of deposits with the Deposit Bureau was not known, the ratio of these funds to the Deposit Bureau funds is just a rough indication. As such, the total may exceed 100%. **The three funds are the fund for replenishing military vessels and torpedo boats, the education fund and the reserve fund for natural disasters (set up with part of the reparations for the Sino-Japanese War). Some of the money in the three funds was transferred to the general account and a special account for extraordinary military spending at the time of the 1904–1905 Russo-Japanese War. As such, the ratio of the money transferred to Deposit Bureau funds at the time was just an approximate indication

Sources The fund planning and operation division, financial bureau, ministry of finance, "*Ōkurashō Yokinbu Shi—Soso Jidai yori Showa Juroku Nen ni Itaru (The History of the Deposit Bureau of the Ministry of Finance—From the Beginning through the 16th Year of the Showa Period)*," first edition, 1941 mimeographed edition, 1964 reprint edition; Koichi Emi et al., "*Choki Keizai Tokei 7 Zaisei Shishutsu (Long-Term Economic Statistics, 7, Fiscal Expenditure)*," Toyo Keizai, 1966

the intention of policymakers to provide a degree of social security whereby the state had to act with a strong sense of responsibility to protect the small-amount savings made by people of the lower- and middle-classes.[11] Very much in line with these intentions, the central famine-relief fund was established in 1890. This was designed to inherit "*gisō*" and "*shasō*" grain-stockpiling warehouses that had been set up in various parts of the country in the early modern period, and which also served as a kind of fund for dealing with natural disasters. These preexisting grain-stockpiling warehouses were officially incorporated into Deposit Bureau funds in 1890 under the "Act No. 21".[12]

The Deposit Bureau was a system designed to transfer and concentrate at the Ministry of Finance the miscellaneous funds of the various separate administrative bodies of the government. As the funds transferred were largely miscellaneous external reserves or deposits, the ministry maintained a strong sense of social responsibility with regards to their management and investment. However, at its inception the Deposit Bureau's funds focused on the purchase of government bonds, following the example of the United Kingdom, where the postal savings system originated and was confined to the investment of postal savings into government bonds.[13] The nature and direction of this investment policy were designed as measures to ensure the stability of funds very much in consideration of the nature of the source of these funds, as was also the case in the United Kingdom.

Nevertheless, investment of Deposit Bureau funds gradually expanded in scope according to government policy. In the wake of the temporary transfer of part of the reparations gained as a result of the Sino-Japanese War and an expansion of postal savings from the 1900s,[14] the significance of Deposit Bureau funds in overall government finance grew.[15] As such, the investment of Deposit Bureau funds in areas other than government bonds came to be viewed more positively (Table 5.2). However,

---

[11] "Chokin Jimu Ōkurashō Chokusetsu Toriatsukai no Bun mo Noshomusho ni Oite Kyoogi Shobun Sento Kou Chosasu (The Request Not Permitted for Consultations and Disposal by the Ministry of Agriculture and Commerce for Savings Work Directly Managed by the Ministry of Finance," *Kōbun Ruiju (Collection of Official Documents)*, Part 9, Volume 21, 1885.

[12] The central famine-relief fund itself was later expended, and, gradually decreasing, ceased to exist. After 1899, the disaster-relief fund was established to replace the famine-relief fund and came to be managed by the Deposit Bureau.

[13] In the United Kingdom, where postal savings originated, all postal savings were used to purchase government bonds. Reflecting concerns over the use of unstable funds that could be subject to request for refunds at any time, the direct use of postal savings for fiscal funds was avoided. William Lewins, *A History of Banks for Savings in Great Britain and Ireland, including a full account of the origin and programs of Mr. Gladstone's financial measures for post office banks, Government Annuities and Government Insurance*, S. Low, son and Marston, London, 1866.

[14] Sugiura Seishi, "Taishuteki Reisai Chochiku Kikan Toshiteno Yūbin Chokin no Seiritsu—Nisshin Sengo no Yūbin Chokin no Tenkai to Sono Seikaku (The Establishment of Postal Savings as a Popular Small Savings Institution—The Development of Postal Savings after the Sino-Japanese War and Its Nature)," *Shakai Keizai Shigaku* (*Socio-Economic History*), Volume 52, No. 4 (1986).

[15] Kamiyama, "*Meiji Keizaiseisakushi no Kenkyu (Research on the History of Economic Policies during the Meiji Period)*," pp. 135–138.

since the collection of postal savings took place mainly in rural areas, their concentration in the Deposit Bureau of the Ministry of Finance for centralized investment meant the withdrawal of funds from rural regions to the central government. This practice was represented by some as depriving rural areas of their own funds and caused a huge controversy at the time. In light of this, the government considered the necessity of "returning funds to the regions" through the supply to the regions of Deposit Bureau funds initially collected as postal savings.[16]

Such measures also reflected the fact that Nihon Kangyō Bank and the prefectural agricultural and industrial banks under it—which had been established with the purpose of supporting agriculture-related finance in rural areas—were unable to respond sufficiently to the demand for funds from small-scale producers due to a lack of funds at these financial institutions, especially among the latter.[17] The Deposit Bureau of the Ministry of Finance was, however, a small organization, and thus it did not have the organizational capacity suitable for actually providing funds to local areas. Therefore, the dispersal of funds to the regions was accomplished through financial institutions that had an actual foothold in the regions themselves, such as Nihon Kangyō Bank and the agricultural and industrial banks.

On the basis of such considerations, official relief lending was provided utilizing Deposit Bureau funds as expenses for measures to deal with crop failures in three prefectures in the northeast region in 1906. "*Ōkurashō Yokinbu Shi* (The History of the Deposit Bureau of the Ministry of Finance)," an official history compiled by the bureau's staff, states that beginning with this relief lending, the return of Deposit Bureau funds to the regions became institutionalized. Later on, it would be defined as "financing for public organizations and a variety of unions for regional development...in Japan".[18]

In 1909, the three Ministries of Communications, Finance, and Home Affairs issued a joint circular, which made the return of Deposit Bureau funds to the regions a permanent system under the two institutional frames of "ordinary funds" and "special funds." The return of funds to the regions under this system were often referred to as "regional funds."

> Influential regional people should strenuously strive in their business ... and be willing to establish private-sector business whilst maintaining austere lifestyles, thereby striving to accumulate surplus funds...If the surplus funds derived from their hard work are spent uselessly, that is without taking measures to investment and thus increase them, this will not serve the goal of advancing private-sector business. If the tiny amounts of funds in the hands of individuals are accumulated and ways opened to use them broadly, then this can help a general advance production. Thus, the true intent to encourage savings is not to encourage only passive thrift, but to earnestly encourage production, accumulate private-sector funds and

[16] "*Ōkurashō Yokinbushi (The History of the Deposit Bureau of the Ministry of Finance),*" p. 2.

[17] Mukai, "1900 Nendai ni Okeru Ōkurashō Yokinbu no Kino to Seikaku (The Function and Nature of the Deposit Bureau of the Ministry of Finance in the 1900s)," p. 34; Research Department, Norinchukin Bank, "*Norin Chuo Kinko 50 Nen no Ayumi (The 50-Year History of the Norinchukin Bank),*" 1973, pp. 4–5.

[18] "*Ōkurashō Yokinbu Shi (The History of the Deposit Fund Bureau of the Ministry of Finance),*" p. 128.

Table 5.2 Breakdown of investments by the deposit bureau

	Total of deposit bureau funds	JGB securities		Offshore funds*		BOJ deposits and cash**		Total of funds related to overseas business expansion	
1909	202,232	129,511	64%			N.A			
1910	275,048	133,611	49%			N.A		4500	2%
1911	248,156	128,188	52%			N.A		3500	1%
1912	269,677	113,912	42%			12,967	5%	2500	1%
1913	248,479	101,875	41%			16,989	7%	3000	1%
1914	262,845	52,526	20%			29,048	11%	8000	3%
1915	307,329	66,173	22%	12,052	4%	47,196	15%	8976	3%
1916	382,702	68,590	18%	120,859	32%	33,485	9%	6700	2%
1917	526,451	58,594	11%	169,349	32%	100,928	19%	34,403	7%
1918	692,265	70,556	10%	407,470	59%	41,083	6%	16,750	2%
1919	870,580	103,788	12%	478,178	55%	31,267	4%	24,727	3%
1920	1,005,577	112,710	11%	404,005	40%	24,002	2%	36,304	4%
1921	1,129,272	168,578	15%	331,012	29%	146,480	13%	17,000	2%
1922	1,248,933	239,779	19%	240,991	19%	186,599	15%	27,668	2%
1923	1,349,131	237,371	18%	276,146	20%	150,085	11%	90,922	7%
1924	1,417,582	309,063	22%	207,801	15%	115,711	8%	40,205	3%

(continued)

Table 5.2 (continued)

	Regional funds							Postal savings		Annual rise in postal savings	Total deposit bureau funds/total of central and local govt finances (%)
	Total***		Ordinary funds		Underwriting of local govt bonds		Total of underwriting of various bonds				
1909	2283	1%	2283	1%				138,703	69%	26,250	19
1910	18,031	7%	9830	4%	7143	3%	1058	172,694	63%	33,991	18
1911	40,181	16%	15,037	6%	15,159	6%	9985	194,374	78%	21,680	21
1912	46,582	17%	13,458	5%	16,112	6%	17,012	204,765	76%	10,391	21
1913	33,595	14%	4954	2%	18,332	7%	10,309	202,010	81%	−2755	18
1914	34,392	13%	0	0%	17,792	7%	16,600	214,193	81%	12,183	21
1915	28,559	9%	5156	2%	15,330	5%	8073	246,965	80%	32,772	26
1916	32,898	9%	955	2%	14,667	4%	8676	333,100	87%	86,135	30
1917	35,927	7%	11,102	2%	16,585	3%	8240	462,904	88%	129,804	34
1918	43,183	6%	16,102	2%	18,878	3%	8203	613,345	89%	150,441	33
1919	66,712	8%	20,261	2%	37,226	4%	9225	748,731	86%	135,386	27
1920	93,980	9%	22,014	2%	61,635	6%	10,331	884,858	88%	136,127	25
1921	116,155	10%	19,873	2%	83,645	7%	12,637	943,838	84%	58,980	27
1922	117,850	9%	13,820	1%	97,039	7%	6991	1,045,441	84%	101,603	27

(continued)

Table 5.2 (continued)

	Regional funds							Postal savings		Annual rise in postal savings	Total deposit bureau funds/total of central and local govt finances (%)
	Total***		Ordinary funds		Underwriting of local govt bonds		Total of underwriting of various bonds				
1923	210,331	16%	10,894	1%	140,430	10%	59,007	1,148,125	85%	102,684	29
1924	219,841	16%	20,000	1%	165,660	11%	34,181	1,137,702	80%	−10,423	28

Unit = ¥1000. Each item shows the total of actual amounts of finance in the FY. % shown without any explanation shows the ratio to the total amount of the Deposit Bureau funds (the FY-end balance). Among items for which financing decisions were made within a FY, as there were changes in both the balance of financed amounts and deposit amounts and not all items financed by the Deposit Bureau were included (extraordinary lending to the ordinary and special accounts, relief lending to companies during the postwar depression, etc.), the total of all the items does not amount to 100%. *Offshore funds = Cash in GBP, foreign currency-denominated treasury securities etc. The Ministry of Finance is aware of the decline in offshore funds as used by the Deposit Bureau since 1920. **There were no records left for "BOJ deposits and cash" for a number of years: it was explained that "cash grew to large amounts after 1885" ["*Ōkurashō Yokinbu Shi (The History of the Deposit Bureau of the Ministry of Finance)*]," p. 226. ***The total of regional funds = ordinary funds + special funds (in addition to local government bonds, the total of Nihon Kangyō Bank debentures and various other bonds underwritten). *Sources* "*Ōkurashō Yokinbu Shi (The History of the Deposit Bureau of the Ministry of Finance)*"; "*Choki Keizai Tokei 7 Zaisei Shishutsu (Long-Term Economic Statistics, 7, Fiscal Expenditure)*"

thereby further build the basis for regional development…As for the harmony between postal savings and regional economies, the government has long taken measures for lending…

How exactly was the supply of these regional funds for the promotion of regional economies designed? First, the supply of "ordinary funds" was set to rise in proportion to the annual increase in postal savings, with an upper limit set at 50% of the increase in postal savings in each region. The Deposit Bureau funds were to be lent out to the regions through Nihon Kangyō Bank and agricultural and industrial banks in the form of underwriting special bank debentures.

…in order to supply funds to public organizations, the way shall be opened to financing via lending from the funds of Nihon Kangyō Bank, agricultural and industrial banks, and Takushoku Bank with the Deposit Bureau underwriting "*Kangyō*" (hypothec) debentures and "*takushoku*" (colonial) debentures within the limits of one-fourth of an increase in postal savings based on natural development since FY1909 (¥12 million) as well as half of the increase in postal savings as a result of this policy of encouragement (however, as this increase begins in FY1909, this shall not be applied unless financing is for FY1910 or later)….[19]

In contrast, "special funds" were funds "to be lent when there is a special need for them, with decisions [and terms to be] made on a case-by-case basis."[20] Though these funds were called "special," they were lent out almost every year via Nihon Kangyō Bank and agricultural and industrial banks. Funds were dispersed for the purpose of disaster relief and disaster recovery, such as storm and flood damage (in Kyoto, Yamanashi and Gunma prefectures in 1908) and for the relief of flood damage and crop failures in the Tohoku region (in Miyagi, Fukushima, Iwate, Yamagata and Aomori prefectures in 1913).[21]

There was another method for the supply of funds by the Deposit Bureau. This came through the purchase of bonds issued by Nihon Kangyō Bank, agricultural and industrial banks, and local governments, showing that the Deposit Bureau's framework of regional funds was actually much broader than at first sight.[22] In

---

[19] The joint circular of the Ministries of Communications, Finance and Home Affairs, "*Hi Dai Hyakunijusan no Ni (Confidential No. 123-2)*," May 1909.

[20] "*Ōkurashō Yokinbu Shi (The History of the Deposit Fund Bureau of the Ministry of Finance)*," p. 130. Because of this, preceding studies found it difficult to accurately grasp the flows of regional funds before the reform of the Deposit Bureau. Kanazawa, "*Kindai Nihon Chiho Zaisei Shi Kenkyu (A Study on the History of Local Finance in Modern Japan)*," pp. 109–110.

[21] "*Ōkurashō Yokinbu Shi (The History of the Deposit Fund Bureau of the Ministry of Finance)*," p. 136.

In 1911, special funds were lent out to Fukushima Prefecture as funds for assisting in the debt consolidation of the Samegawa dam and water-utilization association. The provision of special funds was designed to compensate for the failed redemption of lending of ordinary funds made to the Samegawa water-utilization association through a local government. It is noteworthy that the possibility was opened up during the early period of special funds being provided to items to be covered with ordinary funds from the Deposit Bureau, as seen in the above case, though this involved a loan of ¥450,000 through Nihon Kangyō Bank, a relatively small amount limited to a region and not on a national scale.

[22] The Deposit Bureau funds were used not only for regional development but also as national economic policy funds, with funds often supplied to the Imperial Government Railway and ironworks.

particular, much of the underwriting of local government bonds prior to the interwar period was "mainly for natural disaster relief." This "provided a substantial amount of financing almost every fiscal year," helping to conventionalize the supply of funds for natural disaster recovery in the form of underwriting local government bonds.[23] As a result of fund supply in the various forms described above, the supply of special funds often exceeded that of ordinary funds (Table 5.2).

As seen above, while the Deposit Bureau previously invested mainly in government bonds in principle from the perspective of protecting financing resources, approximately 10–20% of the funds came to be returned to regional economies as regional funds after 1909 (Table 5.2). In addition, the return of Deposit Bureau funds to the regions had the function of providing emergency relief and recovery funds (mainly for natural disasters) as well as that of industry-promoting funds for regional economies. The emergency lending to export industries in 1914, to be taken up in the next section, made even clearer the coexistence of these two aspects in the return of Deposit Bureau funds to the regions.

5.3 Emergency Lending in 1914: An Overview of Relief Lending to Important Export Industries

This section examines relief lending to important export industries by the Deposit Bureau in 1914 in order to ascertain how the supply network and the system of Deposit Bureau funds, still only a few years after its founding in 1909, came to be established. It also examines the nature of the system that they tried to create. At the outbreak of World War I in 1914, international trade encountered difficulties, dealing a severe blow to the Japanese economy. In the wake of this, Deposit Bureau funds were used for relief lending, and this lending was made under the framework of special funds of the regional funds system of the Deposit Bureau established after 1909, as mentioned in the preceding section. Prior to 1914, cases where Deposit Bureau funds were supplied as special funds were almost totally limited to relief for floods and other natural disasters. The emergency lending in 1914 was, in effect, the first case of large-scale lending provided for an economic crisis arising from a cause other than natural disasters, and this, despite being lending to cope with an emergency situation, was later to give a new character to Deposit Bureau lending.

Before considering the actual situation of this emergency lending, let us here look at the situation of the Deposit Bureau immediately before the loans were made.

---

[23] Ministry of Finance, "*Meiji Taisho Zaisei Shi (The History of Government Finance in the Meiji and Taisho Periods)*," Volume 13, 1939, pp. 824–850. When funds were provided for the recovery from storm and flood damage in 1910, the Deposit Bureau initially planned to supply them through Nihon Kangyō Bank, but the bureau also underwrote local government bonds, and afterward, it became the common practice for the Deposit Bureau to provide loans directly to local governments.

Postal savings in 1913 decreased from the previous year,[24] with the Ministry of Communications citing causes such as the interest rates on postal savings relative to market interest rates and inflation. As a result of the actual decrease in postal savings, there was no "increase in postal savings" which the Deposit Bureau was able to supply as "ordinary funds" in FY1913. The supply of regional funds for FY1914 nationwide was thus set at zero. Nevertheless, routes for regional funds other than those derived form of ordinary funds, such as the underwriting of local government bonds, were available in FY1914. In addition, while the supply framework for the Deposit Bureau funds was decided for each fiscal year, the actual supply of funds was often carried over into the next fiscal year,[25] hence there were newly available Deposit Bureau funds to return to the regions in FY1914. These were, however, limited and at the beginning of FY1914, the Vice Minister of Finance stated in a circular that "financing resources of the Deposit Bureau are currently scarce and the bureau finds it necessary to suspend even the supply of low-interest funds it has been providing in recent years,"[26] indicating that the government was well aware of the shortage of funds at the Deposit Bureau.

It was under these circumstances that World War I broke out on July 28, 1914. The temporary interruption of international trade due to the breakout of the war greatly affected Japanese export industries which suffered sharp falls in the prices of silk yarn and cocoons. These trends gave rise to a credit crunch centering on the silk-reeling industry. Though this economic crisis was not caused by natural disaster, since the silk-reeling industry was closely linked to the sericulture industry, it was a severe blow to a large number of farming households and in this way resembled crop failures, frost and flood damage. Contemporary newspapers reported almost daily on the crisis in key yarn-reeling and sericultural areas in Nagano, Gunma and Yamanashi prefectures with coverage focusing particularly on the distressing circumstances of farming households engaged in sericulture.[27]

In response to this crisis, the BOJ, upon a request from The Dainippon Silk Foundation, stated on August 11 that "Even faced with current conditions…there is no difference from normal times in the central bank's stance of lending a large amount of funds according to needs." This introduced flexible silk yarn lending, though within the conventional "special financing" framework, and took measures for the relief of silk-reeling businesses, including an expansion of the financing limits and new approvals. The Japanese financial system comprising private-sector banks that formed the multilayered financial structure, with the BOJ at its summit, took action to relieve the yarn-reeling industry, an important export industry, in this crisis.

---

24 Money Order and Postal Savings Bureau, Ministry of Communications, "*Saikin Yūbin Chokin no Gentai ni Kansuru Sanko Shiryo (Reference Data on the Recent Decrease in Postal Savings),*" 1914. However, the decrease was on a monetary value basis, with the number of users still rising.

25 Kanazawa, "*Yokin Bu Chiho Shikin to Chiho Zaisei (Ichi) (The Deposit Bureau Local Funds and Local Public Finance (1),*" p. 220.

26 Circular by the Vice Minister of Finance, "*Hi Dai Nihyakurokujuni (Confidential No. 262),*" September 19, 1914.

27 "*Jiji Shinpo,*" August 4–18, 1914.

However, these central bank measures failed to cover "small businesses not having banks with which they have conducted transactions for a considerable length of time or small businesses without reliable collateral".[28] "While the Bank of Japan provided funds through regional banks...those who do not have routes for receiving financing from ordinary banks," or small businesses such as silk-raising farmers, were unable to benefit from the relief measures.[29]

> ...Yarn-reeling businesses and silk-raising farmers always stand face-to-face in relentless business competition...when purchases of raw cocoons become speculative, silk-reeling businesses seem unlikely to strive directly for the relief of silk-raising farmers even with the support of banks. If only silk-reeling businesses benefit from relief measures and silk-raising farmers are simply left to continue self-destructive dumping, the relief measures really are extremely unfair...[30]

As reported by "*Toyo Keizai Shimpo*" on August 25, relief lending by banks, led by the BOJ, failed to provide sufficient relief to the sericulture industry. The silk-reeling industry, however, was an especially important export industry for Japan at the time because, unlike the cotton spinning industry, silk was a domestically-produced raw material and thus sourcing inputs did not result in a trade deficit for Japan. In this sense, to many it was obvious that the failure of sericulture farmers meant a crisis for the silk-reeling industry and Japan's silk exports, i.e., the entire sericulture industry.

Jiji Shinpo, dated August 17, 1914, quoted a banker as saying that the relief from this plight was "the central government's responsibility." On September 7, Mutō Kinkichi, a House of Representatives member and a director of the Gunma Prefecture Agricultural and Industrial Bank,[31] together with 28 other House of Representative members, submitted "a bill of proposal concerning the relief of the sericulture industry." In response, the House of Representatives established a committee on the sericulture industry. On September 8, the committee reported the results of "its questions asking for the government's views," telling the Diet that "the government has the intention of taking measures for the relief of, aside from the sericulture industry, general export items, such as "*habutae*" glossy silk cloth, cotton yarn, "*hanamushiro*" figured matting, matches, and other articles."

The committee also reported on the relief methods under consideration by the government, stating, "With respect to these funds, the government intends to take measures to have special banks, such as Nihon Kangyō Bank and prefectural agricultural and industrial banks, provide financing to agricultural, industrial and commercial businesses...and the methods for preparation of the funds for the measures are currently being devised." As the Minister of Finance told the committee, "The

---

[28] Bank of Japan, "*Nihon Ginkō Hyakunen Shi (The Centennial History of the Bank of Japan),*" Volume 2, 1983, pp. 329–331; "*Nihon Ginkō Hyakunen Shi (The Centennial History of the Bank of Japan),*" Reference Data Part, 1986, p. 44.

[29] "*Ginkō Tsushin Roku "Bankers' Magazine),*" No. 348, October 20, 1914.

[30] "*Toyo Keizai Shimpo,*" No. 679, August 25, 1914.

[31] Director of the Gunma Prefecture Agricultural and Industrial Bank, President of Yamaho Wool Weaving Company. In 1904, he was elected to the House of Representatives from the Seiyukai Party. "*Nihon Jinmei Daijiten (The Encyclopedia of Japanese People's Names),*" Kodansha, 2001.

government will work for the best method," the committee adopted an additional resolution to urge "the government to open the way for low-interest financing." With "the committee recognizing that the government consents completely to its intent," the Diet decided to wait and see how relief measures by the Ministry of Finance developed for export industries in general.[32] The low-interest financing here means the Ministry of Finance's Deposit Bureau funds.

Amid these developments, under the following Vice Minister of Finance circular "*Hi Dai Nihyakurokujuni Go (Confidential No. 262),*" dated September 19, 1914, the relief lending to export industries with the Deposit Bureau funds began.

> Though the Deposit Bureau's resources are currently in short supply...the necessary funds have been procured by exceptional methods, including the sale of public bonds held by the Deposit Bureau to the Bank of Japan... In light of the current situation in which extremely adverse effects are being felt in economic quarters...the government recognizes the necessity of providing special relief to manufacturers of important export items and the Bank of Japan has striven to provide funds through regional banks. For quarters with no routes to receive financing from ordinary banks, the Deposit Bureau of the Ministry of Finance shall underwrite *Kangyō* bonds and have Nihon Kangyō Bank, Hokkaido Takushoku Bank and the relevant prefectural agricultural and industrial banks lend relief funds.

The financing of funds was carried out in a manner where the Deposit Bureau used "special funds" to underwrite bonds of special banks such as Industrial Bank of Japan (IBJ) and Nihon Kangyō Bank. This financing method was treated as a short-term measure to avoid the anticipated deepening of the credit crunch, its purpose characterized as "responding to the urgent need to meet the demand for necessary funds, rather than the supply of low-interest funds." The specific breakdown of the amounts supplied included the underwriting of Nihon Kangyō Bank debentures worth ¥5 million and the underwriting of IBJ debentures worth ¥3 million. It is known that Nihon Kangyō Bank extended loans worth ¥4.82 million using the above funds.[33] Nihon Kangyō Bank loans were extended to "manufacturers of important export items ... that do not obtain financing from ordinary commercial banks, mainly small businesses and household-based manufacturers." In other words, the intended targets of the relief measures were sectors normally outside of the financial network and system of BOJ lending.

The problem of the lack of cash at the Deposit Bureau itself was solved with the BOJ purchasing government bonds held by the Deposit Bureau.[34] The Deposit Bureau and the BOJ had a cooperative relationship with regards to emergency relief work. As a result of the decision on special funds, a total of ¥8 million was supplied to

---

[32] "Dai Sanjuyon Kai Teikoku Gikai Shugiin Giji Sokkiroku (Stenographic Records of the Proceedings of the House of Representatives, the 34th Imperial Diet)," No. 3, No. 4, "*Kanpo Gogai (The Official Gazette Extra Edition),*" September 7–8, 1914.

[33] For both Nihon Kangyō Bank and IBJ, the Deposit Bureau's underwriting terms called for an annual interest rate of 7% and a maturity of 10 years, including a grace period of 2 years. "*Meiji Taisho Zaisei Shi (The History of Government Finance in the Meiji and Taisho Periods),*" Volume 13, p. 950; "*Ōkurashō Yokin Bu Shi (The History of the Deposit Bureau),*" p. 162.

[34] Bank of Japan, "*Nihon Ginkō Hyakunen Shi (The Centennial History of the Bank of Japan),*" Volume 2, 1983, p. 331.

regional economies as relief lending from Deposit Bureau funds. The total amount of regional funds in FY1914, therefore, maintained the previous year's level as a whole, though the quota of ordinary funds was reduced to zero due to the shortage of funds (Table 5.2).

These flows of regional funds in 1914 show that in the crisis following the outbreak of World War I which itself caused an interruption to international trade, and at a time when postal savings were stagnating, the Deposit Bureau functioned as a source of crisis relief and promoter of regional economies. This coming despite that fact that it had to cut back on ordinary funds and marked a turning point as the execution of the relief to small producers was prompted by an economic crisis triggered by a cause other natural disasters, hitherto the only circumstance under which a large supply of special funds was provided.

The adoption of this new relief policy, which will be taken up in detail in the next section, signaled that local governments had become as aware of the impact of economic events such as the interruption of international trade as with cases of natural disaster. This recognition was communicated from the regions to the central government, making it possible for the central government to better comprehend the predicament local areas faced in an economic crisis and thus determine the necessary relief measures. From this point onward, the extension of Deposit Bureau special funds to provide lending on a large-scale became normalized not only natural disasters and crop failures induced crises, but also in economic crises such as depressions and business slumps. The case of the 1914 emergency lending served as a precedent for subsequent relief lending in times of economic crises. During the interwar period, the size of relief measures sometimes grew to huge proportions, covering more than one region and extending across the entire country.

5.4 The Invocation Process and Function of Relief Lending: Based on Case Examples of Nagano Prefecture

5.4.1 The Economic Situation in Nagano Prefecture and In-Field Responses: The First Relief Lending

How, then, did the emergency lending of 1914 spread to and influence regional economies? What situation did the areas covered by the lending find themselves in, and what relief measures were implemented in which locations? Did relief lending with Deposit Bureau funds reach the places it was actually needed? In this section I seek to address these questions by focusing on examples from Nagano Prefecture.

Under the impact of the opening of ports to international trade at the end of Edo period and also with the establishment and extension of Japan's railway network in the Meiji period, the silk-reeling industry developed tremendously in Nagano Prefecture. This meant that the weight of the silk-reeling industry and related industries in the prefecture's overall economy increased and created a regional economic structure that was vulnerable to fluctuations in silk exports. The outbreak of World War I, therefore, greatly disrupted Nagano Prefecture's economy, especially as it coincided with the harvest season of summer cocoons, a time when sericulture farmers began transactions with silk-reeling firms.

On August 7, 1914, approximately one week after the outbreak of the war, the Nagano prefectural government, already sensing that the prefecture's economy was about to face a crisis, instructed counties and cities within the prefecture to take stock of the situation and report back. At the same time the prefectural government asked the central government for support.

> We are currently looking into the damage in the wake of the situation (i.e. the war). Regarding sericulture farmers, for the time being, we are urging those who wish to hold on to cocoons to kill silkworms and dry cocoons. Sericulture farmers have an urgent need for funds, and we are requesting county heads and city mayors to inquire as to how much they need. Going forward, we will investigate and execute roughly as follows:

1. With respect to the demand for funds, we will inquire with county heads and city mayors and strive to mediate the procurement of funds.
2. For the mediation of the procurement of funds, we entrust the head of the agriculture and commerce division with the investigation...[35]

As seen above, the Nagano prefectural government was well aware that it was mainly sericulture farmers and silk-reeling firms that were suffering most. The prefecture planned to deal with the difficulties confronting silk-reeling businesses through negotiations with wholesalers and banks, saying, "We will negotiate with the Bank of Japan and wholesalers or commercial banks in Yokohama to provide co-financing to silk-reeling firms." In fact, a few days after this document was prepared, the BOJ decided to provide relief lending to silk-reeling firms. For sericulture farmers, the prefecture's plan called for silk-reeling businesses with some leeway in their finances to help relieve them, saying, "Silk-reeling firms should see the significance of relieving farmers and jointly put up funds to purchase cocoons or provide temporary financing in the form of provisional payments to farmers."

The projected value of the total demand for funds estimated from the reports of local governments in Nagano Prefecture at this point amounted to approximately ¥1.38 million. However, there were big differences in the demand for funds among the various parts of the prefecture, with some counties seemingly without any particular need, while Shimo Ina County had a projected demand for funds of ¥300,000 (Table 5.3). The bulk of the demand for funds came from silk-reeling firms or sericulture farmers for maintaining inventories of silk yarn that could not be shipped out or cocoons whose prices had plummeted.

[35] "Jikyoku ni Tomonau Nōka oyobi Seishika Kyūsai An no Ken (About the Plan for the Relief of Farmers and Silk-Reeling Firms in the Current Situation)," August 7, 1914, included in Nagano Prefecture, "Kobun Hensatsu Taisho San Yen Dai San Ka Sangyō Kumiai (Jikyoku Kyūsai ni Kansuru Shorui) ["*Official Documents Books 1914, Third Division, Industrial cooperatives (Documents Concerning the Relief for the Situation)*]." Unless otherwise noted, materials in this section are documents included these books.

Table 5.3 Original table of the preliminary survey on fund demand in Nagano prefecture

Name of county, city	Amount (¥)	Remarks (descriptions in parentheses are excerpts)
Minami Saku	230,000	Amount for food and clothing of small producers No other means than requesting relief from the central bank
Kita Saku	100,000	As it is impossible to satisfy demand within the region, applications should be made to the governor to ask the central government to provide low-interest funds
Chiisagata	136,000	There is no other way than asking banks and money lenders to lend funds, but at the moment, they remain cautious and are not willing to release funds
Suwa	173,000	Banks and businesses here are in negotiations, and around ¥10 may be lent out
Kami Ina	107,000	Urgently needed funds amount to approximately ¥360,000, of which two-thirds are for disposal of silkworm cocoons. Banks and the silk federation are likely to stave off the distress
Shimo Ina	300,000	(An amount equivalent to half of the estimated output of summer cocoons)*
Nishi Chikuma*	60,000	(Thoroughly implement plans to kill silkworms and dry cocoons.) Temporarily divert basic funds of towns, villages or schools to finance necessary funds, with any shortage to be covered by borrowings from agricultural and industrial banks
Higashi Chikuma	–	No funds required
Minami Azumi	70,000	The county seeks regional funds from the central government or some central financial institutions
Kita Azumi	100,000	Possible to obtain low-interest funds from agricultural and industrial banks
Sarashina	–	The county does not seek external funds and has industrial cooperatives and regional finance companies within the county to exclusively provide required funds
Hanishina	–	The county finds no need to provide funds to farmers. Instead, it recognizes that it is appropriate to relieve silk-reeling firms by lending them low-interest funds
Kami Takai	–	No need for funds for the time being
Shimo Takai	–	The county does not see anyone facing limits requiring relief from the stressful situation
Kami Minochi	100,000	The county believes that one possible way may be to seek the financing of loans, using the killing of silkworms and drying of cocoons under a joint work as collateral

(continued)

Table 5.3 (continued)

Name of county, city	Amount (¥)	Remarks (descriptions in parentheses are excerpts)
Shimo Minochi	–	The country does not recognize the need for urgent relief due to a shortage of funds under the current situation
Nagano	–	The need for funds is unlikely, though no reports have come in
Matsumoto	–	No need for funds for the time being
Total	1,376,000*	

Likely to have been prepared after August 8, 1914, but before August 11
*Due to the lack of descriptions in the original table, this figure was extracted from other tables or original survey slips. The total amount was also changed in accordance with these
Source Transcribed from "Jikyoku ni Tomonau Nōka oyobi Seishika Kyūsai An no Ken (About the Plan for the Relief of Farmers and Silk-Reeling Firms in the Current Situation)," August 7, 1914, included in Nagano Prefecture, "*Kobun Hensatsu Taisho San Yen Dai San Ka Sangyō Kumiai (Jikyoku Kyūsai ni Kansuru Shorui) ("Official Documents Books 1914, Third Division, Industrial cooperatives (Documents Concerning the Relief for the Situation)),*" with some data added independently

In Chiisagata County, for example, "the revenue decline of silk-reeling firms" due to the sharp fall in the silk price was estimated at ¥272,000. While cocoon output reached 16,000 *koku*, the revenue drop resulted in a fall in price from an initial estimate of ¥55 per *koku* to an actual average of ¥38 per *koku*. Based on this, Chiisagata County calculated that the amount of funds "urgently needed" would be ¥136,000, half the "estimated decline in revenue." Regarding the procurement of the necessary funds, the County felt that "requesting banking institutions and other lenders to lend funds is the only method," but it also felt that such lenders "remain cautious and are not willing to release such funds." Thus, Chiisagata County expected that it would be difficult to raise the required funds for relief lending from existing private-sector financial institutions such as banks and money lenders.[36]

Chiisagata County's report "*Ko Dai kyuhyakuyonjunana Go (Ko No. 947),*" reported on the current situation sericulture farmers faced, providing some concrete examples of silk-reeling firms and market observations:

> …As soon as the situation [the outbreak of war] arose, transactions of silk on the Yokohama market were completely suspended and silk prices became chaotic, greatly augmenting the intensity of the crisis. With banks and silk wholesalers halting the supply of funds to silk-reeling firms, these firms lost the ability to purchase summer cocoons and as they were concerned about the sales prospects of their products, they either tried to purchase raw materials using the small amounts of funds they were able to raise, or simply found themselves unable to make any purchases for lack of funds.
>
> …Losses to silk-reeling firms
>
> A variety of plans were in place regarding the summer cocoon price of around ¥5.50, projected on the basis of this year's spring cocoon prices. Following the outbreak of the situation

[36] Chiisagata County "*Ko Dai Kyuhyakuyonjuroku Go (Ko No. 946),*" (Addressed to the Manager of the Home Affairs Department of Nagano Prefecture, August 8, 1914).

[war], however, prices plummeted further right at the peak of cocoon output, and the average trading price up to today stood at approximately ¥3.80. On the basis of the county's projected cocoon output of 160,000 *kan monme*, losses amount to as much as ¥272,000. Given that there still remain cocoons to be harvested. If prices decline further going forward, it is almost impossible to prejudge any end result.

...The situation surrounding the reluctance to sell cocoons

Cocoons that sericulture farmers refused to sell due to low prices and instead entrusted to warehousing firms with cocoon drying and storage amounted to 27 lots at warehouses located in Ueda Town alone since August 3. This is a phenomenon not usually witnessed. Thus, as banks are currently not making funds available for this entrustment, unless farmers have surplus funds, they have yet to find a means of obtaining funds for this method of disposal. In some regions, where farmers undertake household-based silk reeling and have simplified cocoon drying places in place, they kill the silkworms and store dried cocoons on their own...

As pointed out above, as financing for silk-reeling businesses came to a halt following the suspension of the Yokohama market, silk-reeling firms found themselves unable to purchase cocoons as they wished. At the same time, falls in cocoon prices due to market suspension left sericulture farmers without the sufficient financial leeway to refrain from dumping sales of their cocoons on the market, further accentuating the crisis and thereby harming themselves in the process. At this point, the BOJ had yet to come up with relief measures, whilst silk-reeling firms did not have sufficient resources to relieve sericulture farmers.

Faced with these problems, Chiisagata County proposed "the suspension of trading in raw cocoons" and the storing of dried cocoons until market prices recovered. In implementing these measures, the country urged "sericulture farmers to cooperate in their work" as much as possible and expected "towns, villages and their agricultural associations to jointly follow the best method." However, at this time trade in raw cocoons was the most common practice among sericulture farmers in the prefecture and there were few facilities for drying cocoons. In addition, many sericulture farmers already faced financial difficulty. Chiisagata County therefore presented model cases for businesses by citing actual examples of "endurance measures" whereby sericulture farmers received loans from warehouse firms with the use of cocoons as collateral.[37]

Status reports like those quoted show were sent to the Nagano prefectural government not only from Chiisagata County but from many other cities and counties. Amid the economic crisis, cities and counties kept daily tabs on the changing situation including cocoon fluctuations, financial and market conditions in their regional economies, and the conditions of warehousing firms. Besides these reports, agricultural associations and silk-reeling firms also sent in various reports and documents complaining about prevailing conditions.[38] These reports showed that the damage caused by the sharp decline in cocoon prices and silk prices was widespread across

[37] Chiisagata County, "*Ko Dai Kyuhyakuyonjunana Go (Ko No. 947)*" (Addressed to the Manager of the Home Affairs Department of Nagano Prefecture), August 8, 1914.

[38] Bounded books in Nagano Prefecture, "*Kobun Hensatsu Taisho San Yen Dai San Ka Sangyō Kumiai (Jikyoku Kyūsai ni Kansuru Shorui) ("Official Document Books, 1914, Third Division,*

Nagano Prefecture. They also supported the idea that the storage and holding of cocoons and silk were effective countermeasures against this situation, showing that both the public (the prefectural government and counties) and private sectors (silk-reeling firms and sericulture farmers, represented by agricultural associations) were united as to how to respond.

In light of this, the prefectural government adopted a policy to provide emergency relief lending to organizations that could dry and store cocoons. Since the estimated demand for funds was massive, the prefectural government intended to ask the central government for relief funds from the very outset. In doing so, it was assumed that "following the example of the financing of low-interest funds to industrial cooperatives and arable land consolidation after the previous year's cold weather damage to farm products and crop failures in the Tohoku region, negotiations for the borrowing of low-interest funds should be held with the Ministry of Agriculture and Commerce, Ministry of Finance, the Ministry of Home Affairs and Nihon Kangyō Bank[39] The prefectural government clearly had the perception right from the start of the financial crisis induced by the interruption of international trade that the relief effort should involve the central government, following the precedent of relief efforts against cold weather damage and crop failures.

Under these circumstances, the Nagano prefectural government sent officials to Tokyo to visit ministries and agencies of the central government, Nihon Kangyō Bank, and others directly to conduct investigations and negotiations. It did this fully conscious of the possibility that it could secure low-interest funds (the popular name for Deposit Bureau funds being returned to the regions). The negotiations by prefectural government officials with Nihon Kangyō Bank and the Ministry of Agriculture and Commerce were conducted presumably on August 9, judging from the date the report was prepared.[40]

When Nagano Prefecture sounded Nihon Kangyō Bank out, it sensed the bank thought the possibility of extending low-interest funds would be low because of the Deposit Bureau of the Ministry of Finance also lacked funds.[41] Indeed, in FY1914 ordinary funds were not available given the tight finances of the central government

---

Industrial cooperatives (Documents Concerning Relief for the Current Situation)" included various reports with unknown titles.

[39] "Jikyoku ni Tomonau Nōka Oyobi Seishika Kyūsai An no Ken (About the Plan for Relief of Farmers and Silk-Reeling Firms in the Current Situation)," August 7, 1914.

[40] The report did not contain the exact date. However, the "silk foundation" written in the report was believed to be an extraordinary meeting of the Japanese National Silk Foundation held on August 10. As the official who prepared the report wrote that he was going to attend the meeting the following day, it can be assumed that the report was prepared on August 9, 1914. Based on the report's descriptions, it can be concluded that the negotiations between government ministries and agencies and Nagano Prefecture were held on the day when the report was prepared.

[41] "…Since the ministry's intention appears to be to divert funds for industrial cooperatives and arable land consolidation unions, because low-interest funds are in shortage for the current fiscal year, the bank thinks that the ministry may proceed with negotiations about this. Regarding funds for farmers in general, the bank cannot take the initiative, but may do something if the ministry does start negotiations. Further, when we asked about the issue of low-interest funds, the bank replied that if the Ministry of Finance provides such funds, the bank can do anything with the funds, but

and the Deposit Bureau. However, ¥1.6 million of the funding quota from the Deposit Bureau from FY1913 remained. Though this had originally been earmarked for helping industrial cooperatives and arable land consolidation unions, Nihon Kangyō Bank took the view that this funding could be diverted to prefectural industrial cooperatives in order to provide relief funds.

The ¥1.6 million from FY1913 had already been supplied by Nihon Kangyō Bank to prefectural agricultural and industrial banks as funds for agency lending. Thus, after negotiations with Nihon Kangyō Bank, officials of the Nagano prefectural office visited a branch of the Nagano Agricultural and Industrial Bank to check the size of low-interest funds secured by the bank. As a result of this visit, it was found that there were low-interest funds worth ¥52,000 for Nagano Prefecture on hand. Even without additional lending, this could be made available with the consent of the Nagano Agricultural and Industrial Bank[42]

Nagano Prefecture next solicited the opinion of the Ministry of Agriculture and Commerce. As if to back up the line of thinking communicated by Nihon Kangyō Bank, the Ministry of Agriculture and Commerce stated that the government would not provide additional lending of low-interest funds (i.e. Deposit Bureau funds). At the same time, however, the ministry said that "the government is monitoring the damage suffered by Nagano Prefecture this year and treating it in the same way as last year's case in the Tohoku region," strongly hinting that the government recognized that the economic crisis in Nagano Prefecture deserved its support, just like disaster relief in the Tohoku region which was covered by special lending from the Deposit Bureau.

The Ministry of Agriculture and Commerce, however, pointed out that "since the completion of an economic survey on silk yarn-producing areas, surveys on the damage suffered by figured matting in Okayama and peppermint in Hokkaido, Aomori and Chiba, etc. are under way, and, therefore, it is not the case that silk yarn alone has suffered." This indicated that the ministry was well aware that there was the possibility of crises in other industries as a result of the disruption of international trade. This emergency situation, where silk-reeling, sericulture and many other export-related sectors were hit, albeit not by natural disasters, and were on the verge of a crisis, prompted the central government to consider and investigate the need for relief, despite concerns over the lack of funds at the Deposit Bureau.

The Nagano prefectural government also investigated the situation from the perspective of silk wholesalers in Yokohama, and found that "wholesalers would prefer that funds would not come their way." For wholesalers, the falling prices of cocoons were "rather convenient," and it was sericulture farmers who "had been put in a disadvantageous situation" in the wake of the disruption of export markets and falling cocoon prices. A few days after the report was prepared, the BOJ decided on relief measures to ease the urgent credit crunch, but silk and cocoon prices still

---

sees it difficult to come by..." Report prepared by an official of the Nagano prefectural government (presumably prepared on August 9, 1914).

[42] Report prepared by an official of the Nagano prefectural government (presumably prepared on August 9, 1914).

failed to recover. Consequently, silk-reeling firms held down silk yarn production and refrained from making fresh purchases of cocoons, or when they did purchase cocoons the transactions involved prices that were not profitable for sericulture farmers.

> ...Looking at the situation of silk-reeling firms...they usually use revenue from silk reeling operations...to purchase cocoons, as losses from the operations became clear...some of them had no choice but to refrain from purchasing cocoons even after steep falls in cocoon prices. Consequently, many silk-reeling firms...processed only one-third of their cocoons, some of these firms that had no outstanding contracts had to suffer huge losses on the remaining two-thirds...
>
> ...Necessity for the relief
>
> The current conditions in the prefecture were as described above; a situation quite worrisome economically. With farmers in general looking for silk-reeling firms to process cocoons and silk-reeling firms looking to capitalists for investment, there was a panic in maintaining the general economy by obtaining adjustments among these three sectors. If there is any artificial measure at all that can be taken to relieve the situation, then it is of great urgency to push that measure through strongly....[43]

The decline in silk yarn prices hit silk-reeling firms, but there was a structure in place whereby sericulture farmers in Nagano Prefecture ultimately suffered the greatest damage from falls in cocoon prices. Another document, prepared by the Nagano prefectural government, described in detail the difficult situation sericulture farmers faced:

> ...The adverse trend in trade ... gradually affected the silk yarn industry in the prefecture. The economic blow to farmers, besides silk-reeling firms, was unexpectedly wide-ranging. Farmers in particular faced the crises at the time when they were expected to settle *bon* [traditional settlement day in mid-summer] accounts, beginning with payments for fertilizers...and not a few of them were plunged into bankruptcy. The prefectural government recognizes that it will be wholly impossible for some farmers to purchase the fertilizers that they usually buy in autumn and winter....[44]

In advanced sericulture areas it was common for farmer to use purchased fertilizers at the time.[45] As discussed in Chap. 3, even smaller-size sericulture farmers in Nagano Prefecture required substantial operating funds for their business. For this reason, sharp falls in cocoon prices and the credit crunch pushed farmers into a serious liquidity crisis. In response to the crisis in the industry and given the central government's expressed attitude, the Nagano prefectural government prepared the following written petition for a necessary injection of relief funds to relieve farmers,

---

[43] Nagano Prefecture, "*Hi Nagano-ken ni Okeru Nōsangyō to Jikyoku no Kankei (Confidential: The Relationship between the Sericulture Industry and the Current Situation),*" date of preparation unknown. Since the document contained descriptions about relief by the BOJ, it was presumably prepared after August 11, 1914.

[44] Nagano Prefecture, "*Hi Nōka Kyūsai Shikin (Confidential: Relief Funds for Farmers),*" presumably a written request for approval prepared by the prefectural government.

[45] Ikawa Katsuhiko, "*Kindai Nihon Seishigyo to Mayu Seisan (The Modern Japanese Silk-Reeling Industry and Cocoon Production),*" Tokyo Keizai Joho Shuppan, 1998, p. 69.

which, it is believed, was sent to the relevant ministries and agencies of the central government:

> ...Together with an expansion of the war, depending on developments with autumn cocoon prices, the so-called "great economic crop failure" could occur. People within the prefecture could be driven into a situation where they have no means of supporting themselves other than eating the roots of grass and the bark of trees... Payments due could pile up each month and the number of tax payment delinquencies could rise significantly. Under these circumstances, the operations of the autonomous organizations of the various towns and villages could cease and there could be a collapse of confidence. Bankruptcies of smaller producers could culminate in a momentous rise in other unforeseen problems that are hard to quantify, resulting in a deplorable future for many people...These are unbearably alarming developments. Thus, following the precedent of the provision of a portion of postal savings as low-interest funds for the relief of last year's flooding and crop failures in the Tohoku region, the prefectural government will request the central government to disburse approximately the following amount as low-interest funds for industrial cooperatives and Nihon Kangyō Bank in order to encourage agricultural and industrial banks to disburse approximately the following amount to farmers. The prefecture will request that agricultural and industrial banks take steps for financing by forming organizations consisting of over 20 members by the banks' convention, thereby helping farmers overcome this difficult situation. The prefectural government would like to submit the above requests for your kind consideration and approval.[46]

The economic damage suffered by farmers was recognized as an economic issue as well as a social issue. The recognition that low-interest funds (i.e. Deposit Bureau funds derived from postal savings) should be used to deal with the socioeconomic crisis and the relief funds should be extended through the line from the BOJ to Nihon Kangyō Bank was shared by local governments. While submitting the written petition, the Nagano prefectural government responded to the situation within the prefecture without waiting for the central government, including the Deposit Bureau, to respond. On August 22, the Nagano prefectural government issued a circular notice, "*No Ko Hatsu Dai Hyakusanjuroku Go Jikyoku ni Tomonau Nōka Keizai Kyūsai ni Kansuru Ken (No Ko Issue No.136, The Matter Concerning the Relief of the Farm Household Economy Associated with the Current Situation)*," directing county offices to look into funds related to relief for the farm household economy. This circular notice instructed county offices to report on business descriptions of organizations requiring funds, the necessary expenses and shortfalls in funds, and other items for each organization, assuming industrial cooperatives, organizations with over 20 members, philanthropists, and so on, to be eligible borrowers, or the equivalent of those eligible to receive loans from agricultural and industrial banks[47]

In response to the circular notice, a report from Chiisagata County submitted on September 3, included survey slips from five organizations and simplified survey slips from three organizations. The organizations expressed a desire for relief lending and

---

[46] Nagano Prefecture, "*Hi Nōka Kyūsai Shikin (Confidential: Relief Funds for Farmers)*," presumably a written request for approval prepared by the prefectural government.

[47] Nagano Prefecture, "*No Ko Hatsu Dai Hyakusanjuroku Go Jikyoku ni Tomonau Nōka Keizai Kyūsai ni Kansuru Ken (No Ko Issue No. 136 The Matter Concerning the Relief of the Farm Household Economy Associated with the Current Situation)*," August 22, 1914.

Table 5.4 List of organizations desiring loans in Chiisagata County, Nagano Prefecture in 1914

	Required amount (¥)	Reasons for fund demand	
Shimonogō Kangyō credit cooperative	1000	Union silk-reeling /cocoon storage	
Takeishi silk-reeling and marketing cooperative	4000	Union silk-reeling/raw silk sale	
Shimonitasha Soehigumi credit and marketing cooperative	1000	Offering of credit to union members (up to ¥50)	
Muroga credit cooperative	2000	Cocoon warehousing and lending against cocoon collateral to union members	
Nagakubo Furumachi marketing cooperative	2000	Lending to union members for holding on to cocoons	
Kami Shiojiri credit cooperative	1500	Lending of industrial funds	
Urazato marketing cooperative	1000	Purchasing of industrial products	
Urazato credit marketing cooperative	3000	Financing and purchasing of industrial products	
Total amount	15,500	Average	1937.5

Source Prepared based on Chiisagata County, "*Otsu Dai rokusenkyuhyaku Go (Otsu No. 6900)*" (September 3, 1914, included in Nagano Prefecture, "*Kobun Hensatsu Taishō San Yen Dai San Ka Sangyō Kumiai (Jikyoku Kyūsai ni Kansuru Shorui)* [*"Official Documents Books, 1914, Third Division, Industrial Cooperatives (Documents Concerning Relief for the Current Situation)*]"

included an industrial cooperative which had both sericulture farms and members who were also silk-reeling operators; an industrial cooperative planning loans for sericulture farmers for the purpose of cocoon storage; and a warehousing company seeking to refinance users on the premise of taking cocoons as collateral. All of these organizations were related to the retention of cocoon inventories by sericulture farmers. The total amount requested was approximately ¥16,000 and the average amount requested per organization was approximately ¥2000[48] (Table 5.4).

Based on these survey results submitted by county offices, the Nagano prefectural government, in circular notice "*No Ko Hatsu Dai Hyakuyonjuyon Go (No Ko Issue No.144)*" of September 8, stated that "after surveying and inquiring about various firms' complaints about a shortage of funds due to the damage caused by the current situation (i.e. the disruption to trade caused by war), the prefectural government has successfully concluded consultations with the Nagano Agricultural and Industrial Bank. The Bank has raised a substantial amount of funds and will lend them to organizations that need them urgently." While there were reservations attached, such as "loans will be disbursed sequentially" to "various businesses that urgently require funds" and "those businesses that are expected to produce remarkable effects from the

[48] Chiisagata County, "*Otsu Dai Rokusenkyuhayku Go (Otsu No. 6900)*," September 3, 1914.

lending," the Nagano prefectural government and Nagano Agricultural and Industrial Bank were able to agree on the execution of relief lending.[49]

Following the decision to execute the lending program, it was decided to send officials in charge of the Nagano prefectural government and the Nagano Agricultural and Industrial Bank to the relevant areas in the prefecture in order for them to conduct detailed surveys on the lending. Counties were informed of the itineraries of their planned visits. A number of officials from the prefecture and the bank were simultaneously dispatched to different locations between September 15 and September 30. Dispatched officials of the prefecture and the bank conducted surveys through personal interviews with the "parties concerned," or, in other words, those farmers who sought to obtain funds. On these occasions, with respect to those desiring to access loans, individuals and representatives of organizations with 20 members or more were required to bring registered seals and asset reports with them, and industrial cooperatives were required to bring with them registered seals and accounting books. It is believed that in addition to "surveys," specific negotiations and procedures related to lending were actually conducted directly among officials of the prefecture, the bank and those desiring to obtain the loans. This meant that in Nagano Prefecture, the route for tentative emergency lending was already established by the end of September 1914.

Next, on October 13, the Nagano prefectural government and Nagano Agricultural and Industrial Bank set out a detailed outline for the supply of funds.[50] At this point, the lending of approximately ¥39,000 across 30 individual cases was decided of which 16 cases involved lending to industrial cooperatives. As the Nagano prefectural government had ascertained at the outset, the Nagano Agricultural and Industrial Bank had secured approximately ¥50,000 in low-interest funds before the crisis. About 80% of this fund was used initially. The total number of applications for emergency loans at this time stood at 52, which in combination called for loans of over ¥200,000. A total of ¥20,000 worth of loan applications were "rejected" outright, but the remaining loan requests (approximately ¥140,000) were put on hold as "undecided." Later, a selection among the undecided portion of loan applications was carried out and as of October 29, a total of 37 applications had been selected. Even at this point, there still remained many "undecided" applications. While more than 30 applications were canceled, new applications came in, with the total number of effective applications reaching 64 (Table 5.5). Though the Nagano prefectural government was worked smoothly in providing emergency lending in the prefecture, the supply of funds was far from sufficient to satisfy the demand for funds in the prefecture.

[49] Nagano Prefecture, "*No Ko Hatsu Dai Hyakuyonjuyon Go (No Ko Issue No. 144)*," September 9, 1914.

[50] Nagano Prefecture, "*Jikyoku ni Tomonau Nōka Kyūsai Shikin Kashituke Gaku Kettei no Ken (The Matter Concerning the Decision on Lending Amounts of Relief Funds for Farmers Associated with the Current Situation)*," October 13, 1914.

Table 5.5 Applications for the first emergency lending in Nagano prefecture in 1914

County	No. of applications (after Oct. 13)		Lending amounts applied for (¥)	No. of selected applications (As of Oct. 29)		Amounts applied for by selected organizations (¥)	Lending amounts decided (¥)
Minami Saku							
Kita Saku	4		6500	1	1 group	2000	2000
Chiisagata	9		18,500	7	1 individual	8200	6100
Suwa	7		19,500	3		4500	3500
Kami Ina							
Shimo Ina	3		25,000				
Nishi Chikuma							
Higashi Chikuma							
Minami Azumi	10	7 Individuals, 1 Group	17,000	5	4 individuals	2150	2050
Kita Azumi	1		500	4	1 group	6000	4300
Sarashina				5	2 groups	8100	5400
Hanishina	16	2 Individuals 10 Groups	10,900	9	7 groups	15,000	10,900
Kami Takai	6		7800				
Shimo Takai				1		3500	2000
Kami Minochi	8	4 Groups	27,000	1	1 group	5000	35,00
Shimo Minochi							
Nagano							
Matsumoto							
Total	64	40 industrial cooperatives, 15 groups, 9 individuals	132,700	37	20 industrial cooperatives, 12 Groups, 5 Individuals	54,450	39,750

Organizations = Groups of farmers and manufacturers (with at least 10 members) recognized as eligible for obtaining loans from Nagano Agricultural and Industrial Bank, including various trade associations other than industrial cooperatives and arable land consolidation unions, etc.

Source Nagano Prefecture, "Nōka Shikin Yuzu Moshikomisha (Applicants for Financing of Farm Funds)" presumably prepared in October 1914; Nagano Prefecture, prepared the list on the basis of multiple tables and documents included in "*Kobun Hensatsu Taishō San Yen Dai San Ka Sangyō Kumiai (Jikyoku Kyūsai ni Kansuru Shorui)* ["*Official Document Books, 1914, Third Division, Industrial cooperatives (Documents Concerning Relief for the Situation)*]"

5.4.2 The Second Relief Lending: New Supply of Deposit Bureau Funds and Their Effects

While the Nagano prefectural government provided loans using existing low-interest funds already available within the prefecture, the central government determined its relief policy and decided to introduce special funds of the Deposit Bureau. As seen above, on September 19 the Ministry of Finance issued a notice, "*Hi Dai Nihyakurokujuni Go (Confidential: No. 262)*," informing the prefectural government, Nihon Kangyō Bank and other relevant organizations of the decision to inject Deposit Bureau funds. At this point, around 30 types of "important export item" were targeted for relief, but the Ministry of Finance's notice issued on September 23, "*Hi Dai Nihyakunanaju Go (Confidential: No. 270)*," expanded the target items for relief to 32.[51] With respect to silk, the notice clearly specified that the relief target "includes cocoons."

Following the central government's injection of additional funds, the Nagano prefectural government, in "*Nō Ko Hatsu Dai Hyakugojusan Go* (Agriculture *Ko* Issue No. 153)," dated October 1, advised concerned parties that relief lending would be implemented with Deposit Bureau funds. It also provided detailed information about the terms of lending and conducted a survey on loan applicants. The specific terms and conditions for this lending included provisions that any individual or organization seeking funds must put up real estate as collateral as they would not be eligible for unsecured loans, which should only be extended to industrial cooperatives[52] In Nagano Prefecture, the implementation of additional (second) relief lending was decided upon soon after the prefectural government and Nagano Agricultural and Industrial Bank had provided the first round of emergency lending. During the first round of lending, surveys were conducted on the assets held by the targets of the lending, but the exact terms concerning collateral were not specified. It is believed that lending was provided without collateral to organizations of farmers and manufacturers of 20 or more members in accordance with what were the regular lending procedures of the Nagano Agricultural and Industrial Bank.[53]

---

[51] 32 kinds of products: *habutae* silk cloth, raw silk (including cocoons), matches, knitted goods, hemp braid, chip braid, dried cuttlefish, silk handkerchiefs, white cotton, figured matting, straw braid, ceramic ware, glass and glass products, peppermint, string buttons, fish oil and whale oil, towels, toys, seaweed, brushes, bamboo products, agar, cotton crepe, *shiitake* mushrooms, materials for packaging boxes, *mokuro* vegetable wax, lacquer ware, shell ligaments, cotton flannel, taffeta (amber weave), confectionery oil, and soap.

[52] Nagano Prefecture, "*Nō Ko Hatsu Dai Hyakugojusan Go (Agriculture Ko Issue No. 153)*," October 1, 1914.

[53] "When 20 or more farmers or manufacturers by agreement propose joint liability for loans, unsecured lending will be provided to only those with reliable credit under periodic redemptions within 5 years" Act No. 83 "*Nōko Ginkō Hō (The Agricultural and Industrial Bank Act)*," Article 6–4, April 20, 1896.

The Nagano prefectural government's notice dated October 14 also stated that "As earlier informed, these funds should be provided to individuals and organizations other than industrial cooperatives with real estate such as land, buildings and factories, etc. as collateral. The prefectural

On October 13, the Nagano prefectural government received a detailed notice about agency lending of Deposit Bureau funds extended to Nagano Agricultural and Industrial Bank from Nihon Kangyō Bank[54] On October 14, promptly after receiving the notice, the Nagano prefectural government notified the various counties in the prefecture of the details and cautionary notes for the lending of Deposit Bureau funds through its own notice titled, "*Nagano-ken Jikyoku Kyūsai Sangyō Iji Shikin Kyokyu ni Kansuru Ken (Concerning the Supply of Industry Maintenance Funds for the Relief of Nagano Prefecture in the Current Situation)*," advising that a list of loan applicants be drawn up by October 20.

Of particular note here is the condition set for accessing loans derived from Deposit Bureau funds. Deposit Bureau funds were to be "provided to cocoon producers who cannot find ways to sell the cocoons they have produced or who have incurred huge losses due to declining prices and now find themselves in a position to reluctantly abandon their sericulture businesses." The use of these funds was limited to "the cost of repairs of silkworm-rearing rooms, mulberry leaf storehouses, facilities for killing silkworms, sericulture equipment and machinery," or expenses related to the production and manufacture of silkworm eggs, etc. Loans could not be used to cover fertilizer expenses, and instead it was recommended that lending be used for investment in equipment, more specifically cocoon-drying equipment, and warehousing.[55] Since the Deposit Bureau was beset by its own financial difficulties it adopted the "policy of lending funds to a narrow range of borrowers as the amount of new relief funds is limited." As such, the Deposit Bureau created the condition that "funds should not be lent for indirect expenses, such as expenses for fertilization of mulberry fields".[56]

The fact that the loaned funds could not be used directly as payments for fertilizers was a lending condition that greatly inconvenienced sericulture farmers who needed to make payments for fertilizers so as to raise mulberry leaves as working capital. The Nagano prefecture's notice to counties dated October 14 also highlighted this point in red ink by saying that "particular attention is necessary, because some counties appear to be mishandling this matter," indicating that this condition for the use of the funds was probably embarrassing for officials of the Nagano prefectural government and counties.[57] From an early stage, however, the prefectural government, agricultural associations and various industrial cooperatives took countermeasures to respond

---

government would like to add that particular attention must be paid to this point." Thus, it was clearly noted that the lending terms for Deposit Bureau funds differed from those of the previous lending.

[54] Nihon Kangyō Bank, "*Kashitsuke Tetsuzuki (Lending Procedures)*," a copy made by Nagano Agricultural and Industrial Bank, October 13, 1914.

[55] Nagano Prefecture, "*Nagano-ken Jikyoku Kyūsai Sangyō Iji Shikin Kyokyu ni Kansuru Ken (Concerning the Supply of Industry Maintenance Funds for the Relief of Nagano Prefecture in the Current Situation)*, October 14, 1914.

[56] Ministry of Finance (From Vice Minister of Finance Osachi Hamaguchi to Nagano Prefecture Governor Yuichiro Chikaraishi), "*O Dai Hassengohyakugojuroku Go (O No. 8556)*," November 3, 1914.

[57] The Nagano prefectural government prepared a petition to the Ministry of Finance to enable the application for funds for the purpose of fertilizer payments. The document stated that, "We carefully

to the crisis, especially with regards to the drying and storing of cocoons. Deposit Bureau funds, though labeled as relief lending, were never intended to serve as direct compensation for losses and damage, they were funds to be used for investment in equipment and the necessary facilities for drying and storage, etc.

The total amount of special funds provided by the Deposit Bureau to Nihon Kangyō Bank was ¥5 million. From this sum, Nihon Kangyō Bank allotted ¥225,000 to Nagano Prefecture in direct lending to industrial cooperatives; and ¥400,000 to Nagano Prefecture in agency lending through Nagano Agricultural and Industrial Bank. Nagano Prefecture thus received ¥625,000 of the total of ¥5 million available for the entire country, accounting for one-eighth of Deposit Bureau funds dispersed through Nihon Kangyō Bank. The basis for the supply of special funds, it was decided, would be conducted "with the value of exports of important export items... from Hokkaido and prefectures as rough standards... [and that] funds shall be allotted in proportion to these standards, in principle."[58] With its large allocation of funds Nagano Prefecture was clearly an important exporting region. Its silk-reeling and sericulture businesses were, in particular, amongst Japan's principal export industries.[59]

In addition to the funds supplied via the Deposit Bureau, as of November 7, 1914 in Nagano Prefecture, applications for lending sent in by the Nagano prefectural government and forwarded to the Agricultural and Industrial Bank numbered 74 (approximately ¥70,000). Applications forwarded to Nihon Kangyō Bank through the National Federation of Industrial Cooperatives and its Nagano branch totaled 33 (approximately ¥290,000). As of January 1915, applications to the Agricultural and Industrial Bank numbered 1276 (of which 742 actually obtained the funds applied for), and applications to Nihon Kangyō Bank numbered 40 (of which 20 were supplied with funds), with the amount of lending actually supplied or still under assessment reaching the full allotted amount. Besides the above, "the Agricultural and Industrial Bank increased its lending by approximately ¥800,000 over last year, and it can be assumed that the bulk of the increase came from lending under the impact of the [war] situation," instead of agency lending. That is, other than Deposit Bureau funds dispersed via Nihon Kangyō Bank, approximately ¥800,000 was thought to have been used as new lending by Nagano Agricultural and Industrial

deliberated on the Ministry of Finance's latest notice about the lending of relief funds to manufacturers of important export items with the Agricultural and Industrial Bank and the bank's management bureau. Your policy on the relief of cocoon producers is extremely narrow...the procurement of funds for payments for fertilizers for mulberry fields borrowed earlier is not included in the use of funds lent out. It is unfortunate that this policy should interfere with the purchase of fertilizers next year...please give your kind consideration to this matter." It was sent from the governor to the Vice Minister of Finance, but the lending condition was not eased. "*O Dai Hassengohyakugojuroku Go (O No. 8556)*" dated November 3 is presumed to be the reply to this petition.

[58] Vice Minister of Finance notice, "Hi Dai Nihyakurokujuni Go (Confidential: No. 262)," September 19, 1914.

[59] As of 1908, "raw silk was an important product that ranked top among Japan's export items, with the value of raw silk produced in Nagano Prefecture accounting for as much as one-third of the national total." Nagano Branch of the Dainippon Silk Foundation, "*Shinshū no Sanshigyo* [*The Sericulture Industry in Shinshū (Nagano Prefecture)*]," 1908, p. 1.

Bank for the relief of the prefectural economy, with these loans drawn from funds already available within the prefecture.[60]

How were these funds used? The supply of Deposit Bureau funds in 1914 carried the de facto condition that the funds should be directed to investment in equipment. Furthermore, in Nagano Prefecture, where the silk-reeling and sericulture industries were especially prominent, when the crisis brought about by a disruption in trade was felt, there was a general awareness, held by both the public and private sectors, that investment in equipment for cocoon drying and storing facilities had been insufficient. The number of cocoon storage warehouses in Nagano Prefecture consequently increased substantially from 26 (with a storage capacity of 390 *koku*) at the start of the crisis to 51 in 1919, the year after World War I. It then further increased to 61 cocoon storage warehouse in 1924, 89% of which also had cocoon drying equipment.[61]

In the case of an industrial cooperative in Kano Village, Chiisagata County, which took out a loan of ¥10,000 from Nihon Kangyō Bank in January 1915, the cooperative was able to repay the loan in October 1915. During that period, the loan was used as primarily as operating capital, with small-amounts lent to individual cooperative members in response to their need for funds, which usually peaked around February and March, before the summer cocoon raising season.[62] During 1914, Kano Industrial Cooperative responded to the demand for funds from cooperative members by withdrawing the current deposits it had at 19th Bank.[63] The limits of this approach is what likely prompted the cooperative to apply for loans from Nihon Kangyō Bank. Thereafter, Kano Industrial Cooperative frequently transacted with the Nagano Agricultural and Industrial Bank, and in 1918, when it established a new office, it constructed an agricultural warehouse and became engaged in storage operations.[64]

---

[60] Nagano Prefecture, "*Jikyoku Kyūsai Shikin (Funds for Relief of the Current Situation)*" (presumably prepared on January 15, 1915).

[61] Agriculture Bureau, Ministry of Agriculture and Commerce, "*Mayu Soko ni Kansuru Chosa (A Survey on Cocoon Warehouses)*," 1924. It is presumed that warehouses that existed in 1914 were established prior to the outbreak of World War I and four warehouses of which the years of establishment are not known were also established before World War I. Since warehouses that closed before 1924 are not included, the past number of warehouses may be underestimated. Additionally, the storage capacity of warehouses was 390 *koku* in 1914 and 779 *koku* in 1924.

[62] Kanō Industrial Cooperative, "*Taisho Yo Nendo Shiwake Nikkicho (FY1915 Journal Day Book)*," 1915. As confirmed in Chap. 3, when Kanō Industrial Cooperative borrowed external funds in normal times, it borrowed such funds in January–February and repaid them in July–August.

[63] Kanō Industrial Cooperative, "*Taisho San Nendo Shiwake Nikkicho (FY1914 Journal Day Book)*," 1914, Kanō Industrial Cooperative, "*Taishaku Taishohyou (Balance Sheet)*," (by months), 1914–1915.

[64] Kanō Industrial Cooperative, "*Yugen Sekinin Kanō Shinyo Hanbai Kobai Kumiai Jisekisho (Limited Liability Kano Credit, Marketing and Purchasing Union Achievement Report)*" (Manuscript), 1921.

The reopening of the silk trade and its expansion during the war boom were presumably behind the increase in cocoon warehouses and other facilities during World War I. However, the availability of low-interest loan funds, with the condition that they should be used for equipment investment, may have provided a strong incentive to invest in equipment, and, for those businesses whose financial condition soon stabilized, in storage facilities, the need for which became evident during the economic crisis immediately after the outbreak of World War I.

As seen above, it can be concluded that the low-interest funds from the Deposit Bureau lent out mainly to industrial cooperatives through Nihon Kangyō Bank and the Nagano Agricultural and Industrial Bank served as working capital for industrial cooperatives to respond to the demands for funds from union members. In the longer perspective, the funds also significantly raised investment in various equipment and facilities that were necessary for the industry as a whole.

5.5 Summary

This chapter tries to clarify how the system of returning Deposit Bureau funds of the Ministry of Finance to the regions came into being in Japan in the prewar period. In order to achieve this aim it examined the background to and role of the supply of special funds by the Deposit Bureau in 1914 in the specific case of Nagano Prefecture.

Before the Deposit Bureau reform of 1925, the system was characterized by a lack of written investment rules, and the investment of Deposit Bureau funds was left to the discretion of the Ministry of Finance. However, even before the reform of 1925, the system for returning Deposit Bureau funds to the regions was an important part of Japan's financial system and supported local economy.

The return of the Deposit Bureau's special funds to the regions in 1914 was the first case of large-scale relief lending provided for an economic crisis unrelated to a natural disaster. In the process of providing relief lending on a constant basis and in emergencies, the return to the regions of Deposit Bureau funds formed the route for suppling funds to small businesses and farmers organized in industrial cooperatives which acted as intermediaries between Nihon Kangyō Bank, prefectural agricultural and industrial banks, and prefectural and other local governments. This shows the formation of a funding route that differed from the flow of funds in the multi-layered financial structure headed by the BOJ.

Addendum Reform of the Deposit Bureau of the Ministry of Finance–Problems with the Management of Massive Funds and the Advisory Committee.

As the popular funds, the aggregation of small-amount savings by individuals developed in Japanese economy since the beginning of 20th century, Deposit Bureau funds also grew tremendously together with the expansion of postal savings, which was the typical small-amount individual savings.

Considering the fact that postal savings were primarily composed of the small-amount savings of ordinary people, the management of Deposit Bureau funds sought first to maintain them and to secure the interest to be paid on them. However, the design of the system and specific management plans were not predetermined. As such, the management of the Deposit Bureau funds of the Ministry of Finance and the design of that system were highly path dependent.

As postal savings saw a huge increase in a relatively short period thanks to the economic boom during , there emerged a number of large funds with no obvious outlet. The bulk of these funds were poured into the notorious loans. These bad managements induced public criticism after the war-time boom and political actions took place to reform the management system.

In 1925, a package of legislation related to the Deposit Bureau were enacted, known simply as the reform of the Deposit Bureau of the Ministry of Finance. The reform led to the establishment of the Steering Committee of the Deposit Bureau Funds of the Ministry of Finance, an advisory committee that met semi-regularly.

This addendum intends to shed light on the reform that led to the design of a new system for the Deposit Bureau in 1925, and examines the actions and role of the newly established advisory committee.

Chapter 6
Addendum: Reform of the Deposit Bureau of the Ministry of Finance—Problems with the Management of Massive Funds and the Advisory Committee

6.1 Introduction

Part I of this book examined how popular funds, the aggregation of small-amount savings by individuals, were actually managed and how they contributed to Japanese economic development. Individual small savings were accumulated in regional industrial cooperatives which established collaborative ties with ordinary external private-sector financial markets and were able to directly contribute to the flow of funds for the purpose of regional economic development. Postal savings funds, in contrast, though collected and accumulated throughout Japan's regional economies, were less likely to be directly returned to the regions, in part because the central government controlled them.

As Chap. 5 made clear, the Ministry of Finance was granted the authority to invest popular funds accumulated in postal savings accounts as the Ministry's Deposit Bureau funds. However, hitherto there has been little research on the Deposit Bureau of the Ministry of Finance, partly because related information on it was effectively undisclosed until 1925. Despite the fact it managed sizeable funds, even in comparison with the fiscal size of the Japanese government and the combined size of the capital of private-sector banks, the role of the Deposit Bureau of the Ministry of Finance has yet to be fully clarified. This addendum intends to fill this gap and, in so doing, it sheds light on the developments that led to the design of a new system for the Deposit Bureau in 1925, referred to as the reform of the Deposit Bureau, and examines the actions of the newly established advisory committee (full title: the Steering Committee of the Deposit Bureau Funds).

From the beginning of the twentieth century Deposit Bureau funds grew tremendously together with the expansion of postal savings. Furthermore, after 1909 a full-scale system to return these funds to the regions was established and became embedded in the Deposit Bureau. Considering the fact that postal savings were primarily composed of the small-amount savings of ordinary people, the management of Deposit Bureau funds sought first to maintain them and to secure the interest to be

H. Tanaka, *Micro-Credit in Modern Japan*, Studies in Economic History,
https://doi.org/10.1007/978-981-97-6940-7_6

paid on them. The next matter of concern was how to ensure the return of these funds to the regions. However, on this point, the design of the system and specific management plans were not predetermined and were effectively left up to the Ministry of Finance. As noted in Chap. 5, plans were designed in order to establish new and specific funding supply routes in response to natural disasters and economic crises (such as trade disruptions) that occurred intermittently.

Ad hoc responses to crises and the development of a new funding route in reaction to events were the foundations on which fund management guidelines and the system itself were built. As such, the management of the Deposit Bureau funds of the Ministry of Finance and the design of that system were highly path dependent. As postal savings saw a huge increase in a relatively short period thanks to the economic boom during World War I, there emerged a number of large funds with no obvious outlet. The bulk of these funds were poured into the notorious "Nishihara Loans" and other politically determined imperialistic investments overseas, most of which turned into uncollectible debts in the 1920s. These politically-motivated investments overseas and the emergence of bad debts prompted many people in the mass media to criticize the Deposit Bureau of the Ministry of Finance, even referring to it as a hotbed of corruption.[1] Thus, fund management by the Deposit Bureau and its system design became a major social problem in the interwar period.

In 1925, under the Cabinet of Prime Minister Katō Takaaki, the Minister of Finance, Hamaguchi Osachi, took the lead in enacting a package of legislation related to the Deposit Bureau, known simply as the reform of the Deposit Bureau of the Ministry of Finance. The reform led to the establishment of the Steering Committee of the Deposit Bureau Funds of the Ministry of Finance, an advisory committee that met semi-regularly. The Deposit Bureau reform was carried out to ensure transparency in the management of Deposit Bureau funds and to demonstrate to the public that the management of the funds was impartial and that funds were returned to the general public and regional economies. Thus, the Steering Committee of the Deposit Bureau Funds was designed to secure fairness in fund management. However, despite this, the discussions of the advisory committee were held behind closed doors and the covers of the committee minutes were stamped "Confidential." This signifies that right from the outset there was no intention to disclose the work of the advisory committee to the public. In spite of this, however, a number of newspaper articles covered stories concerning the Steering Committee of the Deposit Bureau Funds, often including inside information that corresponded to the content of the committee minutes. Clearly members attending the committee meetings were not prohibited from informing the press what was discussed or chose to do so anyway.

[1] For example, an article in the "Ōsaka Jiji Shinpō"[newspaper] entitled "Truth about the management of the Deposit Bureau funds finally exposed" (February 4, 1925), stated that "the truth about the accommodations of the Deposit Bureau funds, long regarded as a pandemonium of political and business circles, was finally brought to light by a question posed by Mr. Nishimura Tanjirō at a meeting of the special committee on the deposit bill of the House of Representatives on February 3," disclosing "the breakdown of the funds managed by the Deposit Bureau as ¥185.5 million for business funds and ¥152 million for overseas business funds".

How have preceding studies assessed the reform of the Deposit Bureau? Many preceding studies on the reform have examined the idea behind the reform and the legislation itself. In these studies, the establishment of the advisory committee is seen as having enhanced the transparency of the Deposit Bureau's activities, and the reform has been regarded positively as having led to the subsequent stable management of the Deposit Bureau.[2] The fact that Deposit Bureau funds were used for social policies, including measures to counter unemployment in the post-reform 1930s, has been taken for granted, both at the time and in subsequent academic research. In the first half of the 1930s, "Chūgai Shōgyō Shinpō" [magazine] noted that "it is a salient fact that the government is currently mobilizing the Deposit Bureau funds in order to launch civil engineering works to help alleviate economic difficulties and thereby increase the purchasing power of agricultural communities."[3] However, as pointed out in Chap. 5, there has been little research on the Ministry of Finance's Deposit Bureau funds, and thus the reform of the Deposit Bureau itself has received even less attention. To the author's knowledge there has been no detailed analysis which has focused on the specific activities or role (and the impact thereof) of the advisory committee which was created in the course of the reform.

By definition under the system, the Steering Committee of the Deposit Bureau Funds was just an "advisory" committee and the committee itself did not have the function of formulating plans for the management of funds, nor any power to approve or veto the Ministry of Finance's plans. What role then did the Steering Committee of the Deposit Bureau Funds of the Ministry of Finance, positively received contemporaneously and in later years as the achievement of the Deposit Bureau reform, actually play in the management of Deposit Bureau funds? How significant was the establishment of the advisory committee for the financial system of the Ministry of Finance's Deposit Bureau, entrusted with massive popular funds?

This book has sought to clarify how massive small-amount savings, or popular funds, accumulated in the Japanese economy, were collected and managed, as well as

---

[2] Denda Isao, "Yūbin Chokin Seido no Rekishiteki Igi—Ōkura Shō Yokin Bu Shikin no Keisei Katei (The Historical Significance of the Postal Saving System—The Process of Formation of the Deposit Bureau Funds of the Ministry of Finance)," *Kenkyū Kiyō (Research Bulletin)* (The Archival Museum attached to the Faculty of Economics, Shiga University), No. 5, 1972; "Ōkura Shō Yokinbu no Kaikaku—Seisaku Kinyū no Tenkai to Kinō—(Reform of the Ministry of Finance Deposit Bureau—Development and Function of Policy Finance)," *Hikone Rōnsō (Hikone Collection of Treatises)*, No. 156, 1972; Kanazawa Fumio, "Yokin Bu Chihō Shikin to Chihō Zaisei (Ichi)—1920–1930 Nendai ni Okeru Kuni to Chihō no Zaisei Kinyū Kankei (The Deposit Bureau Local Funds and Local Public Finance (1)—Fiscal and Financial Relations between the Central Government and Local Governments in the 1920s–1930s)," *Journal of Social Science*, Volume 37, No. 3 (1985); "Yokin Bu Chihō Shikin to Chihō Zaisei (Ni) The Deposit Bureau Local Funds and Local Public Finance (2)," *Journal of Social Science*, Volume 37, No. 6 (1986); *Kindai Nihon Chihō Zaisei Shi Kenkyū (A Study on the History of Local Public Finance in Modern Japan)*, Nihon Keizai Hyōronsha, 2010.

[3] Kase Kazutoshi, "Senzen Nihon no Shitsugyō Taisaku—Kyūsai-gata Kōkyō Doboku Jigyō no Shiteki Bunseki (Measures to Counter Unemployment in Prewar Japan—A Historical Analysis of Relief-Oriented Public Civil Engineering Works)," Nihon Keizai Hyōronsha, 1998; Chūgai Shōgyō Shinpō, "*Kyohi wo Yōsuru Ōkurashō Yokinbu—Jisetsugara Juyōsei wo Masu (The Deposit Bureau of the Ministry of Finance Holding Massive Funds—The Increasing Importance in These Times)*, May 25, 1934.

the wider impact they had on the Japanese economy and people's lives. This entails an examination of the function of savings closely related to the everyday life of the general public. This addendum, however, is more concerned with political interactions within the central government regarding the Deposit Bureau of the Ministry of Finance, and it therefore deals with a subject different in nature from the other chapters in this book. However, it seems no less important when understanding the function and role of popular funds following the reform of the Deposit Bureau to also understand how the Deposit Bureau of the Ministry of Finance worked, including an understanding of what entities controlled it and their intentions in doing so. The reason is that small-amount savings by individuals, accumulated through postal savings, increased further during the protracted economic slump of the interwar period amid a widespread sense of distrust felt by many towards private-sector financial institutions. As pointed out earlier, the management system of the Deposit Bureau had a highly path dependent nature and largely followed precedents. Thus, an understanding of how the new definitions and system derived from the reform affected the actual management of the funds is indispensable to understanding the subsequent long-term management performance of the system.

6.2 The Pre-reform Shape of the Deposit Bureau

6.2.1 The Initial System Design of the Deposit Bureau of the Ministry of Finance

In order to understand the Deposit Bureau reform, the Bureau's institutional outline should first be considered. This was covered in Chap. 5 to some extent, but in this chapter the focus is more on the institutional and political aspects of the Deposit Bureau.

For the most part, the Deposit Bureau funds of the Ministry of Finance were derived from postal savings. Thus, in terms of institutional origins, the postal savings system was crucial. The postal savings system was started in 1875 as part of poverty relief and alleviation measures aimed at middle- and low-income people who were encouraged to make savings at post offices. Under the "*Fukoku*" Decree No. 13 of May 1885, "Rules for Deposits," the management and investment of these funds were left entirely at the discretion of the Ministry of Finance. Indeed, this served as the only legal basis for the Ministry of Finance to handle postal savings until the reform of the Deposit Bureau with the enactment of Act No. 25 of 1925, the "Act for Deposits of the Deposit Bureau."

Decree to Enact Rules for Deposits and Have Reserve Funds at Government Ministries and Agencies Deposited with the Deposit Bureau of the Ministry of Finance

No. 13

The Rules for Deposits shall be enacted as follows:

The Rules for Deposits

Article 1. The Deposit Bureau shall be established within the Ministry of Finance to take charge of the following savings and reserve funds, hold them, and accumulate interest on them.

1. Savings at post offices
2. Reserve funds as prescribed under official rules of government ministries and agencies
3. Reserve funds of temples, shrines and churches and other funds shared and jointly owned by people, for which petitions are made for deposits with the Deposit Bureau

Article 2. Procedures for handling deposits shall be set by the Minister of Finance.

Article 3. Interest rates on deposits shall be set by the Minister of Finance.

Article 4. Profits and losses on deposits shall be borne by state coffers.

Article 5. Deposit certificates shall not be bought, sold, transferred or pledged as collateral.

Article 6. Investment of deposits shall be entrusted to the Bank of Japan.

Article 7. The Minister of Finance may establish branch offices of the Deposit Bureau at convenient locations or have treasury fund-handling offices receive or pay out deposits.

Article 8. Certificates related to the receipt and withdrawal of deposits shall be exempted from the payment of securities stamp duty taxes.

The above has been proclaimed as of May 30, 1885 (Seal of the Minister of Finance)[4]

The Decree, which enabled the Ministry of Finance to handle not only postal savings but also all "reserve funds as prescribed under official rules of government ministries and agencies." This included the objective of reintegrating (with the Ministry of Finance) the financial resources that various government ministries and agencies had begun to possess in the course of successive reorganizations of the central government's ministries and agencies in the early years of the Meiji period. The intention was to strengthen the powers of the Ministry of Finance by declaring that it should have full authority over the government's financial resources.

Consequently, the Deposit Bureau of the Ministry of Finance, established to manage postal savings and various other funds under the Rules for Deposits,[5] saw a variety of funds come under its control. In 1890, under Act No. 21, Central Famine-relief funds also came officially under the Ministry of Finance. Central Famine-relief

---

[4] Dajōkan (Grand Council of State), "Yokin Kisoku wo Seitei Shi Oyobi Kaku Kanchō no Tsumitatekin wa Ōkurashō Chokin-kyoku e Azukeire Shimu (Enact Rules for Deposits and Have Reserve Funds at Government Ministries and Agencies Deposited with the Deposit Bureau of the Ministry of Finance)," *Kōbun Ruiju (Collection of Official Documents)*, Part 9, Volume 21, May 30, 1885.

[5] Initially, the Savings Bureau, separated from the Government Bond Bureau, was engaged in the management of these funds. After its abolition in 1893, the Budget Bureau took up the task, and from 1897 on, the Financial Bureau took over. It should be noted that there did not exist a bureau called the Deposit Bureau of the Ministry of Finance in the ministry. See Note 9 of Chap. 5.

funds were specifically for dealing with natural disasters, and can been viewed as somewhat inheriting the "*gisō*" and "*shasō*" grain-stockpiling warehouse systems from the previous era. Postal savings were also created in a manner whereby the "profit and loss of post office savings and the responsibility for these savings shall fall under the state coffers" and be "designed to relieve and benefit the poor." In this sense, the Deposit Bureau served to gather the savings of the general public for emergency relief.

Since its inception, the Deposit Bureau system was designed to consolidate the management of government funds as the province of the Ministry of Finance, which would not concede this role to other ministries. At the same time, it was positioned as a system to handle the savings of the general public, which the state had a responsibility to protect and manage. Because of this, the initial investments of the Deposit Bureau funds were not as diverse as seen in later eras, with the bulk of available funds put into government bond purchases. However, at this time, the size of Deposit Bureau funds was hardly substantial, as the use of postal savings was not yet widespread during the nineteenth century.

After the Sino-Japanese War (1894–1895), however, when postal savings reached around ¥20 million, the financial position of the Deposit Bureau was temporarily strengthened when a portion of the war reparations, worth some ¥50 million, were transferred into the bureau as a temporary measure. In terms of fund management following the Sino-Japanese and Russo-Japanese (1904–1905) wars, a portion of Deposit Bureau funds were invested in areas other than government bonds and the Deposit Bureau played a complementary role government finance.

However, these massive funds themselves, named the three post-Sino Japanese War funds, made possible a diverse application of government finances, and were consumed in a series of economic and industrial policies following the Sino-Japanese War and during and following the Russo-Japanese War. An injection of financial resources on this scale, exceeding the size of postal savings, never happened again. The issue of the investment of Deposit Bureau funds in areas other than government bonds, namely the issue of how postal savings should be managed, became a major issue in the twentieth century as the use of postal savings spread across Japan.

As discussed in Chap. 3, following the formation of savings by ordinary people in tandem with developments in regional communities, postal savings surpassed ¥100 million by 1908. The size of the funds managed by the Deposit Bureau also grew accordingly. As postal savings were mainly collected in rural agricultural areas, the government was conscious that the investment of Deposit Bureau funds in government bonds meant the withdrawal of funds from rural regions to the central government. For this reason, the necessity of a "return to the regions" of Deposit Bureau funds came to be discussed within the government from that time onward.[6] In the background to this was the fact that Nihon Kangyō Bank, as well as the prefectural Agricultural and Industrial banks under it, established with the purpose of supporting agriculture-related finance in rural areas, were unable to respond sufficiently to the

6 "*Ōkurashō Yokinbu Shi (History of the Deposit Bureau of the Ministry of Finance),*" p. 2.

demand for funds from small-scale producers due to their own fund shortages.[7] Acutely aware of the Nihon Kangyō Bank and Agricultural and Industrial banks' lack of funds, the Deposit Bureau used its funds to underwrite Kangyō Bank bonds for the first time in 1904, and in 1905, the bureau underwrote Kangyō Bank bonds again for the lending of funds to Agricultural and Industrial banks.

Under these circumstances, in 1906, relief lending was officially provided with Deposit Bureau funds as expenses for measures to deal with crop failures in three prefectures in the Tohoku region. Beginning with this relief lending, the return to the regions of Deposit Bureau funds came to be understood and incorporated into the bureau's management philosophy as "financing for public organizations and a variety of unions for regional development",[8] but this shift was made without any institutional basis at that point of time. The return to the regions of Deposit Bureau funds gained this institutional basis only after the commencement of the system to supply regional funds according to the two quotas of "ordinary funds" and "special funds" under the joint circular of the Ministries of Communications, Finance and Home Affairs in 1909.[9]

In 1910, the supply of funds for recovery from natural disasters led to the issuance of a notice of the Minister of Finance, "Ō Dai Ichiman Yonsen Hyaku Hachijū Ni Gō (Outgoing No. 14182), establishing the supply route of regional funds through the underwriting of local government bonds by the Deposit Bureau. What prompted this were responses to the 1910 flood damage in Tokyo and seven other prefectures. In supplying funds for restoration work on heavily damaged roads and bridges, the Deposit Bureau initially planned to provide lending through Kangyō Bank. In response to requests from the affected local governments, however, the bureau lent funds through the underwriting of prefectural bonds.[10]

In the wake of this case in 1910, the Deposit Bureau "came to broadly decide on conditions and methods for the underwriting of local government bonds across Japan" for all prefectures. However, this was not yet concrete or systematic, the decision reflected "basic principles" rather than anything "final or conclusive." Items such as "the terms and conditions for lending" were not established, and "had to be altered to suit each occasion." Nevertheless, by this Ministry of Finance notice a supply route to "special funds" for local governments through the underwriting of local government bonds was established. Prior to the interwar period, the funds supplied under this formula were "mainly designed for natural disasters relief," and "came to

[7] Mukai, "1900 Nendai ni Okeru Ōkurashō Yokinbu no Kinō to Seikaku (The Function and Nature of the Deposit Bureau of the Ministry of Finance in the 1990s)," p. 34; Research Department, Nōrinchūkin Bank, "*Nōrin Chūō Kinko 50 Nen no Ayumi (The 50-Year History of the Nōrinchūkin Bank)*," 1973, pp. 4–5.

[8] "*Ōkurashō Yokinbu Shi (History of the Deposit Bureau of the Ministry of Finance),*" p. 128.

[9] The joint circular of the Ministers of Communications, Finance and Home Affairs, "*Hi Dai Hyakunijūsan no Ichi (Confidential No. 123-1),*" May 1909, included in Nihon Kangyō Ginkō, "*Teiri Shikin ni Kansuru Meirei Tsūtatsusho Tsuzuri (The Bound Book of Orders and Notices Concerning Low-Interest Funds)*".

[10] "*Meiji Taishō Zaisei Shi Jūsan-kan (History of Government Finance in the Meiji and Taishō Periods Volume 13)*, p. 850.

a considerable amount almost every fiscal year." In this way, for the Deposit Bureau, the supply of funds to local governments became one of the basic frameworks for the supply of regional funds, alongside the route through Kangyō Bank and prefectural Agricultural and Industrial banks.[11]

The "fundamental policy" for the supply of regional funds by the Deposit Bureau was established by the 1909 joint circular of the three ministries, but this was not yet a system with a "final and conclusive form." It had the goal of returning funds to the regions, but the actual supply routes and methods were handled according to the emergency circumstances of each case. Specific ways of providing "regional funds," including the scope of lending, were developed later by adding to and amending the system in response to requests for funds from the Deposit Bureau. For instance, from 1910 onwards, direct lending to industrial cooperatives was permitted.[12]

While the supply of Deposit Bureau funds covered a broad range of recipients, the recipients of these funds never included general financial institutions, such as ordinary commercial banks, or large-scale distributors in the private sector, such as wholesale merchants and trading houses. In addition, the Deposit Bureau tended to lend for specific purposes. "With the intention of laying the foundation for regional development by helping boost private-sector capital," the Deposit Bureau embraced the idea of resolving the shortage of funds in the regions and making loans to provide funds for recovery from natural disasters. As such, it positioned itself as an entity that maintained a distance from the functions of ordinary private-sector financial markets. In this way, by the end of the first decade of the twentieth century, funds from the Deposit Bureau, which had the basic policy of investing mainly in government bonds from the standpoint of protecting its financial resources, came to be returned to regional economies as regional funds at a level of around 10–20% of the Deposit Bureau resources.

6.2.2 Deviation from the Basic Management Policies and Voices Calling for Reform

As seen above, the dual management polices of social and economic support oriented toward the regions and relief and restoration support in times of crisis were already established for Deposit Bureau funds before World War I, but the rapid expansion of financial resources resulting from the economic boom during World War I shook up the bureau's adherence to these management policies. The Deposit Bureau's supply of funds to the regions was not designed to respond promptly to demand for funds in

[11] "*Meiji Taishō Zaisei Shi Jūsan-kan (History of Government Finance in the Meiji and Taishō Periods Volume 13)*, p. 824. However, "ordinary funds" were never provided through the underwriting of local government bonds until 1927. This indicates that throughout the Meiji and Taisho periods, the underwriting of local government bonds was considered as something to be conducted only through the framework of "special funds."

[12] "*Ōkurashō Yokinbu Shi (History of the Deposit Bureau of the Ministry of Finance)*," p. 137.

the private sector, as the supply of funds basically could not exceed the prescribed allocations in proportion to increases in postal savings unless based on requests from local governments and various industry organizations. Because of this, the rapid increase in the bureau's financial resources resulted in a temporary glut of funds. Consequently, during World War I, the Deposit Bureau used its funds as loans to the Chinese government, and newly supplied funds for imperialistic policies, such as investment in Manchuria and Siberia through the Bank of Chosen and the Industrial Bank of Japan[13] As these loans and investments turned into bad debt in the 1920s, the assessment during the interwar period was that "in retrospect, various projects used funds indiscriminately during the war in tandem with the business boom. Some politicians and businessmen with political influence seized the opportunity to withdraw low-interest funds in the name of public interest",[14] with the Ministry of Finance's Deposit Bureau coming under scrutiny for the misuse of funds and having caused a serious social problem.

At the time of the 1925 reform of the Deposit Bureau, its funds totaled about ¥1.5 billion. Of this amount, funds for overseas projects newly lent out during World War I, deemed by some to be misused funds, totaled ¥150 million. While the amount was relatively small in comparison with regional funds of over ¥400 million, it still amounted to 10% of the total. This suggests that when new funds arose before the reform, the Deposit Bureau had no effective mechanism in place to prevent such funds from being invested in risky ventures or those not obviously beneficial to regional economies in Japan.

In the interwar period, the misuse of funds by the Deposit Bureau became a social problem and substantial bad debts arose, throwing the bureau's management into crisis. In response, reform bills related to the Deposit Bureau were passed by the 50th Diet in 1925. These ended up as two acts: the Act for the Special Account of the Deposit Bureau of the Ministry of Finance (March 30, 1925, Act No. 13) and the Act for Deposits of the Deposit Bureau (March 30, 1925, Act No. 25).

The Act for the Special Account of the Deposit Bureau of the Ministry of Finance contained several articles, including the following:

> Act No. 13 Act for the Special Account of the Deposit Bureau of the Ministry of Finance
>
> Article 1. The accounting of the Deposit Bureau of the Ministry of Finance shall be special, and the bureau's revenue shall be appropriated to cover its expenditure.
>
> ...

[13] (Authorship unknown, possibly a Ministry of Finance official), "*Rikenteki Shikin to Taishō Jūyo-nen no Yokinbu Kaikaku (Concession-Hunting Funds and Reform of the Deposit Bureau in 1925)*," possibly 1932; Fukai Isao, (a member of the House of Representatives in 1925), included in "*Shōwa Jūichi-nendo Keizai Kōsei/Fusai Seiri Gai Zatsushorui Tsuzuri (FY1936 the Bound Book of Miscellaneous Documents on Economic Rehabilitation and Debt Consolidation,* etc.)".

[14] Kenseikai Honbu (Head Office of Constitutional Assembly), "*Kensei Kōron (Open Discussion for Constitutional Government)*," 1927, extra edition, p. 21.

Article 3. When prices of assets under management related to Deposit Bureau funds are impaired, such impairment shall be amortized with surpluses arising from the accounting of the Special Account or reserve funds....

Thus, the Act for the Special Account of the Deposit Bureau of the Ministry of Finance obliged the bureau to disclose to the Diet how its funds are managed by positioning the Deposit Bureau funds under the framework of the special account. The act was designed to break through the obscure situation in which the amount and recipients of the bureau's funds were known to only a handful of bureaucrats. On the other hand, the act also established that the account of the Deposit Bureau, while called the special account, should be treated entirely independently of the general account in terms of both revenue and expenditure, positioning it as an account that differed from the government's ordinary finances funded with tax revenues. Deposit Bureau funds were not fiscal funds, but deposits from outside the government entrusted with the bureau.

The other act, the Act for Deposits of the Deposit Bureau, overwrote the Rules for Deposits, the only legal basis for the Deposit Bureau since 1885, and was newly enacted as the legal basis for the Ministry of Finance's management of postal savings.

Act No. 25 Act for Deposits of the Deposit Bureau

Article 1. Cash deposited with the Deposit Bureau of the Ministry of Finance under an imperial ordinance shall become Deposit Bureau deposits and shall be managed by the Ministry of Finance.

Article 2. Cash accepted as postal savings shall be deposited with the Deposit Bureau of the Ministry of Finance and interest on these deposits shall be appropriated as interest on postal savings.

Article 3. The Minister of Finance shall set types of interest on, and the handling of, Deposit Bureau deposits.

Article 4. Deposit Bureau deposits as well as reserve funds and surpluses in payments shall be managed by advantageous and reliable methods for the benefit of the state and public interests with the advice of the Steering Committee of the Deposit Bureau Funds.

The organization and powers of the Steering Committee of the Deposit Bureau Funds as well as rules for the management of the Deposit Bureau funds shall be set by an imperial ordinance.

Article 5. The Bank of Japan shall handle administrative affairs relating to the management of Deposit Bureau funds in accordance with rules set forth by the Minister of Finance.

Supplementary provision

This Act shall be enforced as of April 1, 1925.

As seen above, the Act for Deposits of the Deposit Bureau not only redefined the system for the Deposit Bureau of the Ministry of Finance to handle the management of postal savings but also legally embedded in the Deposit Bureau system the management principle that Deposit Bureau deposits "shall be managed by advantageous and reliable methods for the benefit of the state and public interests." Another important provision in the reform was that the act established a new advisory committee, the Steering Committee of the Deposit Bureau Funds. However, the Act for Deposits of the Deposit Bureau did not contain provisions establishing the details of the Steering Committee of the Deposit Bureau Funds. Therefore, on April 1, 1925, a few days after the enactment of the above two acts, two imperial ordinances were issued to supplement the Deposit Bureau reform-related acts. These were the Rules for the Special Account of the Deposit Bureau of the Ministry of Finance (April 1, 1925, Imperial Ordinance No. 54) and the Rules for the Management of the Deposit Bureau Funds (April 1, 1925, Imperial Ordinance No. 55).

Imperial Ordinance No. 54 The Rules for the Special Account of the Deposit Bureau of the Ministry of Finance

Article 1. A statement of accounts of planned revenue and expenditure shall be adjusted by a competent minister and shall be sent to the Minister of Finance by September 30 of the preceding fiscal year.

A revenue and expenditure plan table and a balance sheet for the fiscal year ending on March 31 of that year, as well as a detailed list of assets under management as of March 31 of that year, shall be attached to the statement of accounts of planned revenue and expenditure in the preceding paragraph.

Article 2. Funds not actually received or spent by the closing of receipts and disbursements of each fiscal year shall be revenue and expenditure of the fiscal year in which they are actually received or spent.

Article 3. Prices of assets under management belonging to the Deposit Bureau funds shall be revised in accordance with market prices as of March 31 of each year. However, this shall not apply to prices that do not exceed market prices.

Article 4. When prices of assets under management belonging to the Deposit Bureau funds are impaired, a surplus to be obtained by subtracting actual payments of expenditure from actual receipts of revenue in the special account shall be appropriated for amortization. When there is still a shortage, reserve funds shall be appropriated for amortization.

(Subsequent articles omitted)

As seen above, the Rules for the Special Account of the Deposit Bureau of the Ministry of Finance provided institutional details for establishing the account of the Deposit Bureau as a special account. Because of this, the Rules did not contain provisions for the advisory committee or the guidelines for the management of the funds, while the Rules for the Management of the Deposit Bureau Funds incorporated such provisions. Below is the full text of the Rules for the Management of the Deposit Bureau Funds:

Imperial Ordinance No. 55 Rules for the Management of the Deposit Bureau Funds

Article 1. The Deposit Bureau funds shall be managed according to the following methods:

1. Subscriptions for the underwriting or purchase of government bonds or local government bonds
2. Lending to the general account or special accounts

3. Subscriptions for, underwriting of, or purchases of corporate bonds or industrial bonds issued by companies established under special laws
4. Lending to banks established under special laws that do not issue corporate bonds
5. Subscriptions for, or purchases of, government bonds issued by foreign governments
6. Designated overseas deposits for the Bank of Japan

Article 2. The Minister of Finance shall determine a necessary plan concerning the management of the Deposit Bureau funds each fiscal year and shall refer the plan to the Steering Committee of the Deposit Bureau Funds. The same approach shall be taken when making any additions or changes to the plan.

Article 3. The Minister of Finance shall prepare a report on the management of the Deposit Bureau funds each fiscal year and submit the report to the Steering Committee of the Deposit Bureau Funds within four months after lapse of the fiscal year concerned.

The report in the preceding paragraph shall describe important matters concerning the status of management of the Deposit Bureau funds and changes in assets under management during the fiscal year.

Article 4. The Minister of Finance shall determine matters necessary for the management of the Deposit Bureau funds other than those provided for in this ordinance.

Article 5. The Steering Committee of the Deposit Bureau Funds shall come under the supervision of the Minister of Finance and shall investigate and discuss matters concerning the management of the Deposit Bureau funds in response to a request for opinions from the Minister of Finance.

Article 6. The Steering Committee of the Deposit Bureau Funds may submit a recommendation concerning the management of the Deposit Bureau funds to the Minister of Finance.

Article 7. The Steering Committee of the Deposit Bureau Funds shall be organized with a chairman and not more than 15 committee members.

When necessary, temporary members may be invited.

Article 8. The Minister of Finance shall serve as the chairman of the Steering Committee.

Article 9. Persons listed below shall be appointed as members.

1. The Parliamentary Vice Minister of Finance
2. The Vice Minister of Finance
3. High officials of ministries and agencies concerned
4. The Commissioner of the Board of Audit
5. The Governor of the Bank of Japan
6. Academic experts

Members listed in 2, 4 and 6 shall be appointed by the Cabinet based on the recommendations of the Minister of Finance.

Temporary members shall be appointed by the Cabinet from among high officials of ministries and agencies concerned and academic experts based on the recommendations of the Minister of Finance.

Article 10. The Chairman shall preside over discussions in the Steering Committee.

When the Chairman becomes unable to perform his duties, a person designated by the Chairman shall take his place.

Article 11. The Steering Committee of the Deposit Bureau Funds shall appoint a manager.

The manager shall be appointed by the Cabinet from among high officials of the Ministry of Finance based on the recommendations of the Minister of Finance. The manager shall organize the general affairs of the committee under the supervision of his superiors.

Article 12. The Steering Committee of the Deposit Bureau Funds shall appoint a secretary.

The secretary shall be appointed by the Minister of Finance from among junior officials of the Ministry of Finance. The secretary shall be engaged in the general affairs of the committee under the supervision of his superiors.

Supplementary provision

This imperial ordinance shall be enforced from the date of its promulgation.

Upon the enforcement of this imperial ordinance, Deposit Bureau funds that are currently under management with management methods that do not correspond to the provisions of Article 1, may continue to be managed by such methods notwithstanding the provisions of Article 1.

As can be seen from the above, the Deposit Bureau system was defined by inheriting the conventional policies that limited the management of Deposit Bureau funds to the underwriting of government bonds, loans to the central government and local governments, and loans to special banks and special financial institutions such as the Central Bank for Industrial Cooperatives.

On the other hand, while the Minister of Finance, or the Ministry of Finance, was to formulate a management plan for Deposit Bureau funds as before, there was a newly prescribed element by which the management plan should be "referred to the Steering Committee of the Deposit Bureau Funds". In addition, the Minister of Finance was obliged to "prepare a report on the management of the Deposit Bureau funds each fiscal year and submit the report to the Steering Committee of the Deposit Bureau Funds within four months after lapse of the fiscal year concerned." In other words, it was prescribed that the Steering Committee of the Deposit Bureau Funds would be able to grasp an overall picture of not only the formulation of the management plan but also the results of the management of the Deposit Bureau funds in advance of its meeting. This arrangement enabled a route to be created to disclose the management status of the Deposit Bureau funds, previously believed to be known only to a handful of bureaucrats even within the Ministry of Finance, to others outside the Ministry of Finance.

6.2.3 The Tone of Contemporary Public Opinion Regarding the Deposit Bureau Reform

How was the new system design of the Deposit Bureau received by the general public? Following the passage of a series of related bills through the Diet, newspapers at the time received the development favorably as the "reform of the Deposit Bureau." However, as the parliamentary passage of the Act for the Special Account of the Deposit Bureau of the Ministry of Finance and the Act for Deposits of the Deposit Bureau came 1 day after the passage of the Universal Manhood Suffrage Act, media coverage was limited. In many cases, press reports on the Deposit Bureau reform were made in tandem with other financial bills.

For example, the Tokyo Asahi Shimbun carried the following article.

> Four financial bills were passed by the Diet. The first was 1. The bill for the Act for Deposits of the Deposit Bureau and the second was 2. The bill for the Act for the Special Account of the Deposit Bureau of the Ministry of Finance. Previously, the management of Deposit Bureau funds was determined at the discretion of the Minister of Finance alone. However, considering that the management of funds soaked up from the regions, in particular from farmers and people below the middle class, were used for the relief of businessmen with political ties and unsound banking corporations, a fact that invited a chorus of criticisms, the government established what was called the steering committee, which drew 14 or 15 members from relevant ministries, the Bank of Japan, Kangyō Bank and Industrial Bank of Japan, the House of Peers and House of Representatives, Industrial Cooperatives, and other public and private-sector quarters. The Deposit Bureau funds are thus to be managed for the interests of the state and public good after seeking recommendations from the steering committee, with rules for their management separately specified. Revenue and expenditure of the Deposit Bureau in the special account shall be incorporated into the main account each year and submitted to the Diet along with the total budget, thereby making the management of the Deposit Bureau funds "fair and square". A section of the treasury division of the Financial Bureau of the Ministry of Finance shall be reorganized into the independent Deposit Bureau, under which the fund division and the management division are to completely and promptly manage and collect the funds defrayed. Though the Deposit Bureau was already covered by the special account prior to these changes, interest on postal savings and fees, previously transferred to the general account, which then paid them to postal savings and others will, beginning in FY1925, be paid out directly from the Deposit Bureau account without going through the general account, allowing the Deposit Bureau to have an entirely independent account. Therefore, starting in FY1925, money transferred from the deposit special account (some ¥60 million) shall disappear from the general account's budget and the same amount shall be entered in the special account of the Deposit Bureau.[15]

As seen above, the mass media, with the understanding that the financial resources of the Deposit Bureau were "soaked up from the regions, in particular from farmers and people below the middle class," appreciated that the reform efforts were for the transparent management of the Deposit Bureau funds. As they understood it, "the government established what was called the steering committee" in a bid to make "the management of the Deposit Bureau funds fair and square," and to be "managed

---

[15] "Kon Gikai wo Tsūkashita Keizai Kenkei hō no Setsumei (Chū)—Kinyū Zeisei—[Explanations about Economy-related Laws (Part 2 of three articles)—Financial Taxation]," *The Tokyo Asahi Shimbun*, March 31, 1925, p. 4.

for the interests of the state and public good after seeking recommendations from the steering committee." Furthermore, they noted that "revenue and expenditure of the Deposit Bureau in the special account [would] be incorporated into the main account each year and submitted to the Diet along with the total budget."

Regarding the composition of the Steering Committee of the Deposit Bureau Funds, Article 9 of the Rules for the Management of the Deposit Bureau Funds enacted a few days later stipulated that the committee's membership consist of the Parliamentary Vice Minister of Finance, Vice Minister of Finance, high officials of relevant ministries and agencies, the Commissioner of the Board of Audit, the Governor of the Bank of Japan, and "academic experts." However, it is noteworthy that the composition of the committee as reported by the media was to consist of "14 or 15 members from relevant ministries, the Bank of Japan, Kangyō Bank and Industrial Bank of Japan, the House of Peers and House of Representatives, Industrial Cooperatives and other public and private-sector quarters." This was reported even before the promulgation of the imperial ordinance. Comparing the contents of the article and the media reports, it is hard to believe that the contents of the press reports that preceded the promulgation of the imperial ordinance had no basis in fact. Rather, the media reports are striking in the clarity in which they report very specific information. This suggests that the mass media obtained certain inside information from officials directly involved in the preparation of the reform bills prior to the passage of the bills related to the Deposit Bureau reform and the imperial ordinance promulgated a few days later.

As seen above, the Deposit Bureau reform in 1925 reaffirmed the premise that the Ministry of Finance, instead of other ministries or agencies. It also made clear that it was the Ministry of Finance that should formulate fund management plans, including investment in government bonds and local government bonds, and conventional methods of indirect lending through special banks, etc. Moreover, with the reform, the idea that Deposit Bureau funds should be managed for the public good in a safe manner was solidified and specified in the legal system.

The system design that emerged can be described as essentially following and inheriting the pre-existing, though unwritten or uncodified, system. However, under the new laws, there were some important changes: the management of Deposit Bureau funds now came under the special account and the Deposit Bureau was newly obligated to disclose the results of its management to the Diet. In this way, the reform was seen as ensuring greater transparency to society. The Steering Committee of the Deposit Bureau Funds was established as an advisory committee in order to reinforce this development. By reporting to the steering committee its management plans and the status of fund management each fiscal year, the Deposit Bureau was subject to greater scrutiny of its fund management, with the committee functioning as an external auditor. The reform also established the legal grounds for the new institutional framework.

6.3 The Role of the Steering Committee of the Deposit Bureau Funds of the Ministry of Finance

What was the actual function of the Steering Committee of the Deposit Bureau Funds of the Ministry? What influence did it have on the actual management of Deposit Bureau funds and the bureau's operations? Institutionally, the Steering Committee of the Deposit Bureau Funds was simply an advisory committee that did not prepare plans for the management of funds per se, and the committee did not have the right to make decisions on the approval or rejection of management plans prepared by the Ministry of Finance. Then, with this limited power, what was the actual role of the advisory committee? These questions will be approached in this section mainly by examining the committee's minutes in its early years.

6.3.1 The Specific Design of the Steering Committee of the Deposit Bureau Funds in the Establishment Phase

How frequently were meetings of the Steering Committee of the Deposit Bureau Funds held? The first meeting took place on May 5, 1925, slightly over a month after the laws related to the Deposit Bureau reform passed the Diet at the end of March. The remaining minutes indicate that the steering committee met eight times in FY1925. After meeting for the first time in May, the committee met twice in June, once in each of July, August, October, and December, and then on March 29, 1926, at the end of the fiscal year.[16]

In FY 1926 the steering committee met in May, July, August, December, January and March, and then in FY1927 it met in May, July, September, December, January and March, indicating that committee meetings were held six times a year with some variation in the months when meetings were held. It is presumed that the Ministry of Finance sought to hold the committee's meeting every other month, somewhat loosely, according to the convenience of its members. With respect to FY1925, the year the committee was established, it is believed that the committee met more frequently than in later years in order to address the large number of pending problems described below. It is presumed that the cycle of meetings of the steering committee in subsequent years and the basics of the committee's functions

---

[16] The date of the 8th meeting is based on Ministry of Finance, "*Shōwa Zeisei Shi (History of Government Finance in the Showa Period),*" Volume 12, p. 93. As long as it can be confirmed at the moment, certain quantities of the minutes of the Steering Committee of the Deposit Bureau Funds are in the possession of the library of the Department of Economics of the University of Tokyo, the Institute of Social Science Library of the University of Tokyo, and the Japan Center for Asian Historical Records of the National Archives of Japan. For minutes in the early years, the minutes of the 8th meeting are missing for some reason.

were designed during the committee's meetings in its inaugural fiscal year. Who, then, were the participants in the committee's meetings?

As seen in the preceding section, members of the Steering Committee of the Deposit Bureau Funds were designated by the imperial ordinance as the Parliamentary Vice Minister of Finance, the Vice Minister of Finance, high officials of relevant government ministries and agencies, the Commissioner of the Board of Audit, the Governor of the Bank of Japan and "academic experts." Media reports assumed that a total of 14 or 15 members would be appointed by recruiting them also from "Kangyō Bank, Industrial Bank of Japan, the House of Peers and the House of Representatives, industrial cooperatives and other public and private-sector quarters" in addition to the people designated above.

Table 6.1 shows the initial steering committee membership, called up on May 5, 1925, which totaled 19 persons. Supposing that the secretaries from the Ministry of Finance took care of clerical work and did not participate in committee discussions, the composition of the steering committee was not much different from the mass media had predicted when the Diet passed the relevant bills.

Committee members included the Minister of Finance, who served as its chairman, and incumbent vice minister-level officials of relevant ministries and agencies. The Director-General of the Financial Bureau of the Ministry of Finance, the official who was actually in charge of the management of the Deposit Bureau funds, was also appointed to the committee. Moreover, from outside the government, the Governor of the Bank of Japan, named as a member of the steering committee under the imperial ordinance, and the president of Nihon Kangyō Bank were appointed together with a few other members as "academic experts." The non-government members comprised the incumbent or former executives of special banks, such as the Bank of Japan, Nihon Kangyō Bank and Industrial Bank of Japan, university professors in the field of economics, as well as incumbent members of the House of Representatives and the House of Peers from both the ruling and opposition parties. Committee members chosen from the Diet included those assumed to be familiar with operations related to the Deposit Bureau's regional funds and general financial business operations, such as executives of the National Federation of Industrial Cooperatives, people experienced in the operations of financial institutions, and former bureaucrats of relevant ministries and agencies (the Ministry of the Interior, Ministry of Finance, and Ministry of Agriculture and Forestry).[17] For that reason, perhaps, of the non-government members, the ratio of former bureaucrats was high, giving the impression that there were only a handful of committee members who could be described as complete government outsiders.

---

[17] Of these initial members, Shimura Gentarō and Shidachi Tetsujirō, together with Ishibashi Tanzan and Wakatsuki Reijirō, colleague members of the Keizai Kōkyūkai, had already announced a reform plan for the Deposit Bureau. They are assumed to have taken an interest in the management of the Deposit Bureau funds even before being selected as members of the steering committee and possessed a certain degree of knowledge about the bureau. Editorial Office of the History of Government Finance in the Showa Period, Ministry of Finance, "*Shōwa Zaisei Shi (History of Government Finance in the Showa Period)*," Volume 12, 1962, p. 11.

Table 6.1 Members of the steering committee of the deposit bureau funds in its early years

Members of the "designated job" group in the rules for management		Attributes of members from the "academic exports" group
Chairman (finance minister)	Hamaguchi Osachi	
Parliamentary vice finance minister	Hayami Seiji	
Vice finance minister	Den Akira	
Vice interior minister	Yuasa Kurahei	
Vice agriculture and forestry minister	Abe Hisanori	
Vice communications minister	Kuwayama Tetsuo	
Commissioner, board of audit	Kōno Hideo	
Governor, bank of Japan	Ichiki Otohiko	
	Sakatani Yoshirō	Ex-finance ministry bureaucrat, ex-finance minister, member of the house of peers
	Yamazaki Kakujirō	Professor of economics at Tokyo Imperial University specializing in monetary theory and financial theory (the first dean of the department of economics)
	Katō Masanosuke	Member of the House of Representative (Saitama Prefecture), the Kenseikai party, member of the House of Peers since 1927, former journalist
	Yamamoto Teijirō	Member of the House of Representative (Niigata Prefecture), the Seiyūkai party, studied in Germany on an Imperial Household Ministry scholarship, former head of the appraisement division at Nihon Kangyō Bank, ex-Agriculture and Forestry Minister
	Kimura Seishirō	Deputy Governor of the Bank of Japan, member of the House of Peers since 1927
	Shimura Gentarō	President of the National Federation of Industrial Cooperatives, member of the House of Peers, former Agriculture and Commerce Ministry bureaucrat, former president of Nihon Kangyō Bank
	Shidachi Tetsujirō	Former President of Industrial Bank of Japan
President, Nihon Kangyō Bank*	Kajiwara Nakaji	President of Nihon Kangyō Bank (as of 1925), former president of Yokohama Specie Bank

(continued)

Table 6.1 (continued)

Members of the "designated job" group in the rules for management		Attributes of members from the "academic exports" group
Director-general, financial bureau, ministry of finance	Tomita Yūtarō	
Secretary, finance ministry	Ueno Isao	
Secretary, finance ministry	Aoki Kazuo	

*The same members served on the committee from the first to the fifth meetings (May 5 to October 9, 1925). The replacement of the Parliamentary Vice Minister of Finance at the 6th meeting was the first change in membership

Source Deposit Bureau, Ministry of Finance, "*Yokinbu Shikin Unyō Iinnkai (Dai Ikkai Kaigi) Gijiroku (Minutes of the Steering Committee of the Deposit Bureau Funds [first meeting]),*" 1925

The initial members of the steering committee were not replaced until the 15th meeting held on May 25, 1927, excepting transfers of bureaucrats or changes in the Minister of Finance. The first change in a non-government member took place at the 15th meeting, when Inoue Kōsai took the place of Yamamoto Teijirō. But the successor, Inoue, like his predecessor Yamamoto, was a member of the House of Representatives belonging to the Seiyūkai Party[18] Inoue was a former bureaucrat in the Ministry of the Interior, who served as governor of Saga, Toyama, Kanagawa and Osaka prefectures successively. He also served as Vice Minister of the Interior just before Yuasa, who was in the same post when appointed as one of the initial members of the Steering Committee of the Deposit Bureau Funds. No documents remain that indicate specified rules for the selection of committee members from outside the government. In changing such members, however, it is believed that the government took the balance among political parties into account and was also conscious to select persons presumed to understand, to some extent at least, the circumstances surrounding the regional funds of the Deposit Bureau.

What, then, was on the agenda of the Steering Committee of the Deposit Bureau Funds? One item was the problem of bad debt, which was already being discussed in the Diet. Given the large number of committee meetings held in its inaugural year, a large proportion of initial discussions are assumed to have focused on the verification and disposal of this problem. There were six points on the agenda of the first meeting of the Steering Committee of the Deposit Bureau Funds held on May 5, 1925 (see Table 6.2) and there were effectively three measures to be decided on the agenda of the initial committee meeting, including the setting of the rules of order. The committee's minutes showed that these were all "passed in their original form", i.e. as prepared by Ministry of Finance officials.

Requirements of "passage" by the steering committee, which per se were decided at the first meeting, were that "items on the agenda shall be decided by a majority

[18] Yamamoto's electoral constituency was Niigata Prefecture, while Inoue's constituency was Gifu Prefecture, an indication that the Ministry of Finance had no apparent intention of arranging committee members by birthplace region.

Table 6.2 Agenda of the first meeting of the steering committee of the deposit bureau funds

	Agenda items	Committee action
1	Remarks by the minister of finance	
2	Decision on the rules of order	Adopted in its original form, except for the issue of a lead time for communicating a schedule
3	Report on the current status of the management of deposit bureau funds	Ministry of Finance officials gave an explanation of the report. There were many questions and answers in response to the explanation
4	Report on the spare capacity for management of ordinary funds of the Deposit Bureau in FY1925	A few questions were asked by members
5	Proposal No. 1 "management plan for ordinary funds of the deposit bureau for FY1925"	A committee member offered his opinion about an increase in regional funds. A Ministry of Finance official replied that though the ministry hopes to increase the amount of funds lent to regions as its basic policy, the present funding condition of the Deposit Bureau does not allow the bureau to increase regional funds any more than in the original management plan. In the end, the management plan was adopted in its original form
6	Proposal No. 2 "matter concerning short-term management of deposit bureau funds"	Adopted in its original form

Source Deposit Bureau, Ministry of Finance, "*Yokinbu Shikin Unyō Iinkai (Dai Ikkai Kaigi) Gijiroku (Minutes of the 1st Meeting of the Steering Committee of the Deposit Bureau Funds)*," 1925, pp. 3–4

of the committee members in attendance. In case of a tied vote, the decision of the committee chairman shall prevail".[19] This means it is fair to assume that the steering committee did not necessarily require the firm approval or a unanimous vote from its members, rather a loose tolerance among committee members in attendance of proposals was all that was required. Under the legal system, however, the advisory committee's right to reject an original proposal was not specifically stipulated. What,

[19] Deposit Bureau, Ministry of Finance, "*Yokinbu Shikin Unyō Iinnkai (Dai Ikkai Kaigi) Gijiroku (Minutes of the 1st Meeting of the Steering Committee of the Deposit Bureau Funds)*," 1925, p. 7. Based on Article 6 of "Y*okinbu Shikin Unyō Iinkai Giji Kisoku An (Draft Rules of Order of the Steering Committee of the Deposit Bureau Funds)*." The proposal was passed in its original form.

then, was the significance of the advisory committee's discussions on proposals and their passage?

6.3.2 Role of the Steering Committee as Seen from Its Minutes: Balance Between Ideal and Actual Practices

In this section the role the advisory committee played in the operations of the Deposit Bureau is considered through a more detailed examination of the contents of the minutes of the first meeting of the steering committee.

Remarks by the Minister of Finance were the first item on the agenda and entailed a description by Minister of Finance Hamaguchi Osachi, chairman of the steering committee, of the idea behind the establishment of the Steering Committee of the Deposit Bureau Funds. Since the remarks reflected the intentions of Minister of Finance Hamaguchi, the central player in the execution of the Deposit Bureau reform, in establishing the steering committee, they are worth quoting at length:

> The government has recently established the Steering Committee of the Deposit Bureau Funds, and its first meeting is being held today. Taking this opportunity, let me briefly explain the background to the establishment of this committee.
>
> The history of the Deposit Bureau of the Ministry of Finance is very long... The amount of postal savings has now become so huge as to match an annual budget of the general account, and it is beyond question that the management of postal savings has an extremely large impact on state finances and the national economy. In particular, the core of Deposit Bureau funds consists of postal savings, more specifically, the small-amount savings of many people. Taking this point into account, it is necessary to ensure that the management of Deposit Bureau funds is conducted very fairly and properly. However, there has been some criticism, with suggestions that the management of funds until now has tended to be sloppy and uncertain. The present Cabinet... recently submitted to the Imperial Diet two bills for the Act for Deposits of the Deposit Bureau and the Act for the Special Account of the Deposit Bureau of the Ministry of Finance... Under the Act for Deposits of the Deposit Bureau, it is now a requirement that Deposit Bureau funds be managed in the interests of the state and public good, according to advantageous and reliable methods by seeking recommendations from the Steering Committee of the Deposit Bureau Funds. Here, the dominant principle for the management of the funds has been legally and clearly established. Also, under the Act for the Special Account of the Deposit Bureau of the Ministry of Finance, the accounting structure of the Deposit Bureau was rectified to clarify the status of its assets. Important amendments were made as well in terms of accounting, including the establishment of a depreciation method. Together with these laws, relevant imperial ordinances and ministerial ordinances were also promulgated, legally completing the first stage of the reform of the Deposit Bureau. Therefore, our forthcoming challenge is to realize the anticipated results these new laws and regulations entail in our actual management of Deposit Bureau funds. On this point, I believe that people place most of their expectations on the function of the steering committee. In other words, since this committee is regarded as the essential part of the latest reform of the Deposit Bureau, I ardently hope that all the members will fully

express their views and strive to ensure that the management of Deposit Bureau funds meet the people's expectations.[20]

As seen above, Minister of Finance Hamaguchi was aware of the enormous size of postal savings and recognized their influence on government finances and the wider Japanese economy. His remarks that "the core of Deposit Bureau funds consists of postal savings, more specifically, small-amount savings of many people... [and thus] it is necessary to ensure that the management of Deposit Bureau funds is conducted very fairly and properly" indicate that he was conscious of both the public nature of and the public interest in the management of the Deposit Bureau funds well before the establishment of the steering committee.

He also thought that in managing Deposit Bureau funds "for the interests of the state and public good," the management of the funds could be conducted "in accordance with advantageous and reliable methods" by "seeking recommendations from the Steering Committee of the Deposit Bureau Funds." To do that, committee members were asked to "fully express their views." It can be said that the advisory committee was expected to play the role of collecting "views," or information, from experts gathered from inside and outside the government.

As the second point on the agenda, the rules of order were set to handle administrative aspects of the committee thereafter. The rules of order were not formulated by participating members of the committee from scratch. They were presented to the participants in the form of a previously codified draft. The draft was assumed to have been prepared by bureaucrats of the Deposit Bureau of the Ministry of Finance in advance.

The Draft Rules of Order of the Steering Committee of the Deposit Bureau Funds

Article 1. The Chairman shall set the date, time, venue and agenda of a meeting at least two days before the meeting and notify committee members of this.

Article 2. A member who is unable to attend the meeting due to illness or other causes shall notify the Chairman to that effect.

Article 3. A meeting of the committee shall not be called into session unless at least half the members are present. However, this shall not apply when an urgent resolution is required.

Article 4. The commencement and closing of a meeting and its proceedings shall be directed by the Chairman. A member who wishes to speak shall seek the permission of the Chairman.

Article 5. When the Chairman deems it necessary or when at least three members in attendance request it, an additional item can be added to the agenda.

Article 6. Items on the agenda shall be decided on by a majority of the committee members in attendance. In the case of a tied vote, the decision of the Chairman shall prevail.

Article 7. Confidentiality shall be maintained regarding discussions at committee meetings.

[20] "*Yokinbu Shikin Unyō Iinnkai (Dai Ikkai Kaigi) Gijiroku (Minutes of the 1st Meeting of the Steering Committee of the Deposit Bureau Funds)*," 1925, pp. 4–5.

Article 8. When the Chairman deems it necessary or when it has been decided at a meeting, the committee may invite relevant government officials and others who are not members of the committee to hear their explanations or opinions.

Article 9. The manager shall prepare a digest record of the proceedings of each meeting.

Article 10. Matters not clearly stated in the Rules of Order shall be decided by the Chairman.[21]

As the minutes show, several committee members asked questions about the draft Rules of Order. In other words, the Rules of Order were not accepted in their draft form without question. Tomita Yūtarō, director-general of the Financial Bureau of the Ministry of Finance, mainly answered questions posed by the committee members, and sometimes Hamaguchi, the committee chairman and Minister of Finance, replied. This indicated that while the Minister of Finance acted as the committee chairman, those who had explanatory abilities were officials of the Financial Bureau in charge of actual administrative aspects of the committee.

The draft Rules of Order, first of all, stated that the holding of a committee meeting shall be decided by the Ministry of Finance, or the organizer of the committee, showing that the holding of a meeting every other month, which later became a near-custom of the committee, was not explicitly stated in the Rules of Order. The Ministry of Finance was also in a position to set an agenda, which was then to be presented to committee members. For that reason, members, who were not incumbent bureaucrats at the time, but former bureaucrats or incumbent executives of various financial institutions, posed questions and voiced opinions about the way an agenda was to be proposed as well as about the adjustment of the schedule.

Kajiwara Nakaji, president of Nihon Kangyō Bank, asked whether "a committee member can request the convening of a meeting" in a bid to clarify whether a member had the right to call a meeting. In response, the Financial Bureau Director-General said that "when a committee member has such request and puts forward that request to the manager, the Chairman will make a decision accordingly." This meant that while a member did not have the right to convene a meeting, he could still propose that a meeting be held.

With respect to a proposal for an item on the agenda, Shimura Gentarō, President of the National Federation of Industrial Cooperatives, asked "whether a member can request the addition of an extra item to the agenda even when he is not present at a committee meeting." An official of the Financial Bureau replied that there should be no problem in making such requests. Thus, the bureau indicated that a member's proposal for an item on the agenda would be accepted regardless of a member's presence at or absence from a committee meeting.

Committee member Sakatani Yoshirō, a former Ministry of Finance bureaucrat, asked "whether a member can propose a management plan." The Financial Bureau avoided a direct reply, and said that "Article 6 of the Rules for the Management of Deposit Bureau Funds gives the committee the right to make a proposal… this provision derives from the spirit of allowing members to add their proposals to

---

[21] "*Yokinbu Shikin Unyō Iinnkai (Dai Ikkai Kaigi) Gijiroku (Minutes of the 1st Meeting of the Steering Committee of the Deposit Bureau Funds)*," pp. 6–7.

the agenda." In effect, the bureau's reply meant that a committee member could not be directly involved in the design of a management plan for Deposit Bureau funds.[22] While member Sakatani did not oppose or object to the bureau's reply, he complained about the adjustment of the committee meeting schedule, saying that "I think the notification of the date of a meeting two days beforehand is too short. As it is a meeting to be held just once a year, I would like, at a minimum, to receive meeting notifications a little longer before the meeting is to be held."

With respect to this issue, members from inside the government but outside the Ministry of Finance, and Vice Minister of Communications Kuwayama Tetsuo voiced views similar to those of members from outside the government on a greater period of notice before the convening of meetings. At this point of time, it became known that committee members appointed from outside the Ministry of Finance, regardless of whether they were from inside or outside the government, did not know how many times a year the steering committee was scheduled to meet. In response to such complaints, the organizer of the steering committee, i.e. the Financial Bureau, changed the draft Rules of Order to lengthen the period from the notification for a meeting to the actual date of holding a meeting from two days to five days.

During the questions and answers above, the Financial Bureau admitted for the first time that the steering committee was due to meet several times a year by saying that "this committee is set to meet several times a year, as necessary, and we expect the committee may need to meet more frequently in the near future." This shows that the Ministry of Finance, in particular the Financial Bureau that actually managed the Deposit Bureau funds in effect had the power to decide on the convening of committee meetings. However, the Financial Bureau, at the first committee meeting, also displayed some flexibility in adjusting according to the expressed opinions of members appointed from outside the government.

After the exchange of views above, the committee took a vote and adopted the Rules of Order without making further amendments. Through these exchanges, it became clear to committee members that they were not provided with important powers to call a meeting or devise a management plan for Deposit Bureau funds.

[22] Sakatani Yoshirō (1863–1941), a member of the House of Peers had already called for the reform of the Deposit Bureau at a meeting of the Budget Committee of the House of Peers in 1923. His career was as follows:

He joined the Ministry of Finance in 1884 upon graduating from the Graduate School of Political Economy, Department of Political Science and Economics, Faculty of Letters, the University of Tokyo.

1897 Director-General of the Budget Bureau, Ministry of Finance.

1903 Vice Minister of Finance.

1906–1908 Minister of Finance (in the first Cabinet of Prime Minister Saionji Kinmochi).

1912–1914 Mayor of Tokyo.

1917—Member of the House of Peers (until his death). When the system of returning the Deposit Bureau funds commenced in 1909, Sakatachi had already departed from the Ministry of Finance. Thus, it is assumed that he did not have any specific information concerning the management of the Deposit Bureau's regional funds at the time of the holding of the first meeting of the steering committee. "*Shōwa Zeisei Shi (History of Government Finance in the Showa Period),*" Volume 12, p. 10.

The government made it clear that Ministry of Finance officials would undertake these crucial functions single-handedly, as they had done previously. However, since it was also made known that the steering committee would meet multiple times a year, the government indicated that the steering committee would be expected to do more than convene once annually in order to approve a Deposit Bureau fund management plan and present results.

6.3.3 Disclosure of the Management Status of Deposit Bureau Funds

The third item on the agenda was the report on the current status of the management of Deposit Bureau funds. The report explained how Deposit Bureau funds had been managed up until that point and drew a large number of remarks from committee members which were met with lengthy responses from the Financial Bureau. Most of the initial explanation of the report was provided by Director-General Tomita of the Financial Bureau of the Ministry of Finance, who served as manager. He first explained that 69% of Deposit Bureau funds were derived from postal savings and further explained that management gains (from which interest and fees had to be paid) amounted to some ¥1 billion. Net profit, he reported, came to around ¥47.5 million. Tomita remarked that "viewed according to purpose, regional funds accounted for the largest amount." He explained that funds classified as regional funds amounted to some ¥450 million, the largest investment destination, followed by government bonds which amounted to some ¥310 million.

As previously noted, the minutes of the Steering Committee of the Deposit Bureau Funds were not disclosed. In principle, they were treated as "confidential", however, the contents of the report presented at the first committee meeting were published in detail, including specific figures, in newspapers the following day. An article in the "Tokyo Asahi Shimbun" dated May 6, 1925, read as follows:

The Secret Door Opened to Show Improvement in the Deposit Bureau: Tough Questions Asked—The 1st Steering Committee Meeting Held Yesterday

The Deposit Bureau of the Ministry of Finance, seen as a hotbed of corruption by the general public as the fund management was hitherto left entirely to the discretion of the Minister of Finance, has been reorganized. The Steering Committee of the Deposit Bureau Funds, empowered to open up the secret window of the Deposit Bureau and promote fair and appropriate management of funds as well as to collect and consolidate funds already lent out, opened its meeting at the official residence of the Minister of Finance in Nagatachō at 3:13 p.m. on May 5. Financial Bureau Director-General Tomita distributed a report on the management status of the Deposit Bureau funds and offered detailed explanations, but committee members remained dissatisfied with Director-General Tomita's explanations alone.

Committee members asked questions about the details of loans including of ¥51.50 million to the Industrial Bank of Japan (IBJ) and IBJ debentures of ¥75.59 million; ¥20 million to three banks, the IBJ, the Bank of Chosen, and the Bank of Taiwan; Tōyō Takushoku (Tōtaku) bonds of ¥28.25 million; and loans of ¥50 million as business funds to the Bank of Chosen, as well as management of these funds by borrowers, collateral offered by borrowers, the status of collections of loans and developments related to loans to China, and so on.

As the committee membership includes many experts, one after the other much tougher questions than those posed at the 50th Diet session were raised and the discussion went into the minutest of details. Director-General Tomita replied to these questions by offering all available materials. The questioning session was temporarily cut off at around 6 p.m. and the meeting proceeded to the second item on the agenda, where Director-General Tomita presented an estimated amount of spare lending capacity for the ordinary funds of the Deposit Bureau (excluding revenue from reconstruction debentures). The committee members held wide-ranging discussions, with a draft offered by the manager as reference.

Disclosed Fund Management List

The following is a Deposit Bureau fund management list ordered by purpose at of the end of March 1925 (in thousands of yen).

Category	Amount [¥]
Government bonds	309,060
Loans to the general account and special accounts	163,450
Regional funds	451,560
Business funds	171,750
Overseas business funds	169,200
Overseas deposits	223,340
Current deposits	115,710
Other	52,300
Total	1,656,300
Government bonds	309,060
Breakdown	
Public bonds with 5% interest	130,480
…(omitted)	

Decision on Management of Ordinary Funds

The Deposit Bureau ordinary fund management plan for FY1925 (excluding revenue from reconstruction bonds) was approved as below at the Steering Committee held on May 5, 1925:

1. Newly issued public bonds	40 million yen
2. Refinancing public bonds underwritten	53 million yen
3. Ordinary low-interest loans extended	
a. Ministry of the Interior	10 million yen
b. Ministry of Agriculture and Forestry	10 million yen
4. Social project funds	10 million yen
5. Central wholesale market expenses	7.25 million yen
6. Yokohama city elementary school restoration expense	4.608 million yen
7. FY1925 Yokohama city reconstruction project expenses	4.608 million yen
8. Draught relief funds for Chōsen Sōtoku-fu (Governor-General of Korea)	1.877 million yen

Short-Term Management of Funds

When spare funds within Deposit Bureau funds are available, the Minister of Finance may manage the funds according to the following methods without consulting the steering committee. In such a case, however, the Minister of Finance shall report it at the next steering committee meeting.

1. Underwriting and purchases of Japanese bonds mature within one year,
2. Loans to the general account or special accounts within one year or redeemable at any time, and
3. Overseas designated deposits within one year or subscriptions for or purchases of treasury securities redeemable within 1 year.[23]

As seen above, though the minutes of the Steering Committee of the Deposit Bureau Funds meetings were undisclosed, the mass media was able to report almost instantly surprisingly detailed information and data on the status of the funds' management. Following the adoption of the special account for the management of Deposit Bureau funds, the government is believed to have already accepted that information on fund management would be disclosed, not only to the Diet but also to news media. Nevertheless, the route by which this information was disclosed remains unknown. Many of those appointed to the steering committee, had, as Diet members, previously pursued the Deposit Bureau issue in the Diet. Therefore, it is possible that they provided information to news media. Whatever the case, it is evident that the route for reporting on the activities of the Steering Committee of the Deposit Bureau Funds to the general public was already in place from the committee's first meeting. Yet, not all of the content of the committee's discussions were reported by news media. Besides management policy and numerical data on bad debt, there was little coverage of the important discussions on the subsequent management of Deposit Bureau funds, which concerned items from the latter half of the third item on the agenda onward. For example, after the report on numerical data, the Financial Bureau

[23] "The Secret Door Opened to Show Improvement in the Deposit Bureau: Harsh Questions Asked The 1st Steering Committee Meeting Held Yesterday," *The Tokyo Asahi Shimbun*, May 6, 1925.

self-reported the existence of lending methods that fell short of the management rules set out in Article 1 of the Rules for the Management of the Deposit Bureau Funds.

> ...if we cite the difference in the scope of management between the above new rules and the conventional practices, first of all, there have been loans to local governments previously. For instance, we financed them through temporary loans until they issued municipal bonds. In the future, however, all financing to them must follow the form of bond issuance. Secondly, we previously financed special banks through loans, but going forward, we are absolutely prohibited from providing loans to banks that issue debentures. Thirdly, previously we were allowed to place designated deposits with banks in Japan, but we certainly will not be allowed to do the same going forward.[24]

In other words, while the Deposit Bureau was previously allowed to provide temporary funds to local governments, Nihon Kangyō Bank and other special banks, in addition to provisions in the form of bonds, these financing methods became impossible following the newly developed legal system after the reform. There appeared to have been recipients of these funds who were considered to have received funds through "management methods incompatible with the rules in Article 1 of the Rules for the Management of the Deposit Bureau Funds" as of 1925. The main recipients of such financing included Tokyo City and Yokohama City, which received earthquake-related loans; IBJ, which received funds for the relief of earthquake-hit industries; IBJ, Bank of Chosen and Bank of Taiwan, which received funds for loans to Chinese Bank of Communications; IBJ (in the form of designated deposits) for financing Taiwan Power Co.; IBJ (in the form of designated deposits) for "the relief of financial difficulties due to delinquent payments on interest on loans to China by the three banks"; and Yokohama Kōshin Bank (in the form of designated deposits) for the relief of the 74th (Shichijūshi) Bank. These funds can be broadly divided into three categories: funds related to natural disaster relief, investment in China and Japan's colonial territories, and funds related to the relief of private enterprises hit by the economic depression. Most of them were loans that turned sour, as described later.

After listening to these explanations, the former President of IBJ, Tetsujirō Shidachi, asked whether "there are some standards by which to distinguish methods of fund management for fund type. For example, funds from postal savings are to be used to finance such and such directions... [etc.]." In response, the Financial Bureau said that "we previously did not distinguish management methods by fund type. But as revenues from reconstruction savings debentures, for which we have been inviting subscriptions since last year, are to be subject to special accounting, they must be used for the two purposes of promoting regional industries and reconstruction in areas affected by earthquakes. The management of other types of funds will be set depending on each particular case, as appropriate".[25]

Deposit Bureau funds were essentially unrestricted in the terms and conditions of loans by funding source. Thus, in response to a question from a committee member

---

[24] "*Yokinbu Shikin Unyō Iinnkai (Dai Ikkai Kaigi) Gijiroku (Minutes of the 1st Meeting of the Steering Committee of the Deposit Bureau Funds),*" p. 22.

[25] "*Yokinbu Shikin Unyō Iinnkai (Dai Ikkai Kaigi) Gijiroku (Minutes of the 1st Meeting of the Steering Committee of the Deposit Bureau Funds),*" p. 23.

from outside the government, the lack of restrictions on a variety of fund uses, including government bonds, regional funds, politically-motivated overseas investment, and the relief of companies was reconfirmed. An awareness among Deposit Bureau officials for the necessity of safe fund management and that the return of funds to the regions should be upheld was also firmly established. These were the factors that had given rise to overseas investment during World War I, and the problem of unrecoverable loans for relief from earthquake disasters and the economic crisis, and social distrust, and were the main reason for the establishment of the steering committee that carried out the reform of the Deposit Bureau.

Committee member Shidachi, former Nihon Kangyō Bank President, who raised the question about the presence or absence of loan terms and conditions depending on type of funding source, continued to seek "an explanation of whether assets under management include loans on which interest payments are in arrears," a question that dived straight into the problem of nonperforming loans. In response to this question, the Financial Bureau replied that "of deposits and other assets under management, needless to say, there are no interest arrears on government bonds and local government bonds," but added that "with respect to business funds and overseas business funds as well, banking corporations acting as intermediaries, regardless of interest payments or non-payments from fund recipients, are legally responsible for payments. Some are experiencing considerable difficulty in interest payments, but up to today, as they have fulfilled their responsibility, interest arrears have not occurred." There was, however, one exception: a loan of ¥20 million to China's Bank of Communications made out of overseas business funds. "The bank paid interest until the year before last… [however] negotiations with the bank face difficulties, and interest payments remain in arrears." In other words, the Financial Bureau admitted that there were problems with overseas investment, though management was trouble-free with respect to government bonds and regional funds.

Committee member Shidachi, based on the above-reported data, asked a further question concerning "whether interest on several types of claims on the Republic of China is being paid without interruption." The Financial Bureau's reply to this question was that "payments of both principal and interest are not coming in as scheduled. But we can still say that interest is barely coming in as a surplus of salt tax is taken as collateral. The principal tends to become delinquent".[26] Officials of the Deposit Bureau were aware that repayments of some overseas investments, even if they were made to a foreign government, were at risk.

In the explanation offered, the Financial Bureau said that loans by the Deposit Bureau were made through special banks and these banks, acting as intermediaries instead of loan recipients, had responsibility for their repayments. At the same time, however, it said that "while the Industrial Bank of Japan is legally responsible for loans to Nichiro Jitsugyō Kaisha (Rosso-Japanese Industry inc.), Kokusai Kisen Kaisha (International Shipping inc.), Bank of Chosen (Korea) and some other companies, the measures that should be taken in the future involve very difficult problems

[26] "*Yokinbu Shikin Unyō Iinnkai (Dai Ikkai Kaigi) Gijiroku (Minutes of the 1st Meeting of the Steering Committee of the Deposit Bureau Funds)*," p. 24.

and we have yet to decide on solutions. With regards to the financial planning of the Deposit Bureau, it would be safe to assume that the principal will not be repaid on them until appropriate final solutions have been worked out." From this it was clear that the Deposit Bureau held no intention to hold the bank responsible for loans to some companies and verged on acknowledging that they would not be repaid to the Deposit Bureau.[27]

Most of these unrecoverable funds were in the categories of "overseas business funds" and "business funds." These were the categories that the mass media often took up and came under public scrutiny at the time. Katō Masanosuke, a member of the House of Representatives and former journalist, noted that "investments of Trust Bureau funds in business areas appear to be attracting public concern" and asked "whether the use of Trust Bureau funds as business funds has been a long-held bureau practice." The point of his question was to establish whether such fund management policy had existed for many years as an established practice of the Deposit Bureau's management.

The Financial Bureau replied that "as you noted, business funds and overseas business funds have drawn public attention as problematic bureau fund management. The lending of these funds goes back many years. Domestically, old loans included rather long-standing ones provided to the Industrial Bank of Japan as funds for disposing of the Hasami gold mine in Nagasaki Prefecture and the Washinosu copper mine in Iwate Prefecture. As we recall it right, the longest-standing overseas loan was the one extended to Hanyeping Company. Many other funds are relief-related, and these were mainly provided after the European war".[28] The category of "business funds" was not necessarily related to highly politically motivated loans and were mostly customary, preceding World War I and indicating the Financial Bureau's unspoken position that these business funds were initially without risk. This issue was not further pursued, at least directly, by committee members, but a question about unrecoverable overseas investments was raised by a committee member from within the government, namely, Commissioner of the Board of Audit Kanano Hideo.

---

[27] "*Yokinbu Shikin Unyō Iinnkai (Dai Ikkai Kaigi) Gijiroku (Minutes of the 1st Meeting of the Steering Committee of the Deposit Bureau Funds)*," p. 27.

[28] "*Yokinbu Shikin Unyō Iinnkai (Dai Ikkai Kaigi) Gijiroku (Minutes of the 1st Meeting of the Steering Committee of the Deposit Bureau Funds)*," p. 28. Business funds were provided to the Hasami and Washinosu mines through the IBJ in 1905. While business operations of the mines deteriorated subsequently, the loans to them with the Deposit Bureau funds themselves had been fully repaid by 1921 after extending the repayment deadline through refinancing ("*Ōkurasho Yokinbu Shi [History of the Deposit Bureau of the Ministry of Finance)],*" p. 182). With respect to overseas business funds, the lending to Hanyeping Company of Deposit Bureau funds, through Industrial Bank of Japan, began in 1907. The real beginning of overseas business funds provided by the Deposit Bureau is believed to have been the underwriting with the Deposit Bureau funds of railway bonds issued by Gyeongbu Railway Company, which operated railways connecting between Seoul and Busan in Korea in 1904. With respect to Chinese Hanyeping Company, prior to the investment of the Deposit Bureau funds in the company, a duo of Yokohama Specie Bank and Industrial Bank of Japan provided financial assistance to the company from 1903, and this was perhaps the perception of the Financial Bureau at the time of the meeting. ("*Ōkurashō Yokinbu Shi [History of the Deposit Bureau of the Ministry of Finance],*" pp. 193, 195).

He asked, "Of the overseas business funds, which of the business funds provided to the Republic of China covers the so-called Nishihara Shakkan (Loans)? Furthermore, what are the objectives and destinations of funds for loans to China? The Deposit Bureau document refers to them only abstractly." This question suggests that even the Board of Audit within the government had no more information than what was reported by the news media about the management of Deposit Bureau funds. To this question, the Financial Bureau replied as follows:

> Of the so-called Nishihara Loans, the investment made by the Deposit Bureau was only ¥20 million in loans to the Bank of Communications. Other funds came from subscriptions worth ¥100 million for government-guaranteed Industrial Bank of Japan debentures and extraordinary revenue from treasury securities.
>
> Of loans made to the Industrial Bank of Japan from overseas business funds, ¥4.67 million represents the underwriting of the first Industrial Bank of Japan debenture of ¥50 million, related to the Nishihara Loans (which had matured but could not be repaid). Thus, of the total face value of ¥50 million, the third and fourth government-guaranteed Industrial Bank of Japan debentures were issued to refinance the first government-guaranteed Industrial Bank of Japan debenture, with the Deposit Bureau of the Ministry of Finance accepting the Industrial Bank of Japan debentures (to supplement the part which no one else would accept)... As this Industrial Bank of Japan debenture was to be issued as a foreign bond... there was a condition attached to the debenture issuance to the effect that it should be sold on overseas markets on the responsibility of the Industrial Bank of Japan... Due to unfavorable market conditions overseas, however, the bank has been unable to make good on this condition.[29]

The Financial Bureau insisted that not too much blame should be placed on the Deposit Bureau for the politically-motivated loans to China, or what were known as the "Nishihara Loans," because the Deposit Bureau's investment stood at "only ¥20 million" and the Industrial Bank of Japan was mainly responsible for the loans. But the bureau acknowledged that the loans were at risk by saying that with respect to the performance of obligations by the Industrial Bank of Japan itself, "due to unfavorable market conditions overseas, the bank has been unable to make implementation." It can be seen that the staff of the Financial Bureau involved in the management of Deposit Bureau funds had a very firm grip on who the ultimate fund recipients were, the amount lent and status of repayments by fund recipients. This was true even when the method of lending did not place the Deposit Bureau into a direct crisis, such as indirect lending via special banks. Yet, the Financial Bureau made no definite remarks which directly admitted that some Deposit Bureau funds were in default.

Following the above explanations, committee member Yamamoto Teijirō, a member of the House of Representatives and former head of the appraisement division at Nihon Kangyō Bank, said that "when I glance through the business funds and overseas business funds, I see a large number of funds that are considered to have repayment difficulties. Some of the funds took the form of underwriting debentures of special banks. If the business operations of borrower companies turn stagnant, they find it difficult to repay the borrowed funds and then, I think, special banks will not be able to perform their obligations. What are you going to do if that happens?"

[29] "*Yokinbu Shikin Unyō Iinnkai (Dai Ikkai Kaigi) Gijiroku (Minutes of the 1st Meeting of the Steering Committee of the Deposit Bureau Funds)*," pp. 36–37.

The Financial Bureau refrained from using the definite term "irredeemable", but it is clear that committee members briefed on the situation took the bureau's explanations as indicating that it was considering the possibility of default.

The reply to Yamamoto's question came not from the Financial Bureau but from Minister of Finance Hamaguchi Osachi, the steering committee's chairman, who had not offered any explanations in the committee's session up to that point. Neither had Hamaguchi been engaged in the management of Deposit Bureau funds up to that point, but he was the very person who spearheaded the reform of the Deposit Bureau. He remarked as follows:

> Honorable committee member Yamamoto's concern is quite understandable. While banks have direct responsibility for the Deposit Bureau in terms of the form of loans taken, I think there could be cases where the Deposit Bureau cannot assert its rights as a matter of fact by sticking to ostensible legal relationships. For example, with respect to loans to Kokusai Kisen, an operator of steamships, which has already emerged as a problematic issue, we may not be able to have intermediary banks perform their obligations as contracted. The Ministry of Finance is currently considering remedial measures on this. Gradually I expect other problematic loans with possibly similar results to come to light. In such cases, as soon as problems occur, we intend to refer them to the steering committee and seek its recommendations depending on contemplated solutions.[30]

The Financial Bureau, the party directly involved in the management of Deposit Bureau funds, offered no explanation that went beyond the institutional principles that the bureau is not to blame for any mismanagement because intermediary special banks would be held responsible for borrowing conditions. However, committee members appointed from outside the Financial Bureau pointed out that even if intermediary banks were responsible for loan repayments, as a practical matter, the fact remained that repayments to the Deposit Bureau were at risk. In the face of such critical views, the Minister of Finance, who was in a position to supervise the Financial Bureau's guiding principles, finally acknowledged the crisis situation.

The Ministry of Finance at last came to admit to committee members appointed from outside the government that "I think there might be cases where the Deposit Bureau cannot, as a matter of fact, assert its rights by sticking to ostensible legal relationships" and "we may not be able to have intermediary banks perform their obligations as contracted," not by explanations by officials in charge of practical work but by remarks from the Minister of Finance supervising them.

As the Minister of Finance stated that "the Ministry of Finance is currently considering remedial measures," it appears that the Financial Bureau recognized that problem loans had to be disposed of prior to the holding of the first steering committee meeting. At the closed-door committee meeting in the presence of committee members appointed from outside the government, however, the Ministry of Finance formally and once again acknowledged the existence of nonperforming loans, paving the way for initiating the process of their disposal. While the Ministry of Finance maintained its stance that the ministry would study ways of disposing of these nonperforming loans, Minister of Finance Hamaguchi also solicited opinions

---

[30] "*Yokinbu Shikin Unyō Iinnkai (Dai Ikkai Kaigi) Gijiroku (Minutes of the 1st Meeting of the Steering Committee of the Deposit Bureau Funds)*," pp. 37–38.

from steering committee members by stating that "Gradually, I expect other problematic loans with possibly similar results to come to light. In such cases, as soon as problems occur, we intend to refer them to the steering committee and seek its recommendations depending on contemplated solutions." This indicates that with respect to the resolution of bad debt, the Minister of Finance attempted to at least solicit opinions and plans broadly from financial experts in and outside the government instead of leaving the matter entirely to the Financial Bureau. Indeed, the "advisory" function of the Steering Committee of the Deposit Bureau Funds was also believed to include the soliciting of opinions from outside professional financial circles.

The report on the current status of the management of Deposit Bureau funds, the third item on the steering committee's agenda, was simply a report and as such it did not involve a particular vote on anything. However, during the discussions on the report, the Steering Committee of the Deposit Bureau Funds attained the unprecedented achievement of having the committee prompt the Ministry of Finance to formally acknowledge the existence of bad debt within Deposit Bureau funds, and initiate the process of its resolution.

News reports already assumed the existence of bad debt in Deposit Bureau funds, though the specific details were not known. Deposit Bureau officials on the other hand, had a grip on the data, but did not recognize nonperforming loans. Considering that data showed the high possibility that some loans made from Deposit Bureau funds would become bad debt, the actual discussions at the steering committee set in motion the process by which Financial Bureau officials came to recognize the bad debt after non-government members indicated its existence and the Minister of Finance made remarks that effectively recognized it. There was a gap in the general public's awareness of the management of the Deposit Bureau funds and its actual management, as indicated by news reports and the Financial Bureau's recognition of the situation ascertained at the Steering Committee of the Deposit Bureau Funds. But the holding of the meeting of the Steering Committee of the Deposit Bureau Funds of the Ministry of Finance worked to narrow this gap considerably. As seen in the news reports cited above, however, the process of the Ministry of Finance's self-acknowledgment of the bad debt was not publicly disclosed.

6.3.4 The Actual Authority of the Steering Committee Over the Management of the Deposit Bureau Funds

Having pressed the Ministry of Finance to take definite steps toward the resolution of the bad debt problem, the steering committee took up the fourth item on the agenda: "Report on the spare capacity for management of ordinary funds of the Deposit Bureau in FY1925." This was not a report on past fund management, rather a report on new management plans as of 1925. This report saw opinions voiced by both committee members appointed from outside the government and non-Ministry of Finance committee members from within the government. The remarks by Vice Minister of Communications Kuwayama Tetsuo indicated that the Ministry of Communications, which was not previously in a position to comment on the management of Deposit Bureau funds, was concerned about and interested in the management situation:

> As Vice Minister of Communications, I would like to say a word or two on postal savings … Postal savings have incurred a net decline… We deeply regret this outcome after the Ministry of Communications has made every possible effort to increase postal savings. Looking at the recent trends in postal savings, we do not see any sign of an upturn. Needless to say, this stems partly from the general business slump, but it cannot be denied that another serious cause of the net drop in postal savings has been an overall increase in other savings vehicles, including postal life insurance, the development of credit cooperatives, and reconstruction savings debenture subscriptions. Thus… the Financial Bureau appears to be withholding reserve funds of around ¥40 million in its funding plan, but that amount of reserve funds may prove insufficient.[31]

The former head of the appraisement division at Nihon Kangyō Bank and a member of the House of Representatives, Yamamoto Teijirō, asked a question about the method of supplying regional funds. When he asked "what is the reason why there are so many funds whose management has been decided but which are not yet disbursed," the Financial Bureau replied that,

> With respect to social project funds and low-interest ordinary regional funds, the Ministry of the Interior and the Ministry of Agriculture and Forestry, the two related ministries, collect and coordinate requests from prefectures and send them to the Ministry of Finance. The Ministry of Finance then makes decisions by taking fund relations, etc., into consideration for the fiscal year concerned, and based on these decisions, the relevant officials in charge determine allocations to prefectural governments, which then need to follow procedures to file bond issuance applications for approval. Since these all involve complicated proceedings, the disbursement of funds tends to be delayed.[32]

This answer indicates that officials in charge of the practical work of the management of Deposit Bureau funds recognized the actual conditions of financial practices, in which procedures for the supply of regional funds by the Deposit Bureau were troublesome and required time for the actual dispersal of funds, rendering the prompt injection of funds difficult.

After the question-and-answer session and the report on the spare capacity for management of the ordinary funds of the Deposit Bureau in FY1925, the committee discussions went on to the next item on the agenda. Items No. 5 and No. 6 required committee members to vote on two proposals. Proposal No. 1 was the "Management plan for the ordinary funds of the Deposit Bureau for FY1925," and proposal No. 2 was the "Matter concerning short-term management of Deposit Bureau funds." Directly following the establishment of the steering committee, the Ministry of Finance assumed it could secure the endorsement of committee members of the

[31] "*Yokinbu Shikin Unyō Iinnkai (Dai Ikkai Kaigi) Gijiroku (Minutes of the 1st Meeting of the Steering Committee of the Deposit Bureau Funds),*" pp. 56–57.

[32] "*Yokinbu Shikin Unyō Iinnkai (Dai Ikkai Kaigi) Gijiroku (Minutes of the 1st Meeting of the Steering Committee of the Deposit Bureau Funds),*" p. 57.

draft fund management plan prepared by the Financial Bureau following its disclosure at the committee meeting, and this process was incorporated into the stage of preparation of the committee agenda. The Financial Bureau attempted to have committee members from outside the government involved in a final confirmation of the management plan after carrying everything solely on its shoulders from the determination of the schedule of committee meetings and the preparation of the agenda to the actual development of the management plan. This process indicates that the Financial Bureau added the function of auditing the management plan to the committee's "advisory" function in a bid to attach value to it.

In the end, these two proposals were carried in their original form, i.e. as prepared by the Financial Bureau, after a committee member offered his opinion about an increase in regional funds. A Ministry of Finance official replied that "though the ministry hopes to increase the amount lent to the regions as a basic policy, the present funding condition of the Deposit Bureau did not allow the bureau to increase regional funds over and above the original management plan." In the end, the management plan was adopted in its original form. But the vote came right after the disclosure of the management plan draft, and some discussions were held before taking the vote.

Minister of Finance Hamaguchi expressed his hope for a speedy settlement by saying that "it would be convenient if, as far as possible, the committee would complete discussions on all items on the agenda today." This statement invited criticism even from committee members appointed from within the government. Vice Minister of Agriculture and Forestry Abe Hisanori complained that "I received the agenda only last night and did not have enough time to form an opinion on it," and on this basis said "I would like to see the vote postponed." Clearly notification of the holding of the committee and its agenda were conducted in a very hurried manner, and information about the Deposit Bureau was not fully shared among members, even those within the government.

With respect to the draft management plan, committee members Yamamoto, former head of the appraisement division at Nihon Kangyō Bank, and Shimura, President of the National Federation of Industrial Cooperatives, the two people believed to have deep understanding of the conditions of regional economies, voiced opinions calling for an expansion of regional funds. But the Financial Bureau explained that an increase in the supply of regional funds was impossible as the Deposit Bureau was currently finding it difficult to lend out additional funds in the face of the decline in postal savings at the time and also because the Bank of Japan and postal life insurance could not afford to provide additional funds, ruling out further discussions on the matter.

As a compromise, the discussions on the matter came to a settlement after obtaining the committee chairman's commitment on the FY1925 management plan and the previous fiscal year's lending plan would be implemented as early as possible—the actual disbursement of funds had been delayed. After the Minister of Finance assured committee members that "the Deposit Bureau will promote the lending of regional funds to the greatest possible degree," the affirmative vote was taken on the first proposal on the agenda.[33] With this, the first meeting of the Steering Committee of the Deposit Bureau Funds came to an end with almost all items on the agenda "adopted in their original form."

The Deposit Bureau had hoped to use the Steering Committee of the Deposit Bureau Funds as a venue for collecting the opinions of committee members on agenda items presented by the Ministry of Finance and for information sharing. The bureau did not, however, anticipate the strong dissenting views that committee members expressed. The anticipated speedy approval of all agenda items by the committee was not exactly forthcoming and the amount and tone of discussion, it is believed, was a surprise to the Financial Bureau and the Minister of Finance, both of whom expected a committee meeting that would pass without requiring any major alteration in the management plan for Deposit Bureau funds as prepared by the Financial Bureau.

The minutes of the first meeting of the steering committee show that a total of 109 separate remarks were made by various speakers. Excluding the remarks by Tomita from the Financial Bureau, who served as the manager, and those by Minister of Finance Hamaguchi, the committee's chairman, the number of remarks by committee members chosen from outside the Deposit Bureau of the Ministry of Finance came to 57. The number of remarks by Tomita and Hamaguchi was particularly high as Tomita offered explanations on almost all agenda items and Hamaguchi made the opening speech. The breakdown of speakers excluding Tomita and Hamaguchi is shown in Fig. 6.1 which indicates that the opinions of members from a variety of positions were voiced at the steering committee. Still, there were a few committee members in attendance who made no remarks not all.

Looking only at the final results of the first meeting of the advisory committee, it appears that all agenda were accepted, including the rules of order and the management plan prepared by the Ministry of Finance, an outcome that was presumably both anticipated and convenient for the ministry and the Financial Bureau. Yet, the minutes examined above paint a different picture. They show that the meeting also brought about some changes to the Deposit Bureau, changes that could not have occurred if the situation had been addressed internally alone. This included the ministry's self-acknowledgement of nonperforming loans within the Deposit Bureau and the ministry's pledge to work hard for the prompt supply of regional funds. In a way the steering committee, as an advisory body, had come to function as an organization similar to an external auditor of a private sector financial institution.

33 "*Yokinbu Shikin Unyō Iinnkai (Dai Ikkai Kaigi) Gijiroku (Minutes of the 1st Meeting of the Steering Committee of the Deposit Bureau Funds)*," p. 76.

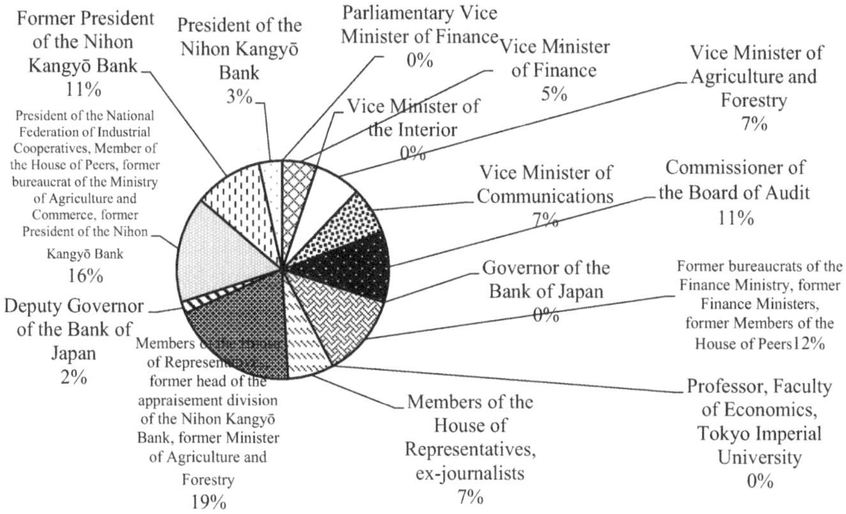

Fig. 6.1 Breakdown of the number of remarks made at the 1st meeting of the steering committee of the deposit bureau funds of the ministry of finance (excluding remarks by the chairman and the manager). *Source* Deposit Bureau, Ministry of Finance, "*Yokinbu Shikin Unyō Iinnkai (Dai Ikkai Kaigi) Gijiroku (Minutes of the 1st Meeting of the Steering Committee of the Deposit Bureau Funds)*," 1925

6.4 Summary

The aggregation of individuals' small-amount savings as postal savings had grown to such an extent that it all but matched state finances before the interwar period. Despite this growth, the entity charged with managing these funds remained just a single bureau of the Ministry of Finance. In the interwar period, overseas investments made mainly during World War I and relief lending to some private-sector companies in response to the postwar depression turned into bad debt. Amid a prolonged economic slump this situation invited public criticism of what was seen as the arbitrary management of Deposit Bureau funds. The reform of the Deposit Bureau was carried out as a response, with the belief that the management of the mass popular funds that were postal savings should be returned to the regions and conducted safely with a high degree of transparency.

Having said that, the emphasis on safe management and the idea of returning funds to the regions were already embedded in the management policy of the Deposit Bureau funds before the reform. The Deposit Bureau reform carried out in 1925, therefore, did not represent a change in the management policy and specific management methods of Deposit Bureau funds. These were still determined by the Ministry of Finance and particularly the Financial Bureau, and the newly created steering committee was not given any important authority over management. Indeed, the fact that the Steering Committee had essentially no power to prepare or reject a management plan was made symbolically clear to committee members selected from outside the government, as indicated by the minutes of the first meeting of the steering committee. Nevertheless, a closer look at the details of the first committee meeting reveal that the voicing of opinions by committee members from both within and outside the government, or at least outside of the Ministry of Finance, led to the process whereby the ministry would recognize failures that would otherwise not have been acknowledged by the Financial Bureau alone. This included the ministry's self-acknowledgement of the existence of nonperforming loans, an important step towards devising a realistic solution for the bad debt problem. Furthermore, in the preparation of an actual bad debt resolution plan, it was possible to make use of the experience and expertise of the people gathered as committee members by providing a platform to hear their opinions.

Committee member appointments hints at the ministry's intention to maintain a balanced membership among political parties. Politics aside though, the committee assembled members who were able to specifically understand the situation in which the Deposit Bureau found itself and who had professional expertise. This included those with experience, past and present, of working at financial institutions, and former bureaucrats of relevant ministries and agencies. In addition, the fact that senior bureaucrats of ministries and agencies related to Deposit Bureau funds other than the Ministry of Finance were recruited as members suggests that the ministry had the goal of opening up and sharing the fund management issue, so far addressed only within the Ministry of Finance. In doing so, it sought to incorporate and make adjustments according to different opinions among ministries and agencies.

This addendum has focused on the reform of the Deposit Bureau from the perspectives of the management of popular funds and their effective utilization for regional economies and society. The reform of the Deposit Bureau, carried out at the end of the Taisho period, when democratic social movements began to flourish, as represented by the term "Taisho democracy," was not something that drastically altered management policy for Deposit Bureau funds already established at the beginning of the twentieth century. The focus on the safe management of funding resources and the return of funds to the regions remained, and so in this sense it can be said that the reform of the Deposit Bureau did not bring about a major change. Yet, the reform did have the effect of accelerating the flow of funds from the Deposit Bureau to the regions. Moreover, after the reform, the supply of funds from Deposit Bureau funds to ordinary private-sector companies declined, whether overseas investments or domestic relief from the economic depression. The Ministry of Finance itself noted the opinions of members of the advisory committee that in some cases opposed plans for providing relief loans to ordinary companies.[34] The existence of the steering committee probably also had the effect of decelerating new lending from the Deposit Bureau to big businesses as such lending might be construed as political and arbitrary lending.

Institutionally speaking, the Steering Committee of the Deposit Bureau Funds was just an "advisory" committee, as it did not function to propose fund management

[34] "*Shōwa Zeisei Shi (History of Government Finance in the Showa Period)*," p. 43.

plans nor did it have any authority to decide or reject the plans presented by the Ministry of Finance. Essentially, the steering committee was expected to "approve in original form" any item on the agenda presented by the Ministry of Finance. Even so, as the minutes of the first meeting of the Steering Committee indicate, the committee's "advice" or recommendations played a role in prompting related bureaus and departments within the Ministry of Finance to be open to opinions and information from outside, including from other ministries and agencies in the government.

In comparison with industrial cooperatives created by local residents in Japan's various regions, the funds accumulated in postal savings prior to the reform of the Deposit Bureau lagged behind in the return of funds to the regions, both in the rapidity of the transfer and the transparency of fund management. It can be said that the reform of the Ministry of Finance's Deposit Bureau, positively evaluated contemporaneously as well as in later years, helped the Deposit Bureau to acquire a greater "fairness" in fund management. This was a achieved through the disclosure of information to the Diet and the establishment of the advisory committee. Through this new analysis of the nature of the 1925 reform of the Deposit Bureau, this addendum has confirmed that there was no change in the fund management principles of ensuring the safety of funding resources and the return of funds to the regions. Instead these fund management principles were more clearly spelled out and emphasized anew, and a greater disclosure and openness to the public was achieved, both in the preparation of fund management plans and reporting results of fund management.

Postal savings grew massively at the beginning of the twentieth century. Following the review of the management system during the interwar period, they were managed for the benefit of regional economies and society as an aggregation of popular funds. How, after the reform, did these popular funds, and the financial network based on them, function for the maintenance and protection of the livelihoods of the poor amid the deepening economic stagnation? This question will be the theme of Part II of this book.

Part II
Share

The shop of the Kanō Industrial Cooperative, in interwar period

Chapter 7
The Expansion of Relief Finance for Predicaments: Industrial Cooperatives in the Interwar Period and the Establishment of the Central Bank for Cooperatives

7.1 Introduction

This chapter closely examines how popular funds-based financial networks were established by the interwar period and contributed to the growth of regional economies, especially in terms of their role of providing a safety net through the reallocation of funds during social and economic crises. It focuses on the development and functioning of this new financial network centered on the Deposit Bureau Fund of the Ministry of Finance (as described in Chap. 5). The Deposit Bureau Fund of the Ministry of Finance was a pool of funds, primarily drawn from postal savings, the management of which was the responsibility of the Ministry of Finance. Japan's system of postal savings, established in 1874 in the early years of Japan's modernization drive, achieved popularization at the beginning of the twentieth century and saw the total amount of funds available for investment increase.[1] These funds were popular funds collected mainly in rural rather than urban areas, and for this very reason they were managed with operational guidelines that they should be invested in such a way as to return them to the regional economies from which they were raised. Although the bulk of these funds continued to be earmarked primarily for purchases of government bonds to ensure their stability in the initial years, after

[1] Sugiura Seishi, "Taishuteki Reisai Chochiku Kikan Toshiteno Yubin Chokin no Seiritsu—Nisshin Sengo no Yubin Chokiin no Tenkai to Sono Seikaku (*The Establishment of Postal Savings as the Popular Small Savings Institution—The Development of Postal Savings after the Sino-Japanese War and Its Nature*)," *Shakai Keizai Shigaku* (*Socio-Economic History*), Volume 52, No. 4 (1986); Postal Savings Bureau, Ministry of Communications, "*Yubin Chokin Kyoku Yubin Chokin Jimu-shi Dai Ippen* (*The History of Postal Savings Administration by the Postal Savings Bureau Part I*)," 1910.

H. Tanaka, *Micro-Credit in Modern Japan*, Studies in Economic History,
https://doi.org/10.1007/978-981-97-6940-7_7

1909 the return to the regions of a portion of these funds came to be established as a permanent mechanism.[2]

As shown in Chaps. 4 and 5 of this book, by the outbreak of World War I the financial systems for popular funds in Japan had effectively taken shape with networks formed in association with operating systems of local funds. While primarily designed for emergency relief in times of disaster, the systems included the underlying objective of promoting regional economies. The Deposit Bureau functioned as a de facto lender of last resort, its funds serving as a kind of core to these financial networks because of their sheer size and given the initial retardation caused by the system.

Nevertheless, the interwar period saw a significant change in the economic situation with a slowdown in the growth of Japan's regional economies and this downturn formed the background to the development of an institutionalized system by which the Deposit Bureau Fund returned funds to rural areas. The Japanese economy in the interwar period was hit repeatedly by depressions and was characterized by "uneven development." Traditional industries and agriculture in particular performed sluggishly.[3] As such, rural regions of the countries in particular became engulfed in poor economic conditions and the changes in the management of popular funds sought to deal with these problems. How did the system for managing popular funds work under these circumstances? How did it succeed the system shaped prior to the interwar period, and how did it further develop that system? The principal task of this chapter is to shed light on these questions and examine the process by which emergency lending to cope with disasters that occurred in times of depression was conducted.

As can be seen in previous studies on measures to counter unemployment, the Deposit Bureau was active in providing relief and public works funds in the interwar period.[4] Studies on the operations of the Deposit Bureau Fund itself, which have used its statistical reports and the minutes of the Steering Committee of the Deposit Bureau Funds, have also shown how the Deposit Bureau Fund provided funds for various anti-recessionary measures in the 1920 and 1930s, though its primary investment target remained Japanese government bonds.[5] However, there are few empirical studies

[2] Fund Planning and Operation Division, Financial Bureau, Ministry of Finance, "*Okurasho Yokinbu Shi—Soso Jidai Yori Showa Juroku Nen ni Itaru* (*The History of the Deposit Bureau of the Ministry of Finance—From the Incipient Era to 1941*)," First Edition, 1941, Mimeograph, Reprint, 1964, p. 2.

[3] Nakamura Takafusa, "*Senzenki Nihon Keizai Seicho no Bunseki* (*Analysis of Japan's Economic Growth in the Prewar Period*)," Iwanami Shoten, 1971.

[4] Kase Kazutoshi, "*Senzen Nihon no Shitsugyo Taisaku—Kyusai-gata Kokyo Doboku Jigyo no Shiteki Bunseki* (*Measures to Counter Unemployment in Prewar Japan—An Historical Analysis of Relief-Oriented Public Civil Engineering Works*)," Nihon Keizai Hyouronsha, 1998.

[5] Kanazawa Fumio, "Yokin Bu Chiho Shikin to Chiho Zaisei (Ichi)—1920–1930 Nendai ni Okeru Kuni to Chiho no Zaisei Kinyu Kankei (The Deposit Bureau Local Funds and Local Public Finance (1)—Fiscal and Financial Relations between the Central Government and Local Governments in the 1920s–1930s)," *Journal of Social Science*, Volume 37, No. 3 (1985); "Yokin Bu Chiho Shikin to Chiho Zaisei (Ni) (The Deposit Bureau Local Funds and Local Public Finance (2)," *Journal of Social Science*, Volume 37, No. 6 (1986); "*Kindai Nihon Chihou Zaisei Shi Kenkyu* (*A Study on the History of Local Public Finance in Modern Japan*)," Nihon Keizai Hyouronsha, 2010.

that explore specific examples in detail or incorporate the viewpoints of the local recipients of these funds. Moreover, few studies have considered the continuity of the system of local fund provision prior to the interwar period and the development of that system.

With regards to changes in the Ministry of Finance's Deposit Bureau system in the interwar period, preceding studies first focused on the 1925 reform of the Deposit Bureau (taken up in the Addendum of Part I), especially analyzing the institutional history and ideology aspects of the reform.[6] The institutional reform, which also encompassed related legislation and the establishment of committees, was carried out in the context of increased operational opacity with the growth of overseas investment following a sharp rise in postal savings during World War I, as well as contemporary social problems caused by postwar failures in the management of some of these investments. Indeed, the misuse of the Deposit Bureau was a major problem taken up in the Diet at the time. It can be said that preceding studies on the Deposit Bureau emerged as a kind of indictment of this period.[7]

However, as examined in the Addendum, the framework for the supply of local funds by the Deposit Bureau and the basic idea of investment itself were maintained in the 1925 reform.[8] Leaving aside the large-scale utilization of Japanese government bonds to ensure the stability of investment funds, the ordinary funds and special funds that made up the framework of local funds, and the principle of the financial network in lending to local government organizations, affiliated hypothec banks and industrial cooperatives remained unaltered through the Deposit Bureau reform.[9] Rather, these financial links and organizational structures were further deepened during the interwar period through the supply of funds by the Deposit Bureau as relief in the wake of a series of depressions and natural disasters. Following on from the establishment of the Central Bank for Industrial Cooperatives in 1923 and the national spread of industrial cooperatives by the interwar period, the links between

---

[6] For example, Denda Isao, "Yubin Chokin Seido no Rekishiteki Igi—Okura Sho Yokin Bu Shikinno Keisei Katei (An Historical Analysis of the Postal Savings Bank System in Japan: The Establishment of the Deposit Bureau Fund)," *Kenkyu Kiyo* (*Research Bulletin*) (The Archival Museum, attached to the Faculty of Economics, Shiga University) No. 5, 1972; "Okura Sho Yoki Bu no Kaikaku—Seisaku Kinyu no Tenkai to Kino (Reform of the Ministry of Finance Deposit Bureau—Development and Function of Policy Finance)," *Hikone Ronso* (*Hikone Collection of Treatises*), No. 156, 1972.

[7] Yamada Kotaro, "*Okura Sho Yokin Bu Ron* (*Discussion on the Ministry of Finance Deposit Bureau*)," 1925; Nakatsumi Tomokata, "*Yokin Bu Hishi* (*The Hidden History of the Deposit Bureau*)," 1928.

[8] Savings Bureau, Ministry of Finance, "*Yokin Bu Shikin Unyo Iinkai* (*Dai Ikkai Kaigi*) *Gijiroku* [*Minutes of The Steering Committee of the Deposit Bureau Fund* (*First Meeting*)]," May 5, 1925.

[9] Saito Hitoshi, "Tokushu Ginko (Special Banks)," included in Sahei Watanabe et al., ed., "*Gendai Nihon Sangyō Hattatsu Shi 26 Kan Ginko* (*The History of Industrial Development in Modern Japan Volume 26 Banks*)," Kojunsha Publishing Department, 1966. With respect to cooperation among Industrial Cooperatives at the national level and the prefectural level, or systematization, its broad outline had been formed by the interwar period, just as with the development of the Deposit Bureau Fund system. I consider anew the formation of the network of cooperative financial institutions in the next chapter.

the financial networks of industrial cooperatives and the Deposit Bureau strengthened further through the relief loans of 1927.[10]

During economic downturns in the 1920s and the 1930s, postal savings, the funding sources of the Deposit Bureau, achieved substantial growth partly due to wider concerns about the solvency of banks. Much of the increase in funds available for investment were appropriated for purchases of Japanese government bonds, partly because of the reaffirmation of the orientation towards stability in investment funds in the process of the Deposit Bureau reform. However, as such developments at the Deposit Bureau gave rise to criticisms of the alleged siphoning off of funds from regions to the central government. The return of Deposit Bureau funds to the regions thus became a government policy partly in response to this criticism. The year 1927, which saw a severe financial crisis, proved to be the only year when the utilization rate of government bond investments of the Deposit Bureau Fund declined—the ratio had otherwise risen constantly from 1925 through to 1936.[11] This indicates that the twin ideas of stability in Deposit Bureau Fund investment and the promotion of regional economies were in a complementary relationship and that the weight of investment by the Deposit Bureau could be changed depending on economic conditions. The provision of funds in times of crisis was one of the most important functions of the Deposit Bureau Fund.

How did the system for the investment of popular funds, based on local funds of the Deposit Bureau Fund, function as economic circumstances changed during the interwar period? Through an analysis of the actual conditions of relief lending in response to widespread frost damage in Nagano Prefecture in the financial crisis year of 1927, which triggered the building of closer ties and cooperation between the Deposit Bureau system and the industrial cooperative system based on regional societies some of which were not yet even by industrial cooperatives, this chapter probes into the development and function of the system for the investment of popular funds in regional economies in the interwar period.

---

[10] Preceding studies recognize that the financial system of the Industrial Cooperative, with the Central Bank for Industrial Cooperative as its central organization, had become increasingly systematized nationally by the latter half of the 1930s and performed the function of supplying policy-based low-interest funds. Having said that, though the point of origin of the national systematization was thought to be the 1920s, there is little accumulation of studies on the process of that systematization. Ōkado Masakatsu, "*Senzen Nihon ni Okeru Keito Sangyō Kumiai Kinyū no Rekishiteki Yakuwari—Kaiso/Chiiki Kan Chosetsu/Kokusai Shōka* (*The Historical Role of System Finance of Cooperative Associations in Prewar Japan—Adjustment between Classes/Regions and Absorption of Government Bonds*)," *Economia*, Volume 57, No. 1 (May 2006).

[11] "*Okura Sho Yokin Bu Shi* (*The History of the Ministry of Finance Deposit Bureau*)," p. 317.

7.2 Supply of Relief Funds to Farm Villages During a Depression: Response to Widespread Frost Damage

7.2.1 The Damage Situation and Responses in Nagano Prefecture

Despite it being springtime, May 12, 1927, saw "horrific cold weather", with temperatures falling to around 10 °C below average for that time of year. Especially focused on Nagano Prefecture, the unusually cold weather resulted in extensive and severe frost damage. In Nagano Prefecture, temperatures below zero centigrade were recorded in many areas. The *Shinano Mainichi Shimbun* [Local newspaper in Nagano Prefecture] extensively covered this damage as an unprecedented natural disaster, reporting on the situation on a daily basis:

> Horrible frost damage throughout the prefecture this morning—30,000 *chō* [approximately 30,000 ha] of mulberry fields damaged—Sericulturists at a loss ahead of spring silkworm rearing
>
> …The damage from the late frost that hit most of the 60,000 *chō* [approximately 60,000 ha] of mulberry fields in the prefecture has been unprecedented in severity and sheer size. It is believed to be more devasting than the frost damage of 1916, with the estimated amount of damage reaching an enormous scale…The prefectural government reported the appalling condition of the prefecture's mulberry fields to the Minister of Agriculture and Forestry, Yamamoto, without a moment's delay and is considering applying for low-interest relief funds… reports reaching the Sericulture Division from branch offices of the sericultural industry regulatory agency, etc. by the morning of May 12 all cited the ruinous damage, with not a few places seeing mulberry fields for spring silkworms almost totally wiped out… The vast majority of ordinary sericulturists were planning to start the rearing of spring silkworms from around May 14–15 to May 20, and many of them are currently in the process of incubating silkworm eggs… but they now have no choice but to substantially reduce the numbers reared due to this sudden frost damage. The number of sericultural unions across the prefecture holding emergency general meetings to consider the best way to cope with the situation is not small.[12]

A large number of sericulture farmers were faced with a critical situation as their mulberry trees withered at their roots and failed to regenerate despite the approaching spring silkworm rearing season.[13] The *Shinano Mainichi Shimbun* reported that "There is no way cocooneries or sericulture farmers can be saved, as after fertilizing and planting mulberry trees, they had to bury the silkworm eggs they had bought with cash."[14] This stark assessment stemmed from the fact that sericulture, even at that time, was an industry that required those engaged in it to maintain a considerable

---

[12] "*The Shinano Mainichi Shimbun*," front page of the evening edition of May 13, 1927.

[13] "Re-germination Not in Good Shape," "*The Shinano Mainichi Shimbun*," May 20, 1927. "Survey on the Major Frost Damage by County and City—The Total Damage Amounting to 1,219,000 Yen," "*The Shinano Mainichi Shimbun*," May 21, 1927.

[14] "A Sad Tale of Frost Damage—Buddhist Monks Asked to Bury Silkworm Eggs—Mashimamura Hondo Kumiai Console Each Other by Drinking Sake to Mourn the Silkworm Eggs," "*The Shinano Mainichi Shimbun*," May 18, 1927.

amount of revolving funds. This meant that a large number of sericultural farmers required financial assistance.

At that moment, however, ordinary financial institutions were under a moratorium in the wake of the 1927 financial crisis. Moreover, in the regions, only upper-class farmers were able to borrow funds from ordinary banks.[15] Therefore, neither the Nagano prefectural government nor sericulture-related industry groups asked ordinary banks for relief loans. Instead, the Nagano prefectural government requested relief loans from the central government immediately after the frost damage occurred, citing the precedent of relief loans granted during previous instances of frost damage. Relief loans from the government in practice meant drawing from Deposit Bureau funds. The supply of such funds entailed lending rates below market interest rates, one of the main reasons the request for relief loans was made to the Deposit Bureau Fund rather than ordinary financial networks.[16]

> Request for Low-Interest Relief Funds—The Prefectural Government Rushing to Thrash Out a Concrete Plan
>
> The prefectural government is currently gauging the exact extent of the frost damage and other matters in order to receive low-interest relief funds from the central government as a remedial measure. For the frost damage in 1924, 450,000 yen in low-interest funds was provided for an estimated 1.03 million yen of damage. For last year's frost damage of 450,000 yen, low-interest funds of 100,000 yen were received. This year's frost damage is estimated at 10 million yen or 5-6 million yen. In any event, the amount of damage is enormous. Based on last year's example, it is estimated that the prefecture needs to obtain low-interest funds of at least 1.3 million yen. In addition, these funds are to be borrowed from the Deposit Bureau of the Ministry of Finance through the Agricultural and Commerce Bank, with the interest rate likely to be set at 6% or lower.[17]

Requests for loans were made not only by Nagano prefectural government but also by sericulture industry-related economic organizations, including the prefectural agricultural association, the federation of sericultural unions, the federation of silkworm egg unions, and the federation of raw silk unions. They decided on May 17 to send a delegation to the Minister of Finance and the Minister of Agriculture and Forestry in Tokyo on May 23 to make a request for the lending of low-interest funds to the tune of 5 million yen.[18] The prefectural government asked the central government for relief loans, and, in consultations with prefectural agricultural experiment stations, also considered remedial measures for affected farmland, ordering counties, cities, towns and villages to look into the damage situation and report their

---

[15] Shirai Kikuo, "*Nihon no Kinyu Kikan—Sono Seisei to Hatten (Japanese Financial Institutions—Their Formation and Development)*," Moriyama Shoten, 1939, p. 267.

[16] In 1927, the average lending rate (real estate mortgage) of ordinary banks stood at 10.4% in the first half of the year and at 10.6% in the second half, higher than the average lending rate of 8.9% by the Agricultural and Industrial Bank and 8.4% by Nihon Kangyō Bank, both secured by real estate, but still not as low as the interest rate on loans from the Deposit Bureau. Research Division, Nihon Kangyō Bank, "*Kinyu Keizai Tokei* (*Financial and Economic Statistics*)," 1939, p. 50.

[17] "*The Shinano Mainichi Shimbun*," front page of the evening edition of May 13, 1927.

[18] "A Loan of 5 Million Yen in Low-Interest Government Funds Requested," "*The Shinano Mainichi Shimbun*," May 18, 1927.

survey results.[19] The damage surveys were conducted not only on mulberry but also fruit trees, and the survey results had essentially been completed by May 16.[20]

On May 19, a "research conference on measures to cope with the frost damage" and a "conference of Nagano Prefecture sericultural operators" were held under the sponsorship of Shinano Yōgyō Hyōron Co. (also supported by Shinano Mainichi Shimbun Co.), with the participation of officials of the Sericulture Division of the Nagano Prefectural Government, Nagano prefectural agricultural experiment stations (including branches) and the sericultural inspection agency of Nagano Prefecture. Though the conferences took place in the northern part of Nagano Prefecture, officials from the southern part of the prefecture also attended, and the number of participants exceeded 1200.[21] The conferences examined ways to cope with the impact of frost damage on mulberry trees, the borrowing of treasury funds and securing of tax exemptions for affected mulberry fields. It ended with the adoption of resolutions requesting low-interest funds to the tune of 10 million yen and the postponement of the payment deadline for the prefectural house tax. On the same day, the prefectural government established its own frost damage committee, with the prefectural governor as its chairman, and began considering what countermeasures should be taken. The measures discussed by the committee included ways to provide low-interest funds, the postponement of prefectural tax payments, the implementation of civil engineering works by taking advantage of farm households' surplus labor, and the encouragement of side businesses.[22]

---

[19] Documents of the Nagano Prefectural Government, included in Agriculture and Commerce Division, "*Showa Ni Nendo Kaju Sogai Teishi Kashitsuke Kankei* (*Related to Low-Interest Loans for the Frost Damage to Fruit Trees in FY1927*)"; Assistant Engineer Hakamada of the Nagano Prefectural Government, "*No Ko Hatsu Dai Hyakugojukyu Go—Nosakubutu no Sogai Taiosaku ni Kansuru Ken* (*Issued by No Ko Agricultural Document No. 159– Concerning Countermeasures to the Frost Damage to Agricultural Produce*)," prepared on May 13, 1927 and enforced on May 14, 1927, the draft of a circular notice on the remedial measures and surveys addressed to the heads of agricultural associations of counties, cities, towns and villages; Nagano Prefectural Agricultural Experiment Station, "*Togai Chosa Hokoku no Ken* (*Concerning the Surveys and Reports on the Freezing Damage*)," addressed to the Nagano Prefectural Government, May 14, 1927; Nagano Prefectural Agricultural Experiment Station, "*Ko Dai Yonju Go* (*Ko No. 40*)," addressed to the heads of agricultural associations of cities and counties, May 16, 1927. All of documents of the Nagano Prefectural Government used in this paper are in the possession of the Nagano Prefectural Museum of History.

[20] Documents of the Nagano Prefectural Government, included in Agriculture and Commerce Division, "*Showa Ni Nendo Kaju Sogai Teishi Kashitsuke Kankei* (*Related to Low-Interest Loans for Frost Damage to Fruit Trees in FY1927*)"; Director Miyazawa, "Kaju Sogai ni Kansuru Ken Hokoku (Report on the Matter Concerning the Frost Damage to Fruit Trees)," addressed to the Minister of Agriculture and Forestry, the Minister of Finance and the Minister of Home Affairs, prepared on May 16, 1927, and enforced on May 18, 1927.

[21] "Research Conference Taking Place Today, Clamoring for Countermeasures against Frost Damage—Attendants Topping 1200 from All over Prefecture—The Full Conference Room Mulls over Remedial Measures in Earnest," "Heated Discussions at Research Conference on Frost Damage—Conference of Sericultural Operators Also Held and Adopts Resolutions and Petition," "*The Shinano Mainichi Shimbun*," May 20, 1927.

[22] "Frost Damage Committee Created with Governor as Chairman—Consideration of Remedial Measures Started," "*The Shinano Mainichi Shimbun*," May 20, 1927.

The fact that various organizations ranging from private groups to local government bodies moved so promptly indicates that the revenues of farming households in Nagano Prefecture plunged considerably. "*The Shinano Mainichi Shimbun*" reported multiple times on suicide victims due to economic losses within a period of around two weeks after the frost damage.[23] Many households complained that they would be unable to pay the prefectural house tax by the payment deadline at the end of June, and delegations from some municipal governments, agricultural associations, sericultural unions and industrial cooperatives directly called on the prefectural government to postpone the tax payment deadline as a relief measure.

> Regarding frost damage relief in Sarashina County, on May 17, the chairmen of the association of village and town mayors, the agricultural association, the federation of sericultural unions and the federation of industrial cooperatives of the county called on Manager Ushijima of the Department of the Interior of the prefectural government and petitioned for the provision of low-interest loans as relief funds and the postponement of the collection of the house tax, originally set for June 30, until September 30…
>
> …the petition claimed that farmers could not rear spring silkworms due to frost damage…and [thus] they cannot possibly be expected to pay the house tax in full. The postponement of the house tax payment is believed to be more appropriate as a relief measure than the provision of low-interest funds.

In response to the above requests, the prefectural government initially hesitated to postpone the tax payment as the prefecture's own coffers were short of funds.[24] Ultimately, however, on May 27, the prefectural government postponed the deadline for the payment of the prefectural house tax as a temporary relief measure.[25] By May 21, the prefectural agricultural association compiled a tentative report on frost damage by county and city,[26] and it was confirmed that Nagano Prefecture, ahead of other prefectures that had suffered similar frost damage, was requesting concrete relief measures.[27]

Already in Nagano Prefecture, however, there were expectations that even if funds were provided from the Deposit Bureau of the Ministry of Finance, "the timing of the provision of such funds would be in August," and there were concerns that the provision of Deposit Bureau funds at such a timing might fail to meet the demand for emergency funds from sericultural farmers who required "urgent funds".[28] Needless

[23] "*The Shinano Mainichi Shimbun*," between May 13 and June 1, 1927.

[24] "Frost Damage Prompts Request for Delay in House Tax Payment—Sarashina the First to Petition the Prefectural Government," "*The Shinano Mainichi Shimbun*," May 18, 1927.

[25] "*The Shinano Mainichi Shimbun*," May 27, 1927.

[26] "Survey on the Damage of the Major Frost by County and City—Total Amount Comes to 1,219,000 Yen," "*The Shinano Mainichi Shimbun*," May 21, 1927.

[27] "Amount of Lending Possibly 2–3 Million Yen," "*The Shinano Mainichi Shimbun*," May 21, 1927.

[28] "Shinren (Federation of Credit Cooperatives of Nagano Prefecture) Starts Lending Funds to Help Frost-Hit Areas over Exigency—With Support of the Central Bank for Industrial Cooperatives, Lending Begins Today at Per-Diem Interest of 2 Sen 1 Rin," "*The Shinano Mainichi Shimbun*," the front page, May 22, 1927. "Exigent funds" meant a variety of demands depending on the financial health of farming households, such as funds to repay operating funds (costs of fertilizers

to say, since May coincided with the beginning of the spring silkworm rearing period, many farming households had already incurred debts related to their sericulture business in order to purchase fertilizers, silkworm eggs, and other materials, and thus they were short of cash. Originally, these debts were to be paid off with proceeds from the sale of spring silkworms,[29] and these proceeds should also have been enough to cover the costs of purchasing food, in which many farmers were not self-sufficient.

Under these circumstances, on May 21, the Federation of Credit cooperatives of Nagano Prefecture, a central organization of industrial cooperatives in the prefecture, decided to lend emergency funds to members. This decision was significant for the relief of crisis-hit farming households in the prefecture.

> In response to the greater part of the widespread frost damage, the Federation of Credit Cooperatives of Nagano Prefecture (Shinren) decided with extraordinary speed to provide affiliated cooperatives with emergency relief funds specifically for purchases of fresh silkworm eggs, mulberry leaves to rear young silkworks, and for urgent additional fertilization of mulberry fields. After consultations on the morning of May 21, the federation decided to start lending emergency funds the same day. The federation also decided to borrow funds from the Central Bank for Industrial Cooperatives if loan requests turned out to be so large that the federation's own funds were not sufficient to meet demand. When Shinren's chairman, Fukai, went to Tokyo for negotiations, the Central Bank readily granted him their consent. With the funds borrowed from the Central Bank, coupled with its own funds, Shinren became able to provide extensive funds to cooperatives requesting them. The lending rate was set at 2 sen 1 rin per diem (7 bu 6 rin per year) [0.021 yen per day per 1 yen borrowed, 7.6% per year], 3 rin lower than the normal lending rate of 2 sen 4 rin per diem and 1 bu 1 rin lower than the normal lending rate of 8 bu 2 rin [8.2% per year]. It was decided that affiliated cooperatives will lend these funds to their members at the interest rate of 2 sen 4 rin or lower per diem... the lending period being May 20 to June 30, for repayment within six months....[30]

As seen above, for these relief measures, individual industrial cooperatives were able to receive support not only from the Federation of Credit Cooperatives of Nagano Prefecture but also from the Central Bank for Industrial Cooperatives. By contrast, at the time of the credit crunch of 1914 and outbreak of World War I, industrial cooperatives did not have a central national organization upon which they could rely for the provision of funds. Moreover, cooperation among industrial cooperatives within Nagano Prefecture was relatively weak at the time and their unique financial network was not yet functioning. For this reason, until the Deposit Bureau provided extensive relief lending, there was no organization that could promptly supply emergency loans. Only the relatively small funds that prefectural agricultural and industrial banks could provide were available to a wide expanse of crisis-ridden

---

and silkworm eggs, etc.) borrowed, new operating funds (costs of purchasing mulberries for raising already existing young silkworms, from areas with minimal damage in the prefecture or other prefectures), and living expenses (food, etc.), though the breakdown was not known. In Nagano Prefecture, rice-growing areas were relatively few, and it was not uncommon for farming households to purchase rice as food, depending on the area.

29 In areas with many sericulturists, peaks in borrowing by members of Industrial Cooperative came in February and March. See Chap. 4 of this book.

30 "Shinren Starts Lending Funds to Help Get Frost-Hit Areas over Exigency—With Support of the Central Bank for Industrial Cooperatives, Lending Begins Today at Per-Diem Interest of 2 Sen 1 Rin," "*The Shinano Mainichi Shimbun*," the front page of May 22, 1927.

Table 7.1 Frost damage to mulberry fields in 1927

	Total mulberry fields (*chō*)	Mulberry fields damaged (*chō*)	Mulberry fields with no cocoon harvest (*chō*)	Estimated damaged mulberry leaves (yen)	Estimated drop in cocoon harvest (yen)
Nagano	64,107.6	46,443.9	33,976.1	10,804,713	16,046,968
Total	206,552.7	70,534.3	50,679	18,239,249	27,973,207

Source Savings Bureau, Ministry of Finance, "*Yokin Bu Shikin Unyo Iinkai (Dai Jurokkai Kaigi) Gijiroku [Minutes of the Steering Committee of the Deposit Bureau Fund (16th Meeting)],*" 1927

areas in Japan's regional economies.[31] By the time of the financial crisis, however, industrial cooperatives in Nagano Prefecture had formed links among cooperatives scattered in various locations, and by having an organization that integrated their functions, they became able, to a certain extent, to procure funds that could be mobilized in times of crisis. Compared to the crisis response in 1914, the response in Nagano Prefecture in 1927, while waiting for assistance by the central government, was more cooperative and organized, and thus was larger in scale.

7.2.2 Supply of the Deposit Bureau Funds and Allocation at the Prefectural Level

As discussed above, after emergency relief measures were promptly taken within Nagano Prefecture, the Deposit Bureau of the Ministry of Finance decided at a meeting of its steering committee on July 13 to provide relief funding in response to the frost damage. It was found that the frost damage extended to eight prefectures, Fukushima, Tochigi, Gunma, Yamanashi, Nagano, Gifu, Okayama and Tokyo, with damaged mulberry fields amounting to approximately 70,000 *chō* (out of a total of 200,000 *chō*), the estimated damage to mulberry leaves standing at about 18 million yen, and an estimated decline in cocoon harvest of about 28 million yen (Table 7.1). For Nagano Prefecture, the area of affected mulberry fields amounted to 46,000 *chō* (out of a total of 64,000 *chō*), the damage to mulberry leaves amounting to around 11 million yen, and an estimated decline in cocoon harvest amounting to around 16 million yen, Nagano alone accounted for more than half the total damage of the combined total for the eight affected prefectures.[32]

[31] Tanaka Hikaru, "*Okurasho Yokinbu Shikin no Chiho Kangen Kino—1914 Nen Kinkyu Kyusai Yushi to Nagano-ken* (*The Function of Return to Regions of Funds of the Ministry of Finance Deposit Bureau—Emergency Relief Lending of 1914 and Nagano Prefecture*)," pp. 129–139. Hereafter, when this paper takes up relief lending by the Deposit Bureau in 1914, I refer to this book, unless otherwise noted.

[32] Savings Bureau, Ministry of Finance, "*Yokin Bu Shikin Unyo Iinkai* (*Dai Jurokkai Kaigi*) *Gijiroku* (*Minutes of the Steering Committee of the Deposit Bureau Fund* (*16th Meeting*))," July 13, 1927.

Table 7.2 Amounts requested and decided for low-rate funds for 1927 frost damage measures

	Amounts requested by prefectures			Amounts assessed by Ministry of Agriculture and Forestry			Amounts decided by deposit bureau
	Mulberry	Others	Total	Mulberry	Others	Total	Total
Nagano	6,150,000	350,000	6,500,000	6,150,000	350,000	6,500,000	5,300,000
Total	13,203,179	1,156,688	14,359,867	10,340,325	856,810	11,197,135	8,330,000

Unit: Yen

Source Prepared based on Savings Bureau, Ministry of Finance, "*Yokin Bu Shikin Unyo Iinkai (Dai Jurokkai Kaigi) Gijiroku [Minutes of the Steering Committee of the Deposit Bureau Fund (16th Meeting)]*"

Following the example of relief provided in previous cases of frost damage,[33] the allocation of relief funds was worked out "on the calculation of about 100 yen per *chō* for fields with no mulberry leaf harvest" at the time of the formulation by the Deposit Bureau. In addition, assuming the new project of mulberry replanting, "only 40 yen per *tan* (approximately 1000 m^2) was allocated for mulberry fields requiring replanting".[34] With respect to this, though there certainly was tremendous damage that actually required replanting, this was believed to have been designed to increase the total amount of funds to be provided. As a result of these calculations, the Ministry of Agriculture and Forestry asked the Ministry of Finance for 11.2 million yen after assessing the requests for funds by prefectures, the Deposit Bureau ultimately decided to inject 8.33 million yen as relief funds (Table 7.2).

Proposal 1 Concerning the Provision of Relief Funds for Hail and Frost Damage

For the allocation of relief funds for the hail and frost damage affecting Fukushima, Tochigi, Gunma, Tokyo, Yamanashi, Nagano, Gifu and Okayama prefectures from April through June 1927, the Deposit Bureau shall provide a total of 8.33 million yen to the Nihon Kangyō Bank, prefectural agricultural and industrial banks and the Central Bank for Industrial Cooperatives:

1. Format of fund provision: The underwriting of debentures issued by Nihon Kangyō Bank, agricultural and industrial banks and the Central Bank for Industrial Cooperatives.
2. Interest rate: The Deposit Bureau's debenture underwriting interest rate is set at 4.8% per annum, or less; the interest on lending by Nihon Kangyō Bank,

[33] In the most recent cases, the Deposit Bureau had disbursed frost damage relief funds, albeit on a relatively small scale, in 1924 and 1926. In the case of the 1924 relief lending, the steering committee did not exist as this was before the reform of the Deposit Bureau, and hence, the committee's minutes are also non-existent. The 1926 frost damage relief lending was approved at the 10th meeting of the steering committee of the Deposit Bureau Fund.

[34] Savings Bureau, Ministry of Finance, "*Yokin Bu Shikin Unyo Iinkai* (*Dai Jurokkai Kaigi*) *Gijiroku* (*Minutes of the Steering Committee of the Deposit Bureau Fund* (*16th Meeting*))," p. 16.

agricultural and industrial banks and the Central Bank for Industrial Cooperatives is set at 5.4% per annum, or less.

Repayment period: Within 5 years for funds for mulberry tree replanting, within 2 years for other funds.[35]

Compared with the relief funds of 1.2 million yen (mainly underwriting of debentures of agricultural and industrial banks) for the extensive frost damage in six prefectures, including Nagano Prefecture, in 1926, the 1927 lending was relatively large in scale.[36] The 6.5 million yen requested by Nagano prefecture was forwarded to the Ministry of Finance without any reductions as a result of the Ministry of Agriculture and Forestry's assessment, and the Ministry of Finance decided to provide 5.3 million yen against the requested amount.[37]

As for specific lending routes, as usual with the previous provision of special funds, the principal methods were through the Nihon Kangyō Bank and prefectural agricultural and industrial banks. For Nagano Prefecture, however, the possibility of a new route was opened, that is, the lending route via the Central Bank for Industrial Cooperatives. "The previous cases of lending were all for financing agricultural and industrial banks... As for Nagano Prefecture, since it is the region where industrial cooperatives were most developed in Japan," an attempt was made to set up a new route for providing funds outside the Nihon Kangyō Bank system.

The provision of Deposit Bureau funds to the Central Bank for Industrial Cooperatives first took place in 1925, when funds totaling 10 million yen had already been supplied as part of measures to cope with a financial crisis. However, this was the first time that the Central Bank for Industrial Cooperatives was used directly within a framework of special funds of the Deposit Bureau in times of natural disasters and other emergencies.[38] Why, then, was the new route via the Central Bank for Industrial Cooperatives sought, when the funding route for lending to industrial cooperatives through agricultural and industrial banks already existed? In the case of the provision of low-interest funds via agricultural and industrial banks, eligible borrowers, even

[35] Savings Bureau, Ministry of Finance, "*Yokin Bu Shikin Unyo Iinkai* (*Dai Jurokkai Kaigi*) *Gijiroku* [*Minutes of the Steering Committee of the Deposit Bureau Fund* (*16th Meeting*)]," p. 4.

[36] Savings Bureau, Ministry of Finance, "*Yokin Bu Shikin Unyo Iinkai* (*Dai Jurokkai Kaigi*) *Gijiroku* [*Minutes of the Steering Committee of the Deposit Bureau Fund* (*16th Meeting*)]," p. 11.

[37] Savings Bureau, Ministry of Finance, "*Yokin Bu Shikin Unyo Iinkai* (*Dai Jurokkai Kaigi*) *Gijiroku* [*Minutes of the Steering Committee of the Deposit Bureau Fund* (*16th Meeting*)]." The underwriting interest rate by the Deposit Bureau was 4.8%, while the lending rates by Nihon Kangyō Bank, agricultural and industrial banks and the Industrial Cooperative Central Bank for Industrial Cooperatives were set at 5.4% or less. For reference, the allocated amount of funds for other prefectures was 130,000 yen for Fukushima, 50,000 yen for Tochigi, 1,430,000 yen for Gunma, 250,000 for Tokyo, 80,000 yen for Yamanashi, 670,000 yen for Gifu, and 420,000 for Okayama.

[38] Norinchukin Bank, "*Sangyō Kumiai Chuo Kinko Shi* (*History of the Industrial Cooperative Central Bank for Industrial Cooperatives*)," 1944, p. 142; Fund Planning and Operation Division, Financial Bureau, Ministry of Finance, "*Okurasho Yokinbu Shi—Soso Jidai yori Showa Juroku-nen ni Itaru—*(*History of the Deposit Bureau of the Ministry of Finance—From the Incipient Period to 1941*)," (the 1941 first mimeographed edition and the reprinted 1964 edition), p. 414, pp. 423–432. Of the relief funds for the frost damage, 2.6 million yen went through the Industrial Cooperative Central Bank for Industrial Cooperatives.

at the time, were limited to industrial cooperatives and organizations with at least 10 members for unsecured loans or collateralized individuals. Moreover, this route earned a negative reputation for its troublesome procedures and for being particularly choosy about to whom it lent. Behind this, it is believed, was the impact of the general deterioration of financial markets across Japan during the interwar period, which made agricultural and industrial banks less-active lenders to new customers.[39] At any rate, it became difficult for low- and middle-income earners to access new funds through the Nihon Kangyō Bank and agricultural and industrial banks.

In the case of 1927, even before the decision on the provision of funds of the Deposit Bureau, an article in a newspaper in Nagano Prefecture was already discussing the potential negative effects from any funds provided through the agricultural and industrial banks route:

> Branches of industrial cooperatives in Nagano Prefecture are in action regarding the supply of relief funds for frost damage, having cooperatives in the prefecture open their doors to cooperative members to make emergency loans to them in the easiest way possible... The emergency lending is designed as providing funds to finance the purchase of mulberry leaves, fertilizer and other supplies for the time being, and industrial cooperatives are now also hastening... to file applications for relief funds with the central government as a fundamental measure. The method of lending low-interest funds provided by the government not only previously required very bothersome procedures through agricultural and industrial banks but was also actually intended only for loans to those in the middle- or higher-income classes in farming villages, with few of these funds being provided to lower-income people who were really in need of funds due to frost damage. Thus, believing that the purpose of the provision of low-interest funds was apparently mistaken, the prefecture is studying ways to provide loans to people in the lower-income bracket via the Federation of Credit Cooperatives of Nagano Prefecture or the agency of the Central Bank for Industrial Cooperatives, in an attempt to make it very easy to take out loans.[40]

There was an expectation in many regions of the rural economy that if relief loans were to be provided through the system of industrial cooperatives, then the scope of relief could be expanded to include low-income earners when compared with the route through agricultural and industrial banks. It was also thought that procedures for providing relief could be simplified through this route. These expectations were likely behind the Ministry of Finance's decision to create the new route for providing Deposit Bureau funds via the Central Bank for Industrial Cooperatives in emergencies.

In Nagano Prefecture, demand for microcredit, even among smaller farming households, had been strong since the Tokugawa period due to the development of sericulture and silk yarn-related industries in the prefecture. Because of this, the

---

[39] Ueda Kinji, "*Nihon Fudosan Kinyu Shi—Toshi Noko Ginko no Rekishiteki Igi (History of Japan's Real Estate Finance—Historical Significance of Urban Agricultural and Industrial Banks)*," Gakujutsu Shuppankai, 2011, Chaps. 4 and 5.

[40] "Greater and Faster Relief Funds for Frost Damage to Have-Nots—Lending Methods Greatly Eased—Bustling with Applications to the Government," "*The Shinano Mainichi Shimbun*," May 17, 1927.

development of industrial cooperatives was dynamic and their organizational institutionalization was ahead of other regions in Japan.[41] As such, Nagano Prefecture was thought to be the most suitable region to measure the potential of the financing function of industrial cooperatives for middle- and lower-income earners. Following the Ministry of Finance's decision, on August 4, the Agricultural Administration Bureau of the Ministry of Agriculture and Forestry and the Deposit Bureau of the Ministry of Finance sent details of lending terms and conditions to the Nagano prefectural government. Earlier, on August 2, the prefectural government decided on the allocation of Deposit Bureau funds by city, town and village.[42] The prefectural government, in "Agricultural Document No.201" dated June 29, had already determined the financing needs in the prefecture through surveys of fund applications at the of city, town and village levels.[43]

Clearly the prefectural government had compiled detailed financing demands in advance of the central government's official decision on the contribution of Deposit Bureau funds. This was not a procedure newly prescribed during the interwar period. A similar step was taken in 1914 in the case of national large-scale relief loans for producers of important export commodities. However, a document titled *"Sōgai Teiri Shikin Kashitsuke Hoho Soan (Draft of the Lending Method for Low-Interest Funds for the Frost Damage),"* apparently prepared by the Nagano prefectural government at the time of the allocation of these funds, included a method for the distribution of relief funds the prefecture had decided to provide, the content of which differed from the precedent set in the response to a crisis in the early years of the World War I period.

The Method of Allocation of Low-Interest Funds for Frost Damage

1. The planned amounts of low-interest loans shall be allocated by city, town and village units.
2. The planned amounts of low-interest loans shall be calculated as follows:
    a. Mulberry fields expected to yield no mulberry leaves shall be further assessed according to the extent of damage, 70% of the total amount of low-interest funds shall be allocated to fields actually damaged.
    b. 30% of the total amount of low-interest funds shall be allocated to cover the the deficit in spring silkworm cocoons...

---

[41] Chapter 4 of this book, Nagano Branch of the Central Association of Industrial Cooperatives, "*Nagano-ken Sangyō Kumiai Enkakushi* (*The History of Industrial Cooperatives in Nagano Prefecture*)," 1927.

[42] Documents of the Nagano Prefectural Government, included in Agriculture and Commerce Division, "*Showa Ni Nendo Kaju Sōgai Teishi Kashitsuke Kankei* (*Related to Low-Interest Loans for Frost Damage to Fruit Trees in FY1927*)"; "Lending of low-interest funds for the frost damage to fruit trees decided as in the first draft," August 2, 1927.

[43] Documents of the Nagano Prefectural Government, included in Agriculture and Commerce Division, "*Showa Ni Nendo Kaju Sōgai Teishi Kashitsuke Kankei* (*Related to Low-Interest Loans for Frost Damage to Fruit Trees in FY1927*)"; "Showa Ni Nen Sōgai Teiri Shikin Kariire An (A Plan for Borrowing Low-Interest Funds for the Frost Damage in 1927)," August 4, 1927.

3. The distinction between long-term and short-term loans from low-interest funds shall be determined by the ratio of amounts designated by the Deposit Bureau of the Ministry of Finance.
4. The distinction between funds provided by agricultural and industrial banks and those provided by credit cooperatives shall be determined under an agreement for each city, town and village (an agreement shall be worked out at a meeting among the prefectural government, agricultural and industrial banks, and the Federation of Credit Cooperatives of Nagano Prefecture).[44]

As described above, the amounts allocated to municipalities were decided by the prefectural government on the basis of reports on damage conditions. The funds allocated to municipalities by agricultural and industrial banks or industrial cooperatives were decided separately, through negotiations between agricultural and industrial banks and the Federation of Credit Cooperatives of Nagano Prefecture. In the case of the 1914 relief loans, though the damage from the credit crunch at that time almost extended across the whole prefecture, the prefectural government did not allocate relief funds to municipalities in advance.[45] This likely left some regions and organizations without any relief measures.

In the case of the 1927 relief loans, however, the amount of funds to be provided were determined from the beginning, though on the assumption that the damage extended to the entire prefecture. This indicated that by this time a mechanism was in place to supply relief funds to a wider range of recipients under uniform criteria, ensuring that the number of those left out was as small as possible. The distinction between short-term and long-term low-interest funds reflects the difference in the classification of ordinary damage restoration funds and funds for replanting, but this also shows that the prefectural government no longer gave much weight to such distinctions in project descriptions.

Since individual industrial cooperatives were local organizations, most of them having been established on the basis of municipalities or hamlets, the allocation of funds by municipality and the specification of amounts to be handled by industrial cooperatives at the same time are presumed to have meant that the decision on the amount to be provided to local industrial cooperatives was made by the Central Bank for Industrial Cooperatives. However, when the time came for farm households to actually receive funds from affiliated industrial cooperatives, as pointed out earlier, they had already been able to receive relief funds from May in Nagano Prefecture. This meant that after the decision on the provision of Deposit Bureau funds, farming households were able to make new applications to cooperatives for low-interest loans.

As outlined above, the 1927 relief lending in Nagano Prefecture consisted of an existing route for providing Deposit Bureau funds through the Nihon Kangyō Bank and agricultural and industrial banks, and a new funding route that used industrial

---

[44] Documents of the Nagano Prefectural Government, included in Agriculture and Commerce Division, "*Showa Ni Nendo Kaju Sōgai Teishi Kashitsuke Kankei* (*Related to Low-Interest Loans for Frost Damage to Fruit Trees in FY1927*)," date of preparation unknown.

[45] See Chap. 5.

cooperatives. The next section, examines how these funds were provided to individual regions and how they affected the local communities concerned.

7.3 Case Studies of the Lending Situation in Nagano Prefecture

7.3.1 Relief Lending Through Industrial Cooperatives: The Case of Kanō Village in Chiisagata County

In this section I analyze the impact industrial cooperatives had on rural areas in Nagano prefecture by examining the specific case of the industrial cooperative in Kanō Village, Chiisagata County, which, as previously discussed, had a high rate of organization across the village.[46] Kanō Village's industrial cooperative was established as early as 1903 and joined the prefectural federation upon its inception.[47] The cooperative was also commended at the national level in 1910[48] and maintained close links with the National Federation of Industrial Cooperatives. How did the existence of the industrial cooperative and its links with systemic lending affect financial conditions in the regional economy? Before addressing this question, I would like to consider the extent of damage in Chiisagata County during the 1927 crisis. The *Shinano Mainichi Shinbun* reported on it as follows:

> In Shinshū [Nagano Prefecture], hit by the unprecedented frost damage, Ueda City and neighboring Shiojiri, Kangawa, Kanō and Toyosato were fortunate to have escaped the damage. These areas suffered little damage and their mulberry fields alone continued to grow lush with green leaves amid the blackened mulberry field zones, helped by rain following the frost damage. The fact that the region of Chiisagata County, the hub of silkworm eggs, incurred no frost damage should be seen in a favorable light in that the region can provide excellent silkworm eggs for the summer and autumn silkworm egg demand, which is expected to increase in the immediate future, as well as for spring silkworm eggs.[49]

---

[46] See Chaps. 4 and 5.

[47] The Nagano branch of the National Federation of Industrial Cooperatives was established in 1906. Central Union of Agricultural Cooperatives, "*Sangyō Kumiai Chuokai Shi* (*The History of the National Federation of Industrial Cooperatives*)," 1988, p. 29. The Kanō Industrial Cooperative was one of the initial members. "*Dainippon Sangyō Kumiai Nagano Shikai Yakuin Oyobi Kaiinn Meibo* (*List of Executives and Members of the Nagano Branch of the National Federation of Industrial Cooperatives*)" (for 1906?), included in Kanō Industrial Cooperative, "*Meiji Sanjuroku Nen San Gatsu Soritsu Zatsu Shorui Tojikomi* (*Established in March 1903 The File of Miscellaneous Documents*)". Hereafter, materials prepared by the Kanō Industrial Cooperative are all in the possession of JA Shinshū Ueda Kanō Store.

[48] National Federation of Industrial Cooperatives, "*Dainiji Hyosho Sangyō Kumiai* (*The Second Commended Industrial Cooperatives*)," 1911.

[49] "We have mulberry leaves, but are afraid of flies and maggots—Silkworm egg producers in the Ueda region," "*The Shinano Mainichi Shimbun*," May 17, 1927.

As described above, immediately after the frost damage, Chiisagata County was seen to have incurred "relatively light frost damage to its mulberry fields." Nevertheless, as of May 18, the spring cocoon harvest was expected to decline 30% from the average annual harvest.[50] Because Chiisagata County was less affected by the frost damage than neighboring regions, harmful insects gathered in the region, causing concentrated pest damage.[51]

Under these circumstances, on May 21, the Chiisagata County Agricultural Association decided to "borrow as much in relief funds as possible for the frost damage".[52] The Chiisagata branch of the (Prefectural) Industrial Cooperative also moved to apply for low-interest funds.

> Industrial cooperatives in towns and villages in Chiisagata County appear likely to apply for around 300,000 yen in total for low-interest funds to cover the latest frost damage. However, as expectations to receive an allocation as requested are not warranted, the Chiisagata branch is seriously concerned about ways to apportion the funds among towns and villages...In addition, industrial cooperatives, pending the receipt of low-interest funds from the Deposit Bureau, intended to use the Federation of Credit Cooperatives of Nagano Prefecture (Shinren) as an emergency measure for the relief of members, and replace these loans with low-interest funds upon their allocation. The Shinren authorities are said to be recently making efforts on this issue.[53]

As a decision had yet to been made about providing Deposit Bureau funds to industrial cooperatives via the Central Bank for Industrial Cooperatives, it is believed that the Federation of Credit Cooperatives of Nagano Prefecture assumed that the provision of low-interest funds would come from agricultural and industrial banks. This shows that even without placing expectations on the provision of funds from the Central Bank for Industrial Cooperatives, federations of industrial cooperatives at the prefectural and county levels already functioned, to a certain extent, as a buffer which provided emergency funds to localities in times of crisis.

According to the final damage survey results prepared by the Nagano Prefectural Government, the prefectural average of the "ratio of decline in the spring silkworm cocoon harvest" was 42.5% and the "ratio of all mulberry fields for spring silkworms with no harvest" was 60%. These compared with ratios of 39 and 62%[54] in Chiisagata County. Thus, according to this assessment, the damage in Chiisagata was by no means substantially lighter than other regions in the prefecture. At the time of the 1927 crisis, Kanō Village's industrial cooperative had 753 members. As the number of households in the village stood at 710, it can be said that the cooperative had

---

[50] "Cocoon harvest forecast in Chiisagata—Likely to drop about 30%," "*The Shinano Mainichi Shimbun*," May 18, 1927.

[51] "Harmful insects concentrate in Chiisagata," "*The Shinano Mainichi Shimbun*," May 21, 1927.

[52] "General meeting of the Chiisagata County Agricultural Association," "*The Shinano Mainichi Shimbun*," May 21, 1927.

[53] "Frost relief funds to Industrial Cooperatives in Chiisagata around 300,000 yen," "*The Shinano Mainichi Shimbun*," May 21, 1927.

[54] Documents of the Nagano Prefectural Government, included in Agriculture and Commerce Division, "*Showa Ni Nendo Kaju Sogai Teishi Kashitsuke Kankei* (*Related to Low-Interest Loans for the Frost Damage to Fruit Trees in FY1927*)".

effectively realized a village-wide membership.[55] Its business report described the overall business situation in that fiscal year as follows:

> Early in the year, public sentiments were depressed amidst a period of national mourning following the passing of the Taishō Emperor, whilst commodity markets remained dull. In this business slump, silk yarn prices declined causing silk yarn producers to incur losses again which further demoralized sericultural households. Wages, fertilizer and other prices gradually declined, financial services were dormant and the business community was overcome with a bleak outlook. During March and April, urban business communities were on the verge of crisis. However, businesses in the prefecture had few transactions with the banks that were forced to suspend operations and thus they felt no acute pain from conditions in the financial market. However, after the implementation of the moratorium, as banks augmented reserves and became more cautious, there was a temporary but substantial credit crunch. Nevertheless, the Kanō Industrial Cooperative, constantly maintaining close contacts with the Central Bank for Industrial Cooperatives as well as the Federation of Credit Cooperatives of Nagano Prefecture, was able to satisfy the demand for funds necessary for industry and economic relief. Despite this, unprecedented cold weather and frost damage hit the region on May 12, blackening the bulk of mulberry fields in the prefecture. This caused the process of transferring baby silkworms to silkworm baskets at the start of rearing to plunge sharply and this saw cocoon prices fall by 20–30% on the previous year. With farm household income from spring silkworms almost halved, farmers were suddenly dispirited and the rural economy fell into severe circumstances. As a result, the collection of prefectural taxes was postponed and the central government was requested to disburse emergency funds in response to frost damage.[56]

As described above in the report, "after the implementation of the moratorium, as banks augmented reserves and became more cautious, there was a temporary but substantial credit crunch." Clearly the region did feel the impact of the wider financial crisis of 1927. The frost damage also had a strong impact. The Kanō Industrial Cooperative submitted a "table on the extent of frost damage" to the Chiisagata branch on June 3. As the business report stated, "unprecedented cold weather and frost damage hit the region on May 12", leaving many farm households with large shortfalls in income from their sericulural activities. In response "the collection of prefectural taxes was postponed and the central government was requested to disburse emergency funds" as a kind of relief measure.

Interestingly, the report also noted that "the Kanō Industrial Cooperative, constantly maintaining close contacts with the Central Bank for Industrial Cooperatives as well as the Federation of Credit cooperatives of Nagano Prefecture, was able to satisfy the demand for funds necessary for industry and economic relief." This points to the significance of the Kanō Industrial Cooperative's (and its members') links with the wider system of finance of industrial cooperatives, specifically the Federation of Credit Cooperatives at the prefectural level and the Central Bank for Industrial Cooperatives.

---

[55] Kanō Village History Editorial Committee, "*Kanō Mura Shi—Gendai Hen* (*Kanō Village History– Modern Times Edition*)," 1963, p. 172.

[56] The FY1927 edition of "Yugen Sekinin Kanō Shinyo Hanbai Kobai Kumiai (Limited Liability Kanō Credit, Marketing and Purchasing Cooperative), "*Dai 25 Nendo Jigyo Hokokusho* (*Business Report for FY1925*)".

Table 7.3 Breakdown of use of loans by the Kanō industrial cooperative in FY1927

Use	Amount lent (yen)	No. of loans
Purchase of fertilizers	105,683	482
Funds for sericulture	26,001	252
Improvement of mulberry fields	13,875	80
Cultivation of mulberry seedlings	3725	30
Land purchase	32,275	50
Old debt redemption	85,315	295
House repairs	27,919	67
Purchase of mountain or forest	10,847	49
Operating funds	29,595	59
Economic funds	34,625	167
Funds for frost damage	17,953	48
Emergency funds for sericulture	6531	49
Total	401,307	1808
Secured loans	22,889	30
Unsecured loans	378,418	1778

The totals do not add up to the gross total due to the omission of some items
Source Prepared based on the FY1927 edition of "Yugen Sekinin Kanō Shinyo Hanbai Kobai Kumiai (Limited Liability Kanō Credit, Marketing and Purchasing Cooperative), "*Dai 25 Nendo Jigyo Hokokusho (Business Report for FY1925)*"

Looking at the purposes of the Kanō Industrial Cooperative's lending activities in FY1927, funds lent as "funds for frost damage" accounted for only 48 loans of the total (1808 loans, see Table 7.3). However, there were a total of 1300 loans for other related purposes, such as the purchase of fertilizers, funds for sericulture, improvements to mulberry fields, old debt redemption and economic funds (i.e. funds for living expenses). While it is unknown exactly when these funds were lent out, this pattern of lending indicates that the Kanō Industrial Cooperative, prior to the decision of the Deposit Bureau on relief loans in July, provided relief loans both from its own funds and with funds accessed through the Central Bank for Industrial Cooperatives.

In 1927, the lowest interest rate on funds the Kanō Industrial Cooperative borrowed externally was 5.4%. The interest rate on Deposit Bureau funds that the Central Bank for Industrial Cooperatives was to provide to affiliated cooperatives was set at 5.4% or lower (it is assumed industrial cooperatives received funds provided by the Deposit Bureau). Following this, the interest rate on funds lent to cooperative members by the Kanō Industrial Cooperative fell from the prevailing rate of 10–5.5% at lowest, and 10.8% at highest.[57] The provision of low-interest funds by the Deposit Bureau had clearly been extended to farm households in the region.

[57] The FY1927 edition of "Yugen Sekinin Kanō Shinyo Hanbai Kobai Kumiai (Limited Liability Kanō Credit, Marketing and Purchasing Cooperative), "*Dai 25 Nendo Jigyo Hokokusho* (*Business*

Unlike loans from agricultural and industrial banks or the Nihon Kangyō Bank, which required lending conditions such as the possession of sufficient collateral, or, in the case of organizations, a minimum number of members. Loans by industrial cooperatives could be borrowed by individual households without collateral[58] (Table 7.3). The effective realization of village-wide membership meant that loans by the Kanō Industrial Cooperative opened the way for almost all households in the village, so long as were members of the cooperative, to borrow funds at relatively low interest rates. The terms and conditions that such loans entailed were advantageous given that unsecured loans by ordinary banks in the same fiscal year carried a highest interest rate of 11.6% and lowest interest rate of 9.7%, with an average rate of 10.4%.[59] Access to these loans was also more widespread as conventional unsecured loans in rural villages were usually limited to wealthy farming households. The cooperative, by contrast, was able to provide low-interest funds to a broader range of borrowers. This was true also in comparison with funds provided via agricultural and industrial banks, which also tended to limit lending to relatively high-income earners.

The case of the Kanō Industrial Cooperative outlined above indicates the significance of the relief lending system during the interwar period with the industrial cooperative serving as a key link in the local community and to the wider financial system. Loans obtained via the industrial cooperative, allowed farming households to obtain emergency funds with the cooperatives' own surplus funds. Whenever the industrial cooperative had a shortage of operating funds, it could procure additional funds from a federation of industrial cooperatives and/or from the Central Bank for Industrial Cooperatives. In terms of the management of rural industrial cooperatives, the links maintained with the systemic financing network of industrial cooperatives were beneficial to operations as they enabled any given industrial cooperative to secure Deposit Bureau funds at interest rates lower than could be otherwise obtained on the market. Industrial cooperatives were able stabilize their operations by replacing their own funds with low-interest funds obtained by loans from the Deposit Bureau system. The existence of this financial network, which was quite different from banks, functioned as a stabilizing presence in regional economies during periods of economic instability. The effectiveness of this network was greatly enhanced by the development of industrial cooperatives at the time.

Report for FY1925)." The cooperative's ordinary borrowings carried an interest rate of 6%, with a highest rate of 8.4%.

[58] The account ledgers of the Kanō Industrial Cooperative show that most of the cooperative's loans were made to individuals, not organizations. Unfortunately, the ledgers for FY1927 were not available, though the ledgers for other fiscal years show that the cooperative lent funds to individuals even when it borrowed funds from the Deposit Bureau system. It is assumed that the cooperative also made loans to cooperative members, that is, individual households in FY1927.

[59] Fumin Kyokai (Association for People's Enrichment), "*Nihon Nōgyō Nenkan* (*Japanese Agricultural Almanac*)," (1933 edition), 1932, p. 143.

7.3.2 *The Case of Seinaiji Village in Shimoina County*

How, then, were the relief loans disbursed in a region where the functioning of the industrial cooperative was weaker? This section examines Seinaiji Village, a case in which conditions differed from Kanō Village. Although Nagano Prefecture among Japan's prefectures had seen the most remarkable development of industrial cooperatives, Seinaiji Village was an outlier in this regard. No industrial cooperative was established in Seinaiji Village, Shimoina County, until as late as 1937.[60] Thus, all relief funds disbursed to the prefecture by the central government for frost damage relief in 1927 were allocated to Seinaiji Village by the prefectural government through the agricultural and industrial banks. The allocated amount was 19,000 yen, and on August 7 the village office prepared a document on relief funds addressed to villagers. The document apparently was a copy of the document from the prefectural government as it contained explanations about items that did not apply to Seinaiji Village residents.

Terms and Conditions for the Lending of Funds.

1. Loan period

Long-term: Within 5 years (funds for replanting damaged mulberry fields)

Short-term: Within 2 years (funds for purchasing fertilizers/silkworm eggs, funds for orchards)

2. Standards for the allocation of funds

For one *tan* of damaged mulberry fields

- Purchase of fertilizers: Up to 5 yen
- Purchase of silkworm eggs: Up to 2 yen
- Replanting of mulberry fields: Up to 50 yen
- The interest rate shall be 5.4% per annum
- The loanees of these funds via agricultural and industrial banks shall be, in principle, sericultural unions and similar organizations as far as possible, and there should be at least 10 members of the organization who have incurred frost damage (at least 20 such members, if possible). However, these standards shall not apply to those whose orchards were damaged.
- Procedures for the loan of these funds shall be as prescribed by the Federation of Credit Cooperatives of Nagano Prefecture or the Nagano Agricultural and Industrial Bank. The required document forms for the Nagano Agricultural and Industrial Bank shall be sent directly by the bank…

Method of Repayments for Frost Damage Relief Funds

1. With respect to the relief funds for frost damage, sericultural unions, farmers' unions and similar organizations or groups organized to borrow funds shall act as follows:

---

[60] Seinaiji Village, "*Seinaiji Mura Shi Gekan* (*Seinaiji Village History, Final Volume*)," 1982, p. 240.

(1) Each union shall save money at the rate of 20 sen per *kan* (0.2 yen per 3.75 kg) from the total amount of silkworm cocoons produced by all union members each year (beginning with spring silkworms in 1928), and shall accumulate this money as the union's cooperative savings;
(2) Each union shall use cooperative savings to pay the interest on relief funds and redeem the principal;
(3) Each union shall continue to accumulate cooperative savings even after the redemption of relief funds for a certain number of years (until 1923);
(4) Each union shall use the cooperative savings to compensate for future losses from frost damage, hail damage, drought damage and other natural disasters or defect silkworms, etc. or to take measures for mutual relief; and
(5) Each union shall use cooperative savings to compensate for losses from declines in cocoon prices caused by fluctuations of silk yarn prices or to prepare funds for adjustments of cocoon prices....[61]

As this shows, when an industrial cooperative did not provide funds to individual households, an arrangement was made to lend funds to individual applicants (including organizations with 10 or more members) through an agricultural and industrial bank. The prefectural government and agricultural and industrial banks assumed that sericultural unions and the like were organizations able to receive loans, and this indicates that they thought that village communities, even when they did not have industrial cooperatives, included organizations that were composed of some kind of local financial or livelihood connection. In Seinaiji Village, local organizations that had existed since the Tokugawa period acted as a receptacle for policy-oriented relief. Regarding the provision of relief funds in Seinaiji Village, prior to individual applications to the agricultural and industrial banks, the village held consultations to designate existing local groups or farmers' unions as applicants and the amounts to be allocated were determined for each of these groups.

Matters for Consultation:

1. Concerning the decision on the amounts of relief funds to be allocated for frost damage:

Following the receipt of the allocation of 19,900 yen in relief funds for frost damage, the disbursal of 10,000 yen to lower Seinaiji district and 9900 yen to upper Seinaiji district is advised.

2. Since the method of borrowing is set as unsecured for a group of at least 10 people, when members of farmers' unions are the same as those of conventional cooperatives, those cooperatives may be accepted as borrowers. If that is not the case, either farmers' unions or organizations formed by qualified members of conventional cooperatives may be acceptable as borrowers.

---

[61] Seinaiji Village Office, "*Nō Dai Kyakugojuyon Go Sogai Kyusai Shikin Kashitsuke Gaku ni Kansuru Ken* (*Nō No. 154 Concerning the Loan Amount of Frost Damage Relief Funds*)," August 7, 1927, documents in the possession of the Seinaiji Post Office (17-2-8). Hereafter, documents of the Seinaiji Post Office are in the possession of the Seinaiji Post Office in Achi Village, Nagano Prefecture.

3. Standard method for a decision on the amounts to be allocated to cooperatives

   (a) 20% shall be allocated on the basis of the number of households.
   (b) 80% shall be allocated on the basis of levies on the number of households and the value of land held.
   (c) Of the funds allocated in the preceding item, the advisability of half being delivered in cash and the other half delivered in kind (conducted by joint purchases of rice and wheat).

4. Concerning the restriction of borrowing by farmers possessing abundant funds:

It is advised that measures be taken to relieve farmers with relatively few funds by restricting the borrowing by farmers in possession of abundant funds. Those who still need to borrow relief funds can do so up to an amount equal to that obtained by dividing the amount allocated by the number of borrowers.

5. Concerning the method of redeeming relief funds:

With respect to the method of redeeming relief funds, under the instructions of the authorities, all cooperative members shall save money at the rate of 20 sen per *kan* (0.2 yen per 3.75 kg) from the total amount of silkworm cocoons produced by all cooperative members each year (beginning with spring silkworms in 1928). If this money is accumulated as the cooperative's savings, it will leave no redemption problems. Thus, this method shall be applied…
Rules under the Code for Cooperative Savings Unions.

Article 1: This union shall be called No. X (Upper/Lower) Seinaiji Cooperative Savings Union and the office shall be located at the residence of the head of the union.
Article 2: This union shall be organized by union members who are qualified as members of an agricultural association…
Article 5: The savings of members …shall be deposited each year with a reliable bank or post office, and the head of the union shall take custody of the passbook….[62]

"Cooperatives" were assumed to be the main entities that would file applications for loans. In Seinaiji Village, "*chien*" groups that were based on local or territorial connections that had existed since the Tokugawa era were prominent.[63] Relief loans were distributed to each cooperative, with 20% of the allocation to be allocated "on the basis of the number of households" and 80% "on the basis of levies on the number of households and the value of land held." Within a cooperative, restrictions were

[62] Seinaiji Village Office, "*Kyōgi Jikō* (*Matters for Consultation*)," believed to have been prepared in August 1927, documents in the possession of the Seinaiji Post Office (17-2-9).

[63] Sakaguchi Masahiko, "*Buraku Yuzaisan Futoitsu Choson no Tenkai to Kiketsu—Taisho ~ Showa Senjiki Nagano Kenka Shimoina-gun Seinaiji Mura no Jirei* (*The Development and Consequence of Towns and Villages with Diverse Non-unified Hamlet-Held Property—The Case of Seinaiji Village, Shimoina County, Nagano Prefecture the Taisho-Showa War Period*)," November 2011, the Society of Japanese Historical Research regular meeting report.

placed on borrowing of funds by "farmers with abundant funds," with the provision of funds to such persons set so as not to exceed the ceiling obtained by dividing the allocation to a cooperative by the number of members.

The amount that a "cooperative" applied for and borrowed was not to be provided according to an application filed by an individual on the basis of individual demand for funds, such as borrowings from an industrial cooperative. A loan amount was determined for each cooperative in advance at the stage of consultations in the village. Under this arrangement, allocations to individuals within a cooperative were also adjusted so that disparities between amounts per household would not become excessive. Furthermore, half of these allocations might have been provided in kind, that is, jointly purchased rice and wheat, instead of cash. Though they were called "loans," it was not the case that only modern pecuniary relations were assumed. In this respect, they were different from relief loans via an industrial cooperative on the assumption of pecuniary relief.

By these relief loans, however, groups of local, territorial connections in Seinaiji Village became connected to the system of the Deposit Bureau funds through the prefectural bank and the agricultural and industrial banks. Furthermore, as the relief loans encouraged the formation of cooperative savings unions, they triggered the reorganization of local groups that led to the formation of postal savings. In fact, a group of 13 members that applied for relief loans in Seinaiji Village in 1927 and formed the Lower Seinaiji Ichiba Cooperative Savings Union was united as a group of local, territorial connections despite its diverse income distribution. It borrowed 1200 yen as an emergency loan and created a covenant savings account in the postal savings system.[64]

When the Deposit Bureau provided low-interest funds as a temporary measure for unemployment relief in 1931, this group applied for the provision of funds as a project implementing body. In this provision of funds for measures to counter unemployment, Seinaiji Village received an allocation of 9100 yen for mulberry replanting and 3500 yen for cultivation. For these loans, the allocation of funds for each cooperative, that is, the decision on fund distribution at village level, was not made, though the loans did not carry the policy-oriented nature of post-disaster restoration.

The Deposit Bureau stipulated that "the lending of funds shall be made to a group of 10 farmers or more deemed capable of jointly undertaking small-scale cultivation or replanting projects," and the village office limited its role to restricting the number of farmers involved in the upper and lower hamlets and to allocating the amounts after applicant groups were determined by "setting the standard of allocation to each union to be based on the number of households and classes."

---

64 Rinzo Hara, Toji Nomura and 12 others, "*Kin Yen Shakuyo Shosho* (*Sogai Taisaku Shikin*) (*Written Acknowledgment of Borrowings* (*Funds for Measures to Cope with the Frost Damage*))," August 27, 1927, Lower Seinaiji Ichiba Cooperative Savings Union, "*Chochiku Kumiai Kiyaku* (*Code of the Savings Union*)," January 1928, included in documents in the possession of the Seinaiji Post Office (17–2-10), and Lower Seinaiji Ichiba Cooperative Savings Union, "*Kumiai Kiyaku Chokin Daicho* (*Ledger for Joint Union Savings Account*)." "*Ichiba*" is the name of the place in the lower Seinaiji district, and this name is believed to have been adopted as the name of the "union".

While groups applying remained unable to freely set the amounts being applied for, whether or not to apply for the provision of funds was left to each respective group in the village.[65] For applications for new Deposit Bureau funds, organizations restructured after the disaster control measures in 1927 again served as the local receptacles. Following the experience of receiving funds from the Deposit Bureau of the Ministry of Finance, an industrial cooperative was established in Seinaiji Village in 1937. This case study of Seinaiji Village helps illustrate the process by which resident organizations that existed within municipalities and had no direct connections with administrative bodies were brought into the financial mechanism of the Deposit Bureau and became connected to the related financial route.

7.4 Summary

The interwar period saw a significant change in the economic situation with a slowdown in the growth of Japan's regional economies. This downturn formed the background to the development of an institutionalized system by which the Deposit Bureau Fund returned funds to rural areas.

This chapter examines how popular funds-based financial networks were established in the interwar period and contributed to regional economies, especially in terms of their role of providing a safety net during social and economic crises. The Deposit Bureau Fund of the Ministry of Finance became the center of this new financial network.

Following on from the establishment of the Central Bank for Industrial Cooperatives in 1923 and the national spread of industrial cooperatives by the interwar period, the links between the financial networks of industrial cooperatives and the Deposit Bureau strengthened further through the relief loans of 1927.

Through an analysis of the actual conditions of relief lending in response to widespread frost damage in Nagano Prefecture in the financial crisis year of 1927, which triggered the building of closer ties and cooperation between the Deposit Bureau system and the industrial cooperative networks, this chapter probes into the development and function of the system for the investment of popular funds in regional economies in the interwar period.

[65] Seinaiji Village Office, "*Shitsugyo Kyusai Rinji Taisaku Teiri Shikin Kashitsuke ni Kansuru Ichi Gatsu Juni Nichi Sonkai Ketsugi Jiko* (*The Matter for Resolution by the Village Assembly on January 12 on the Lending of Low-Interest Funds for Temporary Measures for Unemployment Relief*)," presumed to be on January 12, 1931. The documents are in the possession of the Seinaiji Post Office (17–2-30). The number of farmers for whom the funds were allocated was raised from the initial plan, but the number of applications exceeded that number, an indication that the village assembly presumably narrowed down the applicants.

Chapter 8
Industrial Cooperatives as Safety Nets: The Kanō Industrial Cooperative Coped with the Interwar Economic Depressions

8.1 Introduction

Both this and the following chapter examine certain aspects of how financial networks of popular funds supported regional economies and societies through a method of "sharing" that was well suited to local areas. How did the financial networks of popular funds contribute to regional economy and society? Did they function as a kind of safety net during (prolonged) recessions? This chapter verifies the roles of these financial networks and industrial cooperatives with a micro-study of Kanō Village, Chiisagata County, Nagano Prefecture.

In the 1920s and 1930s Japan experienced a protracted slump. By the latter half of the 1930s, urban areas began to show signs of an economic recovery that centered on the growth of heavy industry, but regional economies, in particular rural areas, remained exposed to crises. Economic growth in modern Japan prior to that, as indicated in previous chapters, was characterized by balanced development. Regional economies, including rural areas and the agricultural sector, experienced robust periods of economic growth.[1] In the interwar period, however, those regions that had experienced expanding income growth led by cash crops such as rice and sericulture, eventually faced declining prices for those goods.

A decline in demand for silk in the U.S. market which became evident from the 1920s, emerged as competition from chemical fiber substitutes gradually became extremely intense. This competition together with the onset of a world depression served a huge blow to the Japanese sericulture industry. Japanese raw silk exports were focused particularly on supplying American silk fabric producers. As the U.S. economy crashed, a large number of farmers in Japan were left exposed as they had

[1] Nakamura Takafusa, "*Senzenki Nihon Keizai Seichō no Bunseki (Analysis of Japan's Economic Growth in the Prewar Period),*" Iwanami Shoten, 1971.

H. Tanaka, *Micro-Credit in Modern Japan*, Studies in Economic History,
https://doi.org/10.1007/978-981-97-6940-7_8

become dependent on silkworm-raising for much of their cash income.[2] In addition to repeated economic slumps, natural disasters such as earthquakes and adverse weather continued and Japan's regional economies were confronted with a variety of crises during the interwar period.[3] Indeed, the persistent crises meant that regional economies were no longer able to support their own communities, an important background in the subsequent drafting of the national program of emigration to Manchuria. Yet not all communities sought to overcome their economic difficulties through the export of population to Manchuria. Some regional communities managed to avoid collapse in the face of the long interwar economic depression. This chapter demonstrates through specific examples how some of Japan's regional communities managed to cope with the economic downturn during the interwar period and maintain social stability.

In the twenty-first century, the socioeconomic function of cooperatives that undertake small-amount financial services as non-profit organizations is being reevaluated. Some point to cooperative organizations, rather than profit-driven private-sector corporate organizations, as a business model that can better confront financial crises and long-term business downturns.[4] This chapter connects to this research trend by examining the industrial cooperative in Kanō Village as a model case of a cooperative that supported its regional economy. This chapter addressed how, in the face of the protracted interwar economic slump, an industrial cooperative in a regional community dealt with the situation from the perspective of its management.

In the interwar period, Nagano Prefecture was the largest center of the sericulture industry in Japan. Despite its status as a relatively isolated rural area the importance of sericulture made it one of Japan's most vulnerable regions to the boom and bust cycles of the world economy. At the same time, Nagano Prefecture was home to a very active industrial cooperative movement. The establishment of the industrial cooperative in Kanō Village can be traced back to 1903, and its successful activity was exemplified by its receipt of an award as an excellent cooperative from the Dainippon Sangyō Kumiai Chūōkai (the National Federation of Industrial Cooperatives) in 1910. In the face of the long business slump and economic depression during the interwar period, the Kanō Industrial Cooperative remarkably never incurred a loss in its operations. Through an analysis of this successful operation, this chapter clarifies

---

[2] Ueyama Kazuo, "*Nihon Kindai Sanshigyō no Tenkai (The Development of Japan's Modern Sericulture Industry)*," Nihon Keizai Hyōronsha, 2016, p. 290, Chap. 7.

[3] Kobayashi Shinsuke, "*Hitobito wa Naze Manshū ni Watattanoka—Nagano-ken no Shakai Undō to Imin (Why did People Emigrate to Manchuria?—The Social Movement and Emigration in Nagano Prefecture)*," Sekaishisōsha, 2015, p. 188.

[4] Muhammad Yunus, translated by Inokuma Hiroko, "*Hinkon no Nai Sekai wo Tsukuru—Sōsharu Bijinesu to Atarashii Shihonshugi (Creating a World Without Poverty: Social Business and the Future of Capitalism)*," Hayakawa Publishing, 2008, (Original published in 2007), p. 55; OECD, translated by JTUC Research Institute For Advancement Of Living Standards, "*Shakaiteki Kigyō no Shuryūka—'Atarashii Kōkyō' no Ninaite toshite (Mainstreaming of Social Enterprise—As the Driving Force of the 'New Public')*, Akashi Shoten, 2010, p. 109; Jacques Moreau, translated by Ishizuka Hideo et al., "*Shakaiteki Keizai towa Nanika—Shin Jiyūshugi wo Koerumono (What is the Social Economy—More Than New Liberalism)*," Nihon Keizai Hyōronsha, 1996 (Original published in 1994), p. 57.

what the well-functioning cooperative could bring to the regional community under economic distress.

8.2 The Background to the Kanō Industrial Cooperative in the Interwar Period

8.2.1 The Perspective of Preceding Research

The interwar period was a time of crisis for farming communities. During the 1920s to the 1930s the price differential between agricultural products and manufactured products widened globally and brought about marked differences between urban and rural areas. Moreover, the change in the global industrial structure itself emerged as an issue for the Japanese economy. With the rapid extension of chemical fibers, invented at the end of the nineteenth century, the competitiveness of silk, Japan's main export item, declined. As a result, many Japanese farmers who raised silkworms as their main sideline business faced increased economic woes.[5]

In 1929, the Great Depression, originating in the United States, triggered a protracted global recession. The Japanese economy had already been experiencing repeated depressions and business slumps from the beginning of the 1920s and so this was only compounded by the global recession. Furthermore, during this period, Japan was visited successively by major natural disasters, including the Great Kantō Earthquake of 1923 and the Shōwa Sanriku Earthquake of 1933. In the Tōhoku region, partly due to the effects of the later earthquake, there were concerned reports of undernourished children and the selling of women and children. The pitiful situation in Tōhoku was reported nationwide and became one of the factors behind political and social crises, such as the February 26 Incident (an attempted military coup) of 1936.

By the time the global depression struck, Japanese society and economy were in a serious condition, and this was particularly stark in Japan's regions. Nonetheless, there were no reports of people dying of starvation or of an immediate exodus from farming villages. One of the reasons why these protracted structural economic difficulties did not trigger a more serious crisis, I argue, was the existence of industrial cooperatives. Their presence in many regions as the providers of relief loans as well as the originator of plans to encourage structural changes in regional industry was an important part of regional resilience.

[5] Asai Yoshio, "*Dokusen Kakuritsuki no Kinyū Kōzō (The Financial Structure in the Period of Monopoly Establishment)*," Itō Masanao, "*Kin Kaikin to Shōwa Kyōkō (The Lifting of an Embargo on the Export of Gold and the Shōwa Depression)*," pp. 150–151; Ushiyama Keiji, "*Shōwa Nōgyō Kyōkō (The Shōwa Agricultural Depression)*," pp. 176–177; Each of the books above are included in Kanji Ishii et al., "*Kindai Nihon Keizai Shi wo Manabu—Ge (Learning the History of the Japanese Economy in the Modern Period—Volume 2)*," Yuhikaku Publishing, 1977.

Many previous studies on interwar industrial cooperatives focused on the relationship between the landlord system and the farmers' movement, examining industrial cooperatives in the context of tenancy disputes and the governance of farming villages, especially the government's interest in promoting industrial cooperatives.[6] Thus, while there has been an abundance of research that analyzes the management of individual industrial cooperatives, for the most part it has lacked the perspective of the effects of the management of these industrial cooperatives on the daily lives of local residents.

The prevalence of the financial network made up of industrial cooperatives, or what was called cooperative financing in the interwar period, has often been acknowledged by researchers in financial history.[7] In particular, the 1920s and the 1930s have been recognized as a period when industrial cooperatives were organized on a large scale, with the establishment and development of national networks taking place simultaneously. As Saeki Naomi pointed out, "the systematization of cooperative financing was all but 100% completed at the time".[8] Ōkado Masakatsu also pointed out that it was during the 1920s that industrial cooperatives "developed cooperative organizations at the national level and created their unique industrial cooperative organization composed of the national federation, prefectural federations, and industrial cooperatives".[9] Preceding research has not, however, gone any further than pointing out that the 1920s was the period when the cooperative financing network was formed and established, and that it often actively began cooperative financing in the 1930s as its presupposed given function.[10] Little attention has been directed to the actual operations of industrial cooperatives and thus preceding research has failed to examine in concrete terms the characteristics and functions that emerged in the new financial network of cooperative financing and the impact it had on regional economies during economic crises.

---

[6] Mori Takemaro, "*Senkanki no Nihon Nōson Shakai—Nōmin Undō to Sangyō Kumiai (Japanese Farming Communities in the Interwar Period—The Farmers' Movement and Industrial cooperatives)*," Nihon Keizai Hyōronsha, 2005.

[7] Kase Kazutoshi, "1920 Nendai ni Okeru Sangyō Kumiai no Fukyū no Igi to Sono Genkai (The Significance of the Spread of Industrial Cooperatives in the 1920s and its Limitations)," *Tochiseidoshigaku (The Journal of Agrarian History)*, No. 68 (1975), pp. 52–72; Asai Yoshio, "*Dokusen Kakuritsuki no Kinyū Kōzō (The Financial Structure in the Period of Monopoly Establishment)*".

[8] Saeki Naomi, "*Nihon Nōgyō Kinyūshi Ron (Theory of the History of Japanese Agricultural Financing)*," Ochanomizushobō, 1963, p. 212.

[9] Ōkado Masakatsu, "Senzen Nihon ni Okeru Keitō Sangyō Kumiai Kinyū no Rekishiteki Yakuwari—Kaisō, Chiiki Kan Chōsetsu, Kokusai Shōka (The Historical Role of Cooperative Industrial cooperative Financing in Prewar Japan—Adjustment between Classes/Regions and Absorption of Government Bonds)," *Economia*, Volume 57, No. 1 (2006), p. 27.

[10] Mori Takemaro, "*Senkanki no Nihon Nōson Shakai—Nōmin Undō to Sangyō Kumiai (Japanese Farming Communities in the Interwar Period—The Farmers' Movement and Industrial cooperatives)*," Nihon Keizai Hyōronsha, 2005.

8.2.2 Activities of the Kanō Industrial Cooperative Until the Interwar Period

Considering its regional characteristics, the industrial cooperative in Kanō Village can be called a "sericulture-type" industrial cooperative according to the classification in preceding research.[11] Kanō Village is now situated in the eastern part of Ueda City and has been known as a sericultural area since the early modern period. The area was connected by railroad to Tokyo and Yokohama, and ultimately to the global market, by the opening of the Shinetsu Line, which enabled the sericulture industry to expand further in the modern period. In Kanō Village, it is said that already "mulberry fields expanded sharply from the end of the Meiji period to the last years of the Taishō period, with mulberry planted in all dry fields except for small tracts of land that were used as private vegetable gardens." The advance of sericulture was so pronounced in Kanō Village that farmers "began to convert their paddy to mulberry fields from around the end of the Russo-Japanese War of 1905".[12]

The Kanō Industrial Cooperative was established as a credit union in March 1903 with the intention of giving financial support for the development of an active sericulture business. The village's population then stood at 4056 and the number of households at 675. The initial union membership numbered 179, meaning that the industrial cooperative was launched with a broad base of participants from its inception. Its membership was drawn from across the village's hamlets and income brackets, as discussed in Chap. 4.

> The Meiji period was a period when loans of money were extremely hard to come by. Even a paltry sum did not change hands without collateral. Indeed, even when farmland was pledged as collateral, interest rates on borrowing ran from 15 to 20% a year, and one of the few stopgap measures for overcoming the tight financing situation was the use of a *mujin-kō* mutual financing association. In many cases, loans could not be repaid and were foreclosed. Even if you wanted to take up some kind of additional productive work as well as continuing to live an ordinary life, you would not have had easy access to the necessary funds.[13]

Residents in Kanō Village at the time faced financial difficulties, as described above, and the Kanō Industrial Cooperative was set up to redress this situation. People in the village at the time complained that "we just want to be in a position to have money to pay for fertilizers at the beginning of spring, even though this is no more than making do for just one year." Among the cash outlays that bothered Kanō residents, "the biggest worry is chemical fertilizers. Only six or seven households in the entire village could buy fertilizers for mulberry fields and paddy fields at the

[11] Mori Takemaro, "*Senkanki no Nihon Nōson Shakai—Nōmin Undō to Sangyō Kumiai (Japanese Farming Communities in the Interwar Period—The Farmers' Movement and Industrial cooperatives)*".

[12] Society for Publication of the Kanō Village History, "*Kanō Mura Shi—Gendai Hen (Kanō Village History—Modern Times Edition),*" 1963, p. 78.

[13] Higashi Fukai Ku (Matsuo Suna), "*Rekishi wa Kataru—Higashi Fukai Ku Shi (History Tells a Story—Higashi Fukai District Magazine),*" 1975, p. 90. Higashi Fukai Ku is a hamlet within Kanō Village. The author, Mr. Suna Matsuo, was born in the middle of the Meiji period.

beginning of spring with cash".[14] Under such circumstances, the Kanō Industrial Cooperative provided its members with unsecured loans on personal credit at the relatively low interest of approximately 10%. Many of the loans provided by the Kanō Industrial Cooperative were actually concentrated around the beginning of spring, and over 70% of the loans were for uses related to agriculture and sericulture, including payments for fertilizers.[15]

The management of the Kanō Industrial Cooperative got off to a good start without incurring any losses. Its revenues grew consistently, and at the time came almost entirely from the interest earned on loans provided to its continually expanding membership base, while the acceptance of savings from cooperative members also increased. With respect to the cooperative's financial situation, the savings-loan ratio showed that the cooperative was considerably over-lending (Table 8.1) prior to World War I. Indeed, not long after its establishment, the Kanō Industrial Cooperative was funding its financing operations by borrowing external funds. As the table indicates, however, the balance of borrowings from commercial banks did not remain high at the end of the fiscal year relative to an aggregate amount of borrowings made within the same fiscal year. The borrowings that made the cooperative's over-lending possible were mostly short-term funds. The cooperative borrowed short-term funds from banks corresponding to the seasonal nature of union members' demand for funds, as discussed in Chap. 4.[16]

According to Mori Takemaro, sericulture-type industrial cooperatives "resolved the over-lending situation temporarily in the 1920s, but their business conditions remained extremely unstable and only stayed alive by relying on financing by cooperative industrial cooperatives".[17] Before World War I, however, the cooperative financial network itself had not yet been established, as discussed earlier. Thus, in the initial stage of its operations, when funds within the cooperative were not plentiful, the Kanō Industrial Cooperative had no choice but to introduce funds from outside the cooperative organization in order to respond to the strong demand for funds from cooperative members.

In other words, the over-lending by the Kanō Industrial Cooperative at the time, I argue, should be positively assessed as proof that the cooperative was able to succeed in the procurement of a large amount of external funds and the expansion of its own lending operations. It is not to be interpreted as evidence of unstable management. The financial conditions surrounding industrial cooperatives prior to World War I were not favorable, and at the time when the National Federation of

[14] Higashi Fukai Ku (Matsuo Suna), "*Rekishi wa Kataru—Higashi Fukai Ku Shi (History Tells a Story—Higashi Fukai District Magazine)*," 1975, p. 43.

[15] Kanō Industrial Cooperative, "*Kashitsukekin Daichō Meiji 40 Nendo (Dai Go Ki) [Loan Ledger for FY1907 (the 5th Term)]*," 1907; Kanō Industrial Cooperative, "*Kashistukekin Daichō Meiji 42 Nendo (Loan Ledger for FY1909)*," 1909, in the possession of the Kanō Office of the JA Shinshū Ueda Tōmi Branch.

[16] Chapter 4, Chart 3.2, Table 3.5.

[17] Mori Takemaro, "*Senkanki no Nihon Nōson Shakai—Nōmin Undō to Sangyō Kumiai (Japanese Farming Communities in the Interwar Period—The Farmers' Movement and Industrial cooperatives)*," p. 31.

Table 8.1 Management of the Kanō industrial cooperative prior the interwar period (1903–1918)

FY	Population	No. of house-holds	No. of cooperative members	Total assets	Paid-in capital	Loans to cooperative members			
						FY-end balance	No. of loans	Average	Total loans within FY
1903	4056	675	179	7632	3090	4525	–	–	7601
1904	–	–	183	7719	4695	5417	83	65	5558
1905	–	–	183	8423	6340	7228	85	85	8488
1906	–	–	197	13,013	7436	8974	98	92	12,804
1907	–	–	208	15,172	8809	8766	110	80	11,178
1908	–	–	211	19,418	10,423	18,356	–	–	24,867
1909	4268	696	212	19,299	11,010	16,710	149	112	18,753
1910	–	–	213	20,416	11,190	17,433	110	158	17,304
1911	–	–	221	25,930	11,430	18,866	105	180	18,977
1912	–	–	223	29,268	11,460	21,282	104	204	19,383
1913	–	–	225	37,215	11,580	24,842	110	225	27,756
1914	–	–	226	43,224	11,700	31,853	131	244	31,501
1915	–	–	223	44,365	11,670	34,614	125	278	27,262
1916	4545	693	247	60,991	12,591	31,772	133	238	23,949
1917	–	–	325	102,726	18,924	35,007	175	200	50,249
1918	–	–	425	156,444	24,874	51,665	202	256	62,863

(continued)

Table 8.1 (continued)

FY	Savings by cooperative members			Savings-loan ratio	External borrowings		Balance of bank deposits	Total profits
	FY-end balance	No. of accounts	Average		FY-end balance of borrowings from banks	Total loans within FY		
1903	821	–	–	551%	500	2700	0	131
1904	869	27	32	623%	0	2055	600	456
1905	958	30	32	754%	0	6350	1000	750
1906	1107	–	–	811%	0	7210	1150	965
1907	1710	–	–	513%	0	6300	4200	1120
1908	629	–	–	2918%	4500	14,200	2000	1301
1909	1100	–	–	1519%	3000	12,950	2400	1572
1910	4037	123	33	432%	0	7100	2800	1615
1911	8584	153	56	220%	0	7500	5900	1502
1912	11,093	173	64	192%	0	6000	5900	1570
1913	17,923	196	91	139%	0	12,500	10,000	1721
1914	22,660	224	101	141%	0	10,800	8800	1873
1915	22,580	220	103	153%	0	12,950	6100	2033
1916	36,333	244	149	87%	0	11,000	24,500	2050
1917	70,761	281	252	49%	0	0	60,022	1926
1918	117,400	544	216	44%	0	0	90,058	2638

Shown in yen, discarding sen (1/100th yen) and below. The numbers of cases and accounts are as shown in the original data
Source Prepared based on "*Jigyō Hōkokusho (Business Report)*" of the Kanō Industrial Cooperative 1903–1918

Industrial Cooperatives held its first national convention in 1906, many industrial cooperatives faced funding difficulties, giving rise to a proposal that a central financial organization for industrial cooperatives was needed.[18] As organizations responsible for providing small-amount financing to regional economies and with the aim of fostering economic development, many industrial cooperatives found it necessary to procure funds externally. In fact, at the time, the Kanō Industrial Cooperative was never regarded as having an unstable management position, despite its temporary over-lending. It was actually commended by the National Federation of Industrial Cooperatives in 1910 for its stable management base that had enabled it to accumulate surplus funds.[19]

The Kanō Industrial Cooperative was able to succeed in building cooperative relations with the ordinary financial network without waiting for a cooperative financial network to develop. Its excellent management was also regarded as an example for other industrial cooperatives to follow. At a time when cooperative financing was yet to be institutionally established, how did the Kanō Industrial Cooperative respond to the strong demand for funds from local union members? It is well-known that in 1906–1907, the president of the cooperative provided assistance using his personal funds, charging no interest, and the cooperative borrowed funds from local regional banks such as the Komoro Bank and the 19th Bank [a prominent bank in silk industry]. At that time, however, obtaining loans from banks was not something that just anyone could do. How did the Kanō Industrial Cooperative succeed in obtaining loans from banks? In order to understand this, it is necessary to examine the cooperative's actions in the years after its establishment.

The oldest record of transactions with other financial institutions made by the Kanō Industrial Cooperative, was the cooperative's application to open a current account with the 19th Bank, dated April 4, 1903.[20] In applying to open the account, Fukai Isao, the cooperative's president, made the application under the title of "*Yūgen Sekinin Kanō Shinyō Kumiai Riji* (Director, Limited Liability Kanō Credit Cooperative)," not under the title of the cooperative's president. In addition, Fukushima Manbei, one of directors, affixed his signature to the application also under the title of director, as Fukai had.[21]

---

[18] Central Union of Agricultural Cooperatives, "*Sangyō Kumiai Chūōkai Shi (History of the National Federation of Industrial Cooperatives)*," 1988, pp. 27–28.

[19] National Federation of Industrial Cooperatives, "*Dainiji Hyōshō Sangyō Kumiai (The Second Commended Industrial cooperatives)*," 1911, p. 110.

[20] Kanō Industrial Cooperative, "*Tōza Yokin Torihiki Mōshikomisho (An Application for Current Account Transaction)*" (addressed to the 19th Bank, April 4, 1903), included in Kanō Industrial Cooperative, "*Zatsu Shorui Tojikomi (File of Miscellaneous Documents)*".

[21] At the time of its establishment, the Kanō Industrial Cooperative had nine executives, including three auditors. Their respective prefectural household tax rate grades in FY1901 (there were a total of 30 grades) were as follows: Fukai Isao (president, Grade 3), Fukushima Manbei (Grade 5), Tanaka Shintarō (Grade 2), Tsuchiya Wasaku (Grade 15), Seki Rinosuke (Grade 8), Tomioka Jukichi (Grade 15), Kodama Hikosuke (auditor, Grade 1), Iijima Rinsaku (auditor, Grade 5), and Seki Manabu (auditor, Grade 3).

There also existed a written acknowledgement of debt believed to have been prepared by the cooperative that apparently tried to borrow ¥500 from the 19th Bank with a repayment period of about six months in December 1903. It did not refer to any collateral, but instead stated that "the debtors shall fulfill their obligations with joint unlimited liability," listing the names of five directors, including the cooperative's president, as joint borrowers. The name of the Kanō Industrial Cooperative was not specified in this transaction, nor was the cooperative's president referred to with the title of "president" or "director".[22] It is presumed that the bank realized that the loan was not provided to the cooperative but to a group of people with pecuniary resources.

Two cases of borrowing, one for ¥500 and another for ¥300, concluded on January 28, 1904, with the 19th Bank, were made jointly in the names of Fukai, Tsuchiya, Tanaka, and Fukushima, or Fukai, Fukushima, Tsuchiya, and Tomioka. When ¥1000 was borrowed on February 26, the names of five men, Fukai, Tanaka, Fukushima, Seki, and Tomioka, were cited as the joint borrowers. The name of the Kanō Industrial Cooperative appeared on none of the written acknowledgements of debt.[23]

As cooperative president Fukai himself later recalled, "When the bank told me that it could lend that amount of funds if I agreed to drop my title as cooperative president, I retorted and told them that they couldn't be serious".[24] The industrial cooperative system, legislated only in 1900, was not yet widely accepted, and thus was not automatically accorded sufficient creditworthiness. Therefore, in order to obtain loans, even from local regional banks, the Kanō Industrial Cooperative had to make use of the personal creditworthiness of individual directors as leverage.[25]

The balance of deposits in the cooperative's current deposit account at the 19th Bank stood at zero at of the end of May 1903, but the balance was ¥310 yen at the end of August, an indication that the account was used actively from the first year after its opening. Other remaining written acknowledgements of debt showed that ¥2000 was borrowed by means of promissory note from Kabushiki Kaisha Itō Shōkai

---

[22] "*Shakuyō Shōsho (Written Acknowledgement of Debt)*" (addressed to the 19th Bank, February 24, 1903), included in Kanō Industrial Cooperative, "*Zatsu Shorui Tojikomi (File of Miscellaneous Documents)*". This was not in the bank's format but was handwritten, believed to have been prepared by the five joint debtors, Fukai Isao, Fukushima Manbei, Tomioka Jukichi, Seki Rinosuke and Tsuchiya Wasaku.

[23] "*Shakuyō Shōsho (Written Acknowledgement of Debt)*" (addressed to the 19th Bank, March 11, 1904), included in Kanō Industrial Cooperative, "*Zatsu Shorui Tojikomi (File of Miscellaneous Documents)*". The prefectural household tax rate grade for Tsuchiya Wasaku was Grade 15 (one of the two lowest graded among the cooperative's executives, but he had once served as village mayor), and also Grade 15 for Tomioka Jukichi (at the time, an incumbent village assembly member).

[24] "*Kanō Mura Shi—Gendai Hen (Kanō Village History—Modern Times Edition),*" p. 171.

[25] The household tax rate grades assessed for the purpose of prefectural taxation in Kanō Village in FY1901 numbered 30 grades. While the cooperative president was assessed at the fairly high Grade 3, cooperative directors included those belonging to the middle-income bracket in the village at Grade 15. However, Tsuchiya and Tomioka, who both served as cooperative director, were assessed at Grade 15 in 1903. Tsuchiya served as Kanō Village mayor until 1902, and Tomioka was an incumbent village assembly member. They apparently had a measure of creditworthiness attributable to something other than income.

on March 11, 1904;[26] ¥1500 from the Komoro Bank on February 13, 1905;[27] and ¥700 from the Komoro Bank on April 14, 1905.[28] But none of the debt documents in this period specify the name of the Kanō Industrial Cooperative, nor were the official titles of those who co-signed their names as joint debtors included. The Kanō Industrial Cooperative in its early years of operation was both unable to obtain credit from the 19th Bank and other regional banks and local trading houses.

8.3 Toward Cooperation Among Industrial Cooperatives: Seeking the Formation of a Network

As seen above, it was necessary for the Kanō Industrial Cooperative in its initial years to overcome the difficult challenge of procuring external funds in order to enable cooperative members to access small-amount financing. The Kanō Industrial Cooperative overcame the challenge by making use of the personal creditworthiness of its cooperative executives. Operators of industrial cooperatives across Japan, including the Kanō Industrial Cooperative, were hoping that these problems would be resolved in the future through cooperation among industrial cooperatives.

In Nagano Prefecture, the prefectural government in 1904 convened a council of union heads, and in 1905, study groups on industrial cooperatives were set up in the Hokushin and Nanshin [Northern and Southern area of Nagano Prefecture] regions. In 1906, these study groups were integrated to become the predecessor of the Nagano Branch of the National Federation of Industrial Cooperatives, and thereafter held a council meeting every year.[29] The Kanō Industrial Cooperative participated in the council of the federation of Hokushin industrial cooperatives from the first meeting in FY1905, indicating that the cooperative was enthusiastic about cooperation among industrial cooperatives over a wider area.[30]

---

[26] "*Yakusoku Tegata (Promissory Note),*" (addressed to Kabushiki Kaisha Itō Shōkai, March 11, 1904), included in Kanō Industrial Cooperative, "*Zatsu Shorui Tojikomi (File of Miscellaneous Documents)*". The three men, Fukai, Tanaka and Seki, co-signed the debt document.

[27] "*Rentai Shakuyō Shōsho (Joint Written Acknowledgement of Debt),*" (addressed to the Komoro Bank, February 13, 1905), included in Kanō Industrial Cooperative, "*Zatsu Shorui Tojikomi (File of Miscellaneous Documents)*". The six men, Fukai, Fukushima, Tanaka, Tomioka, Seki, and Tsuchiya, co-signed the debt document.

[28] "*Shakuyō Shōsho (Written Acknowledgement of Debt)*" (addressed to the Komoro Bank, April 14, 1905), included in Kanō Industrial Cooperative, "*Zatsu Shorui Tojikomi (File of Miscellaneous Documents)*". The four men, Fukai, Fukushima, Tanaka, and Seki, co-signed the debt document.

[29] The Nagano Branch of the National Federation of Industrial Cooperatives, "*Nagano Ken Sangyō Kumiai Enkakushi (History of Industrial cooperatives in Nagano Prefecture),*" 1927, p. 1.

[30] January 21–22, 1905, "Cooperative President Isao Fukai attended a meeting of the council of the federation of Hokushin industrial cooperatives held at the prefectural assembly hall in Nagano City," Kanō Industrial Cooperative, "*Jigyō Hōkokusho Tsuzuri (File of Business Reports),*" FY1905 edition (in the possession of the Kanō Office of the JA Shinshū Ueda Tōmi Branch). The federation of Hokushin [northern area of Nagano Prefecture] industrial cooperatives was organized by industrial

The first council meeting of the Nagano Branch held in January 1906 adopted a resolution to "urge the National Federation of Industrial Cooperatives to establish a central bank of industrial cooperatives".[31] In May 1906, at the second national convention of the National Federation of Industrial cooperatives (a national-level organization of industrial cooperatives established under the leadership of the central government), Kanō Hisayoshi, the association's vice president, advanced a proposal to a similar effect. As this indicates, efforts to establish a means to overcome the limited financial capabilities of individual industrial cooperatives already existed at a regional level prior to proposals from the National Federation.

In March 1907, much earlier than in other parts of the country, the first county-level committee in Nagano Prefecture was created in Chiisagata County.[32] Chiisagata County, a long-standing sericultural area that became connected to the world market for silk with the opening of the railroad, seems to have been particularly positive about cooperation among industrial cooperatives.[33] Moreover, the president of the Kanō Industrial Cooperative, Fukai Isao, was appointed vice president of the Nagano Branch of the National Federation of Industrial Cooperatives in October 1907. What was the impact of this proactive cooperation in Chisagata County on its individual industrial cooperatives?

Kanō Industrial Cooperative President Fukai attended the third national convention of industrial cooperatives held in Tokyo for five days between April 6 and 10, 1908. On April 9, at the end of the meeting, Fukai reported to the convention on the recent activities of the Kanō Industrial Cooperative, and also attended a convivial party of 75 industrial cooperative executives across Japan that night, with Hirata Tōsuke, president of the National Federation of Industrial Cooperatives, also in attendance.[34]

For the first time in its operations, the Kanō Industrial Cooperative succeeded in borrowing funds from the Nagano Agricultural and Industrial Bank on April 11, 1908. The loan amounted to ¥3500 yen, and its period of repayment was about three months (until July 31). The notice of the loan carried with it an attached paper that said that "the nine directors and auditors shall agree to guarantee the debt in their individual capacities," indicating the assumption that the loan was provided on the basis of the personal creditworthiness of the cooperative's executives. This time, however, the borrowing entity was the Kanō Industrial Cooperative itself, not the

---

cooperatives in Minami Saku, Kita Saku, Chiisagata, Sarashina, Hanishina, Kami Takai, Shimo Takai, Kami Minochi, Shimo Minochi, and Nagano City.

[31] "Dainippon Sangyo Kumiai Chuokai Nagano Shikai Kaishoku An (Draft of the Regulations of the Nagano Branch of the National Federation of Industrial Cooperatives)"; the Nagano Branch of the National Federation of Industrial Cooperatives, "*Kyōgi Jikō (Agendas)*," FY1906, included in Kanō Industrial Cooperative, "*Zatsu Shorui Tojikomi (File of Miscellaneous Documents)*".

[32] Chiisagata County Mayor Takei Ichirō assumed the post of the head of the county committee.

[33] "*Nagano Ken Sangyō Kumiai Enkakushi (History of Industrial cooperatives in Nagano Prefecture)*," p. 27.

[34] "*Sangyō Kumiai (Industrial cooperatives)*," May 1908, pp. 92–93.

cooperative's executives as joint debtors.[35] The Nagano Agricultural and Industrial Bank officially extended the loan on April 16, 1908.[36] The "*Taishakukin Keiyaku Shōsho Seishiki Tōhon (the Duly Certified Copy of the Loan Agreement)*," prepared at the notary public office in Nagano City stated that the interest rate on the loan was 9% per annum. The Kanō Industrial Cooperative's business report for 1909 stated as follows:

The Status of Business

> In line with our policy to accommodate cooperative members with the lending of funds necessary for their business as far as possible, we borrowed funds from the Nagano Agricultural and Industrial Bank, the 19th Bank, and the Komoro Bank to provide sufficient loans to those with demand for funds...as interest rates of ordinary commercial banks are high due to the tight conditions of the financial industry, we plan to make use of the agricultural and industrial bank as much as possible.[37]

As is generally believed, borrowing from the agricultural and industrial bank was more advantageous for the Kanō Industrial Cooperative than borrowing from other financial institutions. That the Kanō Industrial Cooperative succeeded in borrowing funds from the Nagano Agricultural and Industrial Bank, and was able to fully repay the loan, allowing it to continue with similar transactions in following years, was of major significance for the cooperative's management. In subsequent borrowing from the agricultural and industrial bank, at least as far as can be gleaned from surviving materials, there was no rider, or provisory clause, that took advantage of the personal creditworthiness of the cooperative's executives as guarantors of debt repayments, as witnessed in the first case of borrowings. Through transactions with the Nagano Agricultural and Industrial Bank, the Kanō Industrial Cooperative established the creditworthiness of the cooperative itself, climbing out of the situation where its financial transactions were based on the personal creditworthiness of the cooperative's executives.

There exist no materials that directly substantiate the impact that the national convention of industrial cooperatives had on the establishment of transactional relationships between the Kanō Industrial Cooperative and the Nagano Agricultural Cooperative. However, it was widely known that many participants other than people related to industrial cooperatives, including officials of government ministries and agencies as well as executives of the Nihon Kangyō Bank and other financial institutions, and members of the press, attended the national convention of industrial cooperatives.[38]

---

[35] Nagano Agricultural and Industrial Bank, "*Tsūchisho (Notice)*," April 11, 1908, included in Kanō Industrial Cooperative, "*Zatsu Shorui Tojikomi (File of Miscellaneous Documents)*".

[36] "*Taishakukin Keiyaku Shōsho Seishiki Tōhon (Duly Certified Copy of the Loan Agreement)*," April 16, 1908, included in Kanō Industrial Cooperative, "*Zatsu Shorui Tojikomi (File of Miscellaneous Documents)*." The form was provided by the notary public office within the jurisdiction of the Nagano District Court.

[37] Kanō Industrial Cooperative, "*Jigyō Hōkokusho Tsuzuri (File of Business Reports)*," FY1909 edition.

[38] "*Sangyo Kumiai (Industrial cooperatives)*," May 1908, p. 1, p. 35.

While industrial cooperatives would not create their central financial institution until 1923, it is believed that in the period prior to that year, through meetings sponsored by the National Federation of Industrial Cooperatives and its branches, industrial cooperatives succeeded in building an information network, including for financial information, that facilitated cooperation between regions and between the central and regional organizations. Most likely the building of such relationships provided an important opportunity for the Kanō Industrial Cooperative to cooperate with subsequent networks of cooperative financing, including the Federation of Credit Cooperatives of Nagano Prefecture and the Central Bank for Industrial cooperatives.

At the sixth national convention of industrial cooperatives held between May 8 and 10, 1910, the Kanō Industrial Cooperative was selected among the "Second Commended Industrial cooperatives".[39] Following the commendation, executives of the Nihon Kangyō Bank in June 1910 and of the National Federation of Industrial Cooperatives in September 1910, respectively, visited Kanō Village to observe operations of the Kanō Industrial Cooperative[40] Fukai, the cooperative's president, was elected a representative director of the newly established Hoshō Sekinin (Warranty) Federation of Credit Cooperatives of Nagano Prefecture in 1913, and then elected vice president of the Nagano Branch of the National Federation of Industrial cooperatives in 1915. Retaining the post of president of the Kanō Industrial Cooperative, Fukai became directly involved in interregional industrial cooperative network organizations.[41]

Perhaps thanks to the building of these relationships, the Kanō Industrial Cooperative obtained its first loan from the Nihon Kangyō Bank in January 1915. The loan amount of ¥10,000 with a one-year repayment period was both much larger and longer than previous borrowing. Thus, it is fair to assume that the loan came from the funds of the Deposit Bureau of the Ministry of Finance, via the Kangyō Bank.[42] As seen above, the Kanō Industrial Cooperative was successful in introducing external funds at relatively low interest rates (compared to market interest rates), while simultaneously actively engaging in the formation of interregional industrial cooperative networks.

---

[39] "Dainiji Hyōshō Sangyō Kumiai (The Second Commended Industrial cooperatives)."

[40] Kanō Industrial Cooperative, "*Jigyō Hōkokusho Tsuzuri (File of Business Reports)*," FY1910 edition.

[41] Fukai Isao, "*Rirekisho (Curriculum Vitae)*," May 1941, included in Kanō Industrial Cooperative, "*Zatsu Shorui Tojikomi, Hyōdai Nashi (File of Miscellaneous Documents, No Heading)*" (in the possession of the Kanō Office of the JA Shinshū Ueda Tōmi Branch).

[42] See Chap. 5.

8.4 The Kanō Industrial Cooperative in the Protracted Recession

8.4.1 An Overview of the Kanō Industrial Cooperative's Management in the 1920s

How was the social structure of Kanō Village affected by the economic boom during World War I? As of 1922, the population of Kanō Village stood at 4115, just a slight increase over its level in 1903 (4056). 3622 of its 1922 population were farmers, who comprised 608 of the village's total of 690 households. Clearly, despite the war boom, Kanō village still maintained an agriculture-centered industry structure.

Rice paddies and dry fields per household stood at 4 *tan* (1 *tan* = approximately 991 square meters) 6 *se* (1 *se* = approximately 99 square meters) and 8 *tan* 2 *se*, respectively, meaning the village's farming was mainly geared towards dry-field cropping. Of the village's total of 495 *chō* (1 *chō* = approximately 9917 square meters, 491 ha) of dry fields in 1922, 359 *chō*, or over 70% of the total, were officially reported as mulberry fields. At the same time, however, it was reported that "mulberry fields at the height of sericulture (the Taishō period) in Kanō Village amounted to 500 *chō* (495 ha) (the number of sericulture households being 600), and cocoon collections under the triple-cropping system amounted to some 60,000 *kan* (1 *kan* = 3.75 kg)",[43] indicating that mulberries were even planted in some rice paddies, not only in dry fields, where mulberries were usually planted. In other words, sericulture was the main industry in Kanō Village even in the interwar period, and the village's economic structure may even be described as a monoculture.

While agricultural business focused on sericulture, most of the village households became members of the cooperative by the interwar period, as can be confirmed in Table 8.1. The number of cooperative members continued to grow even after it reached a number equivalent to the number of households in the village. Perhaps by that time it had become common for more than one cooperative member to be present in each household (Table 8.2).

In order to respond to the strong demand for funds from cooperative members engaged in sericulture, the Kanō Industrial Cooperative provided members with funds procured externally, even to the extent that it fell into a position of over-lending. It managed to climb out of that position, however, by taking advantage of the economic boom during World War I (Table 8.1). Indeed, during this period, it enjoyed some financial leeway and expanded its operations. In 1918, it built a new cooperative office, finally extricating itself from the situation where the cooperative president's house doubled as the cooperative's office. At the time, an agricultural warehouse was constructed along with the office, and began to offer storage services for the cooperative members' agricultural products. Moreover, in 1919, the Kanō Industrial Cooperative launched a marketing and purchase business to handle rice produced

[43] "*Kanō Mura Shi—Gendai Hen (Kanō Village History—Modern Times Edition)*," p. 66, p. 81.

Table 8.2 Kanō industrial cooperative's business structure in the interwar period

	Total assets	Membership	Paid-in capital	Reserves	Loans			
					Total loans within FY	End-FY balance	No. of loans	Per-loan average
1919	271,079	549	34,390	12,154	187,303	122,132	433	282
1921	247,561	648	42,570	17,366	199,884	183,583	618	297
1923	421,372	713	114,540	27,890	299,107	220,167	819	269
1925	610,608	738	115,770	40,174	271,856	273,397	784	349
1927	719,523	753	116,430	64,471	401,307	459,054	969	474
1929	726,335	744	141,600	49,894	439,992	438,835	1012	434
1931	702,340	745	141,570	62,361	254,955	505,971	1089	465
1933	706,188	730	140,970	67,881	126,633	525,123	1288	408
1935	674,127	757	139,380	69,013	112,815	488,455	1238	395
1937	681,065	766	135,570	71,840	161,418	386,883	1039	372
1939	920,653	789	131,795	75,384	87,828	327,038	618	529
1941	1,278,720	823	131,790	83,489	114,367	230,290	515	447

	Savings			Savings-loan ratio (%)	Balance of borrowings	Borrowings within FY	Interest rate on borrowing	Profit
	End-FY balance	No. of accounts	Per-account average					
1919	164,477	1161	142	74	52,000	169,500	N.A	4144
1921	161,814	1709	95	113	13,200	120,600	8.7% (10.2–5.9%)	7209
1923	174,077	2229	78	126	10,886	112,274	7.4% (8.4–5.9%)	14,871
1925	397,309	3354	118	69	11,046	54,000	6% (9–5.4%)	28,669
1927	452,123	4226	107	102	48,355	91,406	6% (8.4–5.4%)	16,664
1929	461,984	4509	102	95	39,156	43,633	7% (7.4–5.4%)	18,215

(continued)

Table 8.2 (continued)

	Savings			Savings-loan ratio (%)	Balance of borrowings	Borrowings within FY	Interest rate on borrowing	Profit
	End-FY balance	No. of accounts	Per-account average					
1931	375,291	4718	80	135	106,320	174,100	6.8% (7.4–5.4%)	8527
1933	372,806	5273	71	141	109,161	136,500	5% (5.9–3.9%)	8722
1935	327,947	5408	61	149	119,484	123,000	5% (5.9–4%)	4061
1937	395,431	5600	71	98	53,230	70,000	4.2% (5.1–3.9%)	4567
1939	651,728	5985	109	50	0	52,100	4.9% (5.1–3.9%)	3885
1941	931,830	5951	157	25	0	4884	5.47%	8556

Source Kanō industrial cooperative, "*Jigyō Hōkokusho (Business reports)*" 1919–1941

by cooperative members, also expanding its activities to cover school supplies and fertilizers.

As can be seen from Table 8.3, however, although the purchasing business to provide fertilizers to cooperative members grew to a relatively large scale, revenues from the purchasing, marketing and warehousing operations did not become large enough to match those from the Kanō Industrial Cooperative's financing operations in the 1920s and 1930s. In the economic boom during World War I, investment gains, including interest income from deposits with external banks, temporarily expanded significantly, but the Kanō Industrial Cooperative's core activities throughout this period remained loans to cooperative members and the interest income they generated.

How then did the downward trend in silk cocoon prices that became noticeable from around 1925 and the frequent depressions affect the sericulture-dependent economy of Kanō Village and the Kanō Industrial Cooperative's operations?

Sericulture-type industrial cooperatives, the most common type of industrial cooperative in Nagano Prefecture, were seen to have resolved their over-lending issues and stabilized their management in the 1920s. Looking at the savings-loan ratio and borrowing, however, it is clear that this assessment was not necessarily applicable to the Kanō Industrial Cooperative. In the first half of the 1920s it again lent out funds in excess of the amount of savings deposits and also borrowed fairly large funds externally. Did this reflect the unstable management of the Kanō Industrial Cooperative at the time?

Examining the breakdown of the ¥13,200 borrowing balance in FY1921, for example, it is evident that ¥7000 had come in the form of low-interest regional funds via the Nagano Prefectural Federation of Credit Unions (i.e. low-interest funds from the Deposit Bureau of the Ministry of Finance allocated by Nagano Prefecture) and the remaining ¥6200 was composed of funds for landed farmers borrowed from the Nihon Kangyō Bank. It is not clear what interest rates applied to each case of borrowing. In FY1921, the lowest borrowing rate was 5.9%, and this rate perhaps applied to the low-interest regional funds.[44] While other ordinary borrowing rates were as high as 8.76% even for the Kanō Industrial Cooperative, with the highest rates rising to over 10% (Table 8.2). The cooperative was able to obtain relatively large funds in a single borrowing, meaning that it had the scope to secure sufficient funding resources to actively offer loans to cooperative members. From the first half of the 1920s the cooperative had once again lent out funds in excess of the amount of savings and thus borrowed externally on a relatively large scale.

The Kanō Industrial Cooperative "requested the Nihon Kangyō Bank to provide long-term funds for landed farmers so that cooperative members in need of funds could refinance their debt with lower interest rates," and to enable them "to use bills for short-term funds for sericulture and purchasing fertilizers." This indicates that

---

[44] Kanō Industrial Cooperative, "*Jigyō Hōkokusho Tsuzuri (File of Business Reports)*," FY1921 edition. Funds for landed farmers were funds designed mainly for the acquisition of land provided actively since the 1920s to help tenant farmers to become landed farmers and landed farmers to maintain their position.

Table 8.3 Kanō industrial cooperative's revenue-expense breakdown in the interwar period

Fiscal year	Profit	Total revenues	Interest on loans	Revenue from bank deposits	Securities revenue	Land revenue	Purchasing dept. revenue	Sales fees	Revenue from processing fees	Revenue from ware-housing
1919	4144	16,287	6569 40%	4026 25%	274	302	1076 7%			
1921	7209	27,818	20,492 74%	4574 16%	68	190	2319 8%			128
1923	14,871	43,562	25,207 58%	13,619 31%	196	279	5652 13%		219	154
1925	28,669	70,129	33,481 48%	16,622 24%	1546	301	7590 11%		90	94
1927	16,664	64,433	41,407 64%	11,509 18%	1518	166	8121 13%	313	1251	111
1929	18,215	66,292	41,442 63%	11,753 18%	1603	406	7628 12%	1055	2218	136
1931	8527	47,705	33,692 71%	4913 10%	1153	148	4013 8%	263	1186	203
1933	8722	46,805	33,177 71%	3911 8%	2070	578	4319 9%	653	1806	180
1935	4061	41,984	30,892 74%	591 1%	178	1455	4513 11%	1376	2149	201
1937	4567	42,299	22,026 52%	1424 3%	692	5849	5738 14%	1641	2822	572
1939	3885	54,839	22,081 40%	2509 5%	517	8941	10,303 19%	4801	4916	340
1941	8556	61,694	14,527 24%	18,202 30%	3019	6373	11,548 19%	1646	4068	1980

(continued)

Table 8.3 (continued)

Fiscal year	Total expenses	Interest on savings	Interest on borrowings	Salaries	Union federation related	Dividends for members	Reserves +accumulated funds*	Special remuneration for executives	Lending rates	Savings rates
1919	12,143	7831	1361	N.A		1693	1312	280	6~9%	6–6.6%
1921	20,609	11,045	2670	4096		2503	4059	395	10% (7–12%)	8% (7–9%)
1923	28,690	15,691	3012	5988		7670	6391	560	10% (7–12%)	7% (6.6–9%)
1925	41,459	24,961	2750	7447	1043	9463	18,526	680	10% (5.5–11%)	6% (5.5–8%)
1927	47,769	30,314	1705	8781	337	10,981	6260	680	10% (5.5–10.8%)	6% (4.7–7.3%)
1929	48,077	27,400	2856	9831	935	11,328	9424	680	8.76% (5.4–9.12%)	4.8% (4.01–6%)
1931	39,177	22,143	3768	8674	310	5662	6777	0	8.76% (5.4~8.76%)	4.8% (4.01–5.6%)
1933	38,082	17,765	5500	8878	299	5638	2655	0	8.4% (6.6–8.4%)	5% (4.6–5%)
1935	37,923	14,818	5715	9292	503	2323	2695	0	7.7% (4–8.4%)	3.6% (2.92–5%, Savings accounts 5%)
1937	37,731	13,587	3430	8449	490	2711	1787	1466	7% (4.2–7.7%)	4% (2.5–4.2%)

(continued)

Table 8.3 (continued)

Fiscal year	Total expenses	Interest on savings	Interest on borrowings	Salaries	Union federation related	Dividends for members	Reserves +accumulated funds*	Special remuneration for executives	Lending rates	Savings rates
1939	50,954	17,338	409	8405	504	0	2389	1886	6.8% (3.6–7.5%)	3.4% (2.6–3.6%)
1941	53,137	23,833	1	9580		3953	4918		6.5% (4.75–7.12%)	2.2% (1.82–3.3%)

As neither expenses nor revenues represent all items in the original data, aggregates of items listed do not correspond to total revenues or total expenses. Securities revenues include dividend revenues

% in some items represents the ratio of the relevant item to total revenues

Source Kanō industrial cooperative, "*Jigyō Hōkokusho (Business reports)*" 1919–1941

*The criterion for dividends is "0.06% per year of capital invested," and the criterion for reserves is "a quarter of retained earnings"

the Kanō Industrial Cooperative acted to supply funds to its members in a manner that would enable them to feel the benefits of interest rate differentials between short-term and long-term funds. In other words, the Kanō Industrial Cooperative "borrowed funds at low interest rates from the Kangyō Bank and the Agricultural and Industrial Bank to strive constantly to improve the daily lives of cooperative members." Moreover, it supplied land-related long-term funds, such as funds for landed farmers, with low-interest long-term funds with limited uses from the Deposit Bureau and the Kangyō Bank, thereby procuring typically large and low-interest land-related loans for its members and for the cooperative's operations.[45]

Table 8.4 shows that in the first half of the 1920s, in 1921 in particular, the cooperative's loans for repayments of previous debts accounted for a relatively large share of its transactions. As already alluded to above, this is thought to have resulted from cooperative members refinancing existing high-interest debts with limited-use but low-interest funds from the Deposit Bureau and the Kangyō Bank. Because they were funds for landed farmers, that is funds for land-related uses, the loans were not to be repaid in the short term, and these low-interest funds remained on the fiscal year-end borrowing balance at the time. On the other hand, the fiscal year-end balance of lending to cooperative members fell short of the annual aggregate amount of loans, pointing to the existence of a smooth flow of funds with cooperative members not falling behind on their repayments.

Under these circumstances, in May 1921, the Kanō Industrial Cooperative was again commended at the (17th) national convention of the National Federation of Industrial Cooperatives. On that occasion, the cooperative received ¥250 in "*onshi*", a kind of imperial gift. The Kanō Industrial Cooperative deposited the whole amount into a newly-created reserve fund, named "the reserve fund commemorating the special *onshi*" and decided to deposit it with the Kangyō Bank or the Nagano Prefectural Federation of Credit Unions. The institutions designated in FY1919 for depositing the cooperative's surplus funds were not limited to these two institutions, but also included regional banks, such as the 19th Bank, Shinano Bank, 63rd Bank, Ueda Bank, Shiga Bank, Kangawa Bank and Komoro Bank[46] indicating that the cooperative adopted different management strategies for the stability-oriented commemorative reserve funds and regular surplus funds.

As shown by the fact that around 20% of the revenues of the Kanō Industrial Cooperative came from interest earned on bank deposits (Table 8.3), the cooperative, while placing priority on the provision of small-amount financing to its members, "constantly maintains contact with the Nihon Kangyō Bank, the Prefectural Federation of Credit Cooperatives, and leading regional banks." Moreover, it had skillfully built a fund management portfolio that took advantage of interest rate differentials by

[45] Kanō Industrial Cooperative, "*Jigyō Hōkokusho Tsuzuri (File of Business Reports)*," FY1921 edition.

[46] Kanō Industrial Cooperative, "*Jigyō Hōkokusho Tsuzuri (File of Business Reports)*," FY1919 edition.

Table 8.4 Kanō industrial cooperative's financial operations in the interwar period

Fiscal year	Total loans within FY	No. of cases	Balance at FY-end	No. of cases at FY-end	Loans made within FY (amount/no. of cases)			
					Unsecured		Secured	
1921	199,884	1182	183,583	618	186,934	1170	12,950	12
1923	299,107	1663	220,167	819	262,137	1636	36,970	27
1925	271,856	1370	273,397	784	245,274	1343	26,582	27
1927	401,307	1808	459,054	969	378,418	1778	22,888	30
1929	439,992	1850	438,835	1012	417,242	1825	22,750	25
1931	254,955	1177	505,971	1089	200,693	1102	54,261	75
1933	126,633	1130	525,123	1288	102,643	964	45,119	166
1935	112,815	1032	488,455	1238	44,053	796	68,762	236
1937	161,418	1183	386,883	1039	108,074	1018	63,343	165
1939	87,828	782	327,038	618	82,208	661	26,177	121
1941	114,367	500	230,290	515	134,932	481	8821	19

Fiscal year	Use of lent funds (ratio to all transactions (amount/no. of cases)											
	Fertilizer purchases		Sericulture-related funds		Land-related funds		Repayments of old debts		Non-farming business funds		Economic funds*	
1921	45%	46%	6%	18%	23%	11%	16%	21%	6%	2%		
1923	31%	26%	13%	21%	12%	10%	13%	11%	4%	1%		
1925	34%	33%	9%	16%	18%	8%	17%	17%	8%	5%	38%	8%

(continued)

Table 8.4 (continued)

Fiscal year	Use of lent funds (ratio to all transactions (amount/no. of cases)											
	Fertilizer purchases		Sericulture-related funds		Land-related funds		Repayments of old debts		Non-farming business funds		Economic funds*	
1927	26%	27%	11%	20%	11%	5%	21%	16%	7%	3%	9%	9%
1929	18%	37%	7%	14%	10%	3%	35%	21%	1%	1%	13%	12%
1931	8%	25%	5%	11%	14%	3%	45%	20%	1%	0%	12%	25%
1933	Industrial funds		73%	65%							27%	35%
1935			69%	63%							31%	37%
1937			66%	65%							34%	35%
1939			60%	40%							40%	60%
1941			60%	38%							40%	62%

Source Kanō Industrial Cooperative, "*Jigyō Hōkokusho (Business reports)*" for each fiscal year. Various items, such as sericulture-related funds, land-related funds, and non-farming business funds, are aggregated with some items in the original data. For example, non-farming business funds include commercial funds, funds for bamboo-ware and paper-manufacturing funds. Since loan uses were narrowed down to the two types, "industrial funds" and "economic funds", after FY1933, uses other than those listed as "economic funds" are considered "industrial funds." Items in "Use of lent funds" in the above table does not include everything in the original data. Thus, the total amounts and the total number of cases do not correspond to the total loans and the total number of cases within the fiscal year. In particular, major loan items in FY1927 included relief funds (funds for the recovery from the frost damage and emergency funds for sericulture) totaling ¥24,484 (6% of total loans) and 97 cases (5% of the total number of cases)

*"Economic" are believed to be funds cooperative members used for users daily lives. As the classification of items was changed into just 2 category (Economic and Industrial) after FY1933, details of uses other than this were unknown

financing route and short-term and long-term funds, leveraging them to enhance its management stability and development.[47]

8.4.2 How Did the Kanō Industrial Cooperative Steer Through the Depression?

As discussed in Chap. 7, in 1927, the year of the Shōwa financial crisis, Nagano Prefecture and a number of other regions were hit by major frost damage. On May 12, 1927, in the midst of a banking moratorium, the sericultural areas of Nagano Prefecture suffered from severe frost which caused many mulberry trees to wither and die from their roots just ahead of the gathering of spring silkworms. In Nagano Prefecture alone, as much as nearly 60,000 *chō* (59,500 ha) of mulberry fields were damaged, according to the initial report into the severe natural disaster.

How did the Kanō Industrial Cooperative manage to overcome the double shock of the financial crisis-induced economic depression and the natural disaster? In this chapter, this question is examined by looking specifically at the work of the Kanō Industrial Cooperative at that time, examining its functions and following the flow of the supply of relief funds by the Deposit Bureau examined thus far.

The supply of funds is a prerequisite for the recovery from natural disasters, but in this case the affected areas were mostly rural and had meagre financial resources, compounded by the fact that many banks at the time had been adversely affected by the financial crisis. Under these circumstances, the Nagano Prefectural Federation of Credit Cooperatives decided to provide emergency funds to affiliated unions on May 21. As funding resources for emergency funds, the federation stated that "since the federation's own funds are absolutely insufficient in the case that requested borrowings prove to be substantial, we decided to borrow funds from the Central Bank for Industrial Cooperatives. [To this end] President Fukai of the Prefectural Federation traveled to Tokyo for negotiations and obtained the Central Bank's ready consent."[48] This statement shows that by 1927 the national financing route for industrial cooperatives ran from Tokyo to the regions in the following chain: central bank to prefectural federations to local individual cooperatives to affected residents.[49]

The lending rate for these emergency funds provided to affiliated cooperatives by the Prefectural Federation of Credit Cooperatives stood at 7.6%, lower than the federation's usual lending rate of 8.7%. The Federation also attached the condition that when affiliated unions provided loans to cooperative members from these emergency

---

[47] Kanō Industrial Cooperative, "*Jigyō Hōkokusho Tsuzuri (File of Business Reports)*," FY1921 edition.

[48] "The credit cooperative federation starts extending loans to save the exigent situation in frost-damaged areas – With the assistance from the Central Bank of Credit Cooperatives, funds are being provided from today at a daily interest of two sen one rin per ¥100," *The Shinano Mainichi Shimbun*, front page, May 22, 1927.

[49] Ōkado Masakatsu, "Senzen Nihon ni Okeru Keitō Sangyō Kumiai Kinyu no Rekishiteki Yakuwari (The Historical Role of Cooperative Industrial Cooperative Financing in Prewar Japan)".

funds, rates should be kept no higher than 8.7%. In the same fiscal year, interest rates on unsecured loans from ordinary commercial banks ranged from a low of 9.7% and a high of 11.6%, averaging 10.4%.[50] Clearly the funds individual industrial cooperatives borrowed from affiliated organizations at low interest rates were then passed on to cooperative members at similarly low interest rates.

Though it is hard to say whether the action taken was prompt enough at a procedural level, subsequently, on July 13, the central government decided on the supply of low-interest funds from the Ministry of Finance's Deposit Bureau funds, which were to be provided as funds for the recovery from the natural disasters. This was the first time that huge relief funds, amounting to as much as ¥8.33 million, were provided via the Central Bank for Industrial Cooperatives, in addition to the supply of Deposit Bureau funds through the Kangyō Bank and agricultural and industrial banks. The lending rate of the Deposit Bureau to financial institutions through which funds were supplied was 4.8%, and the Deposit Bureau attached an additional lending condition that when these financial institutions actually provided the funds to users, the interest rate should not exceed 5.4%.[51] When individual industrial cooperatives in Nagano Prefecture became able to borrow these funds, their borrowing rate would be low enough to refinance their previous borrowings from the Federation of Credit Cooperatives of Nagano Prefecture. Deposit Bureau funds could be used to help reduce the burden on their operations.

No materials survive that specify exactly how much of the Deposit Bureau funds the Kanō Industrial Cooperative borrowed via the Federation of Credit Cooperatives of Nagano Prefecture and the Central Bank for Industrial cooperatives, respectively. Table 8.2 nevertheless indicates that the cooperative's total external borrowing exceeded ¥90,000 in FY1927, nearly double the equivalent in FY1926 and FY1928. The lowest interest rate carried on this borrowing was that charged for the Deposit Bureau funds via the Central Bank for Industrial Cooperatives. Furthermore, the possible reason behind the sharp jump in the balance of borrowings in FY1927 over that of FY1926 or FY1928 may be that the relief funds for the recovery from the frost damage by the Deposit Bureau had longer repayment periods (2–5 years) and thus extended beyond single fiscal years. In addition, as the notes to Table 8.4 indicate, in FY1927 the items for which loans were to be used included those rarely seen in other fiscal years such as funds for recovery from frost damage and emergency funds for sericulture. The Kanō Industrial Cooperative's business report for FY1927 also stated as follows:

> Following the enforcement of the moratorium, banks increased their reserves and remained cautious. As a result, despite a temporary severe credit crunch, the Kanō Industrial Cooperative constantly maintained close contacts with the Central Bank for Industrial cooperatives and the Federation of Credit Cooperatives of Nagano Prefecture, and was able to meet the demand for funds required for industrial operations, including economic funds, without any

---

[50] Fumin Kyōkai (Association for People's Enrichment), "*Nihon Nogyō Nenkan (Japanese Agricultural Almanac)*,"1932, p. 143.

[51] Savings Bureau, Ministry of Finance, "*Yokin Bu Shikin Unyō Iinkai (Dai Jurokkai Kaigi) Gijiroku [Minutes of the Steering Committee of the Deposit Bureau Fund (16th Meeting)]*," July 1927 (in the possession of the Library of the Faculty of Economics, the University of Tokyo).

> delay. However, on May 12 there was substantial frost damage which destroyed a majority of the prefecture's mulberry fields. Because of this, the gathering of silkworms from egg paper declined sharply, and cocoon prices dropped 20-30% on the previous year. Farming household revenues from spring silkworms almost halved, and business suddenly contracted and the rural economy was plunged into an extreme predicament… [Therefore,] we decided to request emergency funds from the government for the recovery from frost damage. In addition, the summer and autumn in succession saw poor silkworms and cocoon prices continued to plunge, causing farming household revenues to decline. This again prompted us to request emergency government funds for sericulture in order to respond to the demand from cooperative members for funds to purchase fertilizers and for wages by offering low-interest loans[52]

As stated above, both are believed to have been covered by the specially named uses of loans that were required to be used when funds were lent from the Ministry of Finance's Deposit Bureau funds. Nearly ¥25,000 was provided to cooperative members under these items alone. The Kanō Industrial Cooperative's success in securing low-interest funds through the national network of industrial cooperatives played an important role in helping the cooperative and its members cope with the multiple difficulties experienced in 1927. In this way, the cooperative ties that the Kanō Industrial Cooperative had established with the Kangyō Bank, agricultural and industrial banks, and the newly-functioning cooperative financial network of industrial cooperatives were greatly reinforced during the 1927 depression period. On the other hand, the relationships with regional banks, with which the Kanō Industrial Cooperative formed ties prior to the interwar period, gradually weakened.

Following the financial crisis, nine banks, including the Komoro Bank and the Chūshin Bank, with which the Kanō Industrial Cooperative transacted up until that time, merged in 1928 to establish the Shinano Bank. In 1926 the Kanō Industrial Cooperative had arrangements with the Komoro Bank, the Chūshin Bank, the 19th Bank, and the 63rd Bank to deposit surplus funds. In 1928 the cooperative's business report stated that "the banks with which the cooperative deposits its surplus funds are the 19th Bank, the 63rd Bank, the Chūshin Bank, the Komoro Bank, and their branches, as in the previous year," but noted that "some of the above banks are currently in negotiations regarding amalgamation." It continued that "in the case of such mergers, the banks with which we deposit our surplus funds shall be the merged bank and its branches".[53] As this indicates, the cooperative had decided to maintain its transactional relationships in anticipation of the banks merger into the Shinano Bank.

Upon its establishment, the Shinano Bank possessed the second largest capital (behind the 19th Bank) in Nagano Prefecture, and held balances of deposits and loans larger than the 19th Bank and the 63rd Bank. It nevertheless declared a moratorium in November 1930. The Shinano Bank handled about 30% of the deposits held by

---

52 Kanō Industrial Cooperative, "*Jigyō Hōkokusho Tsuzuri (File of Business Reports)*," FY1927 edition.

53 Kanō Industrial Cooperative, "*Jigyō Hōkokusho Tsuzuri (File of Business Reports)*," FY1928 edition.

industrial cooperatives in Nagano Prefecture, and thus the bank's failure in 1931 inevitably had an impact on the management of industrial cooperatives.[54]

What was extent of the impact of the Shinano Bank's failure on the Kanō Industrial Cooperative? The cooperative's business report for 1931 stated, "Regarding the handling of deposits with the Shinano Bank, a resolution was adopted unanimously to leave the matter to the discretion of directors," a clear confirmation that the Kanō Industrial Cooperative indeed had deposits with the Shinano Bank upon its collapse. The cooperative's overview of business for the same year, however, also stated that "while the credit crunch was of unprecedented proportions, the Kanō Industrial Cooperative fortunately had only a limited level of transactional relations with the bank that implemented restrictions on payments [the Shinano Bank]." In 1929, the Kanō Industrial Cooperative re-designated banks with which it would deposit its surplus funds to four banks: the 19th Bank, the Shinano Bank, the Yasuda Bank, and the 63rd Bank[55] newly adding the Yasuda Bank [predecessor bank of Mizuho Bank, one of the three megabanks in Japan], with which there were no records prior transactions. It is believed the cooperative took steps to further diversify the locations of its money in advance of the Shinano Bank's troubles.

The Kanō Industrial Cooperative rode out the financial crisis. It minimized the crisis' impact on the cooperative's management through the introduction of low-interest funds obtained via the cooperative financial network and by dispersing risks through the diversification of investment opportunities for surplus funds. In addition, the cooperative successfully supplied low-interest funds in small amounts to the regional economy which had been hit hard by falling cocoon prices and natural disasters. That the cooperative's operations continued in a stable manner and it was able to maintain its function in providing low-interest and small-amount financing was surely a great source of relief for the residents of its community.

The cooperative's business report for 1931 stated that "with respect to the collection of loans, in consideration of falls in income due to the business downturn and the damage it has caused, we have striven to reduce interest rates to mitigate the business community's difficulties." The credit crunch, including the Shinano Bank's moratorium in 1931, together with the decline in cocoon prices, impacted the cooperative's members. As the business report's language suggests, the Kanō Industrial Cooperative most likely saved some cooperative members from defaulting by encouraging them to refinance preexisting loans with low-interest funds. In fact, as Table 8.4 shows, the aggregate amount of loans extended in 1931 plunged, perhaps because of a decline in investment in sericulture caused by the falling cocoon prices. Especially noteworthy, however, is a rise in loans for the repayment of old debts. The rise in this kind of loan indicates a large number of households were unable to repay previous debts in 1931. Also high was the number of loans for cooperative members' living expenses, categorized as "economic funds." These loans accounted for only a small

---

[54] Nagano Prefecture, "*Nagano Kenshi Tsūshi Hen—Dai Kyū Kan, Kindai San (History of Nagano Prefecture, Complete History Part, Volume 9, Modern Period 3)*," 1990, pp. 198–199.

[55] Kanō Industrial Cooperative, "*Jigyō Hōkokusho Tsuzuri (File of Business Reports)*," FY1929 edition.

share of the aggregate lending amount relative to the number of cases, indicating that the amount per loan was relatively small. It nevertheless points to the fact that many households required an injection of a small amount of money for their daily lives.

After 1933, however, as the categories for the classification of loan use shown in business reports were altered and reduced to just "economic funds" and "industrial funds," it unfortunately becomes impossible to accurately understand the amount of funds actually used at the time for productive purposes. The reason is that with respect to the category of "industrial funds," which accounted for over 70% of loans in 1933, the business report stated that "all funds for production, including funds for fertilizers, were accommodated with low interest rates." Nevertheless, given the lending ratios in the old classification for loan use, the "industrial funds" category most likely included the refinancing of old debts with low-interest funds.

Conversely, however, there is the possibility that this is an example of the Deposit Bureau funds that were provided with low interest rates but also with restrictions on usage, such as funds exclusively for the improvement of the sericulture industry. In many cases these funds could not be supplied for the repayment of old debts,[56] but in practice were provided to cooperative members who needed funds to refinance old debts in the name of "industrial funds." This practice came at the discretion of the cooperative in each locality. For example, some years later, around 1936, when low-interest policy loans, called "economic revitalization funds," were provided from the Deposit Bureau funds to the Kanō Industrial Cooperative, a draft prepared by the cooperative for resetting the terms and conditions of lending economic revitalization funds at a time when "the collection of loans is favorable and savings are gradually increasing"[57] indicated that the cooperative had, in fact, eased the lending terms and conditions.

Guidelines for the Lending of Economic Revitalization Funds.

- Funds shall be lent out only to those cooperative members who repeatedly suffered from natural disasters or the business depression and who prepare revitalization plans;
- The amount loaned shall be no more than ¥500 per cooperative member;
- The lending rate shall be set at four *bu* seven *rin* (4.7%) a year;
- The lending of economic revitalization funds shall be repaid periodically within five years or in yearly installments within 10 years; and
- When borrowers fail to abide by the designated use of funds or revitalization plans, the cooperative shall have them repay the funds immediately without the benefit of the time of the application deadline...

[56] For example, "low-interest funds the relief of the unemployed and temporary measures for rural villages" supplied across Japan by the Deposit Bureau could not be lent out to a sericulture village unless their uses were for the cultivation and replanting of mulberry fields, etc. Seinaiji Village Office, "*Shitsugyō Kyūsai Rinji Taishaku Teiri Shikin Kashitsuke ni Kansuru Ichi-gatsu Jūni-nichi Sonkai Giketsu Jikō (The Matter Resolved by the Village Assembly on January 12 Concerning the Lending of Low-Interest Funds for Temporary Measures for the Relief of the Unemployed)*," perhaps January 12, 1931 (in the possession of the Seinaiji Old Post Office [17-2-30]).

[57] Kanō Industrial Cooperative, "*Jigyō Hōkokusho Tsuzuri (File of Business Reports)*," FY1936 edition.

(Note) With respect to debt rules, we shall strive to lower interest rates by investment of specially accommodated funds.[58]

As can be seen above, members of the Kanō Industrial Cooperative were able to borrow economic revitalization funds (low-interest funds supplied by the Deposit Bureau), even during the depression, so long as they could give the appearance of having taken steps to rebuild their farming household's operations.

During the severe depression of farming villages in the 1930s, the Kanō Industrial Cooperative functioned not as an organization to supply investment funds and revolving funds for new production, such as fertilizers and farmland, to cooperative members, but as an organization supplying funds for the settling of their debts and sustaining their daily lives. Had the Kanō Industrial Cooperative not been able to accommodate its members in this way with such funds, it is likely that many people would have suffered greatly. The fact that the Kanō Industrial Cooperative was able to continue providing small-amount financing opportunities indicates that the cooperative functioned as a kind of safety net at the time for local residents. Unfortunately, the lack of referenceable materials makes it difficult to determine the income brackets of those in Kanō Village who utilized these financing opportunities. However, in addition to the supply of low-interest funds, which perhaps included industrial funds, the ratio of economic funds supplied by the cooperative tended to increase in the 1930s. Furthermore, during the 1930s at least, it is evident that the Kanō Industrial Cooperative provided extensive small-amount financing opportunities, with the number of loans exceeding the number of cooperative members.

8.4.3 New Exploration for the Regional Economy: Seeking to Break Away from Monoculture

As can be seen from Tables 8.2 and 8.3, the Kanō Industrial Cooperative managed to record profits even during the long recession in the interwar period, and was able to pay dividends to cooperative members almost every year. As the revenue breakdown in Table 8.3 shows and as was affirmed in the preceding section, this achievement stemmed for the cooperative's success in fund procurement and the investment of surplus funds. Considering that the cooperative earned profits on revenues from loans and investments, it can also be said that the Kanō Industrial Cooperative successfully operated as a profit-seeking financial institution. However, an industrial cooperative is a cooperative union and as an organization it is not specifically designed or driven by the profit motive.

> In getting on in the world, there is nothing more enjoyable than to have sufficient clothing, food and housing, to live within our means, to complete the path of loyalty and filial piety, and to tend to and foster descendants, thereby promoting the country's future prosperity

[58] "Keizai Kōsei Shikin Kashidashi Yōkō (*Guideline for the Lending of Economic Revitalization Funds*)," manuscript (perhaps by Mr. Fukai Isao), perhaps 1936. Fukai (Isao), "*Kanō Kumiai Shorui (Kanō Cooperative Documents)*," FY1936-1937 edition (in the possession of the Fukai Family).

> ...A credit cooperative is formed by a large number of people who each invest a small amount of capital which is then pooled to allow each member to borrow or lend. Though the contribution from each member is extremely small, when put together, it results in a large pool of capital, and a member who is able to borrow money from it can buy fertilizers for cultivation or mulberries for raising silkworms. In this way, even poor people can easily find a means of obtaining capital and can have their share of fair living and follow the path of human righteousness.[59]

As the founder of the Kanō Industrial Cooperative stated in its founding purpose in 1903, the success of an industrial cooperative depends on whether it is able to help union members improve or at least maintain their daily lives and families, as well as foster future generations.

How did these fundamental goals of cooperative activities affect the operations of industrial cooperatives? In the case of the Kanō Industrial Cooperative at least, the cooperative never incurred a loss throughout the interwar period, though it did report a temporary accounting loss on just once occasion. More specifically, in FY1928 the cooperative temporarily reported a loss of ¥9424 on its balance sheet but eliminated it by drawing on reserves, which were transferred to capital. Why did the cooperative make this move?

One plausible reason would be that 1928 was the year after a financial crisis and so it was careful not to give the impression that the cooperative may be incurring losses due to factors such as declines in revenue from interest on loans or interest revenue obtained from deposits. But this was not entirely the case. In FY1928, the Kanō Industrial Cooperative's gross revenue stood at ¥69,825, with the main sources of revenue derived from interest on loans (¥42,396), interest received from bank deposits (¥12,580), and the revenue of the cooperative's purchasing department (¥8590). Overall, revenues in FY1928 were comparable to those in FY1927 and FY1929 (see Table 8.3). The main expenditure items were interest paid on savings (¥30,956), interest paid on borrowing (¥2833), and salaries (¥9831), not much different from expenditures in other fiscal years.

What, then, brought about the excess of expenditures in 1928 (total expenditure of ¥79,250 over revenues of just under ¥70,000)? The excess in expenditures stemmed from ¥23,498 of "*kinen hi* [commemoration expenditure]", a category of spending that only appeared in FY1928. The Kanō Industrial Cooperative marked its 25th anniversary in 1928 and though the specific details are unknown, the above extraordinary expenditure is likely to have covered expenses incurred in the organization of commemorative events. Of the above amount, ¥11,133 was distributed to cooperative members as dividends, and ¥2243 was additionally placed in the reserves set up in commemoration of the "*onshi*[imperial gift award]".[60] Apart from the "commemoration expenditure," additional reserves of ¥4572 were put aside, as in usual years. What is clear is that when "commemoration expenditure" is excluded, the

[59] Fukai Isao, "*Yūgen Sekinin Kanō Shinyō Kumiai Setsuritsu Shushi (The Founding Purpose of Limited Liability Kanō Industrial Cooperative),*" "*Kanō Mura Shi—Gendai Hen Kanō Village History—Modern Edition,*" pp. 168–169.

[60] ¥680 was reported as bonuses for directors.

cooperative operated in the black in FY1928. Thus, the Kanō Industrial Cooperative did not report a loss due to operational failures.[61]

What was the intention of the Kanō Industrial Cooperative in drawing on reserves and transferring nearly ¥10,000 to boost its equity capital in 1928? During the year, the Kanō Industrial Cooperative "established the utilization department by changing the articles of association together with consultations on the grand enthronement ceremony [of the Shōwa Emperor] in this fiscal year" because "the operations of the sales department and the utilization department have the closest relationship with the development of the industrial cooperative." The utilization department "enabled cooperative members to use rice and barley milling machines, a flour mill, barley press rollers and threshing machines, powered by a 15-horsepower electric motor, incessantly every day."

The Kanō Industrial Cooperative's inventory of property for FY1928 newly listed a 32-tsubo (one tsubo ≒ 3.3 square meters) rice milling plant that contained a variety of machines, an asset valued at ¥1400. The inventory also newly listed a 15-horsepower electric motor together with a variety of machines driven by the motor which were valued at ¥3555. It is presumed that the cooperative reported the means of this increase in capital by reporting the loss and then drawing on reserves as a way of processing the accounts for the investment in new business activities.

The cooperative's advance into this new line of business, at least according to the business report, had been planned as early as 1920. This new capital investment, made even though it entailed the reporting of a loss, can be viewed as an indication of what the Kanō Industrial Cooperative intended to do for the regional community beyond the provision of low-interest, small-lot financing opportunities.

As pointed out earlier, the Kanō Industrial Cooperative commenced its sales and purchasing operations in 1919. In 1926, the cooperative assigned full-time specialized staff to a division responsible for selling the products of cooperative members to external markets. Initially centered on the sale of rice, soon after the division's establishment in 1921, the cooperative already recognized the need to "take necessary measures for the advantageous sale of firewood, charcoal, brewing products and other products from cooperative members' side businesses that members have asked the cooperative to market, while the cooperative also encourages members to produce various products for sale"[62]. Of note here is the lack of reference to silk cocoons, a product that underpinned the village's economy. The Kanō Industrial Cooperative's sales operations were not designed to involve transactions in cocoons, rather they aimed at diversifying members' products. Even after full-time dedicated staff were assigned to the sales division, the cooperative expressed its intention to focus on the production and sales of products other than cocoons. A cooperative publication hinted at this, explaining that it was "considering an expansion of general agricultural

---

[61] Kanō Industrial Cooperative, "*Jigyō Hōkokusho Tsuzuri (File of Business Reports)*," FY1928 edition.

[62] Kanō Industrial Cooperative, "*Jigyō Hōkokusho Tsuzuri (File of Business Reports)*," FY1921 edition.

products and side business products, including garden fruits and grass brooms using vacant land, as well as sales channels for them"[63].

Cocoon prices had fluctuated violently on the market since before the interwar period, and even when they were on the uptrend during the Meiji period, the president of the Kanō Industrial Cooperative expressed his apprehension that they would decline, stating: "those who take advantage of new opportunities and methods become increasingly affluent and prosper, and those who are not able to fall behind and could ultimately sink to the extreme of poverty in the end".[64] In April 1914, long before the economic boom of World War I got underway, the Kanō Industrial Cooperative distributed walnut saplings to cooperative members in the belief that growing them on residential land space might prove fruitful.[65] The move was suggested by cooperative president Fukai, who was wary of the harmful effects of farm households' over-specialization, or dependence, on sericulture.

As far as can be gleaned from the cooperative's business reports, the production of walnuts "utilizing residential land space" commenced as part of the Kanō Industrial Cooperative's sales business in 1927, a year after a full-time dedicated staff had been assigned to the sales division to handle the marketing of cooperative members' produce. How significant were the cultivation of walnuts and fruit for the Kanō Industrial Cooperative and Kanō Village?

Clearing Debts with "Shinano Walnuts"—Kanō Village's Sales and Purchasing Cooperative

> Though recently we see cheerful news that Kanō Village's walnuts, labeled "Shinano walnuts," are being sold in large quantities to the Mitsukoshi department store in Tokyo and to foreign countries, enormous efforts had to be made to reach that stage.
>
> That was exactly what happened in Kanō Village, Chiisagata County, the village of residence of Mr. Fukai Isao, the forerunner on the front lines of the industrial cooperative movement, a meritorious figure who warrants a full page in the history of the development of industrial cooperatives in Nagano Prefecture, and who is now serving as president of the Nagano Prefectural Federation of Credit Unions. The Shinano walnuts were the result of his intense efforts. The rural village composed of 690 households has 260 *chō* 9 *tan* (258.74 ha) of paddy fields, 490 *chō* 9 *tan* (486.84 ha) of mulberry fields, 40 *chō* (39.67 ha) of dry fields, 334 *chō* 9 *tan* (332.13 ha) of forests, and 6 *chō* 5 *tan* (6.45 ha) of wasteland. Kanō Village's production statistics include rice of 6688 *koku* (1 *koku* ≑ 180 liters) of rice, of which 2688 *koku* was marketed, 1459 *koku* of barley, of which 226 *koku* was marketed, 750 *koku* of wheat, of which 50 *koku* was marketed, and 248 *koku* of soybeans, of which 68 *koku* were marketed. Also harvested were 25,767 *kan* (1 *kan* ≑ 3.75 kg) of potatoes, 44,981 *kan* of Japanese radishes, 50,007 *kan* of vegetables for pickling, and 61,936 *kan* of cocoons.

---

[63] Kanō Industrial Cooperative, "*Jigyō Hōkokusho Tsuzuri (File of Business Reports)*," FY1926 edition.

[64] Fukai Isao, "*Yūgen Sekinin Kanō Shinyō Kumiai Setsuritsu Shushi (The Founding Purpose of Limited Liability Kanō Industrial Cooperative)*," "*Kanō Mura Shi—Gendai Hen Kanō Village History—Modern Edition*," p. 168.

[65] Kanō Industrial Cooperative, "*Jigyō Hōkokusho Tsuzuri (File of Business Reports)*," FY1914 edition. "*On April 5, as one of the projects to commemorate the new emperor's enthronement, walnut saplings were distributed to all cooperative members*".

However, Kanō Village was also unable to escape the adverse effects of the overreliance on sericulture, and village residents anguished under the burden of heavy debts, amounting to as much as ¥1200 per household due to investments and the non-collection of deposits with the three regional banks of Shinano, Komoro, and Kangawa. The production of "Shinano walnuts" has saved residents from despair and helped them see the light of the dawn, proving an effective resource for the consolidation of their debts. The plans envisioned that against the principal of ¥1000 with an annual interest of 6%, 15 walnut trees would be planted on one tan, which though they bear nothing for the first five years, start to bear walnuts of 1 *tō* 5 *shō* (10 *shō* = 1 *tō* ≑ 18 L = 1/10 *koku*) from the sixth year onward. Walnuts can be sold for an average of 30 sen per *shō* for a total of ¥4.50 per *tan*. This amount is then appropriated to reduce the principal and interest of the debt… In the 24th year, revenue should reach ¥270 and the principal and interest of the debt should be reduced to ¥210.25, leaving a profit of ¥64. In other words, these numbers should ensure debt repayment in installments over 19 years with a grace period of 5 years. In 1934, the entire village's walnut production of 400 *koku* is said to have yielded a total of ¥12,000.

Based on these exact numbers, as part of the projects commemorating the enthronement of the emperor [Taishō], walnut saplings were distributed at the initiative of Mr. Fukai Isao as early as 1912, with one sapling per household. Now, it is said that there are 10 walnut trees per household, totaling 8000 trees planted on residential land and wasteland... All walnut sales are controlled by the cooperative, and also 70,000 saplings are also being cultivated for shipments to Tottori, Fukushima and Shiga prefectures.[66]

Kanō Village's walnuts became well-known products, marketed by 1935 as "Shinano walnuts" as described in the extract above. The regional newspaper, Shin Aichi, in an article in 1934 entitled "the 24-year plan of Kanō Village, Chiisagata," reported on "Debt repayments with the harvesting of walnuts" that "in the 24th year, will see debts that have tormented farm households for many years paid off, leaving a calculated profit of ¥64.87." It further noted that the performance of this initiative "is drawing keen attention from various quarters".[67] The report in Shin Aichi also listed an identical number of walnut trees planted and estimated profits to that in the preceding report referenced above. That these numbers appeared in different media sources can be taken as evidence that the Kanō Industrial Cooperative developed detailed profit plans, or designed business and asset management plans, and explicitly presented information on them, much like a consultancy firm, in order to solicit cooperative members to take up walnut cultivation. At the same time, the cooperative also conducted public relations operations externally. In 1933, Kanō Village boasted the largest production of walnuts in Japan[68] and around the time began sales of "walnut saplings, in addition to the sales of walnuts, nurtured through the improved breeding and cultivation of walnuts".[69]

66 Nagano Branch of the National Federation of Industrial Cooperatives, "*Nagano Ken no Sangyō Kumiai—Shisatsu Meguri (Industrial Cooperatives in Nagano Prefecture—Inspection Visits)*," 1935, pp. 193–196.

67 "*Shin Aichi*," October 24, 1934.

68 Nagano Prefecture, "*Nagano Kenshi Tsūshi Hen—Dai Kyū Kan, Kindai San (History of Nagano Prefecture, Complete History Part, Volume 9, Modern Period 3)*," 1990, pp. 144–145.

69 Kanō Industrial Cooperative, "*Jigyō Hōkokusho Tsuzuri (File of Business Reports)*," FY1933 edition.

Since the 1920s, the agriculture and forestry administration divisions of the central government became aware of the danger of farmers being entirely dependent on sericulture, and it proactively encouraged the diversification of farm management.[70] In the case of Kanō Village, however, the encouragement of production other than sericulture was already under way from the middle of the 1910s at the initiative of the Kanō Industrial Cooperative. In the course of the initiative, the cooperative actively developed walnuts as a new regional brand product and helped them to become firmly established in external markets.[71]

Demonstrating considerable financial skill, the Kanō Industrial Cooperative maintained stable management throughout the course of the long recession. One example of this was the cooperative's efforts to present profit plans to cooperative members for the cultivation of walnuts in which it showed its deft calculation capabilities. When farming households decided to shift their farm management strategies and diversify into new businesses, the Kanō Industrial Cooperative was able to provide the funds cooperative members required so as to make the necessary investments in fertilizers, saplings, and equipment. Ahead of the government's own efforts, the Kanō Industrial Cooperative undertook proactive endeavors to help the regional economy break away from monoculture and was able to provide targeted support to this end. The cooperative's stance that diversification away from a monoculture based on sericulture can be affirmed in a survey on cooperative silk reeling conducted in 1928:

> While the Kanō Industrial Cooperative has been studying the matter of cooperative silk reeling, the central government and the prefectural government recently began to encourage it as a way to promote the development of rural areas. Though the establishment of cooperative silk reeling in this period is a most timely endeavor, there remain many aspects that require further examination. Under these circumstances, the election of 20 members was proposed at a general meeting...With respect to the cooperative silk reeling encouraged by Nagano Prefecture and this County Branch, a study was conducted by members elected at the cooperative's general meeting last year. However, Kanō Village decided to postpone the silk reeling project until we have reconsidered the market trends, as cocoons are now being sold at reasonable prices.[72]

In addition to the requests from the government and higher affiliated organizations of industrial cooperatives, the Kanō Industrial Cooperative itself recognized cooperative silk reeling as a "timely" and potentially profitable endeavor, but it chose to push the cultivation of commercial crops instead of attempting the cooperative silk reeling being touted as a means to further developing sericulture.

---

70 Agricultural Affairs Bureau, Ministry of Agriculture and Commerce, "*Chihō Fukugyō Shuninsha Kaigi Yōroku (Summary Records of the Meeting of Reginal Sideline Business Supervisors)*," 1925.

71 The kind of walnuts cultivated in Kanō Village belong to the family of English walnuts, not the variety traditionally grown in the region, and thus "Shinano walnuts" were an entirely new farm produce. Until the 2020s, these English walnuts remained a local brand specialty.

72 Kanō Industrial Cooperative, "*Jigyō Hōkokusho Tsuzuri (File of Business Reports)*," FY1928 edition.

The value of walnut production, despite gaining "a high reputation as Shinano walnuts" in national markets in the 1930s,[73] never matched the value of production in sericulture or rice. In 1935, for example, walnut production in Kanō Village amounted to 129 *koku* or a value of ¥3225. This could only be considered a small-scale industry and was dwarfed by the village's sericulture industry, which produced 23,000 *kan* of spring cocoons which were valued at over ¥88,000.[74] However, this is somewhat beside the point. The Kanō Industrial Cooperative promoted walnuts from the perspective that "walnuts are not selective in terms of soil property." Because "walnuts are easy to grow," it was possible to grow them on "residential land" and their cultivation would therefore not compete for land with the main production items. Walnuts were also deemed to "have broad export outlets" and enjoy "inexhaustible demand." They were understood to have "extremely high nutritional value" and could "be stored, so they can be sold anytime when cash is needed." With these considerations in mind the cooperative promoted walnuts as "a cornerstone of the diversification of farming management".[75]

At a time when many farming households remained dependent on sericulture and rice for their main sources of cash revenue, it was the local industrial cooperative, ahead of the central government, that pioneered the move away from monoculture in the case of Kanō Village. The shift towards a more prosperous farm management characterized by fruit cultivation in Nagano Prefecture from the end of World War II up to the present was already underway in Kanō Village from the Taishō period. The shift came at the initiative of the local industrial cooperative.

8.5 Summary

In the 1920s and 1930s Japan experienced a protracted slump. By the latter half of the 1930s, urban areas began to show signs of an economic recovery, but regional economies, in particular rural areas, remained exposed to crises. In the interwar period, those regions that had experienced expanding income growth led by cash crops such as rice and sericulture, eventually faced declining prices for those goods Fig. 8.1.

---

73 Agricultural associations of counties and cities, industrial cooperatives of counties and cities, agricultural associations of towns and villages, Ueda Branch of the Nagano Prefectural Federation of Purchasing and Marketing Cooperatives, "*Mamore! Kyōdō (Protect! Cooperatives)*," October 1932, (Isao) Fukai, "*Zatsu Shorui Tojikomi (File of Miscellaneous Documents)*," included in the FY1933-FY1935 edition (in the possession of the Fukai Family).

74 The quantity and value of spring cocoon output were numbers based on a survey conducted at the end of July 1935. As for walnuts, sales of saplings alone came to 45,128 trees for ¥2,708. Kanō Village Office, "*Sangyō Kumiai Tōkei Hōkoku (Industrial Cooperative Statistical Report)*," FY1935 edition (in the possession of the Tōmi Municipal Education Board).

75 The Kanō Village Walnut Sapling Production Cooperative (in the Kanō Village Office), "*Shinano Kurumi Naegi Annai (Guide to Shinano Kurumi Saplings)*," October 1932, included in Fukai (Isao), "*Zatsu Shorui Tojikomi (File of Miscellaneous Documents)*," the FY1933-FY1935 edition.

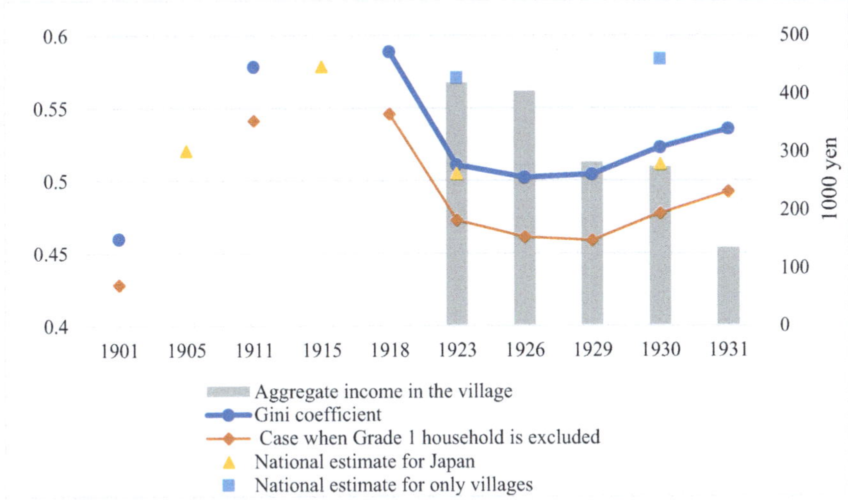

Fig. 8.1 Transition of the Gini coefficient in Kanō Village. Calculated based on amounts of tax payments until 1918 and on amounts of income from 1923 onward. Until 1918, the Gini coefficient was estimated as "the Gini coefficient = 1 − sum of (the relative frequency of the number of households by grade against the total number of households x the cumulative relative frequency of tax amounts by grade against the total amount of prefectural household tax rates) × 2." As progressively high household tax rates were applied to high income earners, if the Gini coefficient in 1923 and onward is calculated using the previous formula based on amounts of tax payments, it would produce relatively higher numbers than those shown in the above chart. Thus, it should be noted that if income data existed prior to 1918, there is the possibility that the Gini coefficient would be lower than that shown in the above chart. *Source* Kanō Village Office, "*Kenzei Kosū Wari Fuka Gaku Tokyū Hyō (Table of Prefectural Household Tax Rate Grades)*" 1901–1931. The national estimates for Japan and all villages are based on Minami Ryōshin, "*Nihon no Keizai Hatten to Shotoku Bunpu (Japan's Economic Development and Income Distribution),*" Iwanami Shoten (1996, p. 108, p. 41)

Industrial cooperatives and their networks which had strong roots in rural area, tried to cope with the severe situation. This chapter verifies the roles of these financial networks and industrial cooperatives with a micro-study of Kanō Village, Chiisagata County, Nagano Prefecture. The cooperative took advantage of low-interest funds provided by the Deposit Bureau and the cooperative financing network of industrial cooperatives in order to supply funds to cooperative members at relatively low-interest.

The case of the Kanō Industrial Cooperative demonstrates the profound impact that a cooperative organization that maintains strong external links and functions for the betterment of the regional economy and society can have in a region. Its varied efforts helped the community to survive a prolonged economic crisis and acted as a kind of safety net.

Chapter 9
The Impact of the Absence of Industrial Cooperatives: Background to the Emigration to Manchuria

9.1 Introduction

The interwar period was a period of rural crisis. The 1920s and 1930s saw the price differential between agricultural produce and industrial products widen globally, while in Japan economic depressions and natural disasters occurred one after another. The decline of the international competitiveness of silk, then Japan's main export industry, directly worsened the economic conditions of farming households dependent on sericulture for much of their cash revenue. Consequently, the economic plight of rural communities became a major social problem at the time, with shocking media coverage of women sold into prostitution and a surge in the number of undernourished children.[1]

Such economic turmoil in the course of time triggered social turmoil. This manifested itself in an attempted coup d'état and a number of political assassinations in Japan, leading to the Manchurian Incident in 1931, and eventually to the Sino-Japanese War and the outbreak of the Pacific War. In the midst of these developments, Japan established a national policy of emigration to Manchuria which saw some 270,000 people migrate to Manchuria as agricultural emigrants, only to meet a tragic end when Japan was defeated in World War II. Many of them died without returning to Japan and survivors often faced up to very tough ordeal before they were repatriated. The tragedy of the Manchurian emigrants has left a lasting imprint on Japanese war memory. Consequently, it is better known than any of the other emigrations to various parts of the world that took place between the Meiji Restoration and the end of World War II.

---

[1] Arai Yoshio, "*Dokusen Kakuritsuki no Kinyū Kōzō (The Financial Structure in the Period of Monopoly Establishment)*"; Itō Masanao, "*Kin Kaikin to Shōwa Kyōkō (The Lifting of the Embargo on the Export of Gold and the Shōwa Depression),*" pp. 150–151; Ushiyama Keiji, "*Shōwa Nōgyō Kyōkō (The Shōwa Agricultural Depression),*" pp. 176–177; the above three papers are all included in Ishii Kanji et al., "*Kindai Nihon Keizai Shi wo Manabu—Ge (Learning the History of the Japanese Economy in the Modern Period—Volume 2),*"Yuhikaku Publishing, 1977.

H. Tanaka, *Micro-Credit in Modern Japan*, Studies in Economic History,
https://doi.org/10.1007/978-981-97-6940-7_9

Despite its tremendous scale it is hard to say that there has been a comprehensive socio-economic assessment of Manchurian emigration. Previous studies have failed to reach a consensus on what factors were behind it and the socioeconomic elements/ actors that prompted so many people to emigrate to Manchuria. Many studies that have been conducted on the topic were collections of records and oral histories of the former emigrants.[2] Research in the historical sciences, including economic histories, on the emigration to Manchuria has largely focused on imperialism and colonial policy, rather than emigration. For that reason, academic knowledge has been accumulated on policy deliberations on Manchurian emigration, including the rural economic revitalization movement, the institutional history of related organizations, including "*gun*" (counties) and legal systems, as well as agricultural policy and production in Manchuria.[3]

Preceding studies claim that "the sending of agricultural emigrants to Manchuria was not significantly influenced by economic factors." Rather they contend that the emigration movement was primarily influenced by the policies of the central government. However, despite this emphasis, most studies about Japanese emigration to Manchuria have been written acknowledging that rural impoverishment was an important background to and consideration of the central government in its policy planning. Whilst the government played a key role, "the project of agricultural emigration to Manchuria was designed to eliminate social unrest by sending out surplus farmers to Manchuria, thereby solving land and famine problems in rural communities".[4]

In other examples of emigration, such as that from Ireland to the United States in the wake of the 1840s potato famine and emigration to advanced Western European nations from former colonies and from Eastern European countries in the latter half of the twentieth century, unemployment and poverty in the sending regions were important background factors to the population flows. In Japan too, it can be argued that aside from central government policy support, emigration to Manchuria just before World War II was prompted by the fact that rural communities across the country could no longer maintain their socioeconomic living standards. Emigration is not something that can be explained by policy measures or the political environment alone. The conditions that confronted those who actually became emigrants should also be considered.

[2] Yamada Shōji ed., "*Kindai Minshū no Kiroku: 6. Manshū Imin (The Records of Modern People: 6. Emigrants to Manchuria)*" (Shin-Jinbutsuōraisha, 1978), Nozoe Kenji, "*Umi wo Watatta Kaitaku Nōmin (Frontier Farmers Who Traveled across the Sea)*" (NHK Publishing, 1978), etc.

[3] Study Group on the History of Emigration to Manchuria, "*Nihon Teikokushugi Ka no Manshū Imin (The Emigration to Manchuria under Japanese Imperialism)*," Ryūkeishosha, 1976; Takahashi Yasutaka, "*Shōwa Sengoki no Nōson to Manshū Imin 1 (Rural Communities in the Shōwa Postwar Period and the Emigration to Manchuria 1)*," Yoshikawa Kōbunkan, 1997; Tama Shinnosuke, "*Sōryokusen Taisei Ka no Manshū Nōgyō Imin (The Agricultural Emigration to Manchuria under the All-Out War System)*," Yoshikawa Kōbunkan, 2016.

[4] Kobayashi Nobusuke, "*Hitobito wa Naze Manshū ni Watattanoka—Nagano Ken no Shakai Undō to Imin (Why People Crossed the Sea to Travel to Manchuria—Social Movements and Emigration in Nagano Prefecture)*," 2015, p. 188.

However, this chapter, like preceding studies, questions the assumption that poverty automatically leads to emigration. For example, while Nagano Prefecture became impoverished as its sericulture industry slumped and subsequently sent out a particularly large number of emigrants to Manchuria[5] preceding studies have demonstrated the importance of the effectiveness of the Manchuria emigration administration in Nagano Prefecture and the influence of policies in prompting people to emigrate to Manchuria.[6] Considering poverty as the push and various policies as the pull factors behind emigration, it would follow that all areas across Nagano Prefecture would send out emigrants to Manchuria. In practice, however, regional differences in the actual numbers of emigrants can be observed. In Kanō Village (subject of the preceding chapter), in which a well-established industrial cooperative existed, emigration to Manchuria was a topic little discussed despite the economic decline and impoverishment seen across the village. This may have been due to the existence of a community safety net, such as an effectively functioning regional cooperative that contributed to maintaining social stability in times of economic plight and thus mitigating the poverty-driven push factor.

Previous studies on Japanese emigration, including emigration to Manchuria, have analyzed socioeconomic factors in the sending regions and have sought to understand imbalances in the regional distribution of emigration.[7] Particular attention has been paid to economic cycles within individual villages, including in the agricultural sector, and the relative strength of communal ties. While preceding studies have been aware of the function of communal ties (that might be termed social capital), they have assumed such communal ties could only function within a given region and have overlooked the economic function, including financial, of such ties within a given community. Thus, this chapter focuses on the economic functions performed by organizations and communities as well as their connections and cooperation with wider external networks.

In considering the background of the emigration movement, this chapter examines the effects of new economic organizations, such as cooperatives, established in the modern period, and their financial networks. This is because regionally-based industrial cooperatives during the interwar period did more than simply collect deposits locally, they also became able to connect themselves to a national network of popular funds, a network of cooperative financial organizations centering on the Central Bank for Industrial Cooperatives and the Deposit Bureau Funds of the Ministry of Finance. This book has shown that reginal economies became able to secure and advance the funds required for maintaining and improving their livelihood through cooperation with national financial networks, and that this was an important element underpinning the stability of regional economies. Networks of popular funds, so to speak,

[5] Publication Society for the History of the Development of Manchuria of the Self-Promotion Society of Nagano Prefecture ed., "*Nagano-Ken Manshū Kaitakushi (History of the Manchuria Development By Nagano Prefecture)*," 1984.

[6] Araragi Shinzou, "'*Manshū Imin' no Rekishi Shakaigaku (The Historical Sociology of the 'Emigration to Manchuria')*," Kohrosha, 1994, pp. 105–117.

[7] Araragi Shinzou, "'*Manshū Imin' no Rekishi Shakaigaku (The Historical Sociology of the 'Emigration to Manchuria')*," pp. 83–87.

emerged in Japanese society and could function as a kind of safety net for local communities in times of unprecedented rural economic crises, as occurred during the interwar period. However, this positive assessment is derived from successful examples. In this chapter, therefore, the question of how rural communities without cooperative organizations addressed the economic plight of the interwar years. How did they manage without a cooperative organization in their village which could accumulate and manage popular funds, and that could connect them to external networks of popular funds? Furthermore, this chapter seeks to ascertain what responses the networks took to rural regions that were isolated from such networks of popular funds.

9.2 The Case of Seinaiji Village

9.2.1 An Overview of Seinaiji Village in the Modern Period

This chapter examines the case of Seinaiji Village in Shimoina County, Nagano Prefecture, which was referred to briefly in Chap. 7. Seinaiji Village was located in an area where the industrial cooperative movement was active, though for many years it did not have its own industrial cooperative. Furthermore, as the administrative districts of the early modern period were carried over into the modern period, the organizations and customs of the early modern period remained relatively strong in Seinaiji Village compared to other villages.[8]

Seinaiji Village was a mountain village near Iida, in the southern part of Nagano Prefecture. The village, which had consisted of upper and lower areas since the early modern period, went through temporary mergers with other villages in the Meiji Period, but ultimately remained as Seinaiji Village from 1889 into the twenty-first century, maintaining the administrative district of the early modern period. In 1889, the village's population stood at 1401, with the number of households totaling 259 and the arable land area totaled 97 chō, 9 tan, 26 bu (≒ 97 ha), with rice paddies and dry fields combined. Since Seinaiji Village is a mountain village, the bulk of the arable land was made up of dry fields, with few rice paddies. The arable land area per household was 3 tan 7 se (≒ 0.37 ha), and tobacco was mainly produced on this small arable land area during the nineteenth century. In the twentieth century, mulberry leaves for sericulture became the chief crop in the village.

---

[8] The continuity can be seen evidently in the relationship of accession from youth to a young men's association and the continued existence of "*kukai*," lower autonomous organizations of the village. For details, see Tanaka Hikaru, "Kinsei kara Kindai Shoki ni Okeru Kyōdōtai Kinō no Hensen—Seinenkai to Kukai ni Chūmoku Site (The Transition of Community Functions from the Early Modern Period to the Beginning of the Modern Period—Focusing on Young Men's Associations and *Kukai*)," Yoshida Nobuyuki ed., "*Yamazato Seinaiji no Shakai Kozo (The Social Structure of Mountain Village Seinaiji)*" (Yamakawa Shuppansha, 2018).

In addition to the above, the main village industry had been forestry since the early modern period. Sales of lumber and charcoal-making had long been a significant source of cash income.[9] By the 1910s, the livelihoods of Seinaiji Village's inhabitants were based on cash earned from sericulture and charcoal-making which was then used to purchase food from outside the village.

In laborious tasks such as road development and the tending of common forests, administrative work was borne not by the village but by its lower organizations, namely, the "*kukai*" of the village's upper and lower areas. After the Taisho Period, the village became the owner of the common forests instead of the "*ku*," albeit nominally, as the management of the common land property was still borne by the "*ku*".[10] The "*ku*" put together and executed each year's budget, and as the source of revenue in that budget, the "*ku*" also had the authority to impose taxes on "*kukai*" members.[11] In Seinaiji Village, the "*ku*," a geographically-based organization, played a significant role as an unofficial administrative organization and also as a powerful livelihood community.

What then was the situation in Seinaiji Village in the 1920s and the 1930s? According to the "*Sonsei Ichiran (Table of Village Conditions)*" for 1933, prepared by the village office of Seinaiji Village,[12] the population as recorded in local family registers stood at 2149, while the resident population stood at 1933. This shows that the population had increased over its level in the Meiji Period, but that about 10% of the population recorded in family registers had left the village for work, perhaps in the wake of the recession in the 1930s. The number of households was 389, with five to six persons per household on average. There were 452 children of school age, meaning that, on average, each family had at least one child who was attending elementary school. The development of sericulture from the Meiji Period to the Taisho Period and the booming economy influenced by World War I made it possible for the people of Seinaiji Village to afford an expansion of their household size.

In terms of occupations, the village was made up of 308 landed-farmer households and 64 tenant-farmer households. No figures were available for sub-categories of tenant-farmer households. In the village, there were no farming households could be recognized as pure tenant farmers. In any case, there existed little of the confrontation between farmland owners and tenant farmers that was prevalent in many Japanese farming villages prior to World War II. Indeed, it could be characterized as a community of relatively equal small-scale farming households.

---

[9] Seinaiji Village, "*Seinaiji Mura Shi Gekan (Seinaiji Village History Volume 2)*," 1982, pp. 9–10.

[10] Lower Seinaiji Kari Kukai, "*Hōkokusho (Report)*," January 18, 1918, documents owned by Seinaiji Shimo (Lower) Ku 14–42.

[11] Kari Kukai, "*Taishō Go Nen Ichi Gatsu Kai Shimo Seinaiji Kiyaku (January 1916 Revised Lower Seinaiji Rules)*," 1916, documents owned by lower Seinaiji *Ku* [14–42].

[12] The following statistical data were based on Seinaiji Village, "*Shōwa Hachi Nen Shi Gatsu Shirabe Nagano Ken Shimoina Gun Seinaiji Sonsei Ichiran (Table of Village Conditions in Seinaiji, Shimoina County, Nagano Prefecture, Surveyed in April 1933)*" (1933, documents [2–11-5–9] possessed by the Seinaiji Post Office).

In Seinaiji Village, there were a total of 23 small farmers' cooperatives, whose establishment was encouraged by the government at the time. Since the number of members of these cooperatives stood at 372, the same as the number of farming households, it is highly likely that all farming households had joined. Similarly, the agricultural association's membership stood at 373, with 20 persons named as representatives, and thus it can be fairly assumed that it too mustered support from all farming households in the village. On the other hand, there were only three sericulture unions in the village, and membership was much smaller, amounting to only 41 persons. Given that a total of 254 households were engaged in the sericulture industry, the organization rate of sericulture unions was much lower than other agriculture-related cooperatives.

Table 9.1 provides evidence of the industrial structure of the village. Agriculture along with cocoon and silk thread accounted for most of the village's total production. However, between 1930 and 1932, the value of output from sericulture declined significantly despite relatively little change in the volume of output volume. This reflected the adverse effects of the sharp drop in cocoon prices at the time which greatly affected the village's economy. Nevertheless, at the beginning of the 1930s, sericulture remained the main industry of Seinaiji Village. While dry fields in Seinaiji Village in FY1932 totaled 1163 tan (≒ 115.4 ha) in terms of land registers, the land area planted with mulberries reached 1312 tan (≒ 130.1 ha), indicating that, in order to support sericulture, mulberries were planted in areas that were not originally dry fields. Conversely, planted areas for vegetables accounted for only 287 tan (≒ 28.5 ha) and fruits only 45 tan (≒ 4.5 ha). With a relatively small rice paddy area, most farming households in Seinaiji Village stuck with the business model of securing cash income from sericulture even in the face of the declining cocoon prices.

The village's main manufactured products included "*giri*," a mechanical part used in the silk-reeling industry. While the number of *giri* factories stood at 20, there were only 21 mechanics. The value of *giri* output in FY1933 totaled ¥2400, indicating household-based small-scale production.[13] Combs, one of the village's specialty products since the early modern period, were produced at 10 factories with output valued at ¥1258. The village's industrial output was not a substantial part of its economy. There were 14,206 tan (≒ 1408 ha) of village-owned forests and 5939 tan (≒ 589 ha) of privately owned forests, and firewood and charcoal from publicly owned forests amounted to 1500 kan (≒ 5625 kg). Lumber from privately owned forests amounted to 560 koku (≒ 156 m^3) and the firewood and charcoal from them 3300 kan (≒ 12,375 kg). These forestry products combined had a total output value of ¥25,146, making up for the fall in sericulture and agricultural production. Having said that, as can be seen from Table 9.1, it was impossible for the forestry industry to completely replace sericulture-related revenues.

The decline in the output value of sericulture at the beginning of the 1930s was due to a drop in market prices, not due to reductions in the volume of output, and in that sense, it was not a problem that sericulture farmers in Seinaiji Village could solve on their own. This dire situation was not limited to Seinaiji Village alone, it stemmed

[13] Seinaiji Village, "*Seinaiji Mura Shi Gekan (Seinaiji Village History Volume 2)*," 1982, p. 294.

Table 9.1 Total output in Seinaiji village and arable land area per household

	Total value	Agriculture	Cocoon and silk threads	Manufacturing	Forestry	Total value of output per household	Arable land by tan (rice paddies, bu)	Arable land by tan (dry fields, bu)	Cocoon output (kan)	Mulberry fields by tan* (bu)
1930	162,995	76,650	60,400	3345	21,250	409	6	37	61	48
1931	109,374	53,149	50,532	3658	12,800	260	6	37	71	48
1932	130,646	50,012	53,730	1329	25,146	326	6	37	Unknown	48

Unit: Yen; *Source* Seinaiji village, "Showa Hachi Nen Nagano Ken Ina Gun Seinaiji Sonsei Ichiran (Table of Village Conditions of Seinaiji, Shimoina County, Nagano Prefecture, Surveyed in March 1933)" (1933, documents 2-11-5-19 possessed by the Seinaiji Post Office). Prepared on the basis of multiple tables. Fishery and livestock industry items were omitted in total output as they represented only tiny amounts. Discrepancies in total output reflect those in the original data. Item marked * shows per-household figures

from a wider slump in the Japanese silk-reeling industry due to a fall in exports to the United States in the 1930s. Opportunities for female migrant labor work in the silk-reeling industry, much of it located within Nagano Prefecture, also decreased.[14] While the exact number of female workers in the silk-reeling sector from Seinaiji Village at the time is unknown, the decline in such migratory labor opportunities is believed to have compounded the reduction of farm household earnings caused by the fall in sericulture revenues.

Sericulture products tended to become subject to erratic market prices even when the economy boomed. The sericulture industry required substantial cash outlays to purchase silkworm-egg cards and fertilizer for mulberries, and many small and medium-sized farm households borrowed funds temporarily to meet these payments and engage in sericulture. Before the long-term recession, however, all borrowed funds could be repaid thanks to rising cocoon prices. Thus, many farming households relying on sericulture as their main source of earnings faced an economic crisis during the interwar period when prices of silk yarn and cocoons continued to fall. Seinaiji Village was no exception.

9.2.2 The Impact of the Financial Crisis and the Village's Responses

Declines in cocoon prices had already become conspicuous across Japan from around 1925, and the economy of Seinaiji Village appears to have been adversely affected from that time. How did the financial crisis of 1927 and the extensive frost damage in Nagano Prefecture and other places in Japan at around the same time affect Seinaiji Village? Though the consequences of these unfortunate developments have already been taken up in other chapters, here it is worth covering them again in relation to Seinaiji Village.

After the Shōwa financial crisis occurred in 1927, a moratorium was introduced to calm the financial panic. During this moratorium period, extensive frost damage hit Nagano Prefecture and other areas in the country. The affected areas were the main production areas of Japan's silk industry and the frost damage principally affected mulberry leaf growing by sericulture farming households.

The sericulture industry required the seasonal revolving of funds for purchases of silkworm-egg cards and fertilizers for mulberries. Farming households often found themselves pressed for cash to make their tax payments and food purchases in addition to maintaining the funds required for business-related outlays. They also faced a reluctance on the part of banks and other lenders to lend funds in the wake of the financial crisis, which was compounded by disruption to sericulture revenues that season due to the frost damage. As a result, Nagano Prefecture encountered a major financial crisis.

---

[14] Vocational Division, Nagano Prefecture, "*Nagano Ken Sangyō Rōdō Jijō (Industry and Labor Situation in Nagano Prefecture)*," 1938.

As detailed in Chap. 7, in response to the financial crisis the central government provided relief financing through the Ministry of Finance's Deposit Bureau funds. In part because of the sheer extent of the frost damage, especially on the crucial sericulture industry, the total amount of financing reached an unprecedented scale for such relief financing (i.e. in response to frost damage).

Proposal 1 Concerning the Provision of Relief Funds for Hail and Frost Damage.

For allocation as relief funds for the hail and frost damage that affected the prefectures of Fukushima, Tochigi, Gunma, Tokyo, Yamanashi, Nagano, Gifu and Okayama from April through June 1927, the Deposit Bureau shall provide a total of ¥8.33 million to the Nihon Kangyō Bank, prefectural agricultural and industrial banks and the Central Bank for Industrial Cooperatives:

1. Format of fund provision: The underwriting of debentures issued by the Nihon Kangyō Bank, agricultural and industrial banks and the Central Bank for Industrial Cooperatives.
2. Interest rate: The Deposit Bureau's debenture underwriting interest rate at an annual 4.8%; the lending interest by the Nihon Kangyō Bank, agricultural and industrial banks and the Central Bank for Industrial Cooperatives at 5.4%.

Repayment period: Within 5 years for funds for mulberry tree replanting, within 2 years for other funds.[15]

Following the decision by the Deposit Bureau, in Nagano Prefecture, the prefectural government allotted amounts of relief funds to the local governments concerned based on the reports they had submitted on the damage in their respective areas. As ascertained in Chap. 7, the relief financing in 1927 marked an important beginning of the emergency connection of the two largest networks of public funds, namely Deposit Bureau funds and cooperative financing of industrial cooperatives, to ensure prompt procedures and convenience in fund provision. In Seinaiji Village, however, these funds were provided through the Nagano Agricultural and Industrial Bank. As there existed no industrial cooperatives in the village, there was no way to obtain finance through the Central Bank for Industrial cooperatives, through which relief funds were supplied. The allocation of relief funds, amounting to ¥20,000 for the entire village, was carried out nevertheless.

Nō[Agriculture] No. 154

August 7, 1927 Seinaiji Village Mayor

To [Addressee left blank]:

Concerning the Loan Amount of Frost Damage Relief Funds……

1. ¥19,900 Allotments of frost damage relief funds

Breakdown

[15] Savings Bureau, Ministry of Finance, "*Yokin Bu Shikin Unyō Iinkai (Dai Jurokkai Kaigi) Gijiroku (The Minutes of the Steering Committee of the Deposit Bureau Funds [16th Meeting])*," July 13, 1927.

1. **¥19,900 Allotment related to mulberry fields (handled by the Agricultural and Industrial Bank)

Lending terms and conditions

1. Lending period.

- Long-term: 5 years or less (funds for replanting damaged mulberry fields).
- Short-term: 2 years or less (funds for purchasing fertilizers and silkworm eggs, funds for fruit farms).[16]

Without an industrial cooperative in Seinaiji Village, relief funds were first allotted to the two upper and lower "*ku*" areas after discussions at the village assembly, and the respective "*ku*" then decided on how to distribute the allotted funds. Each "*ku*" distributed the funds by having its affiliated regional organization in the same "*ku*", called "*kumiai*," borrow them. It was impossible for individual households to directly borrow funds from the Agricultural and Industrial Bank, because the bank essentially required a potential borrower to be a juridical person or to be a group of ten or more members.

The "*kumiai,*" which were present in each area of Seinaiji Village, were regional organizations that had existed in the village since the early modern period.[17] This organization was a subsidiary body of the "*ku,*" which itself was an autonomous organization, undertaking preparations for the village's festivals and day-to-day issues such as road maintenance. Thus, the "*kumiai*" that composed each "*ku*" were essentially neighborhood organizations, and each "*kumiai*" was composed of more than ten members.

The following document describes the consultations in the lower "*ku*" regarding the distribution of relief funds.

Matters for Consultation

1. Concerning the decision on the allotment of frost damage relief funds
   As we received frost damage relief funds totaling ¥19,900, we wish to consult about the advisability of allotting ¥10,000 to the Seinaiji upper "*ku*" and ¥9900 to the Seinaiji lower "*ku*" for borrowing.
2. Since the borrowing method calls for unsecured borrowings by ten or more persons, if members of a farmers' cooperative and members of a conventional cooperative are the same, that cooperative can borrow the funds. When this is not the case for the cooperative concerned, either a farmers' cooperative or a cooperative organized only by members of a conventional cooperative qualified for borrowing can borrow the funds.
3. The standard method concerning the decision on the amount of funds allotted to each cooperative

   (a) 20% shall be allotted on the basis of the number of households,

[16] Documents in possession of the Seinaiji Post Office [Ya 17].

[17] Mori Kenji, "*Dezukuri no Sato—Sono Minzoku to Rekishi (Villages Cultivating Farmland Away from Home—Their Folk Customs and History),*" Shinyosha, 1989, pp. 17–22.

(b) 80% shall be allocated on the basis of levies on the number of households and the value of land held.
(c) Of the allocated funds in the preceding item, the advisability of half being delivered in cash and the other half delivered in kind (by joint purchases of rice and wheat).

4. The method of restricting the borrowings of funds by sufficient funded farmers:
   If any sufficient funded farmer still needs to borrow relief funds, his cooperative should supply him up to an equal amount of the funds, by dividing the allocated amount to the cooperative concerned by the number of borrowers and taking measures to relieve farmers with considerably few funds...[18]

As can be surmised from the consultations of the Seinaiji lower "*kukai*," special care was given to provide a greater portion of the available relief funds to impoverished members within the cooperative. It is also especially noteworthy that there is a high likelihood that half of the funds supplied as relief funds were distributed in kind through the joint purchases of rice and wheat. When the financial crisis and the frost damage in 1927 struck, Seinaiji Village faced an economic crisis that was accompanied by a food shortage. Importance was given to assistance measures that entailed a relatively low degree of freedom for those individuals receiving them. Distribution of relief in kind in Seinaiji Village as food meant that relief could not be used for the rebuilding of self-employed farmers nor for debt repayments.

Why then were such assistance measures taken? To understand this, it is necessary to look back at how Seinaiji Village responded to times of crisis, particularly famine, in the early modern period. A document (quoted below) presumed to have been prepared by village executives and submitted to a local magistrate's office in 1842 suggests that village executives borrowed external funds, which were then distributed within the village for individuals to borrow, a format nearly identical to the one adopted in 1927.

> Following the poorer than expected harvest and high rice prices of recent years in Seinaiji Village, prices having increased further lately, impoverished people are facing greater difficulties. The local lord, terribly worried about the situation, wished to offer some assistance, but local financial officials failed to accommodate the lord's request for help due to the strained fiscal position. As no rice was planted in Seinaiji Village, farmers found the difficult situation no longer bearable. Under these circumstances, one of the local officials, Nakae, was instructed by the lord to borrow 10 bales [≑ 600 kg] of rice each month despite the difficult and stringent fiscal position. In the current month, the lord had already paid out 40 ryō [a little under ¥50,000 in the present day] in rice payments. Local village officials identified very hard-pressed farmers and had them borrow rice individually. Farmers who faced hardship because of their laziness or indulgence in farming were not allowed to borrow rice until they had truly reformed themselves. After careful scrutiny, if lazy farmers were found to have changed, they were allowed to borrow rice. Village officials followed this procedure and handled everything honestly. Those farmers allowed to borrow rice, as described above,

[18] Documents in the possession of the Seinaiji Post Office, [Ya 17]. "*Kyōgi Jikō (Matters for Consultations)*," which may have been prepared in August 1927.

under the lord's instructions were placed under surveillance to see whether they were diligent in their farming work, and village officials kept a close watch over them.[19]

The above document notes that an appeal for relief was made to the local lord and that "no rice was planted in Seinaiji Village". Evidently, the rural mountain village had long not been self-sufficient in food. In this case in the first half of the nineteenth century, the local lord offered assistance by providing "10 bales of rice each month" or by supplying rice in kind in the form of loans despite the difficult and stringent fiscal position faced in his domain. As the document stated that "local village officials identified very hard-pressed farmers and had them borrow rice individually," the administrative organization in Seinaiji Village must have distributed this rice in kind after examining the degree of poverty of individual households. In other words, already in the early modern period, Seinaiji Village had designed a mechanism under which the autonomous administrative organization of farmers in the village could receive external relief funds or relief supplies in kind, decide on allotments to individual households and then distribute them through smaller subsidiary groups in the village. As seen above, this mechanism was designed to function in times of emergency.

In the early modern period, warehouses for stockpiling grain, called "*gisō*" or "*shasō*," and "*machi-gaisho,*" in the Edo Period, were established across Japan to deal with natural disasters and famine. They provided "*bikō chochiku*" provisions derived from contributions made by local residents as a kind of preparation or countermeasure for famine or other crises.[20] These stockpiles often consisted of rice and other grains in kind. In other words, it was common not only in Seinaiji Village but also across Japan in the early modern period for relief measures in times of emergency to be taken in the form of the supply of food in kind.

In the Meiji Period, on the other hand, these local stockpiling systems were, in effect, gradually abolished, under the government's policy to turn them into common property, or assets, of individual local governments, rather than stockpiles as measures to respond to natural disasters. In place of the stockpiling system, the "*Bikō Chochiku Hō* (the *Act for Famine-Preparation Stockpiles)*" was enacted in 1880. This too was abolished in 1899, and the Deposit Bureau of the Ministry of Finance inherited the central famine-preparation reserves. As the Deposit Bureau would later do, in the modern period it became common across Japan for relief financing in times of emergency to be provided in cash instead of in kind (i.e., grain).

In the wake of the 1927 financial depression and the frost damage crisis, however, Seinaiji Village distributed relief financing from the Deposit Bureau within the village in the form of the supply of food in kind, following, in a way, the crisis response customs that had been in place since the early modern period. The difference was,

---

19 Documents of Tosaya, Seinaiji Village, Seinaiji Village, "*Seinaiji Mura Shi Jōkan (Seinaiji Village History Volume 1)*," 1982, p. 432.

20 Kikuchi Isao, "*Kinsei no Kikin (Famine in the Early Modern Period)*," Yoshikwa Kōbunkan, 1997; Yoshida Nobuyuki, "*Kinsei Kyodai Toshi no Shakai Kōzō (The Social Structure of Huge Cities in the Early Modern Period)*," University of Tokyo Press, 1991.

however, that the relief funds had been provided by the Deposit Bureau, through long-term low-interest financing. As such they were simply loans that had to be repaid in cash. Despite a grace period of up to 5 years, these loans were due for repayment in 1932 at the latest. If a booming economy had followed in subsequent years, it would have been another story. But a worldwide depression broke out in 1929, and as the Japanese government lifted the embargo on the export of gold, causing a new financial crisis, the Japanese economy failed to recover during the period.

9.3 For the Relief from the Depression: The Central Government's Policies and Local Communities

With the overall economic conditions failing to improve, how did Seinaiji Village, with its heavy debt burden, manage to cope with the situation having ridden out the initial emergency by converting its relief financing into food supplies?

In 1931, Seinaiji Village again received a supply of Deposit Bureau funds, this time called "Low-Interest Funds for Temporary Measures for the Relief of Unemployment in Farming, Mountain and Fishing Villages." This measure was part of what is often called Takahashi Fiscal Policy, a kind of Keynesian policy led by Minister of Finance Takahashi Korekiyo that sought to stimulate troubled regional economies, with rural areas particularly targeted.[21] The selection of Seinaiji Village as a recipient of these low-interest funds meant that the central government recognized the village's plight and its need for positive assistance.

Consultations on the distribution of funds supplied in the village were as follows.

> The Matter for Resolution by the Village Assembly on January 12 [1931] Concerning the Lending of Low-Interest Funds for Temporary Measures for the Relief of Unemployment
>
> 1. The standard for the allotment of the funds to the upper and lower *ku* shall be based on the grade of local taxes imposed on each household.
>
> 2. An eligible recipient of the lending of the funds shall be the first registrant in the family register who can be recognized as a responsible person to be engaged in farming in the future.
>
> 3. The funds shall be lent out for small-scale cultivation and replanting by a group of ten or more individuals taking joint responsibility and who can be recognized as capable of administering farming business.
>
> However, an individual may borrow the funds, albeit only for small-scale cultivation, when putting up collateral.

[21] Kase Kazutoshi, "*Senzen Nihon no Shitsugyō Taisaku—Kyūsai-gata Kōkyō Doboku Jigyō no Shiteki Bunseki (Measures to Counter Unemployment in Prewar Japan—An Historical Analysis of Relief-Oriented Public Civil Engineering Works)*," Nihon Keizai Hyōronsha, 1998. The major feature of the supply of the Deposit Bureau funds in 1931 was that the funds were provided directly to local governments without going through related financial institutions such as the Nihon Kangyō Bank. However, preceding studies point to the limits of the policy effect of this supply of the Deposit Bureau funds because of the fact that the funds did not go through financial institutions, including industrial cooperatives.

4. The standard for the allotment of an amount to each group shall be based on the grade of local taxes imposed on each household [...]

10. Financing standard based on the grade of local taxes imposed on each household

From Grade 1 to Grade 4 ¥55

From Grade 6 to Grade 10 ¥50

From Grade 11 to Grade 15 ¥45

From Grade 16 to Grade 20 ¥40

From Grade 21 to Grade 25 ¥35

From Grade 26 to Grade 30 ¥30

From Grade 31 to Grade 35 ¥25

1. Allotted Amount of Funds

• ¥9100 Funds for replanting

• ¥3500 Funds for small-scale cultivation[22]

At the national level, Takahashi Fiscal Policy is associated with the implementation of public works projects in regional areas as unemployment relief measures. In Seinaiji Village, however, the Deposit Bureau funds provided for the sake of unemployment relief were not used for public works. Applications for the funds were made to bolster sericulture, the village's main industry. As a result, the village allotted ¥9100 for replanting mulberry trees and ¥3500 for the cultivation of farmland. The Deposit Bureau funds at the time were lent out directly to local governments, without having to go through the Nihon Kangyō Bank or other financial institutions. Thus, the Seinaiji Village Office provided the funds to individuals by way of lending the funds to residents and business operators within the village.

In the actual distribution of funds to individuals, the village made use of existing local organizations, just as it had done in 1927. A "*kumiai*," a subsidiary organization of the "*kukai*," served as an intermediate receptacle by receiving the funds from the village office. The village assembly had decided in advance that the amount of borrowing by each group should be allotted on the basis of the local tax grades levied on "*kumiai*" members. In other words, it was basically impossible for individual "*kumiai*" or individuals to borrow the amounts required according to their respective demands.

How, then, were the funds distributed within a "*kumiai*"? This is indicated in a written acknowledgment of debt prepared by one of the village's "*kumiai*."

[...]

[22] Documents in possession of the Seinaiji Post Office, [Ya 17]; Seinaiji Village Office, "The Matter for Resolution by the Village Assembly on January 12 Concerning the Lending of Low-Interest Funds for Temporary Measures for the Relief of Unemployment," believed to have been prepared on January 12, 1931.

1. **The borrowed money shall have a period of deferment until August 31, 1932, and shall be repaid in equal installments over 5 years up until 1936.
2. Interest shall be 4.2% a year, which is also applicable to the period of deferment, and the amount repaid calculated at that rate shall be as shown in a yearly table in an accompanying paper.

......

May 15, 1931

Obligor 87 Seinaiji Village, Shimoina County

Hara Tsunegorō (Seal)

Ditto 83 Seinaiji Village, Shimoina County

Nomura Tōji (Seal) ... [11 further persons omitted][23]

The above written acknowledgement from the "Ichiba" *kumiai* listed 13 people of the lower *ku* area, including Hara Tsunegorō and Nomura Tōji. It shows that the *kumiai* allotted funds to *kumiai* members according to the local tax grade imposed on each household.[24] In accordance with the decision by the village assembly, the funds were distributed to *kumiai* members individually in amounts that ranged from ¥43 to ¥73. This does not mean, however, that the *kumiai* was solely an organization that delivered the relief funds received. Existing documents show that the *kumiai* was a territorial group that submitted data on land for cultivation and replanting, as well as business plans, to the village. It is not entirely clear from the documents retained by the Ichiba *kumiai* whether these cultivation and agricultural improvement projects were actually carried out, but they still show that in receiving the Deposit Bureau funds, the ability to plan projects and prepare necessary documents were required of regional fund recipients, even if the receiving organization contained no members with secondary or higher education. The absence of an industrial cooperative in Seinaiji Village meant that small-scale territorial groups were the only entities that could manage the required paperwork. It can be assumed, as seen in 1927, that the *kumiai* also had the capacity to distribute food and funds since the early modern period.

It was not allowed, at least ostensibly, to use funds borrowed from the Deposit Bureau as a makeshift relief fund for the purchase of food or redemption of older debts. Deposit Bureau funds were supposed to be provided as investment funds, or loans that were expected to be recovered from business operations.

Another set of documents reveals that in 1932 the economy of Seinaiji Village remained financially hard-pressed, so much so that it was unable to repay the Deposit

---

[23] Documents in possession of the Seinaiji Post Office, [Ya 17]; A group of 13 persons, including Nomura Tōji and Hara Tsunejirō, "*Shakuyō Shōsho (Written Acknowledgment of Debt)*," (addressed to the Seinaiji Village Mayor) May 15, 1931.

[24] The standard for the allotment of an amount per capita is altered from the village assembly decision above. It is believed that the numbers were changed when actually providing the funds later.

Bureau funds. The repayment deadline of the Deposit Bureau funds borrowed in 1927 came in 1932 and the local authorities of Seinaiji Village received a notification to that effect from the Nihon Kangyō Bank[25], which had absorbed the Nagano Agricultural and Industrial Bank. Seinaiji Village circulated this notification throughout the village, most likely addressing it to the representatives of groups that had received the loans.

Nō[Aguriculture] No. 166

June 10, 1932 Seinaiji Village Mayor

To Mr. Nomura Tōji and another representative,

With respect to the repayment of frost damage relief funds borrowed in 1927, we received a notification from the Matsumoto Branch of Nihon Kangyō Bank, as shown in the copy of the attachment to the notification. Please give due consideration to the notification.

Copy of the Attachment June 8, 1932 The Matsumoto Branch of Nihon Kangyō Bank

Dear Mayor of Seinaiji Village

We hope this letter finds you well. In light of the current plight of rural communities, the government recently decided to supply emergency funds for fertilizers and sericulture, and our bank, the Nihon Kangyō Bank, was designated to handle this financing. Seinaiji Village has outstanding borrowings of ¥11,800 (the breakdown by borrowing group is as shown in the attachment) from the 1927 frost damage relief funds, which are due in July this year. As the government has decided not to extend the repayment deadline for these outstanding borrowings, your village is required to repay the full amount by the deadline. In view of the current recession, however, there might be some borrowers who find it impossible to repay the whole amount, and thus we were instructed to make arrangements for borrowing groups unable to redeem the above to refinance the existing debts with the latest low-interest funds under the following conditions. With the above understanding from the groups that borrowed the frost damage relief funds listed in the attachment, we have been instructed to pay due heed to allot on a priority basis the latest low-interest funds to groups unable to make full repayments.

Therefore, please be advised that we will send application forms for new borrowing after the prefectural government decides on allotments to each of the towns and villages.

Conditions for the refinancing of the 1927 frost damage relief funds:

1. **Interest shall be paid in full amount at the July payment period.

For the principal amount due in July, at least 10% shall be repaid in cash and the remainder refinanced using the current new low-interest funds.[26]

---

[25] During the interwar period, Nihon Kangyō Bank absorbed agricultural and industrial banks nationwide. The absorption of the Nagano Agricultural and Industrial Bank took place in 1930, and following this the Nihon Kangyō Bank took over Seinaiji Village's relief financing debt. Nihon Kangyō Bank, "*Nihon Kangyō Bank Nanajū Nen Shi (The 70-Year History of the Nihon Kangyō Bank)*," 1967, p. 25.

[26] Documents in possession of the Seinaiji Post Office, [Ji 2–11-9].

The notification given by the Nihon Kangyō Bank indicated that of the ¥19,900 of the frost damage relief funds provided to Seinaiji Village, ¥11,800, or more than half of the total amount, was borrowed for 5 years. Furthermore, it showed that the government was aware that the economic conditions of rural communities at the time, not only in Seinaiji Village but across the country, made it difficult to repay relief funds. Despite that awareness, the government could not treat them as bad debts, since the relief funds in 1927 were provided from Deposit Bureau funds which were not government fiscal resources raised through taxation or government bond issuance. Deposit Bureau funds were principally funded with postal savings, and as such, the government was obliged to ensure the repayment plans of those relief funds be achieved without delay. The government attempted to ensure the fulfillment of the repayment plans by allotting "on a priority basis the latest low-interest funds to groups unable to make full repayments" of funds borrowed previously for frost damage relief. In other words, the government offered an opportunity for groups deemed unable to repay the relief funds to first repay their outstanding debt to the Deposit Bureau with new low-interest funds from the Deposit Bureau, or alternatively a possibility to refinance the old debt with new funds. Through this measure, the government tried to temporarily eliminate the debt repayment obligations of rural communities and thereby prevent a worsening of the repayment status of the Deposit Bureau funds and its balance of payments.

In the actual documents on the lending conditions of the Deposit Bureau funds to be returned to regions during FY1932, the funds concerned were actually supplied under the name of "funds related to the refinancing of high-interest debts". This suggests that as the Japanese economy was in the doldrums, the government sought broad temporary relief from Deposit Bureau fund debt repayment through further lending and refinancing. However, it is believed that the refinancing funds offered by the Nihon Kangyō Bank to Seinaiji Village were not from the quota of "funds related to the refinancing of high-interest debts," because the lending conditions noted were as follows:

> Funds for refinancing old debts, with interest rates of 6% or higher, borrowed for the same purpose as the existing Deposit Bureau funds provided. However, old debts from Deposit Bureau funds cannot be refinanced with these new funds.[27]

These lending conditions suggest that the government considered the refinancing of Deposit Bureau funds with newly provided Deposit Bureau funds an undesirable measure. In FY1932, however, the Deposit Bureau of the Ministry of Finance lent out funds to regions via the Nihon Kangyō Bank and agricultural and industrial banks under many other names, including "emergency funds to deal with unemployment," "emergency funds for sericulture" and "industrial funds for small and medium-sized commercial and industrial businesses." Through these variously named funding facilities, the de facto refinancing of existing Deposit Bureau funds borrowed with new Deposit Bureau funds occurred across Japan. In the case of Seinaiji Village, as the

---

[27] Deposit Bureau, Ministry of Finance, "*Shōwa Hachi Nen Ku Gatsu Shirabe Yokinbu Chihō Shikin Yūzū Jōken Ichiranhyō (List of Lending Conditions of the Deposit Bureau Funds for Regions, Surveyed in September 1933)*," 1934, p. 22.

official document Nō [Agriculture] No. 166, cited above, referred to "the supply of emergency low-interest funds for fertilizers and sericulture," it is believed that the funds to Seinaiji Village were provided via the quota of "emergency funds for sericulture."

For Deposit Bureau funds, there were a variety of uses and limitations on organizations through which the funds were supplied under their respective names. However, during the business depression in the first half of the 1930s, most of the Deposit Bureau funds provided to regions, though supplied under a variety of names, were in practice used as temporary relief funds including to defer the repayment of outstanding debts. Under these circumstances, Seinaiji Village, which in the previous year had obtained Deposit Bureau funds as industrial investment funds, was still unable to afford the complete repayment of old debts and applied for the central government's temporary relief measures for rural economies.

9.4 Limitations on the Offering of the Safety Net and the Manchuria Emigration Policy

9.4.1 The Absence of the Safety Net: Relief with the Supply of Products in Kind

As the preceding section describes, at the beginning of the 1930s, the central government fully recognized the crisis in rural communities. Thus, it provided relief financing in various formats, a safety net with popular funds, making active use of the Deposit Bureau funds of the Ministry of Finance. This supply of funds by the government, discussed in the preceding chapter in the case of Kano Village, could serve as a lender of last resort, albeit with less mobility, securing lower interest rates than otherwise available via cooperative financing, with the industrial cooperative in the village linked to the cooperative financing network of popular funds. In this way, a double financing buffer, that is the buffer of the funds of the industrial cooperative accumulated within the village and the Deposit Bureau funds nationally accumulated and distributed, existed in the local community.

At the beginning of the 1930s, however, an industrial cooperative did not yet exist in Seinaiji Village. This meant that no deposits or accumulated capital existed in an industrial cooperative within the village and that the village had no access to funds for borrowing at the county level, the prefectural level, or from cooperative financing institutions such as the Central Bank for Industrial cooperatives. Thus, in the case of Seinaiji Village, as we have seen up to the preceding section, the only reliable external source of funds was the slow-moving Deposit Bureau. On top of this, the village lacked an organization with professional staff who could handle the procedures for accessing these funds, even then known for being notoriously cumbersome.

These circumstances in Seinaiji Village meant prolonged livelihood difficulties, which in terms of the food situation could be traced back to 1927. With respect to the repayment deadline for Deposit Bureau funds and the deferment of that deadline through further lending of Deposit Bureau funds, a notification to that effect was delivered in early June 1932. However, Seinaiji Village did not only lack funds for repayment at the time. Beginning in April 1932, the agricultural association of Seinaiji Village repeatedly circulated a notice about the sale of government-owned rice within the village, indicating that the food situation in the village had already become strained by the spring. The first delivery of government-owned rice arrived on June 8, 1932.

June 8, 1932 The Agricultural Association of Seinaiji Village

To Heads of the Small Farmers' Cooperatives,

The first consignment of the rice sold off by the government has finally arrived for distribution (however, 50 bales of rice have yet to arrive due to bad road conditions) ...[28]

As mentioned above, the central government provided both funds and food in kind. In a way this action amounted to a revival of the practice of early modern poverty relief supposed to have been abolished in the modern period. Nevertheless, this action had a real significance for local communities like Seinaiji Village facing difficulties in securing food. Indeed, in 1932 Seinaiji Village repeatedly applied for the supply of government rice through the agricultural association.

Agricultural Association No. 127

June 20, 1932 The Agricultural Association of Seinaiji Village

To the Heads of Small Farmers' Cooperatives,

Concerning Mediation for Government-Owned Rice

Regarding the above subject matter, since April, we have already made requests for quantities [of rice] twice and relayed them to the county agricultural association. As the country agricultural association this time asked us to compile a third request for quantities [of rice], please deliberate on the matter below and disseminate to everyone in your cooperative. Please fill in the quantity [requested] in the attached application form, sign and stamp your seal on it, and submit the application by June 26, together with a deposit of ¥1 per bale.

1. Be advised in advance that the rice will be distributed one-and-a-half months to two months after the application.
2. Please fill in the application form clearly including the house number.
3. Please ensure that you stamp your seal on the application very clearly.

Agricultural Association No. 125

June 20, 1932 The Agricultural Association of Seinaiji Village

[28] Documents in the possession of the Seinaiji Post Office, [Ji 2–11-12].

To the Heads of Small Farmers' Cooperatives,

Concerning the Arrival of Government Sold Rice

Regarding the above subject matter of Government sold rice, for which an application was previously filed, please be advised as follows. We were notified by the country agricultural association of information provided by the prefectural agricultural association. Please disseminate this to members of your cooperatives, and ensure that they have payments ready for the rice.

1. **The rice to be distributed on this occasion is all polished rice.
2. The warehouse from which the rice sold off is to be dispatched from: Osaka (polished rice)
3. The dispatch from the warehouse is expected in mid-July
4. The price per bale for delivery at Iida Station is expected to be around ¥7.15

(Deduct the deposit of ¥1 put up at the time of application from the above price)

Please bear in mind that we will let you know the exact price and the date of arrival of the rice as soon as the country agricultural association notifies us.[29]

It appears that the sale of government-owned rice in the 1932 fiscal year came to an end with the third distribution in mid-July. The document indicates that Seinaiji Village was unable to afford purchasing rice on the regular market in July, when summer cocoons were put on sale.

Just ahead of the government relief measure, on May 20, 1932, the aforementioned "*kumiai*" and the small farmers' cooperative in Lower Seinaiji jointly borrowed from the *kukai* of the lower area *ku*.[30] This loan was not for cash but for rice in kind. This demonstrates that the relief system in the Village functioned with the *kukai* securing food in kind and then distributing it among villagers, a practice reminiscent of measures taken in times of famine in the early modern period.

Written Acknowledgment of Debt

The amount of ¥110.56 as the price of 16 bales of rice lent out by the *ku*

We recognize that we have borrowed and received the above amount and will be certain to repay it by July 10, 1932. We hereby submit to you a written acknowledgment of debt.

---

[29] Documents in the possession of the Seinaiji Post Office, [Ji 2–11-11].

[30] Judging from the "lending book of the rice sold off by the government," the territorial groups "*kumiai*" carrying such names as "Ichiba" and "Dai Ichiban" were the same groups as the small farmers' cooperatives that were newly created around 1930, having identical members. This shows that the same territorial group was given two different meanings by having a head of the *kumiai* and a head of the small farmers' cooperative. Lower Seinaiji *Kukai*, "*Seifu Haraisage Kome Kashitsukechō Dai Ikkai Bun (Lending Book of the Rice Sold off by the Government: The First Sale)*," May 1932; Lower Seinaiji *Kukai*, "*Seifu Haraisage Kome Kashitsukechō Dai Nikai Bun (Lending Book of the Rice Sold off by the Government: The Second Sale)*," September 1932, Documents owned by the lower *ku* area, [22–27].

May 20, 1932

Lower Seinaiji

Head of the Dai Ichiban Kumiai: Hara Tsunegorō

Head of the Small Farmers' Cooperative: Nomura Tōji

Addressed to Lower Seinaiji *Kukai*[31]

The rice the *kukai* stocked up on its own before the government rice arrived was lent out to the respective subsidiary *kumiai* within the *ku*. For example, the Dai Ichiban *kumiai*, represented by Hara Tsunegorō, was composed of 16 members and borrowed 16 bales of rice from the lower *ku*. The price was ¥110.56, with interest set at ¥1.60. The borrowing was ostensibly made in money, but in practice each *kumiai* member received a bale of rice in kind in the name of financing from the lower *ku* area. This suggests that it was judged that Seinaiji Village households could not afford to pay the approximately ¥7 in cash.

The lower *ku* area, which acted as the execution entity for the relief measure by procuring rice with its own funds and distributing it to the respective *kumiai*, did not seek to earn much interest through the lending. This fact is indicative of the real conditions of the financial and food crises in Seinaiji Village at the time. For the purchase of the rice, the lower *ku* area withdrew postal savings, eking out the required funds by liquidating the savings or common assets of cooperative members.[32] These collective savings of the local community, instead of personal savings, functioned to relieve those community members suffering from harsh livelihood circumstances.

In Seinaiji Village, the *kukai* was an organization that had its own economic base as well as a political and administrative authority. It was not limited to a tax-collecting function but also had the right to collect forestry revenue and fees for the use of charcoal-making kilns in common forests. Even when the *kukai* made use of its own funds to secure food to provide to its members, it is thought that the *kukai* alone was unable to resolve the deteriorating food situation in Seinaiji Village. Therefore, from the latter half of May to early June, Seinaiji Village, instead of relying on settlement via *kukai* and other communities in the region, finally opted to take advantage of the central government's relief measure in the form of the supply of government-owned rice.

In the wake of the economic crisis brought about by the world depression, Seinaiji Village required a two-stage bailout: a relief measure within the village and another from the central government. While relief within the village was provided as rice in kind, the assistance made use of Deposit Bureau funds and took the form of loans ostensibly for investment in industry. The acceptance of external funds to help

[31] Documents in the possession of the Seinaiji Post Office, [Ji 2–11-22]. In the documents, the amount of money, the number of bales, persons' names and the number given to the *kumiai* were handwritten, and a note in the margin read "of 16 bales of rice, four bales of unpolished rice were delivered.".

[32] Lower Seinaiji *Kukai*, "*Seifu Haraisage Kome Kashitsukechō Dai Ikkai Bun (Lending Book of the Rice Sold off by the Government: The First Sale)*," May 1932; Documents owned by the lower *ku* area, [22–27].

rebuild the village's economy was similar to the case of Kano Village taken up in the preceding chapter. However, the government relief measure still failed to improve economic conditions in Seinaiji Village, which depended heavily on sericulture. While the *kukai*, which operated as an organization underpinning the economic foundation in Seinaiji Village, had revenue from mountain forests, the village's common assets, it did not have sufficient internal deposits or an accumulation of capital and had no links to external financial networks. Unlike the industrial cooperative in Kano Village, the *kukai* thus failed to bolster the village's economy on its own as it could not afford the outlays the serious economic crisis required.

9.4.2 The Reality of the Rural Economic Revitalization Movement in Seinaiji Village

Needless to say, in view of the critical situation, since the middle of the 1930s, Seinaiji Village obtained loans and subsidies from the government to undertake rationalization, including various productivity enhancement, industrial diversification, and cost-cutting measures. After the government launched the "Rural Economic Revitalization Movement" policy in response to the agricultural depression in 1932, Seinaiji Village was designated an "economic revitalization village" in 1933.[33]

The government believed that the problem of rural economies across Japan lay in falling cocoon prices due to the slump in the silk-reeling industry and the decline in rice prices due to an expansion of imported rice. In other words, a decline in farmers' cash earnings because of the worsening balance of income and expenditures in sericulture and rice, the two main products of Japanese farm households, was behind the crisis. There were only two options for improving this situation: improve profitability of existing industries or establish new industries in rural areas.

The Japanese government provided policy support for plans that sought to develop new sideline businesses, including the growing of fruit-bearing trees, livestock raising, as well as farmers' expansion into handicraft industries. At the same time, the improvement of mulberry fields and silkworm breed varieties, and the rationalization of sericulture through improved silkworm nurturing methods were also encouraged. Regarding the fertilizer issue, the government proposed a reduction in fertilizer purchases, urging farmers to produce fertilizers themselves. Faced with a high incidence of agrarian disputes and the issue of raising the productivity of farmland, an attempt was made to reform the existing land ownership status. Measures to expand the number of landed farmers were encouraged, such as a review of the existing tenancy system and bringing new arable land under cultivation.

However, while the government presented and outlined its policy goals, it provided much less fiscal backing for them, and effectively left the implementation of some

---

[33] Ultimately, Seinaiji Village was designated as an "Economic Revitalization Specially Subsidized Village" in 1938. Seinaiji Village, "*Seinaiji Mura Shi Gekan (Seinaiji Village History, Volume 2)*," 1982, pp. 99–100.

plans up to the ideas of individual local governments. That was, in fact, how the rural economic revitalization movement proceeded.[34] Lying behind these problems were the loss of land by farmers under pressure to repay their debts in the aftermath of the depression and unemployment. These economically destabilizing factors led to the state supported Manchuria emigration program, and new farmland cultivation project.

What actions did local governments then take as practical measures? In terms of policy measures for the improvement of sericulture, the government declared the commencement of the rural economic revitalization movement in 1932, and Nagano Prefecture, in response, devised a "Five-Year Plan for the Renewal of the Sericulture Industry" in 1933. In accordance with the plan, the Nagano prefectural government decided to provide a total of ¥730,000 in financial incentives in 1934, including ¥300,000 for the improvement of mulberry fields, ¥180,000 for mixed cropping in mulberry fields, and about ¥250,000 for the conversion and replanting of mulberry fields. Of these policy measures, Nagano Prefecture had already received government subsidies for mulberry field conversion/replanting in FY1932, and the 1933 measure entailed an increased subsidization in this activity.[35]

A leaflet entitled "Concerning Facilities for the Improvement of Mulberry Fields," prepared by Nagano Prefecture in September 1934 details the countermeasures the prefectural government considered necessary for the sericulture industry at the time:

- [There is] No need to be so pessimistic about the sericulture industry

……

- Growing mulberry leaves cheaply and improved management are the keys to self-revitalization

If you grow mulberry leaves cheaply and get a bountiful harvest of silkworms, you can naturally produce cocoons cheaply. Generally speaking, mulberry fields in Nagano Prefecture are very inefficient. There are many blighted mulberry fields, and the recent decline in cocoon prices has caused growers to neglect their mulberry fields. Some are in bad shape and the quality of land has declined severely. Moreover, the biggest reason [for inefficiency] is that as much as 45% of all mulberry fields in the prefecture have been planted with a mulberry breed variety that has a very low yield. Therefore, blighted mulberry fields that are still good enough to be replanted should be replanted, and those mulberry fields that can be converted to grow other crops should be converted to make way for other appropriate crops. Above all, ordinary mulberry fields planted with the inferior mulberry breed varieties should be replanted with superior varieties as soon as possible… Since an excess production of cocoons is also problematic, the cocoon output should be first kept at the current level, and the resulting surplus area of mulberry fields should be converted, diverting the converted surplus area to the production of green manure crops, food crops and feed crops. The most

[34] Hiraga Akihiko, "*Senzen Nihon Nōgyō Seisakushi no Kenkyū (A Study on Japanese Agricultural Policy in the Prewar Period)*", Nihon Keizai Hyōronsha, 2003, pp. 157–159.

[35] Nagano Prefecture, "*Sōen Kaizen no Shisetsu ni Tsuite (Concerning Facilities for the Improvement of Mulberry Fields),*" September 1934. Multiple sheets of the leaflet were included in the documents in possession of the Seinaiji Post Office [Ji 2–11], an indication that a large number of leaflets were distributed.

important task of sericulture farmers under current circumstances is to improve sericulture operations through the aforementioned measures.

At the time, Nagano Prefecture had Japan's largest silk-reeling industry and sericulture industry. Phrases like "No need to be so pessimistic about the sericulture industry" and wording such as "self-revitalization" appear to reflect the prefectural government's intent to preserve the sericulture industry. However, the prefectural government at the same time stated that "mulberry fields that can be converted to grow other crops should be converted," indicating that Nagano Prefecture was hoping to achieve a reduction in the area planted under mulberry and diversify toward other crops in the prefecture's economy. Recognizing that it would be difficult to achieve a rapid restructuring of rural output when the prefecture's economic base was underpinned by the two main industries of sericulture and silk-reeling, the prefectural government nevertheless hoped to see a phased conversion of some fields to other crops and a transformation of the industrial structure.

Against this background, what, specifically, was the "improvement" in the sericulture industry that Nagano Prefecture sought? The leaflet quoted above clarified this vision by explaining the behavior of subsidized farming households as follows:

(1) The newly encouraged method for improving mulberry fields is to "dig out one ridge after every two ridges."

    (i) Mulberry fields in the prefecture are basically densely planted...The method now encouraged by the prefecture to improve mulberry fields is to widen the spacing between ridges by digging out 33% of the mulberry stumps.
    (ii) What are the benefits of this method?
        (a) In around the third year, the harvest will come back to almost the same as it was, and some mulberry fields will perhaps yield more than before.
        (b) In the wider area between the ridges in the mulberry fields, intercropping of green manure crops, food crops and other crops becomes possible...
        (c) When green manure crops are planted for intercropping, inputs of chemical fertilizers can be reduced.

    ......
    (iii) What about the payment of financial incentives?
        (a) Financial incentives are paid when densely planted mulberry fields of two ares or larger per complex are transformed into fields where one ridge is dug out after every two ridges. The amount of the financial incentive is ¥4 per 10 ares.
        (b) Sericultural unions are naturally entitled to receive financial incentives, and even sericulture farmers who are not members of such unions can receive financial incentives in the same way as long as they are engaged in the sericulture business.

(c) Applications for financial incentives should be submitted by the end of October through the municipal office for cities, the town office for towns, and the village office for villages, or through the branch of the local sericulture control office. Sericulture work needs to be completed by March 15 of the following year.

(2) The newly encouraged method of mixed cropping in mulberry fields is to "dig out one ridge after every other ridge."

(i) What sort of method is this?

The encouragement of mixed cropping in mulberry fields is the new policy the government has adopted, and the prefectural government has also decided to follow this policy and encourage mixed cropping…

(ii) What are the benefits of mixed cropping?
(a) The quality of mulberry leaves improves…
(b) The intercropping of green manure and food self-sufficiency is assisted…
(c) It becomes easier to adjust the scale of sericulture management.
(iii) What about the distribution of financial incentives?

Financial incentives are paid at the rate of ¥6 per 10 ares when a sericultural union engaged in sericulture transform mulberry fields of two ares or larger per complex into fields where one ridge is dug out after every two ridges and the total area improved by one sericultural union amounts to 10 ares or more.

The "improvement" of the sericulture industry advocated by Nagano Prefecture essentially meant a reduction in the acreage of mulberry fields. The guidance provided encouraged farmers to desist from the dense planting of mulberry trees so as to increase the yield per tree. Thus, "improvement" meant raising productivity per mulberry tree and reducing the total mulberry acreage, while other crops were to be grown in the space opened by the mulberry acreage reduction. In a bid to help farming households respond to the decline in cocoon prices, the prefecture attempted to have villagers control the consumption of cash inputs by reducing the use of purchased fertilizers in sericulture and increasing the production efficiency of farmland. The prefecture aimed to help farming households break away from their dependence on income from sericulture by urging them to reduce and convert mulberry fields and grow other crops. This policy to rationalize the sericulture industry was shared by both the central government and the prefecture, as seen by the fact that subsidies came not only from the prefectural government but also from the central government.

The improvement of mulberry fields was also carried out in Seinaiji Village with subsidies from both the prefectural and the central governments in 1934. What were the entities that actually received funds in this project to convert and replant mulberry fields? Both the central government and the prefecture assumed that local small sericultural unions would receive the subsidies and also carry out the conversion of mulberry fields.

- Planning and implementation of projects and tasks of sericultural unions… Good plans cannot be expected to simply appear, and thus projects cannot be so effective when individual sericulture farmers separately undertake the planning and implementation of projects. Therefore, this fall, sericultural unions should become more united and enhance their cooperative power to accomplish these projects satisfactorily and produce their full effects.[36]

The expectations placed on sericultural union by the authorities were did not match their actual importance. As mentioned earlier in this chapter, in April 1933, a year before the subsidization policy was formulated, Seinaiji Village was had 245 households engaged in sericulture, but only 41 members spread across three sericultural unions. Membership fell well short of covering the whole the village. A likely result was a 1934 drive to establish additional sericultural unions in Seinaiji Village in order to qualify for the subsidies. Indeed, the number of sericultural union in Seinaiji Village surged to 11.[37]

These sericultural unions are believed to have been formed by taking advantage of small pre-existing *kumiai* in each area. For example, "Kyōei Sericultural Union" was established on June 12, 1934, in the lower *ku* area, by electing *kumiai* executives. The head of the Kyōei [co-prosperity] Sericultural Union was Hara Tsunegorō, then postmaster of the third-class post office who belonged the *kumiai* in the "Ichiba" district in the lower *ku* area. In the case of this sericultural union, there were eight members at first, and after new members joining later and some dropouts, it is known to have had at least 19 people involved in it.[38]

The Kyōei Sericultural Union drew up a plan to implement such projects as the conversion and replanting of mulberry fields and the encouragement of mixed cropping, and to that end received subsidies from the prefecture and the central government. However, as far as the remaining documents show, this sericultural union did not appear to have acted as the main entity implementing improvement projects, which was the reason it received the subsidies. This sericultural union distributed the subsidies received to its members directly. The sources related to this sericultural union and project included, aside from the written plan for sericulture improvement, documents stating the subsidy amounts its members received, with their receipt stamps, but there were no documents on the actual implementation of mulberry replanting or mixed cropping.[39]

This indicates that individual sericultural unions were established in Seinaiji Village as the receivers of subsidies and were not the actual working units or organizations that implemented projects. Sericultural unions were consolidated into an organization called "Shimoina County Sericultural Union Seinaiji Branch" and were

[36] Nagano Prefecture, "*Sōen Kaizen no Shisetsu ni Tsuite (Concerning Facilities for the Improvement of Mulberry Fields)*," September 1934.

[37] Shimoina County Sericulture Union Seinaiji Village Branch, Mayor Sakurai Sōjūrō, "*Shōwa Kyū Nendo Shimoina Gun Yōsangyō Kumiai Seinaiji Shibu Keihi Shūshi Kessannsho (FY1934 Shimoina County Sericultural Union Seinaiji Branch Statement of Settlement of Accounts)*,"1934, Documents in the possession of the Seinaiji Post Office, [Ji 2–11-5–3].

[38] Lower Seinaiji Kyōei Sericulture Practice union, "*Shōwa Kyū Nen Roku Gaku Yakushokuin Kumiaiin Meibo (June 1934, Name List of Executives, Employees and Kumiai Members)*," 1934, Documents in possession of the Seinaiji Post Office, [Ji 2–11-5–27].

[39] "*Jigyō Betsu Seisannsho (Statements of Accounts by Business Sector)*," 1934–1936, Documents in the possession of the Seinaiji Post Office, [Ji 2–11-5–26].

thereby absorbed into the larger organization that covered Shimoina County in its entirety.[40] Specific actions taken by individual organizations within the village were mostly left to the discretion of individual sericulture farmers.

The Shimoina County Sericultural Union Seinaiji Branch collected membership fees of ¥1 from the village's 11 unions and an additional 15 sen per union member. As the amount collected from members totaled ¥30, the total number of sericultural unions members had probably risen to 200 in 1934. Given the number of farming households engaged in sericulture was 245 in 1933, it is apparent that the sericultural unions in the village drastically increased their organization rate in order to receive subsidies.[41] Yet the organization rate had yet to reach 100%, and thus it appears that several farming households engaged in sericulture in Seinaiji Village maintained a degree of independence. The trend towards greater organization through sericultural unions in this period is, however, undeniable, sparked though it was by the effort to cope with the recession through the receipt of subsidies from the central and prefectural governments.

9.4.3 The Establishment of an Industrial Cooperative as the Receiver of External Funds

Despite the procurement of various external supportive funds, the household income in Seinaiji Village remained low. In 1933, when the Japanese economy had reached the trough of its economic downturn, average income in Seinaiji Village stood at approximately ¥185 per household.[42] However, the Gini coefficient on the basis of the estimated income in Seinaiji Village was 0.47. Considering that in 1930, the estimated national Gini coefficient was 0.51, and the estimated Gini coefficient

[40] Since they paid membership fees to the Shimoina County Union Federation, they apparently came under its aegis officially in 1935 at the latest. Shimoina County Sericultural Union Federation Head Fukushima Yoshio, "*Shōwa Jū Nendo Shimoina Gun Yōsangyō Kumiai Keihi Shūshi Kosei Yosansho (FY1935 Shimoina County Sericultural Union Statement of Settlement of Accounts and Corrected Budget)*," 1936, Documents in the possession of the Seinaiji Post Office, [Ji 2–11-5–23].

[41] Shimoina County Sericultural Union Seinaiji Village Branch Mayor Sakurai Sōjūrō, "*Shōwa Kyū Nendo Shimoina Gun Yōsangyō Kumiai Seinaiji Shibu Keihi Shūshi Kessannsho (FY1934 Shimoina County Sericultural Union Seinaiji Branch Statement of Settlement of Accounts)*," 1934, Documents in possession of the Seinaiji Post Office, [Ji 2–11-5–3]; Shimoina County Sericultural Union Seinaiji Village Branch Mayor Sakurai Sōjūrō, "*Shōwa Jūichi Nendo Shimoina Gun Yōsangyō Kumiai Seinaiji Shibu Shūshi Kessannsho (FY1936 Shimoina County Sericulture Industry Kumiai Seinaiji Branch Statement of Settlement of Accounts)*," 1936, Documents in the possession of the Seinaiji Post Office, [Ji 2–11-5–4].

[42] Seinaiji Village, "*Shōwa Hachi Nendo Shimoina Gun Seinaiji Mura Tokubetsuzei Kosū Wari Fukagaku Hyō (FY1933 Table of Special Tax Amounts Assessed on the Basis of the Number of Households in Seinaiji Village, Shioina County)*," 1933, Documents held by the lower *ku* area [3–98-23].

for villages was 0.58 and thereafter likely deteriorated,[43] Seinaiji Village, despite its economic hardship, maintained a relatively high level of equality.[44] With its high level of equality intact, Seinaiji Village attempted to break through the period of economic hardship by successively establishing small farmers' cooperatives and sericultural unions, organizations whose establishment was encouraged by the government to improve agriculture. It was under these circumstances that the idea of establishing an industrial cooperative ultimately arose.

The Seinaiji Credit Sales, Purchasing and Use Cooperative was established in 1937. In the latter half of the 1930s, regionally-based industrial cooperatives could receive funds from the Central Bank for Industrial Cooperatives, not to mention the Deposit Bureau, and indeed many had long since been established in autonomous communities across Japan. As has already been discussed, the industrial cooperative system introduced into modern Japan, in addition to its credit function, also offered the joint use of facilities and equipment, such as warehouses and farm equipment. Some also came to have marketing and purchasing functions, selling the crops produced by union members externally and selling fertilizers, food, and other daily necessities to cooperative members.

The most widely utilized of these functions was the credit function which helped cooperative members form deposits and provide small-amount loans to fellow cooperative members. This was because agricultural development in modern Japan was characterized by the need for initial investment, for items such as fertilizers and sericulture inputs, and thus the majority of farmers had a strong demand for cash. Rather surprisingly, until 1937 Seinaiji Village, despite its heavy reliance on sericulture, managed to find sufficient funds for operations even without the collection of savings in the village through an industrial cooperative.

Once established, how did the Seinaiji industrial cooperative perform in a village long characterized by the independence of its farming operations? According to the 1939 account book, the only account book now in existence, the union's credit operations were limited in scale. The size of profits from credit operations for the entire year was small, though a detailed examination is not possible as the rate of interest on lending is unknown (Table 9.2). The balance of loans at the end of the fiscal year (the union's third year since establishment) shows that outstanding loans were in very small amounts, less than ¥100 in loans given on personal credit, and less than ¥600 in loans secured by collateral. This gives the impression of a union that was not particularly active in its credit operations.

---

[43] Minami Ryōshin, "*Nihon no Keizai Hatten to Shotoku Bunpu (Japan's Economic Development and Income Distribution)*," Iwanami Shoten, 1966, p. 108, p. 41.

[44] In Kano Village, which had had long-standing industrial cooperative, as seen in Chapter 10, the average income per household was about ¥190 in 1931 and about ¥53 in 1932, with a higher Gini coefficient and inequality higher than in Seinaiji Village. Regarding the degree of poverty measured by the income of village residents, there existed little disparity between the two villages, or it may be presumed that Kanō Village found itself in a more difficult situation. Kanō Village Office, "*Kenzei Kosū Wari Fukagaku Tōkyū Hyō (Table of the Grades of Prefectural Tax Amount Assessed on the Basis of the Number of Households)*" for each fiscal year.

Table 9.2 FY1939 balance sheet of the Seinaiji industrial cooperative

Debits		Credits	
Investment	11,200	Paid-in investment unsettled	6069
Reserves	446	Building cost	10,198
Special reserve fund	1431	Investment in Central Bank for industrial cooperatives	300
Investment in national purchasing sales cooperative federation unsettled	900	Investment in National purchasing sales cooperative federation	1000
Investment in credit cooperative federation unsettled	200	Investment in credit cooperative federation	400
Investment in purchasing cooperative federation unsettled	792	Investment in purchasing sales cooperative federation	1200
Investment in Tenryūsha unsettled	6570	Investment in Tenryūsha [County's silk reeling cooperative company]	9000
Annual installment borrowings	4400	Current deposits in Shinren[the Federation of Credit Cooperatives of Nagano Prefecture]	1838
Borrowings on bills	23,000	Securities	98
Overdraft	8991	Loans on credit	68
Term borrowings	3500	Secured loans	569
Reserve fund for capital increase	2657	Loans for tobacco-growing funds	3467
Current savings	5396	Cocoon department account	4344
Hōkoku [patriot] savings	1484	Goods purchased	10,541
Charcoal branch savings	86	Payments for sale of goods purchased accrued	2272
Subsidies from the prefecture	3200	Provisional payments for cocoons	84,103
Cocoon department savings	61,728	Provisional dividends for cocoons	1394
Accrued fares	637	Advances paid	801
Accrued goods purchased	1281	Payments for charcoal accrued	314
Refund equity	83	Payments for farm products accrued	22
Earnings retained	390.53	Goods sold	41
		Cash	331
Total	138,376		138,376

Unit: Yen; units of sen rounded off
Source The Seinaiji Credit Sales, Purchasing and Use Cooperative, "Receipts and Expenses Ledger," FY1939 edition

The Seinaiji industrial cooperative instead was active in purchasing and sales, which could be described as its main activities. Entrusted by union members, the union sold cocoons and charcoal and supplied food to its members. Considering that in charcoal production, the lending of charcoal kilns by the *kukai* and the securing of materials in common forests for firewood and charcoal operations were carried out by individuals, it is presumed that the Seinaiji industrial cooperative had to seek strong cooperation with the *kukai*.

Was the Seinaiji industrial cooperative not required to fulfill its financial function? On this point there is some uncertainty. The ledger lists items of advances paid, apart from loans. Indeed, the itemized advances paid take up more pages than do loans in daily account books. These entries describe the counterparties to whom funds were provided as advances, the pretexts for the advance, and the repayment situation. There was no description of interest rates, and this makes it possible to presume that advances paid were in effect equivalent to interest-free loans.

As can be seen from Table 9.3, few individuals received advances, though it must also be said that some of the recipients are unknown. Advances paid to individuals were mostly made for mulberry leaves and amounted to several tens of yen. What also stands out is the fund contributions to agricultural associations, village offices and other public institutions in the village, with some given to joint recipients. The total amount of advances paid within the fiscal year exceeded ¥4000 and the balance at the end of the fiscal year surpassed ¥800, both indicating movements of cash exceeding the ordinary credit granted by the Seinaiji industrial cooperative.

The payment of advances of funds to individuals and regional organizations by industrial cooperatives was not a common practice. That the industrial cooperative granted subsidies for individual emigrants, a role that under normal circumstances would be played by the village office, indicates that the recently established Seinaiji industrial cooperative shows the close relationship between it and the village administration and agricultural association. Indeed, it may be aptly described as an auxiliary body of the administrative organizations that took on some of the normal functions of the village office, the *kukai*, and other groups under its aegis. The 1939 account books of the Seinaiji industrial cooperative, the only ones that have survived, were retained among the documents held by the lower ku area, not by the current Seinaiji agricultural cooperative. This points further to the close relationship held between administrative organizations in Seinaiji Village and the industrial cooperative[45].

On the other hand, the Seinaiji industrial cooperative joined the National Federation of Industrial Cooperatives in addition to a prefectural federation. In this way, the establishment of the industrial cooperative made it possible for Seinaiji Village to finally link itself to the public funds network (besides Deposit Bureau funds), and the sales channels for agricultural products and other goods formed by industrial cooperatives. These links were utilized as can be seen in the balance sheet which shows subsidies from the prefecture provided to industrial cooperatives. By establishing an industrial cooperative in the latter half of the 1930s, Seinaiji Village had

[45] Seinaiji Credit Sales, Purchasing and Use Cooperative, "*Suitō Motochō (Receipts and Expenses Ledger)*," the FY1939 edition, the lower *ku* Documents [14–17].

Table 9.3 Breakdown of advances paid by the Seinaiji industrial cooperative in FY1939

	Total number	Number of advances paid	Amount of advance paid	Recipient	Pretext
January	5	1	100	Agricultural association	Funds for Rabbit fur business [for munitions]
February	4	2	200	Sakurai Satoru	Payments for charcoal
			80	Sakurai Takaharu	Related to emigration to Manchuria
March	5	1	114	Agricultural association	Rabbit fur/Emigration to Manchuria
April	4	1	29	Agricultural association	Wire
May	4	0			
June	2	1	100	Sakurai Ikoma	Village office subsidies (Emigration to Manchuria)
July	13	7	100	Treasurer	Related to the village office
			100	School principal	Related to the elementary school
			20	Village office	Advances for travel expenses
			58	Sakurai Seikichi	Payments for mulberry leaves
			90	Sakurai Tamitoshi	Payments for mulberry leaves
			70	School principal	Related to the elementary school
			250	Village office	Related to the village office
August	4	3	230	Treasurer	Related to the village office
			9	Kimura	Payments for mulberry leaves
			75	Village office	Manchuria visitation cost
September	9	4	160	Secretary	Travel expenses for emigrants

(continued)

Table 9.3 (continued)

	Total number	Number of advances paid	Amount of advance paid	Recipient	Pretext
			91	Agricultural association	Receipts of payments for mulberry leaves from the county agricultural association
			150	Treasurer	Related to the village office
			11	Branch office	Payments for mulberry leaves
October	7	4	6	–	Automobile lending
			200	Agricultural association	Funds for sheep
			228	Rōbundō [variety store]	80 sheets of [n.a.]
			150	School principal	Related to the elementary school expense
November	7	5	148	Rōbundō	Payments for petroleum
			84	Agricultural association/ Village assembly	Village assembly travel expenses/ agricultural association advances paid
			100	Agricultural association	Rabbit fur funds
			50	Agricultural association	Rabbit fur funds
			35	–	Transfer of provisional payments for November 1938
December	12	8	50	Agricultural association	Rabbit fur funds
			150	Village office	Related to the village office
			50	Village office	Related to the village office
			50	Village office	Related to the village office
			100	Village office	Related to the village office

(continued)

Table 9.3 (continued)

	Total number	Number of advances paid	Amount of advance paid	Recipient	Pretext
			40	Agricultural association	Payments for rabbit hair/skin
			150	Agricultural association	Payments for rabbit fur
			198	Rōbundō	Payments for gasoline
Total amount of advances made (loans) within the fiscal year				4149	
Balance of advances made (loans) at the end of the fiscal year				802	

Unit: Yen; units of sen rounded off
Source Compiled from the 1939 edition of the Seinaiji Credit Sales, Purchasing and Use Cooperative, "Receipts and Expenses Ledger"

finally transferred the financial and distributional functions hitherto conducted by the village's territorial groups to an industrial cooperative.

In the initial years after its establishment the expectation that the Seinaiji industrial cooperative would offer credit to individuals was not particularly high. The establishment of the industrial cooperative made it easier for Seinaiji Village to receive external funds (without dismantling conventional community organizations), as the presence of an industrial cooperative was a prerequisite to qualify for external funds. However, it was unclear whether such an organization and institutional arrangement could improve the village's economic situation. The fact is the industrial cooperative supported village subsidies to residents wishing to emigrate to Manchuria, a movement which was pursued enthusiastically by the village in the latter half of the 1930s.

9.4.4 The Seinaiji Village Manchuria Emigration Plan

In September 1938, the Seinaiji Village office established a 3-year "economic revitalization" project. The plan sought the improvement of sericulture; enhancing productivity in other agricultural products; the rationalization of the forestry industry (firewood and charcoal); mechanization (the introduction of wheat and rice milling machines); and infrastructure development (waterway and forest road maintenance). The plan also stated that the village would work to "achieve the goals of the Manchuria emigration [program] in accordance with state plans and village revitalization, and to improve agricultural management".[46] The Manchuria emigration plan was formulated within the village as an economic policy equivalent to measures for productivity enhancement, industry promotion measures, and infrastructure development.

In March 1938, the central government announced its "Implementation Guidelines for Phase 1 of the Plan for Emigration to Manchuria". In response, Nagano Prefecture drew up a document entitled "Guiding Principles for the Establishment of the Plan for Emigration to Manchuria" in November that year.[47] The fact that the economic revitalization plan of Seinaiji Village, developed in September 1938, included the Manchuria emigration plan demonstrates that the village was acting well ahead of the prefectural government. Why was Seinaiji Village so proactive in the plan to send emigrants to Manchuria? The written plan of the village provides an insight into the thinking in Seinaiji Village at the time:

> The cultivated acreage in the village is an average 3 tan 2 se per household, and there are no rice paddies, which makes food self-sufficiency impossible. The bulk of arable land has been converted into mulberry fields making sericulture the main source of income. During winter, the charcoal making side business helps make a living, but the population simply continues to grow year-on-year. When we think of the village's future and villagers' agricultural management, we cannot help but tremble […] the village will work to "achieve the goals of Manchuria emigration in accordance with the state plan"[48]

As described earlier, while Seinaiji Village must have carried out measures to improve sericulture in the latter half of the 1930s, village administrators clearly concluded that such measures alone could not feed the village's growing population. Seinaiji Village also promoted the forestry industry, centering on firewood and charcoal production, to supplement villagers' income from sericulture, but even this was judged as insufficient to maintain living standards. Consequently, Seinaiji Village decided to pin its hopes for the village's economic recovery on the migration of part of its population overseas where they could acquire new lands to cultivate.

The encouragement of emigration to Manchuria was made alongside the promotion of forestry. In 1937, a year before the village set out the economic revitalization movement, the village assembly of Seinaiji Village already regarded these two initiatives on an equal footing in the village's economic policy.

> Proposal No. 11
>
> Concerning the Expenditure of Village Subsidies

[46] Seinaiji Village Office, "*Gian Dai Yonjūroku Gō Nagano Ken Shimoina Gun Seinaiji Mura Keizai Kōsei Tokubetsu Josei Shisetsu Hi (Proposal No. 46, Expenses for the Specially Subsidized Facilities for Economic Revitalization)*" (September 1938), Documents in the possession of the Seinaiji Post Office [Ji 2–2-16–2].

[47] Motojima Kazuto, "'Seinaiji Sonpō'—Sonpō to Manshū Imin no Jidai—(Seinaiji Village Bulletin—Village Bulletin and the Era of the Emigration to Manchuria), "*Iida Shi Rekishi Kenkyūsho Nenpō 12 (The Iida City Institute of Historical Research Annual Bulletin 12)*," 2014.

[48] Seinaiji Village Office, "*Gian Dai Yonjūroku Gō Nagano Ken Shimoina Gun Seinaiji Mura Keizai Kōsei Tokubetsu Josei Shisetsu Hi (Proposal No. 46, Expenses for the Specially Subsidized Facilities for Economic Revitalization),*" Documents in the possession of the Seinaiji Post Office [Ji 2–2-16–2].

Subsidies to the sanitary association ¥26

Subsidies to the village's agricultural association ¥200

Subsidies to the local veterans' association branch ¥105

Subsidies to the charcoal union branch ¥40

Support subsidies to agricultural emigrants to Manchuria ¥450

The village shall disburse subsidies to various groups, as above.

Submitted on February 28, 1937.

Proposal No. 14

Concerning the Sale of Timber from Seinaiji Village-owned Forests

......The village shall sell miscellaneous small trees at reduced prices to produce charcoal for unemployment relief.

• Proceeds of the sales shall be appropriated for afforestation under an operation plan. Regarding the sale at reduced prices, an appropriate method shall be devised to equally benefit village residents at large.

Submitted on February 28, 1937[49]

As seen above, Seinaiji Village sought to deal with its problems of unemployment and insufficient income by felling the village's common forest to produce charcoal and equally allocate its opportunities to village residents. It also promoted the Manchuria emigration project as one of its subsidized projects. The village administrators treated both measures together as a means for lifting Seinaiji Village out of its economic hardship. These developments evolved not only at the level of the village administration, which was relatively susceptible to the instructions of the central and prefectural governments, but also at the level of lower administrative organizations such as the *kukai*, or at levels closer to ordinary citizens.

Rules for the Encouragement and Subsidization of Agricultural Emigrants to Manchuria

This article shall be called the Lower Seinaiji Rules for the Encouragement and Subsidization of Agricultural Emigrants to Manchuria.

The Regulations are designed to have 50 households emigrate to Manchuria over 3 years by providing subsidies to existing *ku* residents pursuant to the regulations [...] encouraging agricultural emigration to Manchuria for the revitalization of Seinaiji Village.

The financial resources for subsidies under the Regulations shall come from the sale of miscellaneous small trees from forests owned by the lower Seinaiji *ku*. The miscellaneous small trees shall be cut down from appropriate places in the forests after consultations at the *kukai*, and they shall be sold sequentially as necessary to raise a total of ¥2500 over 3 years.

The subsidies shall be ¥50 per household as a standard and shall have three types, A, B, and C. The subsidies shall be ¥50 for A, ¥40 for B, and ¥25 to ¥30 for C.

[49] Documents in the possession of the Seinaiji Post Office [Ki 27–27].

A shall be the head of a household planning and beginning to execute emigrate to Manchuria by the whole family as agricultural emigrants, and a person who fulfills his obligations to pay taxes and conduct works as a genuine *ku* resident.

B shall be the head of a household planning emigrate to Manchuria by the whole family and a person who fulfills his obligations to pay taxes and conduct works with a lapse of 5 to 20 years behind the head of the household of a branch family.

C is a second or third son who has yet to do his duty to the *ku* independently, and a person who does not have an obligatory tax and labor relationship even if he has a spouse.

A person who is planning to emigrate to Manchuria shall apply for the subsidies pursuant to the preceding article verbally or in writing to the head of the lower Seinaiji *ku*.

When deciding on subsidies for a village resident going to Manchuria, the head of the *ku* shall call a meeting of a committee to take fair and strict action. The committee shall be composed of all *kukai* executives and *kukai* assembly members as well as the heads of various relevant groups.

A person who has received subsidies but has returned to Seinaiji Village under unavoidable circumstances or some other reasons shall return the subsidies, and when he fails to perform his obligations under Article 4 of the *ku* rules, he shall not have rights to land under public ownership.

Would-be emigrants must absolutely not hold farewell parties. The granting of subsidies shall be suspended to those who violate this prohibition.

Any change or abolition of the Regulations shall require a resolution by the general assembly after a decision by the committee.

Supplementary Regulations

The Regulations shall be enforced as of April 1.

April 1, 1937 Lower Seinaiji *Kukai*[50]

As can be gleaned from the above, Seinaiji Village supported the emigration project by utilizing its common forests or *ku* as source of finance for emigration costs. This was taking place even before the village administration had officially formulated its project or received subsidies from the central government. In Seinaiji Village, the higher and lower *ku* existing since the early modern period functioned strongly in the modern period as communities and as administrative organizations. The *kukai*, even though its fiscal conditions were not necessarily robust, disbursed supporting subsidies for emigration to Manchuria. Indeed, even before it was able to receive monetary support from the central government, Seinaiji Village was undertaking practical measures to pursue the national plan for emigration to and the colonization of Manchuria.

The economic stagnation in the local community at the time was so pronounced that it was determined to export a portion of its population and seek to expand

[50] Lower Seinaiji *Kukai*, "*Manshū Nōgyō Imin Shōrei Josei Kitei (Rules for Encouragement and Subsidization of Agricultural Emigrants to Manchuria)*," April 1, 1937, Documents in the possession of the Seinaiji Post Office [Ki 27–26].

the farmland cultivated by its residents overseas. Presumably, this could have been avoided if the funds for the safety net to prevent the collapse of livelihoods had been supplied, either internally or externally, to residents. However, the economic situation became an insurmountable plight in the absence of an effective organization for the provision of funds and without the connections such organizations bring to external funding networks. In the case of Seinaiji Village, the provision of funds to residents within the local community was, as a result, used not only to sustain life within the village but also to support emigration out of the village. In the latter half of the 1930s, Seinaiji Village came to acknowledge that it could no longer sustain its society as it was. In FY1937, with support funds provided by the lower *ku* area, 14 representatives and their family members, a total of 56 people, left Seinaiji Village for Manchuria[51]

9.5 The Subsequent Situation and Summary

In the second half of the1930s the Japanese economy recovered due to an expansion of public investment (intended as an unemployment relief measure) and a military-demand induced revival of heavy industry. The increase in public investment, stimulated by the fiscal and monetary policies of Minister of Finance Takahashi Korekiyo in the 1930s, meant not only a fiscal expansion but also an increase in the supply of low-interest funds from the Ministry of Finance's Deposit Bureau, lent out as expenses for unemployment measures and for recovery from natural disasters. These measures were underpinned by the savings of ordinary citizens, since the fiscal expansion was financed at the time by the issuance of government bonds, which were actively bought by individual investors and banks, burdened with massive amounts of personal deposits that could not be invested elsewhere amid the recession. In this way, the Japanese economy was bailed out through the effective utilization of the savings of ordinary citizens.

However, after the outbreak of the Sino-Japanese war in 1937, fiscal funds raised by government bonds were diverted to expanding military expenses. Most of the popular funds, including postal savings, were now required to be used to purchase government bonds and thus became a military funding source. This was an era which was characterized by slogans like "Let Us Join the Savings War!" and "Defend Our Country, Get Savings Ready"[52] which appeared in people's daily lives through leaflets and savings passbook bags.

The pumping of funds into the military resulted in a shortage of funds for regional economies and for economic development measures. This led to declines in public

[51] Seinaiji Village, "*Seinaiji Mura Shi Gekan (Seinaiji Village History Volume 2)*," 1982, pp. 131–133, p. 64.

[52] Ministry of Communications, "*Chochiku Sen ni Sanka Simaseu (Let Us Join the Savings War)*," 1938; Ministry of Communications, "*Aikoku Chokin Tsūchō Bukuro (Patriotic Savings Passbook Bag)*," in the possession of the Seinaiji Post Office.

works budgets in the regions and in investment by private-sector companies in non-military industries. Until then, people's personal acts of savings served as the foundation which supported people's livelihoods, not only as funds for the individual savers themselves, but also as popular funds for investment. During the war, however, personal savings were deprived of this function, no longer could they serve as a safety net for people's livelihoods through the supply of low-interest funds.

As the war intensified, controls were tightened amid the short supply of not only funds but also labor. By 1940, Seinaiji Village began receiving notifications about the mobilization of labor.

> Concerning the Notice on the Holding of the Labor Mobilization Conference
>
> Under the state general mobilization plan for the objective of strengthening the long-term wartime posture, it has been decided to establish a comprehensive plan to take all possible measures to ensure the mobilization of important supplies, labor, transportation and electric power, and controls of funds and trade. The mobilization of labor is aimed at systematically mobilizing workers required by the so-called industries of these difficult times, such as satisfying military demand, execution of production capacity expansion plans, promotion of exports, and the securing of people's daily necessities. Hence, this notice was issued to establish the labor mobilization conference by selecting well-qualified representatives from every town and village in order to achieve these objectives…[53]

Evenamid the labor shortage Seinaiji Village recruited emigrants to Manchuria. From the end of 1939 to the end of 1940, the "*Seinaiji Mura Shi (Seinaiji Village Magazine),*" issued by Seinaiji Village, carried articles entitled "*Takumin Genchi Hōkoku (Field Reports by Settlers)*",[54] which included letters from people who had already emigrated to Manchuria. The reports also solicited further emigration. In total, Seinaiji Village sent 71 settlers and 247 of their family members to Manchuria (settlers were presumed to be household heads). This number ranked Seinaiji among the largest sending communities in Nagano Prefecture. As of November 1945, the number of households in Seinaiji Village stood at 409 and the village population was 2092. Thus, nearly 20% of the village's households and nearly 10% of the village population emigrated to Manchuria.[55]

These large numbers suggest that while emigration was encouraged as national policy at the time, the economic plight during the long recession of the interwar period had also put much stress on the community. A variety of economic policies and relief support carried out by various administrative organizations, ranging from the central and prefectural governments to the village and *ku,* were insufficient to stabilize the economy and society of Seinaiji Village. Though there were no reports of people who starved to death, as seen by repeated efforts by the *kukai* and the village to secure food, the economic conditions in Seinaiji Village were so severe

---

[53] Seinaiji Village Major Matsushita Tanezane, "*Shoku Dai Nanajūnana Go Romu Doin Kyogikai Kaisai Tsuchi no Ken (Shoku No. 77, Concerning the Notice on the Holding of the Labor Mobilization Conference),*" April 13, 1940.

[54] Seinaiji Village, "*Seinaiji Mura Shi (Seinaiji Village History),*" August 10, 1939.

[55] Seinaiji Village, "*Seinaiji Mura Shi Gekan (Seinaiji Village History Volume 2),*" 1982, pp. 131–133, p. 64.

as to cause strong anxieties among residents about their livelihoods. In comparison with the case of Kanō Village, the people of Seinaiji Village, which did not have an internal accumulation for the circulation of funds or links with external networks of funds, found themselves more vulnerable to external market fluctuations.

From the mid-1930s, under the central government's policy to rebuild agricultural communities, it became possible to receive not only low-interest loans from Deposit Bureau funds but also subsidies for the rationalization of various industries, including agriculture, and the implementation of public works. Nevertheless, even these Keynesian-style unemployment measures and attempts at agricultural improvement were not enough to sustain local communities in regional economies that failed to create an alternative to sericulture. Seinaiji Village was a case in point; no entity was able to present a vision for agriculture in the village that could supplant sericulture and provide financial support for such a task. After many efforts to break through the economic difficulties, Seinaiji Village gave up in a sense. Instead of seeking to sustain its community while maintaining its population, Seinaiji Village opted to export a portion of its population, enthusiastically embracing the emigration movement promoted by the central government.

The example of Seinaiji Village shows that a modern community that maintained the customs and systems of the early modern period could still utilize them in the modern period for social stability. Maintaining its communal ties kept the conventional crisis-response function in place. At the same time, however, the example also shows that by failing to design a new organization such as an industrial cooperative, the village was unable to enhance its financial liquidity. The crisis-response capability of the village was thus difficult to link with the massive external financial network newly born in the modern period. As a result, the community of Seinaiji Village was economically vulnerable to a series of large-scale economic crises, such as the financial crisis and the world depression, in the 1920s and the 1930s.

As noted in Sect. 9.3 of this chapter, when the Japanese economy was at a low ebb in the first half of the 1930s, it was difficult to say whether households in Kanō Village (Chap. 8) or Seinaiji Village (this chapter) were better off in terms of the estimated average income and assets. In FY1931, the average income per household was about ¥190 and the average assets about ¥113 in Kanō Village, but these plunged to ¥53 and ¥64, respectively in the following year. In Seinaiji Village in 1933, the average income was ¥186 and the average assets ¥309. In terms of the Gini coefficient, the degree of equality within the village was higher in Seinaiji Village, and in that sense, it is possible to argue that Seinaiji Village's residents were both more affluent and equal than their counterparts in Kanō Village.

However, these income and asset data for a single year do not include the financial accumulations that residents built up at local financial institutions—not only their savings per se but also their creditworthiness to obtain loans. Furthermore, the access to external financial networks and creditworthiness that local institutions had built up as a single organization cannot be measured by the income and a total amount of assets within the village alone.

Though Seinaiji Village suffered in 1930s and sent out a large number of emigrants, it survived as a village thereafter, and the *kukai* also continued to operate as an important institutions in the region up until the twenty-first century. The *kukai* and its subordinate organizations such as *kumiai* and youth associations stood together and did their best to mitigate Seinaiji Village's economic difficulties during the interwar period, a point demonstrated in this chapter. It can be argued, however, that the example of Seinaiji Village clarified that the inability to invest accumulated savings funds within the community, at least during the period of the long recession following the world depression prior to World War II, and the inability to link with the national financial networks served to bring a considerable degree of instability to the local community and its economy.

Previous research has stressed that mass emigration emerged not because of economic poverty itself but because of a deterioration in the subjective economic conditions felt by people in the wake of economic changes.[56] That is in interwar Japan, changes in the market structure related to the sericulture industry and the world depression gave rise not only to absolute poverty among sericulture farmers across Japan, but also generated increasing subjective feelings or expectations of poverty, and that these were an important background to the national plan for mass emigration to Manchuria.

Given the sizable economic weight of sericulture and silk-reeling industries in Nagano Prefecture's regional economy at the time, it is presumed that the prefecture suffered relatively larger declines in income levels and also greater subjective feelings of poverty, hence Nagano Prefecture sent out the largest number of emigrants to Manchuria among Japan's prefectures. On the other hand, however, the facts demonstrated in this and the preceding chapter suggest that the existence of basic small-lot financing opportunities in the regional economy, even compared with other social and community-based ties, more efficiently mitigated not only the objective economic difficulties of local residents but also the subjective perception of poverty. Built up in the modern period, the financial system of popular funds, except in the case that their return to the local community was hampered by government policy, succeeded in functioning as a financial safety net for local society in modern Japan. Such popular funds played the role of enhancing the capabilities of individuals along the lines proposed by Cambridge University economist Amartya Sen.

9.6 Summary

The economic turmoil in the interwar period triggered social turmoil in Japan. This manifested itself in an attempted coup d'état and a number of political assassinations in Japan, leading to the Manchurian Incident in 1931, and eventually to the Pacific War. In the midst of this process, Japanese government established a national policy of emigration to Manchuria which saw some 270,000 people migrate to Manchuria, only to meet a tragic end.

---

[56] Araragi Shinzo, "*'Manshū Imin' no Rekishi Shakaigaku (Historical Sociology of 'Emigration to Manchuria',*" pp. 105–106.

Many studies about Japanese emigration to Manchuria have been written acknowledging that rural impoverishment was an important background to and consideration of the central government in its policy planning. Emigration is not something that can be explained by policy measures or the political environment alone. The conditions that confronted those who actually became emigrants should also be considered.

However, this chapter, like preceding studies, questions the assumption that poverty automatically leads to emigration. Considering poverty as the push and various policies as the pull factors behind emigration, it would follow that all areas across Nagano Prefecture would send out emigrants to Manchuria. This chapter examines the effects of new economic organizations, such as cooperatives and their financial networks on emigration policy with the case of Seinaiji village in Nagano prefecture, which didn't have it until the late 1930s and sent huge numbers of emigrants to Manchuria.

Chapter 10
Postwar Japan—Postal Savings and Agricultural Cooperatives as the *Alternative Financial System*

10.1 Introduction

Thus far this book has examined how from the Meiji period onwards Japanese society, a mostly rural and not particularly wealthy society, tried to deal with the risks and opportunities that emerged in the wake of the industrial revolution and integration with international markets; or, in other words, how Japan managed the potential destabilization of society that can result from economic development. One important aspect of this, as discussed, was the attempt to foster a habit among individuals to form small savings so as to protect their livelihoods. These efforts led to the formation of popular savings, which provided, in effect, a new financial system that differed from the regular financial market, and had at its core the return of the popular funds to regional communities.

The supply of funds through the new financial system thus developed with a nature differing from the conventional banking system that was made up of several big banks under the Bank of Japan (BOJ) at its apex. The new system operated as a financial market with the function that its huge accumulated funds, collected from ordinary people, should be returned to regional economies and companies with limited capital, and in this way benefit society at large. The system, while placing importance on protecting the fund resources, was not primarily driven by profit. Though these funds were composed of small savings, in combination they formed a huge pool of capital, one that essentially remained without direct connections to ordinary big capital corporations.

The successful industrialization and economic development of modern Japan was not limited to the development of heavy industries in urban areas and industrial zones. It also involved the growth of export-oriented light industries, whose development was in turn based on the advancement of regional economies. Indeed, many of these light industries were linked to the agricultural sector which also saw its production increase during industrialization. The financial system built on a funding network of popular funds was a fundamental pillar underpinning the development of Japan's

H. Tanaka, *Micro-Credit in Modern Japan*, Studies in Economic History,
https://doi.org/10.1007/978-981-97-6940-7_10

regional economies, especially in terms of the provision of funds for the development and maintenance of smaller businesses with limited capital.

The objective of this book has been to shed light on the nature and formation of the financial system financed with popular funds. Clarifying its development after World War II is beyond the scope of this book. However, the financial system with popular funds still exists up to the present, and an outline of how it developed through the postwar period and into the twenty-first century is necessary in order to further support the assertions made in this book. In the course of Japan's postwar economic recovery and the subsequent period of high economic growth, the postal savings and industrial cooperatives covered in this book continued to expand financially. The alternative financial system undoubtedly grew in step with this.

What developments did this financial system, initially built up in the early modern period to counter the instability of the commercial or capitalist market economy, witness after World War II? To what extent were its functions in the postwar inherited from the prewar period, or were they altered- or abandoned entirely? Though a full analysis of these questions is a subject for future research, this chapter presents an institutional overview of the postwar development of Japan's alternative financial system covered in this book.[1] In addition, this chapter seeks to reposition the functions and roles of postal savings and cooperative unions in the postwar Japanese economy from a medium- and long-term perspective by re-examining contemporary studies on the FILP, as well as agricultural cooperatives, accumulated after the war by viewing them as studies related to the network of popular funds.

[1] While this chapter attempts an analytical overview of the Japanese economy after World War II, there have been few studies on the economic history of individual sectors in postwar Japan. This is partly a result of the problem the disclosure of historical materials, but it is also because the transition from the modern to the contemporary period has rarely been the subject of historical analysis even in the 2000s. In the twenty-first century, however, the recognition is beginning to spread that the postwar Japanese economy now falls within the scope of historical analysis with an eye on developments before and after. Studies on rural regions, which this chapter mainly refers to, are beginning emerge and attempt a historical analysis of the era of high economic growth by leveraging postwar primary source materials for example, those written and edited by Nishida Yoshiaki and Kase Kazutoshi, "*Kōdo Keizai Seichōki no Nōgyō Mondai—Sengo Jisakunō Taisei heno Chōsen to Kiketsu (Agricultural Problems in the High Economic Growth Period—The Challenge of the Postwar Owner Farmer System and its Consequence)*," Nihon Keizai Hyōronsha, 2000, which covered the situation in Azuma Village, Inashiki County, Ibaraki Prefecture, around the 1960s). There are also attempts to explore new angles for historical analysis, including oral history, by adopting interviews and other methods of analysis of the current situation (Aoki Hiroyuki, "Oraru Hisutorii niyoru Rōdō Kenkyū heno Kōken—Kibōgaku Kamaishi Seitetsujo Chōsa wo Chūshin ni—(Contribution to Labor Research by Oral Histories—Focusing on the Social Sciences of a Hope Survey at the Kamaishi Ironworks)," *Shakai Seisaku (Social Policy and Labor Studies)*, Volume 4, No. 1, 2012).

10.2 Statistical Overview

10.2.1 Structural Change in the Postwar Japanese Economy and the Network of Popular Funds

In 1956 the Economic Planning Agency declared that "we are no longer in the postwar period".[2] The Japanese economy, which had shrunk to 30% lower than its prewar peak level following Japan's defeat, had recovered, surpassing its prewar size by the mid-1950s.[3] Having passed through the initial confusion immediately after defeat in World War II, the Japanese economy was soon propelled into the so-called era of high economic growth.

It was often pointed out by contemporaries that domestic demand was an important factor in Japan's recovery and high economic growth, as was large-scale domestic investment by corporations, particularly in the heavy and chemical industries[4] Regarding how the financial system responded to the tremendous demand for funds by these corporations, it has been argued that the main bank system based on corporate cross-shareholding, loans by the banking system, and the government's policy-based financing or "signaling effect" from industrial policy were particularly important.[5] The strong demand for funds during the high economic growth period was met mainly by indirect financing by banks under the so-called convoy system, rather than direct financing through the securities market.[6] When considering the financial system in the postwar Japanese economy attention has been directed to the banking system more than anything else. The network of popular funds covered in this book has received little attention, effectively going under the radar.

As this book has repeatedly pointed out, studies on the financial system in postwar Japan have more or less overlooked the existence and functions of the network of popular funds. For many years, economists and historians paid little attention to the Deposit Bureau or the cooperative financial network of cooperative unions, despite the fact that they had already, even before World War II, managed massive funds, and supported regional economies by investing in infrastructure and functioning as

---

[2] Economic Planning Agency, "Nenji Keizai Hōkoku (Annual Economic Report)," 1956.

[3] The real gross national product (GNP) in 1946 was equivalent to 69% of the 1934–1936 average GNP (Andrew Gordon, translated by Moriya Fumiaki, "*Nihon no 200 Nen (Japan's 200 Years)*," Misuzu Shobo, 2013, p. 521). The real gross national expenditure (GNE) in 1946 was equivalent to that of 1939 (Statistics Bureau, Management and Coordination Agency, "*Nihon Chōki Tōkei Sōran (Historical Statistics of Japan)*," Volume 3, 1988, Tables 13–10.

[4] Nakamura Takafusa, "Sengo Nihon Keizai—Seichō to Junkan (The Postwar Japanese Economy—Growth and Cycles)," Chikumashobo, 1968, Chapters 3 and 4.

[5] Teranishi Jūro, "Nihon no Keizai Shisutemu (Japan's Economic System)," Iwanami Shoten, 2003, pp. 200–202.

[6] Sugiura Seishi, "Sengo Fukkōki no Ginkō Shōken—'Mein Banku Sei' no Keisei wo Megutte (Banks and Securities Firms in the Postwar Restoration Period—The Establishment of the 'Main Bank System')," Hashimoto Jurō ed., "*Nihon Kigyō Shisutemu no Sengo Shi (The Postwar History of the Japanese Corporate System)*," University of Tokyo Press, 1996.

a safety net for regional communities in natural disasters and economic depressions. However, this poor coverage in preceding historical research of research does not mean that the network was insignificant, unable to grow or function effectively. While it has not attracted as much attention as the banking system did after the war, it is worth asking how the network of popular funds grew and functioned as the Japanese economy experienced high economic growth and as the corporate-sector expanded? The very large growth the alternative financial system achieved in this era, I argue, renders the lack of scholarly attention it has attracted a curious oversight.

10.2.2 Statistical Overview of the Postwar Network of Popular Funds

This sub-section seeks to address several key questions: What was the financial position occupied by postal savings and cooperative unions in the postwar economy? How large were the funds formed by the savings of the general public (not corporations, the fiscal sector or the wealthy) as the postwar Japanese economy expanded? Was the network of popular funds sizeable enough, when compared with the general financial system comprised mainly of companies and banks, for it to be called an alternative financial system even after World War II?

From the turbulent period immediately after Japan's defeat in World War II until the late twentieth century a consistently high household savings rate, usually between 10 to 15% (sometimes even exceeding 20%), was a notable characteristic of the Japanese economy (Fig. 10.1). In the immediate years after the war, reconstruction funds from the United States, such as GARIOA (Government Appropriation for Relief in Occupied Areas) and the EROA (Economic Rehabilitation in Occupied Areas) funds, loans from the World Bank, and foreign capital raised by overseas bond issuances were injected into the Japanese economy. However, about half of domestic gross savings from the 1950s to the 1960s were provided from the household sector, and it can therefore be said that most of the investment funds that supported Japan's era of high economic growth were supplied by domestic household savings.

Throughout the high economic growth period, the corporate sector was the largest borrower in the Japanese financial market, and the household sector was both the core entity forming savings and the largest lender. Furthermore, the domestic demand-led growth during this period, and massive capital spending by the manufacturing sector that drove much of that growth, was financially supported by companies reorganized as corporate groups and banks. These facts, as discussed above, were well recognized at the time and in previous research and became a commonly accepted key factor in understanding Japan's high economic growth.[7]

[7] Teranishi Jūrō, "*Senzenki Nihon no Kinyū Shisutemu (The Financial System of Japan in the Prewar Period)*," Iwanami Shoten, 2011, p. 4; Tezuka Masao ed., "*Nihon no Kinyū 100-nen (100 Years of Japan's Finance)*," Kinzai Institute for Financial Affairs, 1968, p. 197; Research Department, Bank of Japan, "*Wagakuni no Kinyū Seido (The Financial System of Japan)*," 1962, p. 44.

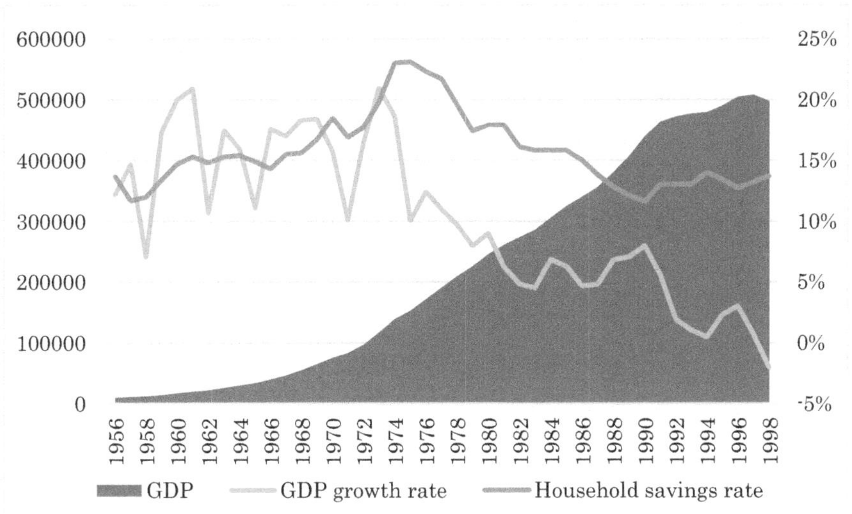

Fig. 10.1 Japan's postwar economic growth and household savings. Monetary unit = ¥1 billion. *Source* Compiled from on the economic planning agency, "*Keizai Hakusho (Economic White Paper)*," FY2000 edition, and the Economic and Social Research Institute, Cabinet Office, "*Kokumin Keizai Keisan Kakuhō (Revised Report on National Economic Accounting)*," http://www.stat.go.jp/data/chouki/03.htm (accessed on September 22, 2017)

The status of banks, however, declined almost consistently. The structure in which the smooth supply of funds to affiliated companies based on the networks of corporate groups with major banks and regional banks serving as main banks and the share of banks in the deposits and loans of all financial institutions gradually dwindled after World War II (Table 10.1). During this period, cooperative unions and postal savings became increasingly prominent in terms of deposits and loans. Postal savings and financial institutions affiliated with cooperative unions also continued to expand after World War II, and their growth often outpaced that of private-sector banks. Funds possessed by financial institutions affiliated with cooperative unions, mainly consisting of agricultural cooperatives and credit cooperative banks, as well as post office-related services, composed of postal savings, postal life insurance, and postal annuities, together amounted to a scale equivalent to banks. For example, the share of deposit-taking institutions affiliated to cooperative unions or related to postal services together reached a combined 29% of total deposits in 1958, just over half the 57% share of banks, but reached a combined 40% by 1978, exceeding the 36% share of banks. Loans extended by these institutions expanded similarly, closing in on the scale of lending operations by banks in 1979, when the high economic growth period came to an end.

In the postwar Japanese economy, popular funds as an accumulation of personal small savings became much larger than before World War II. The reason was that during the high economic growth period, average income increased amid improving

Table 10.1 Financial institutions' share of total deposits, loans

Fiscal year	Share of total deposits			Share of total loans		
	Banks (%)	Cooperative unions (%)	Postal services-related (%)	Banks (%)	Cooperative unions (%)	Postal services-related (%)
1930	61	0	17	77	0	8
1934	52	4	22	75	8	0
1938	54	5	19	71	6	6
1942	56	10	20	77	6	6
1946	50	21	25	88	8	5
1950	65	14	17	70	9	9
1954	59	13	18	58	12	12
1958	57	12	17	57	11	14
1962	49	14	15	53	13	13
1966	48	16	14	51	13	14
1970	43	17	17	47	13	14
1974	40	17	19	46	14	16
1978	36	17	23	42	13	21
1982	34	16	26	40	12	25

Note Cooperative unions = Total of agricultural cooperatives, credit cooperative banks, Nōrinchūkin Bank and Shōkō Chūkin Bank; Postal services-related = Total of Trust Fund Bureau, postal savings, postal life insurance, and postal annuities. Loans do not include those by securities
Source Compiled based on statistics bureau, management and coordination agency, "*Nihon Chōki Tōkei Sōran (Historical Statistics of Japan)*," Volume 3, 1988, Tables 11-17-ab

economic equality in Japanese society and the general public preferred more familiar financial institutions, such as postal savings and cooperative unions, as places to deposit their household savings rather than private-sector banks. Therefore, it can be said that the financial system underpinned by popular funds and its network came to occupy a more important place during the high economic growth period than before the war in terms of the total amount and share of savings and deposits.

Did this network retain its prewar function of transferring funds to regional economies in the postwar period? With respect to the banking system and its fund-providing network, under the impact of the dissolution of "*zaibatsu*" conglomerates during the Allied Occupation of Japan after the war, the network went through a reorganization process, including the rebuilding of the main bank system. Did a reorganization process also occur in the network of popular funds? How much of the cooperation built before the war and functions of each network remain in the postwar years and what new were they given? These questions are the subject of the next section.

10.3 Institutional Continuity and Discontinuity: From the Deposit Bureau of the Ministry of Finance to the Trust Fund Bureau of the Ministry of Finance

10.3.1 The Postwar Financial Status of Postal Savings

How were postal savings and their management system, and the Deposit Bureau system of the Ministry of Finance reorganized after the war? How did postal savings develop in the postwar period? The quantitative financial status of postal savings in the Japanese economy is shown in Fig. 10.2. It shows that while popular funds came to account for over 40% of total savings, postal savings alone almost always exceeded 10% of the total. Table 10.1 (above) further indicates that postal savings constantly accounted for close to 40–50% of popular funds in the postwar Japanese economy. While postal savings were an accumulation of small-amount personal savings, they grew to hold the largest amount of any independent savings-accumulating institution in Japan. Further, in the postwar period, the financial status of postal savings did not decline but rather gained in stability and importance.

What was behind the stable development of postal savings? The accumulation of small-amount savings by postal savings was not considered a threat by private-sector banks as they were thought to be targeted at a social class differing from the typical customers of banks. This was exactly the case before the war, and this thinking seems to have persisted at least until the 1970s, resulting in a kind of social consensus that there was a sort of social segmentation between postal savings and banks.[8] Furthermore, some analyses attributed the steady growth of postal savings in the postwar period to the remarkable growth of the use of the "fixed-amount postal savings" system introduced as a formal system in 1941. Lying behind this was the major premise that people's income increased nationally throughout the high economic growth period, creating some leeway for households to accumulate financial assets, thereby leading to an increase in household savings in general.[9]

Since the government recognized this increase in household income, it set the policy goal of helping domestic financial institutions to hold abundant funds derived from household savings and to help industries to access these abundant investment funds. This was to be achieved by urging people to put a significant proportion of their increases in income into savings rather than spending them directly on consumption. At the time, the government was fearful of "excessive consumption" with the sharp inflation induced by goods shortages immediately after the war still fresh in the memory. In order to induce saving preferences among households, the government

[8] ITō Mariko, "Kōdo Seichōki Yūbin Chokin no Hatten to Sono Yōin—Yūbin Chokin Zōkyō Mekanizumu no Keisei wo Megutte (The Development of Postal Savings during the High Economic Growth Period and the Factors behind It—Concerning the Formation of the Postal Savings Augmentation Mechanism)," *Yūsei Shiryōkan Kenkyū Kiyō (Postal Archive Research Bulletin)*, the inaugural issue (2010), p. 49.

[9] Ministry of Posts and Telecommunications, "*Yūsei Hyakunen-Shi (100-Year History of Postal Services)*," Yoshikawa Kobunkan, 1971, pp. 879–888.

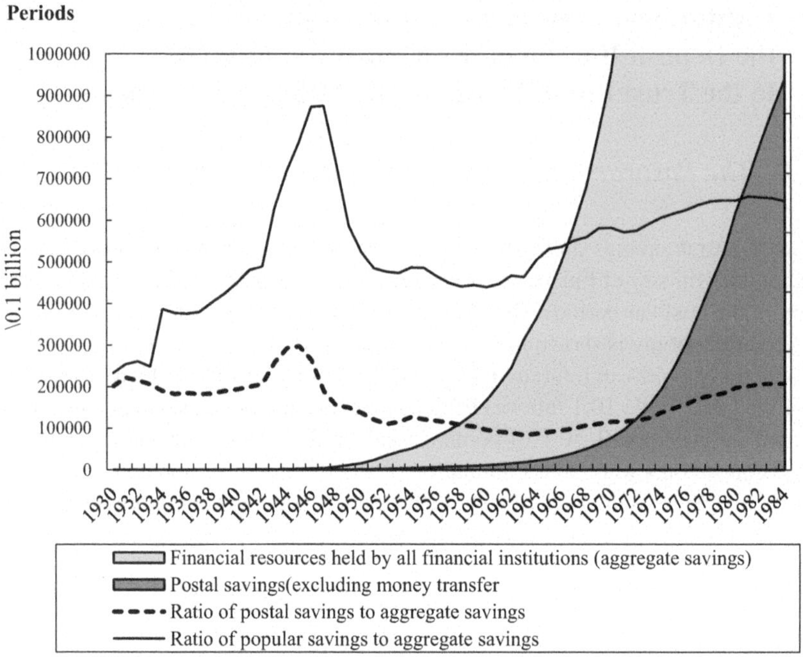

Fig. 10.2 Position of postal savings in the financial market in the prewar and postwar periods. *Note* Aggregate savings = Overall total of savings of private-sector and public-sector deposits and bonds issued. Popular savings = Postal savings + deposits at financial institutions affiliated with cooperative unions (agricultural cooperatives, credit cooperative banks and Nōrinchūkin Bank). *Source* Compiled from statistics bureau, management and coordination agency, "*Nihon Chōki Tōkei Sōran (Historical Statistics of Japan)*," Volume 3, 1988, Tables 11-17-a, 11-15

encouraged savings through awareness-raising activities, such as poster campaigns and lecture meetings, just as it had done before the war.[10] The fact that savings-encouraging campaigns were conducted by enlisting the cooperation of the "Children's Post Office" and youth and women's organizations signifies that in the postwar period as well, savings education, particularly education to make a habit of the use of postal savings, was carried out in elementary schools and in regional organizations. As shown in Chap. 3, the targeting of elementary school education and regional communities had a lasting influence in Japanese society that persisted long into the postwar period.[11]

In addition to the above, postal savings carried advantageous conditions such as a favorable interest rate. Because of "the policy factor that deposit and savings interest rates were kept lower due to the low interest rate policy under the high

[10] Sheldon Garon, *Beyond our means; Why America spends while the world saves*, Princeton University Press, 2012, pp. 276–281.

[11] Ministry of Posts and Telecommunications, "*Yūsei Hyakunen-Shi (100-Year History of Postal Services)*," Yoshkawa Kobunkan, 1971, p. 878.

economic growth program adopted by the cabinet of Prime Minister Ikeda Hayato," interest rates paid by other private-sector financial institutions were held low, and consequently, among the financial assets households could choose from, interest rates on fixed-amount postal savings tended to be advantageous compared with bank deposit rates.[12] An increase in the number of post offices during the same period, or an increase in the number of post office branches handling postal savings, was also a factor behind the growth of postal savings. The increase in the number of post offices itself, following an increase in population in urban areas, was accelerated by a public-interest factor in the communications network to provide postal services to all the people of Japan. Consequently it also meant an expansion in opportunities to make use of postal savings.

This physical increase in savings opportunities was in sharp contrast to the situation of private-sector banks at the time. After the war, the government adopted a policy of promoting the rationalization of the management of private-sector companies and issued a notice to private-sector banks in 1949 and again in 1953 to prohibit them, in principle, from establishing new outlets. While a "notification of liberalization" was issued in 1963, a large expansion of the number of branches never materialized in the wake of a securities crisis in 1965. Private-sector banks were thus unable to achieve favorable results in expanding the number of their branches in the 1960s.[13]

Postal savings, however, did not achieve much growth in rural and farming areas in the 1960s. According to "a survey on the state of use of postal savings" made by the postal savings system itself, when the category of households (which accounted for 99% of the balance of postal savings) were classified into the three categories: wage-earning workers, farming households, and ordinary households, the 1955 composition ratio stood at 48.6% for wage-earning workers, 22.8% for farming households, and 28.6% for ordinary households. In 1961, the composition ratio came to 52% for wage-earning workers, 18.6% for farming households, and 29.4% for ordinary households, showing a noticeable drop in the proportion of farming households in the total. As the ratio of farming households itself to the total number of users of postal savings was higher than the above composition ratio, it does not mean that postal savings failed to gain users among farming households. The analysis of the authorities concerned pointed instead to a relative failure to attract new or additional savings by farming households, hence the decline of the 1961 composition ratio for farming households.

As can be seen in Table 10.2, during the period of high economic growth, postal savings grew more rapidly in urban rather than rural areas. Postal savings officials stated that the uphill battle faced in rural areas was "due to the prevalent use of agricultural cooperatives," acknowledging honestly and without pretense that agricultural

[12] Itō Mariko, "Kōdo Seichōki Yūbin Chokin no Hatten to Sono Yōin (The Development of Postal Savings during the High Economic Growth Period and the Factors behind It)," p. 52.

[13] Itō Mariko, "Kōdo Seichōki Yūbin Chokin no Chiikiteki Tenkai—Sengo 'Yūcho Zōkyō Mekanizumu' no Keisei—Kanagawa-ken no Jirei wo Chūshin to Shite (Regional Expansion of Postal Savings during the High Economic Growth Period—Formation of the Postwar 'Postal Savings Augmentation Mechanism'—Centering on Case Examples in Kanagawa Prefecture)," *Yūsei Shiryōkan Kenkyū Kiyō (Postal Archive Research Bulletin)*, No. 8 (2017), pp. 32–36, pp. 38–39.

Table 10.2 Composition ratio by area of the postal savings balance in the postwar period

Classification		Composition ratio			Rate of increase (times)		
Fiscal year		1955 (%)	1960 (%)	1965 (%)	1955–1960	1960–1965	1955–1965
Balance of postal savings	Six major urban areas	19	37	38	4.1	2.5	10.2
	Other	81	63	62	1.6	2.4	3.8
Population	Six major urban areas	30	33	36	1.1	1.1	1.3
	Other	70	67	64	1.0	1.0	1.0

Source Ministry of Posts and Telecommunications, "*Yūsei Hyakunen-Shi (100-Year History of Postal Services)*," Yoshikawa Kobunkan, 1971, Table 7-5

cooperatives were a competitor in rural areas for the collection of small-amount savings. Postal savings officials at the time noted that "it can be said that since the decade from 1955, the core customer segment for postal savings increasingly shifted to wage-earning workers in urban areas." During the period of high economic growth, postal savings gradually began to segment their operations, letting financial institutions affiliated with cooperative unions rooted in rural areas dominate there, while priding themselves in handling savings of the general public in urban areas. This made sense as it also corresponded to urbanization and changes in the employment and industrial structures of the Japanese economy.[14]

Financial institutions affiliated with cooperative unions in rural areas, i.e. agricultural cooperatives in the postwar period, had at least one outlet in each local government area by inheriting prewar industrial cooperatives. This meant that both postal savings and financial institutions affiliated with cooperative unions remained closer to people's lives and provided them with more savings opportunities than private-sector banks in postwar Japanese society. As people became more affluent as Japan experienced rapid economic growth, all the various institutions within the networks of popular funds, obtaining the cooperation of local schools and a variety of other regional groups, grew into gigantic financial institutions which nevertheless remained close to local communities. This was a situation that was, at the time, unlike any other place in the world.

[14] Ministry of Posts and Telecommunications, "*Yūsei Hyakunen-Shi (100-Year History of Postal Services)*," Yoshikawa Kobunkan, 1971, pp. 880–881.

10.3.2 Organizational and Institutional Transformation of the Ministry of Finance's Deposit Bureau: The Impact of GHQ Reforms

As seen in the preceding section, in the postwar period postal savings retained their nature as an accumulation of small-amount personal savings while shifting the focus of their business activities to urban areas amid industrial and demographic change. Indeed, they continued to grow, accumulating more household savings, in total, than private-sector banks were able to. What transformation, if any, did the management aspects and functions of postal savings and the Deposit Bureau of the Ministry of Finance undergo after World War II?

As this book has already indicated, the massive funds that the Deposit Bureau of the Ministry of Finance, designed as the management division of postal savings, came to manage and the financial function of the management of these funds grew. Already in the interwar period the extent of their scale and importance had grown to the extent that the Deposit Bureau was referred to as "the second central bank".[15] Along with stable management, such as constant purchases of government bonds, the funds of the Deposit Bureau had a variety of functions. They were used not only as funds for the promotion of industry and infrastructural investment for regional economies under the concept of returning the funds to the regions, but also as extraordinary relief funds in times of natural disasters and economic depression. Furthermore, as most Deposit Bureau funds were derived from postal savings, even after reforms saw information on its management disclosed to the Diet in a similar manner to general government finances, Deposit Bureau funds were characterized by a management philosophy that differed from fiscal finances. Here the greatest importance was given to the protection of the funding resources.

World War II and the subsequent period of Allied occupation were unprecedented periods of institutional transformation in Japan's politics and economy. How much did the functions of the Deposit Bureau system remain after such dramatic periods of change in the Japanese economy? To jump to the conclusion, the Deposit Bureau still managed postal savings after war's end, though it had undergone a name change becoming the Trust Fund Bureau, and it certainly inherited many of its prewar functions. Indeed, even after postal savings were removed from government management under the privatization of postal services, the basic management policy and system continue to exist in the twenty-first century as part of the Japanese government's Fiscal Investment and Loan Program (FILP). However, with Japan's industrial and social structure changing so drastically in the era of high economic growth, it is assumed that the role required of the management of postal savings naturally changed as well. What functions were the government-controlled postal savings required to (an actually) perform in the rapidly changing postwar economy?

---

[15] Asai Yoshio, "Dokusen Kakuritsuki no Kinyū Kōzō (The Financial Structure in the Period of Monopoly Establishment)," Ishii Kanji et al., "*Kindai Nihon Keizai Shi wo Manabu—Ge (Learning the History of the Japanese Economy in the Modern Period—Volume 2)*, Yuhikaku Publishing, 1977.

Preceding studies on the prewar Deposit Bureau are limited, and the same is true of the postwar Trust Fund Bureau system. While there is an accumulation of contemporary analyses of the present situation with respect to the FILP as the Trust Fund Bureau system was incorporated into this program, there are few studies that examine the transition from the prewar Deposit Bureau system to the Trust Fund Bureau and whether there was much continuity in the process.[16] In terms of the task set for this book in particular, several questions remain to be considered. How did the "regional funds" built before the war for Deposit Bureau funds, that is the financial network of popular funds, in coordination with financial institutions affiliated with cooperative unions, perform and function in the postwar period? What role did they play amid the Japanese economy's postwar recovery and subsequent rapid growth? This section first provides an overview of the management policy for Deposit Bureau funds and aspects of institutional change that took place from World War II and under the Allied Occupation. Under the Japanese government's wartime policy and under GHQ (General Headquarters of the Allied Powers), the Deposit Bureau underwent several institutional transformations. Understanding these institutional transitions is essential to grasp the function of the Deposit Bureau in the postwar period.

In the 1930s, when rural areas suffered multiple depressions, Deposit Bureau funds came to be proactively used for various measures to deal with unemployment and for the promotion of regional economies.[17] Also, in response to major natural disasters that occurred successively during the same period, including the Great Kanto Earthquake of 1923 and the Shōwa Sanriku Tsunami of 1933, the Deposit Bureau provided massive reconstruction funds. In providing these funds to affected areas, the bureau took steps to ensure closer cooperation with local organizations such as industrial cooperatives. The development of these systems made it possible to supply funds through effective small-amount financing to actual local sites in

---

[16] Denda Isao, "Shikin Unyōbu Ron (The Theory of the Trust Fund Bureau)," *Hikone Ronsō*, Volume 240, 1986. Yanagase Kōzō, "Senryōka Nihon Zaisei no 'Gōrika' Katei to Zaisei Tōyūshi—Sengo Nihon no Zaisei Tōyūshi Seido no Keisei Katei (1) (The 'Rationalization' Process of Japan's Public Finance under the Occupation and the Fiscal Investment and Loan Program—The Formation Process of the Fiscal Investment and Loan Program in Postwar Japan (1)," *Keizai Ronsō* (Kyoto University), Volume 108, No. 1, July 1971. Yanagase Kōzō, "Kaigin, Yugin, Shikin Unyōbu Seido no Keisei no Jijō to Sono Yakuwari—Sengo Nihon no Zaisei Tōyūshi Seido no Keisei Katei (2) (Circumstances Leading to the Formation of the Japan Development Bank, Export-Import Bank of Japan and the Fiscal Investment and Loan Program—The Formation Process of the Fiscal Investment and Loan Program in Postwar Japan (2)," *Keizai Ronsō* (Kyoto University), Volume 108, No. 2, August 1971. Yamada Hirofumi, "Kokusai Shōka Kōzō no Hikaku Bunseki—Kokusai Shōka ni Okeru Senzen, Sengo no Nichigin Shinyō to Shikin Unyōbu (Yokinbu) Shikin (Comparative Analysis of the Government Bond Absorption Structure—Prewar and Postwar Bank of Japan Credit for the Absorption of Government Bonds and the Trust Fund Bureau (Deposit Bureau) Funds," *Shoken Keizai (Economic Studies of Securities)*, No. 153, 1985. Takehara Norio, "Shōwa 30 Nendai Kōdō Seichō Ka no Shikin Unyōbu (The Trust Fund Bureau during the High Economic Growth Period in the Decade from 1955)," *Shokei Ronsō (Commerce and Economic Debate)* (Osaka Gakuin University), Volume 7, No. 1, 1981.

[17] Kase Kazutoshi, "*Senzen Nihon no Shitsugyō Taisaku—Kyūsai-gata Kōkyō Doboku Jigyō no Shiteki Bunseki (Measures to Counter Unemployment in Prewar Japan—The Historical Analysis of Relief-Oriented Public Civil Engineering Works)*," Nihon Keizai Hyōronsha, 1998.

regional economies and at the household level, as the previous chapters in this book have shown.

As the government moved to an all-out war footing after the outbreak of the Sino-Japanese war in 1937, however, the Deposit Bureau expanded the underwriting of wartime government bonds and cut back on the return of funds to the regions. Preceding studies have focused on this function of the Deposit Bureau during wartime and have come to see it as the principal function of the Deposit Bureau of the Ministry of Finance in the prewar period. That is, the Deposit Bureau has been largely regarded as an institution that primarily functioned for the absorption of government bonds. Deposit Bureau funds were indeed utilized as a funding source for the conduct of the war by the Japanese government, providing an unrivalled fund for the purchasing of wartime government bonds.[18]

Consequently, after the war, the Allied occupation forces considered the Deposit Bureau to had been part of the Japanese war machine. Thus, as the occupation forces pursued a policy of democratization and demilitarization in Japan, GHQ remained wary of the existence of the Deposit Bureau. However, GHQ came to recognize that the presence of the Deposit Bureau system itself was essential for the management of the massive postal savings funds and so tentatively the Deposit Bureau continued to exist under the occupation, though the management of the funds was subjected to significant restrictions.

Under ESS/FI, "Concerning Management Plans for the Deposit Bureau Funds as well as Postal Life Insurance and Postal Annuities," issued to the Minister of Finance by on January 29, 1946, the Economic and Scientific Section (ESS) of the General Headquarters of the Allied Powers ordered that "Going forward, the Deposit Bureau must not invest in or make loans to government-controlled companies, *tōseikai* control associations, *eidan* corporations or other corporate bodies" and "the Deposit Bureau must not make loans to or purchase corporate bonds of special banks unless GHQ grants approval after meeting the demands of the state and local governments".[19] Thus, the management policy for funds of the Ministry of Finance's Deposit Bureau immediately after the end of the war was not only demilitarized but also reconfigured to prevent the bureau from contributing to regional economies as it had before the war. As the Deposit Bureau's investments were limited to government bonds and local government bonds, it became impossible for the bureau to lend funds to regional economies through loans to the Central Bank for Industrial cooperatives and Nihon Kangyō Bank.

During the war, the Deposit Bureau had already ceased, in principle, to provide any new funds to the Central Bank for Industrial cooperatives or Nihon Kangyō Bank after 1937. It was certain that as of 1941, ¥7.4 billion, or over 80% of ¥8.8 billion, and as of March 1945, ¥32.4 billion or almost all of the ¥33.6 billion Deposit Bureau funds had been appropriated for the purchasing of government bonds for

[18] Yamada Hirofumi, "Kokusai Shōka Kōzō no Hikaku Bunseki (Comparative Analysis of the Government Bond Absorption Structure)".

[19] Financial Bureau, Ministry of Finance, "*Hi Shikin Unyōbu Seido Gaisetsu (Confidential: An Overview of the Trust Fund Bureau System),*" 1955, p. 78.

military spending.[20] Nevertheless, despite this wartime situation, no institutional element existed that prohibited the Deposit Bureau from recycling funds to regional economies. Considering these points, it can be said that it was the GHQ directive that, in effect, recognized and stipulated that the Deposit Bureau was an organization that functioned to absorb government bonds. In this way the Deposit Bureau of the Ministry of Finance lost the function that had led it to be referred to as the second central bank, and it no longer formed the core of the network of popular funds that had been built up in the interwar period and which provided funds in times of crises to regional economies.

This change in the institutional design and limitations on loan recipients caused some problems for the Deposit Bureau system as a management entity. The implementation in February 1949 of the belt-tightening policy, known as the "Dodge Line" after its proponent Joseph Morrell Dodge, then chairman of Detroit Bank and an economic adviser to GHQ, caused a deficit in the management of the Deposit Bureau funds. Postal savings began to show an increase as rapid inflation came to an end following the implementation of the Dodge Line, a large amount of surplus funds soon accumulated in the Deposit Bureau. Yet there were no appropriate places to put such surplus funds, as recipients of the bureau's investments remained limited to government and local government bonds[21] However, as the source of Deposit Bureau funds were postal savings, that is the savings of the general public, any loss-making management of postal savings meant the impairment of the assets of ordinary people. This was a situation that could not be allowed to continue. Because of this, the Ministry of Finance in May 1949 requested permission from GHQ to permit greater flexibility with regards to the recipients of Deposit Bureau funds:

> Concerning the Management of Economic Funds of the Deposit Bureau in FY1949
>
> 1. ....The Deposit Bureau is expected to have a surplus fund of an amount of over ¥30 billion even after underwriting ¥23.3 billion of local government bonds.
>
> 2. From the standpoint of the Deposit Bureau, however, the bureau now finds it necessary to transfer a little over ¥3.7 billion from the General Account to make up for a deficit under the FY1949 budget. Furthermore, from the perspective of financial independence of the Deposit Special Account, the bureau finds it necessary to invest the above surplus funds in profitable and secure locations.
>
> 3. Further, looking at the overall financial condition, the shortage of funds is quite significant. As important industries needed to secure the state and public interest, [such as] agriculture, forestry and fishery industries and smaller businesses, etc., are all finding it difficult to secure necessary funds, it is considered desirable to provide them with Deposit Bureau funds. This

[20] Norinchukin Bank, "*Nōrin Chuō Kinko 50-nen no Ayumi (The 50-Year History of Norinchukin Bank)*," 1973, p. 86.

[21] Yanagase Kōzō, "Senryōka Nihon Zaisei no 'Gōrika' Katei to Zaisei Tōyūshi—Sengo Nihon no Zaisei Tōyūshi Seido no Keisei Katei (1) (The 'Rationalization' Process of Japan's Public Finance under the Occupation and the Fiscal Investment and Loan Program—The Formation Process of the Fiscal Investment and Loan Program in Postwar Japan (1)," p. 43.

> is deemed to be appropriate when considering that the bulk of Deposit Bureau funds comes from the small-amount postal savings of the general public.....[22]

As the Ministry of Finance's request stated that it is desirable to provide the Deposit Bureau funds to "agriculture, forestry and fishery industries and smaller businesses, etc.," the Japanese government, even after the wartime period when the Deposit Bureau had functioned, in effect, as an institution that absorbed government bonds, still retained the belief that the Deposit Bureau of the Ministry of Finance should function as a financial institution for the general public and for regional economies especially.

On July 5, 1949, in response to the ministry's request, GHQ permitted the Deposit Bureau to provide loans to five public corporations handling mainly products related to agriculture, forestry and fisheries.[23] But these public corporations were government-owned organizations created during the occupation period along the lines of the wartime control economy. Therefore, what GHQ permitted fell well short of allowing the Deposit Bureau to reconnect with the private-sector networks of popular funds as had been established before the war, including special banks and financial institutions affiliated with cooperative unions.

In consideration of the situation in which the Deposit Bureau funds remained severed from the financial networks built before the war, in July 1949 the Ministry of Finance again requested that GHQ permit further diversification of the funds' management. Permission was sought from GHQ for loans to the Industrial Bank of Japan, Nihon Kangyō Bank, Nōrinchūkin Bank and Shōkō Chūkin Bank. The Industrial Bank of Japan and Nihon Kangyō Bank were special banks that had served as routes to supply Deposit Bureau funds from the initial years after the establishment of the system for returning the bureau's funds to the regions at the beginning of the twentieth century. Nōrinchūkin Bank and Shōkō Chūkin Bank were the successors to the Central Bank for Industrial Cooperatives and the Central Bank for Commercial and Industrial Associations. These two banks were the central financial institutions affiliated with cooperative unions through which the Deposit Bureau provided its funds in the prewar period. Thus, the Ministry of Finance was clearly making an attempt to reconnect the government-run and private-sector popular fund networks.

According to the explanation the Ministry of Finance provided GHQ, the Deposit Bureau's loans to these financial institutions assumed ultimate borrowers to be "those small-scale farmers, etc. who cannot get loans from collateral funds and/or from commercial banks because of the risks involved." This makes it clear that the bureau's loans were aimed at small-scale self-employed business owners and individual farming households. The management idea of returning Deposit Bureau

---

[22] Following Japan's defeat, the Deposit Bureau suffered impairment losses in securities held and outstanding loans and drew on its reserve funds to cover these losses. But it still had to take out ¥3.6 billion from the General Account to make up for the remaining losses and also write off 30% of the double blocked postal savings. Financial Bureau, Ministry of Finance, "*Hi Shikin Unyōbu Seido Gaisetsu (Confidential: An Overview of the Trust Fund Bureau System)*," p. 79.

[23] The five public corporations are the Foodstuff Distribution Public Corporation, Oil Distribution Public Corporation, Fertilizers Distribution Public Corporation, Feed Distribution Public Corporation, and Food Distribution Public Corporation.

funds to the regions, set out at the beginning of the twentieth century, had not vanished in the Ministry's thinking. However, GHQ at first did not have a good understanding of the existence and function of this other financial network. GHQ simply responded that "our stance is quite clear. That is, governmental funds should be used only for the government and governmental organizations and private-sector financial institutions must meet private-sector demand," urging the Deposit Bureau to restrict itself to acting as an institution to purchase government bonds. GHQ thought that even if loans were for small businesses and farmers, meeting the demand for funds in the private sector should be left to private-sector financial institutions.

In response, the Ministry of Finance tried to persuade GHQ by explaining that small business owners "cannot get loans from commercial banks due to the risks involved," but GHQ argued that "the same risks are involved when the Deposit Bureau provides funds." GHQ was displaying a greater reluctance to allow the Deposit Bureau to, in its view, experiment in small-amount financing. By way of rebuttal, the Ministry of Finance replied that "we made indirect investments with trustworthy special banks acting as intermediaries to ensure that the Deposit Bureau would avoid taking risks," explaining the indirect lending formula the Deposit Bureau had used to provide funds before the war.[24]

These exchanges between GHQ and the Ministry of Finance indicate that GHQ, which was supposed to have conducted an analysis of the Japanese economy during wartime, failed to recognize the function of the financial system of the network of popular funds built before the war by the Deposit Bureau in coordination with special banks and financial institutions affiliated with cooperative unions. GHQ thus had little understanding of the importance of the Deposit Bureau as a financial institution for rural areas and small businesses.

It was not only the Japanese government that contacted GHQ on the matter. The Federation of Bankers' Associations of Japan, a private-sector organization, submitted a "Statement of Position on the Recent Fiscal and Economic Situation," which was addressed to Dodge in October 1950. It asked GHQ to release Deposit Bureau funds into the private-sector economy. As this statement indicated, it can be assumed that as the share of postal savings in the American economy was around 2% of total deposits, an entirely different share for postal savings to that in the Japanese economy, Dodge and GHQ underestimated the functions of the Deposit Bureau.[25] In view of the fact that studies on the history of finance as well as contemporary analyses

[24] Office of the History of Finance, Ministry of Finance, ed., "Showa Zaisei Shi—Shūsen kara Kōwa made (The History of Showa Finance—From the End of the War to Peace), "Volume 10 (National Treasury System. National Treasury Balance, Prices, Salaries, Trust Fund Bureau Funds), 1980, pp. 813–820.

[25] Federation of Bankers' Associations of Japan, "*Saikin no Zaisei Kinyū Jōsei ni Kansuru Ikensho (Statement of Position on the Recent Fiscal and Economic Situation)*," October 23, 1950.

Industrial funds required recently...under the influence of the occurrence of special demands, ...are truly unavoidable, such as growing working capital and necessary funds for rationalization for economic reconstruction...while there is vigorous unavoidable demand for funds, governmental funds are recording an excess of withdrawals over payments and the release of accumulated funds, including collateral funds and the Deposit Bureau funds, etc. is far from smooth....

(3) Concerning the Deposit Bureau of the Ministry of Finance

of the current state of affairs, as this book has discussed earlier, often disregarded the functions and importance of these networks of popular funds, it was perhaps only natural that officials of another country would find it more difficult to grasp their importance. Under these circumstances, as the outbreak of the Korean War in 1950 made the financial difficulties of the private-sector economy ever more pronounced, there arose a change in the perception of the function of the Deposit Bureau within GHQ. On November 21, 1950, Dodge sent a memorandum to the Minister of Finance that presented a new guideline for loans by the Deposit Bureau:

> The source of funds for the Deposit Bureau is the savings of ordinary Japanese people...made up of deposits and payments to other accounts in relatively small amounts.
>
> If there is a certain principle to regulate the management of these funds, it is to ensure the absolute safety of owners of individual funds.
>
> The savings of Japanese people amassed by the Deposit Bureau have been protected by limiting their investments to loans by the government and local governments or public bonds. This should be commended rather than denounced.
>
> Complaints about this policy are coming from those who need funds, not from depositors.
>
> Those who need long-term investments argue that these funds should be used for direct loans to industries, to expand or improve businesses and other similar objectives.
>
> ...Of savings by the Japanese people, Deposit Bureau funds represent the most concentrated, massive accumulation. Therefore, the bureau's funds are usually considered to be a particularly appropriate source of funds for healthy, long-term investments in securities....Recognizing that it is desirable to use a limited portion of the Deposit Bureau funds for healthy purposes other than government bonds and local government bonds, GHQ considered and approved one plan to achieve this purpose. Detailed complements necessary for amending laws must be planned later and decided upon through consultations.
>
> ...The Trust Fund Bureau shall be permitted to use some of its funds for safe and constructive usages that are helpful for the development of the Japanese economy.
>
> This shall be carried out by way of acquiring bank debentures up to a certain limit. ...The absorption of bank debentures means that the use and scope of funds shall be broadly distributed and banks as intermediaries shall take on the usual financial risks and provide security. Furthermore, there shall be an advantage that funds shall be used through usual routes of private-sector financial institutions.
>
> In order to secure a maximum stability, investments by the Trust Fund Bureau need to be cautiously selected and limited under law. Investment of funds should not be influenced by where they come from. Funds cannot be allowed to be used for political usages, other than necessary, constructive and secure purposes.
>
> The primary duty of the Trust Fund Bureau shall be to protect small-amount depositors and provide them with safety and security. No credit must be given to those who are vigilantly

---

When looking at Deposit Bureau funds, while the ratio of postal savings to all bank deposits in the United States is just around 2%, that ratio in Japan is from 20% to as high as 40%. Even in recent years, the ratio ranges from 15 to 16%, indicating that a considerable portion of national income is being accumulated in the Deposit Bureau. Therefore, economic circulation would be inhibited significantly unless these funds are efficiently released into the private sector....

watching for opportunities to use part of these funds for their own business purposes or benefits.[26]

It can be confirmed from the Dodge proposal that during this period, GHQ had come to appreciate the Deposit Bureau's original philosophy that postal savings are composed of the personal small-amount savings of ordinary people and that their management as popular funds should place importance not only on their stability but also as a source of investment as public funds.

The Ministry of Finance interpreted the Dodge memorandum as indicating GHQ would allow, to some extent, a diversification in the scope of recipients of Deposit Bureau funds. In exchange, GHQ requested a legal reorganization of the bureau. In the following year, GHQ moved to develop a new legal system for the institutional reorganization of the Deposit Bureau.[27] Under the Trust Fund Bureau Fund Act (Act No.100 of 1951) enacted on March 31, 1951, it was decided that a new organization, called the Trust Fund Bureau, would manage postal savings, taking over from the Deposit Bureau. Did the actual conditions and the policy for the management of postal savings undergo any change with the name change of the managing organization?

The text of the Act, in part, says, "Article 1—This Act is designed to contribute to the advancement of public interests by integrating and managing postal savings (including postal transfer savings, the same shall apply hereinafter)...reserves and surplus funds in the government's special accounts and other funds deposited with the Trust Fund Bureau pursuant to provisions of laws and government ordinances as well as reserves and surplus funds in the special account of the Trust Fund Bureau as the Trust Fund Bureau funds and by managing these funds with reliable and advantageous methods." In other words, it is clear that this new Act was not intended to alter the basic idea of postal savings management which upheld the principles of stability of fund sources and investments for the public interest. This was very much in line with the provisions of the Act for the Deposits of the Deposit Bureau enacted in 1925 that "postal savings shall be managed for the interests of the state and the public with advantageous and reliable methods".[28]

The new Act also clearly spelled out that when the Trust Fund Bureau incurs a deficit in its fund management, funds to cover the deficit shall be transferred from the General Account of the Japanese government. It was explicitly clarified, for the first time since postal savings were created at the end of the nineteenth century, that the government shall bear the responsibility of protecting the personal small-amount savings it takes care of by ultimately making up for losses with government finances. Thus, it can be said that the postwar postal savings system, with its management

[26] J. Dodge, "*Yokinbu Shikin no Unyō ni Tsuite (Concerning the Management of the Funds of the Deposit Bureau)*," November 21, 1950 (included in Financial Bureau, Ministry of Finance, "*Hi Shikin Unyōbu Seido Gaisetsu (Confidential: An Overview of the Trust Fund Bureau System)*," pp. 92–94). As the original English document from Dodge is undiscovered, the text is re-translated from Japanese document for Japanese officilas.

[27] Financial Bureau, Ministry of Finance, "*Hi Shikin Unyōbu Seido Gaisetsu (Confidential: An Overview of the Trust Fund Bureau System)*," p. 82.

[28] Financial Bureau, Ministry of Finance, "*Hi Shikin Unyōbu Seido Gaisetsu (Confidential: An Overview of the Trust Fund Bureau System)*," pp. 123–124.

rules, more strongly ensured the character of postal savings to protect the foundation of peoples' livelihoods.

Furthermore, pursuant to Article 7 of the Trust Fund Bureau Fund Act, limitations on fund recipients were reclarified and re-designated. The following were designated as recipients of funds of the Trust Fund Bureau:

1. Government bonds, loans to the government,
2. Bonds issued by juridical persons whose budgets require resolutions of the Diet, loans to such juridical persons,
3. Local government bonds, loans to local governments,
4. Of juridical persons established under laws and regulations, bonds issued by juridical persons that do not have investments by the central government, local governments or juridical persons designated in 2., loans to such juridical persons, and
5. Bonds issued by banks, Nōrinchūkin Bank and Shōkō Chūkin Bank[29]

The coordination of the networks of popular funds between postal savings and the private sector, as had existed before the war, was once again made possible. On the other hand, purchases of foreign bonds, frequently conducted as one of the stable investments during the period of the Deposit Bureau, were restricted, together with stocks of juridical persons overseas. Compared with the prewar period, it can be said that fund management by the Trust Fund Bureau in the postwar period was required to focus on the provision and return of funds within Japan, rather than efficient fund management as a financial institution.

The new restriction was also imposed to limit the amount of funds the Trust Fund Bureau could use to purchase bank debentures to one third of the total. With respect to the amount of underwriting of bonds by financial institutions, a new restrictive framework was created to limit the amount the Trust Fund Bureau could underwrite to up to 50% of bonds to be issued by one financial institution and up to 60% of an amount of a single issuance. Under these limitations, from the standpoint of borrowing financial institutions and companies, it became institutionally impossible to procure the full amount of funds necessary for a new business project from the Trust Fund Bureau, a practice frequently seen with the Deposit Bureau during the prewar period.

From the government's perspective, this was not only a measure designed to dissuade the private sector from relying heavily on funds from the Trust Fund Bureau but also an institutional design for producing the pump-priming effect by signaling that the Trust Fund Bureau is involved at the time of fund procurement,

[29] Juridical persons in 2. = Japanese National Railways (JNR), the Japan Development Bank, the Housing Loan Corporation and the People's Finance Corporation, etc., juridical persons in 4. = Teito Rapid Transit Authority, etc. Following the revision of the Trust Fund Bureau Fund Act (Act No. 283) of July 31, 1952, loans to the Electric Power Development Co. were added. With respect to fund management overseas, since 1965, the possibility of the Trust Fund Bureau's fund provisions to the Overseas Economic Cooperation Fund was newly opened. Fund Operation Division, Financial Bureau, Ministry of Finance, "*Zaisei Tōyūshi Kankei Oboegaki Shū (Collection of Memoranda on the Fiscal Investment and Loan Program),*" 1967, p. 52.

thereby promoting loans by private-sector financial institutions, activating operations of private-sector financial institutions, and seeking to reduce investment risks.[30]

> Investment in the private sector [the supply of industrial funds] by the Trust Fund Bureau is not simply intended to have a bank bear the risk as an intermediary agency but also to protect the bank itself from a management crisis if the worst should occur.[31]

As discussed above, the institutional framework of the Trust Fund Bureau, replacing the Deposit Bureau, inherited the ideas of stable fund management and the return of funds to the regions from the prewar Deposit Bureau system. With this prewar precedent as its foundation, the new institutional framework also partially incorporated GHQ's way of thinking that the provision of funds to the private sector should be left to private-sector financial institutions, confining the funds of postal savings and other domestic small-amount savings to domestic management.

10.3.3 The Trust Fund Bureau in the High Economic Growth Period

Following the abolition of the Deposit Bureau and establishment of the Trust Fund Bureau in 1951, the Trust Fund Bureau, together with pensions and other funds managed by the government, came to be incorporated into the so-called Fiscal Investment and Loan Program (FILP) from 1953. Within FILP's institutional framework, the function of providing ad hoc funds for relief in times of emergency was maintained as one of the management functions of Trust Fund Bureau funds. In 1959, for example, the Trust Fund Bureau provided disaster relief funds to the Agriculture, Forestry and Fisheries Finance Corporation, a government-affiliated financial institution newly created in the postwar period.[32] However, while the Deposit Bureau in the prewar period used financial institutions affiliated with cooperative unions as conduit institutions to supply funds to the actual sites of their use in regional economies, the Trust Fund Bureau under FILP was unable to maintain the level of coordination with such private-sector organizations as had existed in the prewar period.

How did the Trust Fund Bureau supply funds to regional economies and for infrastructure development? In the first place, it was impossible for the Ministry of Finance to directly screen loan applications from numerous small-scale business entities, including small businesses and farming households, given the paperwork involved and its own credit screening capabilities. During the interwar period, the Deposit

---

[30] Economic Research Institute, Economic Planning Agency, "*Zaisei Tōyūshi Kaikaku heno Teigen (Proposal for the Reform of the Fiscal Investment and Loan Program),*" 1997, p. 8.

[31] Financial Bureau, Ministry of Finance, *"Hi Shikin Unyōbu Seido Gaisetsu (Confidential: An Overview of the Trust Fund Bureau System),"* p. 134.

[32] Fund Operation Division, Financial Bureau, Ministry of Finance, "*Zaisei Tōyūshi Kankei Oboegaki Shū (The Collection of Memoranda on the Fiscal Investment and Loan Program),*" 1967, pp. 180–182.

Bureau overcame these problems by cooperating with the network of financial institutions affiliated with cooperative unions which enabled it to supply small-amount funds to regional economies. In the postwar period, the return of funds to regional economies by the Trust Fund Bureau was carried out mainly through loans to large corporations undertaking infrastructure projects. In 1962, for instance, the Trust Fund Bureau lent equipment investment funds to nine electric power companies as funds for emergency measures to cope with power shortages by way of purchasing bonds issued by the Industrial Bank of Japan and the Long-Term Credit Bank of Japan[33] When the Japan Development Bank and the Export–Import Bank of Japan extended loans to shipbuilding companies in accordance with tonnages to be built in the building of large ships in the first half of the 1960s, the Trust Fund Bureau supplied the necessary funds to the two banks.

In extending these loans, the Trust Fund Bureau adjusted the ratios of its fund provisions by paying heed to the involvement of ordinary commercial banks, acting so as not to deprive private-sector financial institutions of lending opportunities. It is believed that by indicating the provision of funds by the Trust Fund Bureau, the bureau intended to show that seemingly high-risk investment plans such as the construction of large vessels were trustworthy ones.[34] For the Japanese economy, which had suffered a large loss in its merchant shipping during the war, construction of large-sized ships represented a fundamentally important investment for the fostering of shipbuilding and upgrading the industry technologically, as well as for facilitating international trade.

This period also saw an energy transition from coal to petroleum. As many industries converted from coal-based to petroleum-based technology, the coal mining industry faced a crisis. The Trust Fund Bureau in 1965 provided funds to major coal mining regions for the purpose of industrial rationalization, industrial transformation, and job creation for displaced workers. This supply of funds was designed to "promote particularly exhausted coal-producing regions" and "seek fund management under the lending limits that makes it possible to extend loans suitable for the promotion of medium-sized companies that can serve as the core of regional development in coal-producing areas".[35]

Aside from the supply of funds to individual industries, the Trust Fund Bureau became involved in supplying funds for numerous infrastructure construction projects that supported the enhancement of living standards for the entire population. These included, for example, loans for the construction of various types of

[33] "*Zaisei Tōyūshi Kankei Oboegaki Shū (The Collection of Memoranda on the Fiscal Investment and Loan Program)*," p. 59.

[34] Fund Operation Division, Financial Bureau, Ministry of Finance, "*Zaisei Tōyūshi Kankei Oboegaki Shū (The Collection of Memoranda on the Fiscal Investment and Loan Program)*," 1967, pp. 26–33.

[35] "*Zaisei Tōyūshi Kankei Oboegaki Shū (The Collection of Memoranda on the Fiscal Investment and Loan Program)*," pp. 42–51, p. 46, included in "*Santanchi Shinkō Jigyōdan no Gyōmu ni Tsuite (Concerting Operations of the Coal Producing Area Development Corporation)*," addressed to the Financial Bureau, Ministry of Finance, from the Coal Bureau, Ministry of International Trade and Industry, March 11, 1965, p. 50 of the above.

power plants[36] direct loans to the Japan Highway Public Corporation, Metropolitan Expressway Public Corporation and Hanshin Expressway Public Corporation, etc.,[37] and fund provision to JNR and the Japan Railway Construction Public Corporation[38] The bureau provided these loans to a variety of road construction corporations to help develop a network of expressways across Japan, excavate tunnels, and build bridges. The funds provided to JNR were also injected into the development of the world's first high-speed railroad such as the *Shinkansen* or "bullet trains". In this way, popular funds were involved in the development of Japan's transportation infrastructure much of which has remained a key component of the Japanese economy in twenty-first century.

Investment in infrastructure meant more than the introduction of new technologies such as the *Shinkansen*, it also entailed the direct provision of funds to foster small businesses and their technological development. In 1963, for example, specific small businesses were targeted for nurturing by the "Small and Medium-sized Enterprise Investment Business Corporation" and provided with low-interest funds from the Trust Fund Bureau through the Japan Finance Corporation for Small Business. These funds carried a long repayment period of 15 years.[39] The bureau also supplied funds to Japan Airlines Co. for the development and manufacturing of domestically-produced aircraft.[40] An examination of the postwar management plan of the Trust Fund Bureau leaves no doubt that the bureau's funds were managed with the same philosophy as in the prewar period, i.e. that funds should be used not only for the agricultural sector and for relief from regional economic crises but also for social stability and economic promotion. Compared with the prewar period, on the other hand, the management philosophy of the bureau was more geared towards the supply of funds to accomplish the transformation of Japan into a technology-oriented nation.

From the mid-1960s, by which time the development of high-speed railroads and a network of expressways had ran its course, the focus of the supply of funds by the Trust Fund Bureau shifted from transportation infrastructure and industrial investment to projects that contributed to the improvement of living standards, such as the construction of housing and leisure facilities.[41] The Trust Fund Bureau began to

---

[36] "*Zaisei Tōyūshi Kankei Oboegaki Shū (The Collection of Memoranda on the Fiscal Investment and Loan Program)*," pp. 64–68.

[37] "*Zaisei Tōyūshi Kankei Oboegaki Shū (The Collection of Memoranda on the Fiscal Investment and Loan Program)*," pp. 87–119.

[38] "*Zaisei Tōyūshi Kankei Oboegaki Shū (The Collection of Memoranda on the Fiscal Investment and Loan Program)*," pp. 221–226.

[39] "*Zaisei Tōyūshi Kankei Oboegaki Shū (The Collection of Memoranda on the Fiscal Investment and Loan Program)*," pp. 78–82.

[40] "*Zaisei Tōyūshi Kankei Oboegaki Shū (The Collection of Memoranda on the Fiscal Investment and Loan Program)*," pp. 234–276.

[41] Fiscal Investment and Loan Program Coordination Division, Financial Bureau, Ministry of Finance, "*Zaisei Tōyūshi Ripōto 2010 (Fiscal Investment and Loan Program Report 2010)*" (2010), Yamada Hirofumi, "Kokusai Shōka Kōzō no Hikaku Bunseki (Comparative Analysis of the Government Bond Absorption Structure).

provide funds to the Japan Housing Corporation and Housing Loan Corporation[42] and also to state-run hospitals, the Environmental Pollution Control Service Corporation, national universities, and the Private School Promotion Association[43] These developments also followed the idea that the role required of the Trust Fund Bureau was to contribute to the stability and improvement of people's livelihoods. While the networks of popular funds administered and managed by the Ministry of Finance lost much of the coordination with the network of private-sector financial institutions that had existed in the prewar period, the bureau underpinned Japan's high economic growth and development. It played an important role in Japan's advance as a technology-oriented nation, the improvement of people's living standards, the provision of funds for infrastructure development, education, and basic technological development, aside from the government's fiscal expenditures.

10.4 Development of Financial Institutions Affiliated with Cooperative Unions: From Industrial Cooperatives to Agricultural Cooperatives

This next section turns to the case of industrial cooperatives, i.e., financial institutions affiliated with cooperative unions, which built another massive network of popular funds. In the postwar period what were the sources and providers of funds? What experiences did they go through in the course of the transition from the wartime to the postwar period, and up to the present? As seen at the outset of this chapter, the collection of savings and provision of loans by financial institutions affiliated with cooperative unions also grew steadily during the postwar high economic growth period. This growth was not only in absolute terms, it was also an astonishing relative expansion in comparison with the growth in deposits at other financial institutions. Consequently, at the end of the high economic growth period, financial institutions affiliated with cooperative unions expanded their share of the financial sector in both the total amount of savings and the total amount of outstanding loans (Table 10.1).

Despite the strong growth described above, in the postwar period the cooperative unions that followed in the footsteps of industrial cooperatives faced different conditions. Japan's rural society, the very base of cooperative unions in rural areas, went through a dramatic structural transformation between the occupation period and the era of high economic growth. The GHQ-driven agricultural land reform dismantled the landlord system, reorganizing the land ownership structure so as to increase the prevalence of relatively small-scale owner-farmers in Japanese agriculture. This had an effect of equalizing the rural social structure, but at the same time the land reform

---

[42] "*Zaisei Tōyūshi Kankei Oboegaki Shū (The Collection of Memoranda on the Fiscal Investment and Loan Program)*," pp. 123–149.

[43] "*Zaisei Tōyūshi Kankei Oboegaki Shū (The Collection of Memoranda on the Fiscal Investment and Loan Program)*," p. 151, pp. 167–168, pp. 169–175.

embedded the smallness in the scale of land cultivated per household in Japan's agricultural sector.[44]

With manufacturing proving the engine of growth in the Japanese economy during the era of high economic growth the number of employment opportunities in urban areas expanded. As a result, the urban areas increasingly absorbed inflows of population from the countryside. The number of farmers who engaged in side-jobs also increased. The development of domestic heavy and chemical industries brought chemical fertilizers and agricultural machinery into Japan's agriculture at relatively cheap prices, prompting agricultural mechanization. Furthermore, the eating habits of Japanese people underwent gradual change, and in response to changing demand, the items cultivated in the agricultural sector also changed. On the other hand, under the government's determined policy to support rice prices, many farming households remained oriented toward growing rice.[45]

Sericulture, which together with rice had been a pillar of the rural economy in the prewar period, underwent even more dramatic changes. During the war Japanese silk exports had been suspended in 1941 and the production of raw silk was significantly restricted under the wartime control economy. While raw silk was revived as an export item after the war, the development of the domestic chemical fiber industry brought about a decline in the silk-reeling sector. The number of households who engaged in sericulture as a side business or as second jobs drastically declined.[46]

While the employed population in agriculture became older and working hours in agriculture shortened due to mechanization and farmers taking on side jobs in other industries, agricultural production contrastingly increased. Furthermore, from the 1950s to the 1960s, as prices of agricultural products continued an upward trend, production volume and the income gained from agricultural output increased. Considering that farming households with side jobs sometimes obtained a larger income from their side jobs than their agricultural income, the economic conditions faced by farming households in the postwar period significantly improved. This was a very different situation to the interwar depression and farming households enjoyed the "income-doubling" high growth period along with households employed in other industries.[47] Amid these changes in the social and economic conditions, financial institutions affiliated with rural cooperative unions, or industrial cooperatives that

---

[44] Research Department, Norinchukin Bank, "*Nōrin Chuō Kinko 50-nen no Ayumi (The 50-Year History of Norinchukin Bank)*," 1973, p. 110. Starting from the agrarian reform immediately after the war, the tenancy system and other legal constraints concerning agricultural land were imposed to prevent the revival of the landlord system, and the institutional possibility of large-scale farmland management entities arising spontaneously was completely swept away from the postwar Japanese economy.

[45] Toguchi Tomoaki, "*Sengoki ni Okeru Nōgyō Seisan Kōzō no Keiryō Bunseki (The Quantitative Analysis of the Agricultural Production Structure in the Postwar Period)*," the Association of Agriculture and Forestry Statistic, 1997, p. i.

[46] Ōhara Sōichirō, "*Kagaku Seni Kōgyō Ron (A Discussion of the Chemical Fiber Industry)*," the University of Tokyo Press, 1961, pp. 23–25, Ueyama Kazuo, "*Nihon Kindai Sanshigyō no Tenkai (The Development of Japan's Modern Sericulture Industry)*," Nihon Keizai Hyouronsha, 2016, Final Chapter.

[47] Nakamura Takafusa, "*Sengo Nihon Keizai (The Postwar Japanese Economy)*," pp. 215–217.

had existed in rural areas in the prewar period, continued to collect small-amount savings. What functions were these institutions required to play and how did they perform?

10.4.1 Financial Institutions Affiliated with Cooperative Unions in the Postwar Period: Focusing on the Actions of the Central Bank for Cooperatives

This section examines the financial function that industrial cooperatives performed from the interwar period through to the postwar period, with a particular focus on the actions of their central bank. During the interwar period many industrial cooperatives in rural areas acted as diversified business entities, involved not only in small-amount financing but also in handling the distribution and sales of agricultural products produced by union members, as well as retail operations for fertilizers and food in response to the demand of union members. However, as this chapter seeks to present an overview of the function of popular funds networks from the occupation period to the era of high economic growth, the working of the Central Bank for Industrial Cooperatives is the main focus. This is because the bank offers the most suitable institution to ascertain the actions of financial institutions affiliated with cooperative unions as a whole during the relevant periods. Since the main operations of cooperative unions from the final years of the interwar period to the wartime period were concerned with distribution rather than financing, the consumption and purchasing operations during the relevant periods will also be treated.

Industrial cooperatives had spread throughout Japan by the interwar period and provided small-amount financing opportunities in regional economies, particularly in rural areas. Reflecting their proliferation and given that individual small industrial cooperatives sometimes showed funding vulnerabilities, the Central Bank for Industrial Cooperatives was established with the government's assistance as the core of the financial network of industrial cooperatives in 1923. The central bank came to coordinate with funds of the Deposit Bureau of the Ministry of Finance from around the financial crisis of 1927, and through this financial coordination, regional economies in Japan's rural areas were able to deal with the economic crises in the 1930s. Under these circumstances, industrial cooperatives in various places proceeded with the nurturing of new commercial crops and the expansion of sales channels through individual management efforts.

Into the latter half of the 1930s, however, as the war intensified, the government began controlling the distribution of agricultural products and required industrial cooperatives in rural areas to serve as the terminal organization for the centralized collection of food. The Food Control Act enacted in 1942 required farmers to deliver a certain amount of rice and wheat and legislated the principle of centralized collection by industrial cooperatives. This made it impossible for farmers to freely buy and sell the main agricultural products, and the competence of industrial cooperatives to control the distribution of farm produce came to have legal enforceability at a stroke. But this development imposed restrictions on industrial cooperatives as well, forcing individual industrial cooperatives to suspend their efforts to diversify sales channels and build brands. The creation of a free market for the distribution of agricultural products by individual industrial cooperatives and private-sector companies had to be dropped.[48]

The war influenced not only the sales operations of industrial cooperatives but the management policy of their credit operations too. Savings newly collected by industrial cooperatives at the time were larger even than the increase seen at other financial institutions, but long-term lending to cooperative members was constrained after the outbreak of the Sino-Japanese war in 1937. The Central Bank for Industrial Cooperatives poured most of the popular funds collected into purchases of government bonds to raise money for the military. The central bank later looked back on the transformation of its role during the wartime period, saying that "the function of the bank, which used to have the mission of supplying low-interest funds to rural areas, changed significantly and its most important tasks were now to mop up funds from rural areas and manage them".[49]

As described above, the operations of industrial cooperatives, originally private-sector organizations independent from the government, came to be greatly influenced by the government during the war. In 1943 legislation was implemented that proclaimed industrial cooperatives should be merged with agricultural associations and newly reorganized as agricultural societies. The Agriculture Organizations Act was designed to promote agricultural associations, public organizations set up under the Agricultural Association Act of 1899 as bodies to provide farming guidance with the premise of participation by all farming households in each village. This would be achieved by consolidating them with industrial cooperatives to become cooperative union organizations with a different principle of voluntary participation. Following this, they further merged with forestry unions and other agricultural, forestry and fisheries groups, and the Central Bank for Industrial Cooperatives was then renamed to become the (current) Nōrinchūkin Bank[50] However, agricultural societies as organizations in which local residents were practically forced to participate, were judged to be undemocratic after the war. GHQ ordered that they be disbanded as part of its democratization policy. As the cooperative union system itself was deemed democratic, however, agricultural cooperatives (*nōkyō*, Japan Agricultural Cooperatives, JA) were established in rural areas. In truth, they were not really new organizations, just a reorganized form of the disbanded agricultural societies.

Under the Agricultural Cooperatives Act and the Agriculture Organizations Liquidation Act of 1947, agricultural societies were liquidated as organizations, thus

[48] Research Department, Norinchukin Bank, "*Nōrin Chuō Kinko 50-nen no Ayumi (The 50-Year History of Norinchukin Bank),*" pp. 66–68.

[49] Research Department, Norinchukin Bank, "*Nōrin Chuō Kinko 50-nen no Ayumi (The 50-Year History of Norinchukin Bank),*" p. 77.

[50] Research Department, Norinchukin Bank, "*Nōrin Chuō Kinko 50-nen no Ayumi (The 50-Year History of Norinchukin Bank),*" pp. 93–94.

disposing of the bad assets incurred during the wartime. Agricultural cooperatives were launched in the form of new cooperative unions that inherited the assets of agricultural societies excluding nonperforming assets. Most of the liabilities incurred by agricultural societies across Japan did not result from the managerial failures of individual agricultural societies, rather they largely stemmed from the fact that government bonds as well as corporate bonds of government-affiliated financial institutions and government-controlled companies related to distribution, which agricultural societies were asked to buy and support, became "closure assets" after the war. The government extended no assistance for the disposal of these assets or the inauguration of agricultural cooperatives.[51] In this way, industrial cooperatives (i.e. prewar cooperative union organizations) were temporarily forced to accept the mandatory participation of residents in rural areas across the country during the wartime period and undertook activities as cooperative organizations at the end of the governmental line in terms of distribution and finance. At war's end, however, the government provided no assistance. Nevertheless, agricultural societies inherited fixed assets such as their union membership, they organizations and retail outlets they had built up previously, and they could be regrouped as agricultural cooperatives independent of the government.

Following the legal and institutional reorganization and the disposal of liabilities during wartime, the financial operations of agricultural cooperatives already in 1946 "were rapidly transformed as the supplier of funds to agricultural, forestry and fisheries sectors from the fund-absorptive nature that had existed since the wartime period." The role as an organization to cooperate with the government in the purchasing of government bonds was abandoned at the end of the war, and the financial network of cooperative unions in Japan, or the so-called cooperative financing, was promptly restored as a network of non-profit private-sector financial institutions with its original mission of collecting and managing popular funds for regional economies.

As explained in the preceding section, however, as of 1946, as the Deposit Bureau of the Ministry of Finance, under GHQ instructions, was prohibited from extending loans other than the provision of funds to the government and local governments through the underwriting of government bonds and local government bonds, the linkages between the dual networks of popular funds built during the prewar period by financial institutions affiliated with cooperative unions on the one hand, and postal savings on the other, remained severed. The regionally-based financial networks, which enabled public–private cooperation in meeting the financial needs of regional communities smoothly and promptly with postal savings, directing funds from across the country to government institutions and providing funds to financial institutions affiliated with cooperative unions, were shredded. Because of this situation, from 1946 to 1947, Nōrinchūkin Bank, the central financial organization of agricultural cooperatives, was forced to supply funds to rural regions with only its own funds accumulated within agricultural cooperatives available. Nōrinchūkin's loans included

[51] Research Department, Norinchukin Bank, "*Nōrin Chuō Kinko 50-nen no Ayumi (The 50-Year History of Norinchukin Bank)*," p. 111.

large-scale lending to Shōkō Chūkin Bank, the central organization of another line of financial institutions affiliated with cooperative banks. This was caried out to relieve Shōkō Chūkin's funding difficulties and for lending to agricultural cooperative unions and fisheries cooperatives for new investments in projects needed for recovery from the war.

On the severed cooperation with the Deposit Bureau, Nōrinchūkin Bank lamented "losing the source of long-term, low-interest funds the bank had used since its establishment", which it felt was "a heavy blow to the bank during the subsequent period of tight funding." During the initial period of confusion right after war's end, farming households were unable to make investments amid the rising prices of agricultural products and material shortages. While the agricultural sector had a fund surplus during this period, various loans to regional economies and small-scale business entities were funded with Nōrinchūkin's funds on hand, or funds collected from agricultural cooperatives in each respective region. Clearly financial institutions affiliated with cooperative unions had sources of funds and organizational bases to supply the necessary funds to regional economies on their own even after their financial ties were severed with the Deposit Bureau, which was virtually a state-run financial institution holding the mass of postal savings collected from across the country. Furthermore, financial institutions affiliated with cooperative unions were able to maintain a management policy that provided funds to small business owners (often farmers) in their regions, even in the initial postwar chaos.[52]

On the other hand, they continued to explore renewed cooperation with government-affiliated funds. One of the specific actions to that end was the underwriting of Nōrinchūkin Bank bonds by the Reconstruction Finance Corporation. With this lending as the source of funds, Nōrinchūkin provided medium- and long-term loans to cooperative unions under its aegis for the recovery of agriculture, forestry and fisheries. Loans amounting to ¥2.1 billion during FY1948 were set to continue in subsequent years, but were suspended in 1949 because of the Dodge Line. Despite the suspension, however, the loans from the corporation played an important role as Nōrinchūkin recalled that "the corporation's loans pioneered the way for medium- and long-term loans for the agriculture and fisheries sectors that had completely dried up due to the suspension of funds from the Deposit Bureau and other reasons, even though there was an enormous need for funds in the postwar period".[53]

Finally, in December 1950, the underwriting of bonds issued by Nōrinchūkin by the Deposit Bureau, or the fund supply route that existed in the prewar period, made a comeback. However, this underwriting was only for a portion of bonds issued at the time. "Until then, all bonds issued by Nōrinchūkin were underwritten by the Deposit Bureau of the Ministry of Finance or the Reconstruction Finance Corporation as low-interest long-term bonds. After the reopening of underwriting, however, the bank's bonds were issued as a public offering in the market, in principle, a major departure

[52] Research Department, Norinchukin Bank, "*Nōrin Chuō Kinko 50-nen no Ayumi (The 50-Year History of Norinchukin Bank),*" pp. 106–111.

[53] Research Department, Norinchukin Bank, "*Nōrin Chuō Kinko 50-nen no Ayumi (The 50-Year History of Norinchukin Bank),*" p. 116, p. 134.

from previous offerings." In addition, issuance terms differed from those set during the prewar period. Interest rates, for example, were no longer as low as they had been before the war.[54]

As described above, after 1951, when the Deposit Bureau of the Ministry of Finance was renamed the Trust Fund Bureau, it officially became possible, institutionally speaking, for the new bureau to provide funds to Nōrinchūkin Bank and other financial institutions affiliated with cooperative unions. However, the new system neither reopened the way for the total amount of bonds issued to be underwritten, as they had been before the war, nor allowed noticeably lower interest rates. Thus, the close cooperation between the two types of networks of popular funds that existed during the prewar period did not revive.

It can also be said that, unlike the prewar era, in the postwar period the two networks of popular funds, i.e., postal savings and financial institutions affiliated with cooperative unions, came to undertake relatively independent operations, with the Trust Fund Bureau refraining from newly underwriting ordinary bank debentures in and after 1955. During the interwar depressions, the financial network of cooperative unions received funds from the Deposit Bureau, and in wartime, financial institutions affiliated with cooperative unions supplied funds to the government. In the postwar period, the direct financial links between these two networks was limited.

However, despite the absence of financial assistance, including preferential treatment, by government-affiliated financial institutions, financial institutions affiliated with cooperative unions continued to receive government requests to provide financial assistance to the regions. When natural disasters, including typhoons and frost damage, occurred in succession from 1953 to 1954, regional economies called for relief financing, and financial institutions affiliated with cooperative unions provided damage-relief loans amounting to ¥48.7 billion. It was reported that "the government asked the network of cooperative unions to procure all funds for disaster-relief loans on their own." For the restoration from disasters, the government adopted the stance that cooperative unions, even without any funds supplied by the government, were supposed to respond to compelling demands in the regions. In fact, cooperative unions did respond. Nōrinchūkin Bank, as the central financial institution for agricultural cooperatives and fisheries cooperatives, collected funds from agricultural cooperatives in regions not affected by natural disasters and provided relief loans to agricultural cooperatives in affected regions that required support funds.[55]

---

[54] Research Department, Norinchukin Bank, "*Nōrin Chuō Kinko 50-nen no Ayumi (The 50-Year History of Norinchukin Bank)*," p. 129.

[55] Research Department, Norinchukin Bank, "*Nōrin Chuō Kinko 50-nen no Ayumi (The 50-Year History of Norinchukin Bank)*," pp. 129–130.

10.4.2 The New Development of Financial Functions of Agricultural Cooperatives

As Japan was entering the high economic growth period, industrial cooperatives in rural areas were reorganized as agricultural cooperatives. They began to function again as locally-based financial institutions supporting farming households in local communities now characterized by greater equality and smaller land holdings as a result of the agricultural land reform. In the wake of high economic growth, savings in rural areas also grew and this saw a further accumulation of savings by union members in financial institutions affiliated with cooperative unions. The funds held by Nōrinchūkin Bank, the financial central institution of agricultural cooperatives, also experienced increasing growth.

As its funds grew from within, Nōrinchūkin Bank began to provide short-term funds to relevant industries and purchase corporate bonds as places to put these funds. The most noteworthy among these investments was Nōrinchūkin's purchases of ¥35.9 billion of the BOJ's bills drawn for sale. The bills were issued as part of the BOJ's monetary tightening at the time, and the purchases of the bills by Nōrinchūkin came at the request of the central bank. In addition, the issuance of the bills drawn for sale marked the beginning of the BOJ's so-called selling operations in the postwar period.[56] In the prewar period, the Deposit Bureau of the Ministry of Finance cooperated with the BOJ in its monetary policy, but financial institutions affiliated with cooperative unions never became directly involved. The fact that Nōrinchūkin cooperated with the implementation of the BOJ's operations, i.e., the state's monetary policy, from the beginning of the postwar period indicated the stronger presence and financial power of financial institutions affiliated with cooperative unions in that period.

From the latter half of the 1950s, on the other hand, as demands for investment funds in agriculture under private management did not grow as much as investment in equipment by companies in the manufacturing sector, both Nōrinchūkin and the agricultural cooperatives under its aegis needed to reconsider where they should invest the everincreasing funds under their management. Of the total lending of some ¥80.0 billion in 1954, Nōrinchūkin lent ¥50.0 billion to agriculture-related organizations under its aegis and ¥13.0 billion to fisheries-related organizations. In 1958, of the total of ¥170.0 billion of loans outstanding, Nōrinchūkin lent only about ¥30.0 billion to agriculture-related organizations and about ¥20.0 billion to fisheries-related organizations. Some ¥120.0 billion had been lent to recipients other than cooperative unions, mainly comprising short-term loans to private-sector financial institutions, including call loans[57] In other words, financial institutions affiliated with cooperative unions that augmented their financial power on the strength of rising incomes in rural areas during the high economic growth period were no longer

---

56 Research Department, Norinchukin Bank, "*Nōrin Chuō Kinko 50-nen no Ayumi (The 50-Year History of Norinchukin Bank),*" p. 131.

57 Research Department, Norinchukin Bank, "*Nōrin Chuō Kinko 50-nen no Ayumi (The 50-Year History of Norinchukin Bank),*" p. 147.

the main recipients of support financing from the Trust Fund Bureau, government-affiliated financial corporations, or other government-affiliated financial institutions. They had grown into entities providing support funds to financial institutions in the financial markets.

Financial institutions affiliated with cooperative unions that supported the network of popular funds during the high economic growth period not only supplied funds to recipients outside the scope of borrowers covered by the ordinary financial system, they also became supporters of the regular banking system and financial markets. It is well established that the robust demand for funds from the industrial sector during the era of high economic growth period was satisfied by the banking system rather than the stock market. The source of these funds, however, was not limited to private-sector banks that came to adopt the main bank system and convoy system, it was also satisfied by the provision of popular funds collected from rural areas across Japan.

Lying in the background to the supply of funds to the general financial markets by financial institutions affiliated with cooperative unions, or funds of the alternative financial system, was the problem of the emerging competition over the provision of funds to agriculture- and fisheries-related borrowers, the primary recipients of funds of financial institutions affiliated with cooperative unions. The main competition was with the Agriculture, Forestry and Fisheries Finance Public Corporation, whose main source of funding was the Trust Fund Bureau, i.e. the former Deposit Bureau. Thus, government-affiliated financial institutions funded by postal savings and financial institutions affiliated with cooperative unions found themselves in a competitive relationship in rural areas.

After consultations, the problem of competition for agriculture- and fisheries-related financing between the two was settled late in 1958 with an accord that "the financing in these sectors should be gradually shifted to funds affiliated with cooperative unions".[58] After classifying the Agriculture, Forestry and Fisheries Finance Public Corporation and Nōrinchūkin Bank into two different networks of "institutional finance" and "finance affiliated with cooperative unions," the Trust Fund Bureau in 1961 continued to consult over the supply of Trust Fund Bureau funds to these two systems. While leaving the supply of funds to local sites to cooperative unions, the Trust Fund Bureau explained that the bureau itself would provide funds in cases in which the financial network of cooperative unions did not extend, confirming its policy of continuing to offer funds to agriculture- and fisheries-related sectors from the old Deposit Bureau funds.

The competitive relationship stemmed from the impact of institutional changes to the Trust Fund Bureau. While the Trust Fund Bureau recognized the supply of regional funds for the sectors related to agriculture, forestry and fisheries, one of the raisons d'être of the Deposit Bureau system, the bureau lost all specific routes or contact points to directly provide its funds to actual local sites other than through

[58] Research Department, Norinchukin Bank, "*Nōrin Chuō Kinko 50-nen no Ayumi (The 50-Year History of Norinchukin Bank)*," pp. 147–149.

government-affiliated financial corporations as the Deposit Bureau was reorganized into the Trust Fund Bureau.

Consultations within the bureau indicated that the Trust Fund Bureau recognized that cooperative unions were much more likely to have a good grasp of the actual conditions in rural areas in comparison with government-affiliated financial corporations. As pointed out in the preceding section, however, even if the Trust Fund Bureau sought the return to the regions of its funds, institutionally it was no longer possible under the fund management plan to pursue whole-amount lending to financial institutions affiliated with cooperative unions. It is believed that the competition for fund recipients and the segregation problem stemmed from the Trust Fund Bureau's inability to have direct cooperation with financial institutions affiliated with cooperative unions, a result of the postwar institutional changes.[59]

While the government adopted a policy of essentially leaving agriculture-related small-amount financing to agricultural cooperatives, in accordance with the structural changes of the Japanese economy from the 1960s, rural areas experienced a rapid outflow of population and the number of farmers decreased. For this reason, the composition of agricultural cooperative memberships changed, and instead of regular cooperative members who were farmers, the number of associate family members increased. Amid these developments, mergers among individual cooperative unions were encouraged in policy and the number of general agricultural cooperatives declined from 7320 in 1965 to 5488 in 1972. The geographic coverage of the average cooperative management units grew accordingly.[60]

The expansion of financial institutions affiliated with cooperative unions as financial institutions did not stop, and agricultural cooperatives as small-amount financial institutions for the benefit of the general public and regional economies continued to develop throughout the era of high economic growth. The life insurance business (currently JA mutual aid), begun in earnest after the war, also grew to gain the second largest share of Japanese life insurance market. While Nōrinchūkin's fund management became diversified, including loans to private-sector companies in relevant industries, Nōrinchūkin itself supplied low-interest funds to cooperative unions under its aegis and set out guidelines for implementing structural improvements in agriculture.

Nōrinchūkin's low-interest loans to the cooperative unions under its aegis for the agriculture- and fisheries-related sectors centered on medium- and long-term loans. Aside from these loans, what was characteristic of Nōrinchūkin's loans to

---

[59] Fund Operation Division, Financial Bureau, Ministry of Finance, "*Zaisei Tōyūshi Kankei Oboegaki Shū (The Collection of Memoranda on Fiscal Investment and Loan Program)*," pp. 183–184. Aside from financing for the agriculture, forestry and fisheries sectors, the Trust Fund Bureau in 1962 issued a "Memorandum on Disaster-Relief Financing of Shōkō Chukin Bank," confirming that the Trust Fund Bureau will "facilitate (Shōkō Chukin Bank) in taking measures for low-interest loans similar to those by the People's Finance Corporation and the Japan Finance Corporation for Small Business." ("*Zaisei Tōyūshi Kankei Oboegaki Shū (The Collection of Memoranda on the Fiscal Investment and Loan Program)*," p. 71).

[60] Norinchukin Bank, "*Nōrin Chuō Kinko 50-nen no Ayumi (The 50-Year History of Norinchukin Bank)*," p. 178.

Table 10.3 Breakdown of the balance of *Nokyo* (JA) loans by use

	Agriculture (%)	Livelihood (%)	Non-agricultural businesses (%)	Local governments (%)
1961	53.1	17.2	12.0	
1975	26.5	28.2	24.2	7.5
1980	27.5	31.4	20.9	7.0
1985	26.9	31.9	18.8	6.1
1990	20.2	51.3	17.7	6.1
1993	16.3	54.1	18.7	7.7

Note For 1961, based on prefectural data at the end of September. For other years, based on national data at the end of respective fiscal years

Source Excerpts from Table 10.3, Morozumi Kazuo, "*Nōkyō no Chiiki Kinyū to Soshiki Unei (Agricultural Cooperatives' Regional Financing and Organizational Management)*"

relevant industries outside the sphere of cooperative unions was that most of them were short-term funds, even in the case that they were provided for industries such as fertilizers and agricultural materials.[61] After the era of high economic growth, financial institutions affiliated with cooperative unions adhered to the principle that they were primarily for cooperative unions members. This had not changed despite their greatly increased presence as financial institutions.

Yet the nature of agricultural cooperatives had been altered in other ways. Their role "as financial institutions specializing in agriculture weakened", while "their nature as regional financial institutions to provide funds for supporting people's livelihoods was enhanced".[62] From the 1960s to the 1970s, the main part of the demand for funds from union members shifted from agricultural investment to housing construction. Loans by agricultural cooperatives across Japan amounted to about ¥900.0 billion in 1963 and the total increased to about ¥4 trillion by 1972. Most of this was composed of loans for new builds or home renovation, in rural areas and indeed in urban areas. Into the 1970s, loans to non-union members expanded, in particular to local governments and companies, also expanded. Loans for agricultural use decreased significantly[63] (Table 10.3).

As seen above, many of the characteristics of financial institutions affiliated with cooperative unions in rural areas changed in the postwar period. These changes included: the loss of points of contact in local areas for the supply of Deposit Bureau funds, a feature of the interwar network of popular funds; and the abandoning of cooperative institutions serving at the end of the government's control policies in

---

[61] Research Department, Norinchukin Bank, "*Nōrin Chuō Kinko 50-nen no Ayumi (The 50-Year History of Norinchukin Bank)*," pp. 184–193.

[62] Morozumi Kazuo, "*Nōkyō no Chiiki Kinyū to Soshiki Unei (Agricultural Cooperatives' Regional Financing and Organizational Management)*," Morozumi Kazuo ed., "*Nōkyō Saihen to Kaikaku no Kadai (Reorganization of Agricultural Cooperatives and Reform Agenda)*," Ie-no-Hikari Association, 1998, p. 214.

[63] Research Department, Norinchukin Bank, "*Nōrin Chuō Kinko 50-nen no Ayumi (The 50-Year History of Norinchukin Bank)*," pp. 182–183.

the fields of both distribution and finance during wartime. Financial institutions affiliated with cooperative unions that accumulated household savings grew during the era of high economic growth and came to function as a massive national financial network of popular funds. Remarkably, this happened even without the cooperation of government-affiliated financial institutions. Furthermore, while they prioritized the provision of investment funds to primary industries and loans for the improvement of the livelihoods of union members, financial institutions affiliated with cooperative unions also came to play a supporting role for the BOJ and private-sector companies in broader financial markets.

10.5 Subsequent Developments: The Network of Popular Funds and the Modern Japanese Economy

10.5.1 Summary: Continuity and Discontinuity Before and After World War II

After experiencing the disturbances of the wartime control economy and the tumultuous institutional reforms of the occupation period, industrial cooperatives in rural areas passed through a rebuilding process as agricultural cooperatives and the Deposit Bureau of the Ministry of Finance was reorganized into the Trust Fund Bureau. While going through this organizational transformation, by the mid-1950s, as the era of high economic growth period commenced, the networks of popular funds, inheriting the logic of their operation in the prewar period, reestablished themselves as two financial networks with mechanisms differing from the prewar period.

What respective roles did the reorganized and independent networks of government-affiliated and cooperative union-led popular funds play during the era of high economic growth? This chapter has attempted an overview of these networks by focusing on the actions of the Trust Fund Bureau and Nōrinchūkin Bank, the respective central organization of each network. Based on this overview, it can be affirmed that in the postwar period both the Trust Fund Bureau and Nōrinchūkin continued to maintain the management goals of the prewar period, namely to support and promote regional economies, and to provide relief from natural disasters and improve people's livelihoods. This book has sought to ascertain how the financial networks of popular funds in modern Japan prior to the outbreak of World War II were built and elucidate the functions they performed. It can be confirmed that these financial networks subsequently performed the functions of providing funds for the stability and improvement of people's living standards, a role established in the prewar period, albeit performed thereafter in different forms. Despite the chaos of the wartime and initial postwar period and the institutional reorganizations that took place, the principles behind the network of popular funds remained the same.

However, in the postwar period, the Trust Fund Bureau (or FILP) provided funds for relatively large projects in comparison with the prewar period. In particular, support was provided for upgrading and developing new technology, and for large-scale infrastructure projects, with an eye on the improvement of people's living standards. One of the reasons behind FILP's retreat from offering small-amount finance opportunities, a major departure from its predecessor's prewar role, was the institutional inability of the Trust Fund Bureau to supply funds to small business owners via cooperative unions. In the first place, the Trust Fund Bureau, as in the era of the Deposit Bureau, was just a small division within the Ministry of Finance and could not perform the function of screening large numbers of potential loan recipients. Given this fact, it may be deemed only natural that the postwar targets of the Trust Fund Bureau's fund supply moved toward a small number of large-scale projects which could be screened with relative ease within the bureau.

On the other hand, financial institutions affiliated with cooperative unions that accumulated enormous amounts of funds from household savings growing amid rising incomes during the era of high economic growth, continued to supply business funds and investment funds as they had during the prewar period. These were mainly for the management of the primary industries operated by union members. However, the expansion of demand for funds from primary industries did not keep pace with the increases in funds available for cooperative union management. This allowed the financial institutions affiliated with cooperative unions the leeway to provide surplus funds temporarily on the general financial market.

Cooperative unions provided union members with medium- and long-term funds and supplied short-term funds to the general financial markets, at times also offering support to the BOJ's market operations. Thus, the portfolio of financial institutions affiliated with cooperative unions consequently became one that provided the general financial markets with funds different in nature from those of the banking system that supplied medium- and long-term investment funds to affiliated companies under the convoy system and the main bank system. Popular funds accumulated within cooperative unions in the postwar Japanese economy, while maintaining a degree of segregation from the regular banking system in postwar financial markets, performed the role of underpinning the general financial system.

10.5.2 The Period of Low Growth

Thus far this chapter has examined the role that the financial networks of popular funds built from the beginning of the twentieth century performed in the era of high economic growth. It has shown that even after experiencing wartime and postwar reorganization they maintained their traditional purpose, namely the stabilization and improvement of people's livelihoods. In the 1970s, however, as the Japanese economy moved into the so-called era of low growth, conditions surrounding the financial networks of popular funds changed drastically. The organizations and systems of the financial networks of popular funds, including postal savings, FILP, and agricultural cooperatives, etc., became the subject of social criticism.

From the latter half of the 1970s to the first half of the 1980s, when the balance of postal savings continued to grow steadily as the balance of deposits at private-sector financial institutions slackened, postal savings faced complaints from private-sector financial institutions which claimed that postal savings were "pressuring the private sector".[64] The "*Shūkan Tōyō Keizai (Weekly Toyo Keizai)*," in an editorial in 1981, argued for a reduced role for postal savings stating that "the basic policy for economic management should aim for a private sector-driven liberal economy, with the public sector steadfastly adhering to the role of complementing the private sector with a certain appropriate market share".[65]

Such criticism against postal savings in the 1970s and the 1980s, however, only came from a portion of the private sector, more precisely from financial companies, which were still out of touch with the opinions of users. Much of the mass media, including newspapers, were in favor of people being able to use the relatively stable postal savings and consequently supported the growth of postal savings relative to private-sector banks.[66] The criticism against postal savings reflected complaints expressed by other financial institutions against the strong power of postal savings to attract new household savings when financial institutions found it more difficult to do the same as the era of high economic growth came to an end. In other words, this was criticism leveled at the stronger player in the competition. It was aimed at gaining a larger slice of a shrinking pie.

Nevertheless, criticism voiced against postal savings gave rise to new discussions among bureaucrats and within the financial industry on the pressures that state-run financial institutions had on private-sector financial institutions. While the core issue in the criticism of postal savings was postal savings' expanding share in the collection of people's savings, the criticism soon extended to the expansion of FILP, the fund management division of postal savings, and its alleged inefficiency.[67] In fact, the size of postal savings derived FILP, which had one of the world's largest savings pools in a single financial institution, reached about ¥417 trillion as of 1994 after the burst of the economic bubble. This amount far exceeds the combined balance of deposits at all city banks (¥285 trillion) and is equivalent to three-fourths of the balance of deposits at all private-sector banks, including regional banks (¥553 trillion). Even including the balance of deposits at credit cooperative banks and credit cooperatives, financial institutions affiliated with cooperative unions and formed with popular funds, as are postal savings, the total combined balance of deposits of all private-sector financial

[64] Itō Mariko, "Antei Seichōki no Yūbin Chokin—Yūbin Chokin Zōkyō Mekanizumu no Henka to Sono Yōin (Postal Savings during the Stable Growth Period—Change in the Postal Savings Augmentation Mechanism and Its Factors)," *Yūsei Shiryōkan Kenkyū Kiyō (Postal Archive Research Bulletin)*, No. 2 (2011), p. 75.

[65] "*Shūkan Tōyō Keizai (Weekly Toyo Keizai)*," August 8, 1981 issue, p. 55.

[66] Gotō Shinichi, "*Yūcho Minei Ron—Yūcho Ginkō Ronsō Shi (The Idea of the Privatization of Postal Savings—The History of Arguments related to Postal Savings and Banks)*," Yuhikaku Publishing, 1987, pp. 144–145.

[67] Gotō Shinichi, "*Yūcho Minei Ron—Yūcho Ginkō Ronsō Shi (The Idea of the Privatization of Postal Savings—The History of Arguments related to Postal Savings and Banks)*," Yuhikaku Publishing, pp. 146–147.

institutions in Japan stands at ¥675 trillion, which further underlines the massive scale of postal savings.

In the 1990s, these funds and their management were criticized as a system for "maintaining and expanding vested interests"[68] and functioning as ""a system for making ends meet in Japan's government finances by providing gigantic sums to paper over the cracks in distortions in government finance." These critiques came despite FILP being assessed elsewhere as "the driving force behind Japan as an economic powerhouse" and "the great driving system of economic growth." From around this time, the "*zaitō* (FILP) problem" was severely criticized for its inefficiency. Criticisms were leveled at weak incentives for public sector cost-cutting, the pressure the program put on private sector financial markets, the program's lack of investment effects, inefficient management, and the inefficient selection of investment targets.

The "inefficiency" critique was also cast against agricultural cooperatives from the 1980s, although agricultural cooperatives could not be described as being in the public sector. This stemmed from the generally deteriorating financial condition of agricultural cooperatives in the 1980s. Loans of funds from financial institutions affiliated with cooperative unions in rural areas, mostly provided to local businesses in rural regions with funds collected in rural areas, shrank due to slack agricultural investment. Changing conditions in general financial markets made it impossible for Nōrinchūkin Bank and other central institutions to conduct profitable management of short-term funds[69]

Already from the 1960s the government began to criticize the lending of funds to union members by agricultural cooperatives for purposes other than agriculture. With the proactive expansion of the provision of funds for areas other than agriculture, forestry and fisheries, such as housing construction funds for union members, which rose significantly from the 1970s, the government complained that agricultural cooperatives "are tilting toward businesses other than those related to agriculture" and "deviating from the primary objectives and nature of agricultural cooperatives." Later in the 1980s, the Ministry of Agriculture, Forestry and Fisheries once again issued notifications of warning on the matter.

On the other hand, however, another kind of criticism emerged in the 1990s from the standpoint of agricultural economics. The government's calls for restrictions on the financial operations of agricultural cooperatives and the easing of qualifications for union membership, was seen as somewhat contradictory to "expectations that

68 Miyawaki Atsushi, "*Zaisei Tōyūshi no Kaikaku (Reform of the Fiscal Investment and Loan Program)*," Toyo Keizai, 1995, pp. 10–15.

69 Morozumi Kazuo ed., "*Nōkyō Saihen to Kaikaku no Kadai (Reorganization of Agricultural Cooperatives and Reform Agenda)*," Ie-no-Hikari Association, 1998, pp. 10–11.

agricultural cooperatives, as regional financial institutions, are supposed to proactively contribute to local residents or regional development".[70] The falling loans-to-savings rate of agricultural cooperatives and their relative inactivity in their role as regional financial institutions in the 1980s can also be attributed to the institutional constraints that did not allow agricultural cooperatives the flexibility to adequately respond to the actual needs of regional economies. Agricultural cooperatives were also subjected to criticism from within their memberships and from many of the key players in regional economies. Criticism was especially directed toward decisions to divert surplus funds under cooperative management to the securities market, which had become relatively disadvantageous.

Until the 1990s, agricultural cooperatives had tried to solve the issue of organizational inefficiency by ensuring economies of scale and rationalization, which in many cases meant the implementation of mergers of cooperatives across wider areas. However, this solution "led to a 'distance divergence' in terms of both consciousness and business development between farmers and agricultural cooperatives". The growing sense of distance felt by users from their agricultural cooperatives meant "farmers felt that agricultural cooperatives have now become organizations resembling but actually quite different from what they should be as organizations organized by farmers themselves". Many felt that the wave of agricultural cooperative mergers had been a negative development and had "prompted farmers to lament that they [agricultural cooperatives] had become a distant entity to farmers".[71]

Nevertheless, the Trust Fund Bureau promptly mobilized relief funds for the Great Hanshin Awaji Earthquake of 1995, funds that it could divert without going through long-term procedures within the bureau's system. In the Great East Japan Earthquake and Tsunami of 2011, the first financial institution that began the provision of funds to affected areas was JA mutual aid.[72] Beyond the era of low growth and amid the bubble economy in late 1980s and the lost two decades (1990s and 2000s), the networks of popular funds, despite frequent social criticism, particularly against organizational inefficiencies, recognized their respective roles as safety nets and continue to strive to perform their functions.

[70] Morozumi Kazuo, "*Nōkyō no Chiiki Kinyū to Soshiki Unei (Agricultural Cooperatives' Regional Financing and Organizational Management)*," pp. 217–218; Miwa Masao, "Nōkyō to Chiiki Kinyū (Agricultural Cooperatives and Regional Finance)," (*Nōrin Kinyū (Agriculture and Forestry Finance)*, Vol. 43, No. 8, 1990), p. 27.

[71] Nakagawa Soshichirō, "*Nōsei Kaikaku no Kadai—Nōgyō, Nōson Kasseika heno Michi (Agenda of Agricultural Administration Reform—The Path to Activation of Agriculture and Agricultural Regions)*," Association of Agriculture and Forestry Statistics, 1997, p. 4.

[72] Fiscal Investment and Loan Program Coordination Division, Financial Bureau, Ministry of Finance, "*Zaisei Tōyūshi Ripōto 2010 (Fiscal Investment and Loan Program Report 2010)*," 2010.

"Chiiki ni Okeru JA Kyōsai no Yakuwari—Higashi Nihon Daishinsai kara 1 Nen wo Mukaete (The Role of JA Mutual Aid in Regions—1 Year after the Great East Japan Earthquake)," *Nōgyō Kyōdō Kumiai Shinbun (Agricultural Cooperative Union Newspaper)*, March 22, 2012, http://www.jacom.or.jp/tokusyu/2012/tokusyu120322-16467.php.

10.6 Summary

The chapter overviews the transition and development of the financial system financed with popular funds after World War II. The financial system with popular funds still exists up to the present, and an outline of how it developed through the postwar period and into the 21st century is necessary in order to further understand. In the course of Japan's postwar economic recovery and the subsequent period of high economic growth, the postal savings and industrial cooperatives continued to expand financially. The alternative financial system undoubtedly grew in step with this.

What developments did this financial system, initially built up in the early modern period to counter the instability of the commercial or capitalist market economy, witness after World War II? To what extent were its functions in the postwar inherited from the prewar period, or were they altered- or abandoned entirely? This chapter presents an institutional overview of the postwar development of Japan's alternative financial system covered in this book. In addition, this chapter seeks to reposition the functions and roles of postal savings and cooperative unions in the postwar Japanese economy from a medium- and long-term perspective by re-examining contemporary studies on the FILP, as well as agricultural cooperatives, accumulated after the war by viewing them as studies related to the network of popular funds.

Chapter 11
Alternative Financial System as a Bulwark Against the Fluctuations of the Modern Market Economy

11.1 Popular Funds Networks as a Social Bedrock

This book has shown that the small-amount savings of ordinary individuals, made to underpin their livelihoods, were accumulated as massive funds within the Japanese economy from the modern period. The enormous flow of funds that was created by these individual savings may be fittingly called "alternative financial system" of the Japanese economy. While the regular financial system centering on banks and the stock markets encouraged industrialization in advanced sectors and the expansion of markets led by large corporations, the massive financial network formed through the accumulation of popular funds conversely worked to protect people's livelihoods in the face of sometimes violent fluctuations in the market economy. It acted as a kind of safety net which served to mitigate the disruption that the market economy's sharp fluctuations could cause to people's livelihoods.

The development of these non-bank, non-profit financial organizations, such as the postal savings system and cooperative unions, contributed to the growth of regional economies and the stability of regional communities during Japan's industrialization. It ensured that economic development took place nationwide and became the social infrastructure that mitigated the inherent risks and fluctuations of market expansion. It can be argued that the creation of the financial system based on popular funds for non-profit purposes, in parallel with the market-oriented financial system led by banks and large corporations, led to the creation of inextricably linked financial systems that prompted economic modernization and market competition on the one hand and mitigated social risks brought about by them on the other.

Part I of this book, entitled "Collect/Manage," examined how personal small-amount savings were formed and became the funding sources of a network of popular funds that returned funds to regional communities for the promotion of their economies. Chapter 2, based on macro-level statistics, showed that the savings of ordinary households provided the main sources of funding for Japan's economic development. Japan's high savings rate has drawn keen attention as one of the key

H. Tanaka, *Micro-Credit in Modern Japan*, Studies in Economic History,
https://doi.org/10.1007/978-981-97-6940-7_11

elements that underpinned the country's successful industrialization and economic development. However, the core of these savings was not derived from the internal reserves of the corporate sector or the savings of wealthy individuals, such as securities, it was the growing savings and deposits at financial institutions by ordinary households. Though the "Japanese savings habit" is often regarded a long tradition these days, it actually emerged with modernization at the beginning of the twentieth century.

The growth in household savings saw a rapid rise in deposits at popular financial institutions such as postal savings and industrial cooperatives. These accumulations of savings came to rival the deposits held at private-sector financial institutions, and the continuous growth of these popular savings formed the foundation of the high savings rates observed in the modern Japanese economy at the macro-level.

Chapter 3 examined how savings habits took root in Japanese society by focusing on postal savings which served as a catalyst for the formation of savings habits nationwide. As has often been pointed out, government efforts to encourage savings had a major impact on the propensity to save and the spread of postal savings across the country. Behind the success of government policy was the cooperative and positive response seen in Japan's local regions. With respect to postal savings, in addition to the government's provision of physical infrastructure, such as increasing the number of places that could handle postal savings, but this alone was not enough. The voluntary cooperation of elementary schools and various new and old rural communities through the use of postal stamp savings and *kiyaku* [covenant] savings also had a significant bearing on the development of savings habits among ordinary people. Several factors were likely behind this local cooperation including the spread of educational opportunities in the modern period; household-level opportunities for investment in new businesses, including agriculture; and heightened market instability as national integration progressed and as local markets became susceptible to volatile international markets which made individual households increasingly aware of the necessity of holding their own funds.

Ordinary people's voluntary participation in the savings formation movement was encouraged, normalized, and activated by the various organizations they belonged to in modern Japanese society. Education-related organizations, including elementary schools and their alumni associations, contributed greatly to the formation and consolidation of savings habits among young people. In addition, it is worth noting that it was not only the new organizations that had arisen in the modern period that played a role. Traditional financial systems such as "*kō*" mutual assistance associations and "*mujin*" mutual loan associations that had existed since the early modern period were also incorporated and absorbed into the modern savings system. Postal savings and savings with industrial cooperatives, for which almost anyone could obtain a passbook, were able to subsume funds from ordinary people who otherwise found it difficult to form and manage financial assets and had until that time done so in traditional organizations such as "*kō*" and "*mujin*". This also meant that people who organized "*ujiko*" shrine parishioner unions and the various kinds of "*kō*" turned instead to the use of institutions like postal savings and industrial cooperatives.

What did this formation of savings by the general public in regional communities entail for them and their economies? Chapter 4 examined the case study of Kano Village in Nagano Prefecture and specifically verified the significance of the collection of funds and their return to the regions. What did it mean when ordinary people saved funds locally? What did the accumulation of these funds in industrial cooperatives or cooperative unions (non-profit organizations, albeit with financial functions) mean for the demand for funds in local economies? Chapter 4 addressed these questions by examining the process by which local industrial cooperatives were established and the roles they played. It was found that such local financial institutions were in the first place established to reflect strong local demand for funds and were supported by local people. In the case of the industrial cooperative of Kanō Village, young people who returned to their rural regions after receiving higher education in urban areas established the cooperative by recruiting supporters throughout the village as a means to promote livelihood stability and the local economy. Their activities took advantage of the network of young people based on elementary school alumni associations. The cooperative initially included some influential people in the village as cooperative executives, but though influential these executives were not necessarily from the wealthy class. In this way, the industrial cooperative of Kanō Village was created under the leadership of the relatively young members of the village's middle-income class.

There were high expectations among local people for the Kanō Village industrial cooperative on its establishment and it soon became a favored destination for individual savings. In the same way as postal savings and the nationwide spread of savings habits, industrial cooperatives succeeded in involving various local groups ranging from elementary school alumni associations to "*ujiko*" unions of local shrines. Indeed, it can be argued that obtaining social participation from such local groups in the new system was necessary for the stability of industrial cooperatives in the regions.

Once a stable industrial cooperative was formed, various financial opportunities such as small-amount financing and modern savings opportunities were provided to various organizations and the local members that cooperated with the industrial cooperative of that region. The industrial cooperative in Kanō Village, in response to demand for funds from cooperative members, provided seasonal, small-amount loans that were not available from ordinary private-sector banks at the time. These loans, it is believed, enabled members to make stable investments in the sericulture industry in Kanō Village. The counterflow and expansion of the servicing of accumulating personal small-amount savings as they returned in the form of funds to meet local needs were carried out in ways that were visible to participants.

The expansion of small-amount financing opportunities was not limited to Kanō Village; it occurred in various parts of Japan in a manner corresponding to the expansion of markets linked to the global economy after the country's opening-up to international trade. As small-amount financing opportunities at the household management level were required in regional economies, the nationwide spread of industrial cooperatives was achieved amid voluntary social participation by local people. Amid this movement, the interpersonal creditworthiness extended by financial institutions only to the wealthy class in the regions came, in many cases, to be granted to individual industrial cooperatives as organizations. As a result, industrial cooperatives succeeded in creating new flows of popular funds by collecting and recirculating funds locally.

How did postal savings managed by the central government handle the massive accumulation of popular funds? Chapter 5 sought to address this question, covering the popular funds collected as postal savings and verifying the mechanism by which they were returned to the regions, including how this came to be built and managed by examining the design and functioning of the Ministry of Finance Deposit Bureau fund system. With respect to postal savings, whose position was established as the institution for the collection of popular funds at the beginning of the twentieth century and which continued to grow rapidly thereafter, the government was aware from the start that postal savings funds should be stably managed and that funds should be returned to regional economies, the source of postal savings. Thus, the Ministry of Finance Deposit Bureau incorporated the return of these funds to the regions into its management system in 1909.

In 1914, amid the economic crisis following the outbreak of World War I, the Deposit Bureau provided relief funds, leading to the creation of a mechanism for returning Deposit Bureau funds to the regions as financing for regional industries. These developments came about as local governments communicated to the central government the impact that regional economic crises were having. These crises were not as easily seen by the government when compared to natural disasters and so the necessity of relief was not self-evident. The relief financing of 1914 became the first example of relief funds supplied from the Deposit Bureau in response to economic fluctuations not caused by natural disasters. The adherence to this precedent marked the institutional beginning of low-interest financing in subsequent economic depressions. In the interwar period, relief financing from the Deposit Bureau in response to economic crises came to have an increasing importance as the crises faced in Japan's regions began to assume more serious proportions amid long recessions, structural change and the slowing growth of agricultural productivity.

Before turning to an analysis of the interwar period in Part II, Chapter 6 as an Addendum analyzed the impact of the 1925 reform of the Deposit Bureau in reference to the bureau's management and organization. The reform itself was necessitated after the management of Deposit Bureau funds became subject to claims of political misuse during and immediately after World War I. Ambiguities in the bureau's management method and a lack of transparency and accountability (the bureau was not obliged to disclose information on its management details to the Diet) generated sharp criticism at the time.

With the reform, the Deposit Bureau's management of funds became more transparent, the performance of management was disclosed and became subject to auditing by an advisory committee, a panel of experts officially called the Steering Committee of the Deposit Bureau Funds. Following the advisory committee's report, the nonperforming claims, formed mainly during the buoyant economy during World War I and the subsequent postwar depression, were recognized as policy failures by the government, though somewhat imperfectly, and procedures for the disposal of bad debts commenced. In this way, the reform prompted the government to reaffirm the importance and legitimacy of the principles of stably managing Deposit Bureau funds and returning them to the regions, principles to which it would strictly adhere.

Deposit Bureau funds were not mere fiscal resources; they represented funds derived from the accumulated small-amount savings of the general public that the government was simply entrusted to manage and protect. Therefore, it was considered only natural to use them for regional economies and the public good rather than for political investments or to provide relief to large private-sector companies. This notion was reaffirmed before Japan entered the full-blown depression period in the 1930s, and was held widely among government authorities, Diet members and large financial institutions.

Management networks of popular funds were formed for industrial cooperatives and Deposit Bureau funds and developed during World War I which also saw the first steps toward cooperation. Subsequently, however, the Japanese economy was very suddenly plunged into a long depression. Structural changes in industry and employment saw shifts in the main targets of social policy from rural to urban areas. However, while the population of workers in urban areas increased amidst the progressing industrialization, a large rural population still existed as a result of the development of regional economies up until that time and the enhancement of agricultural productivity. The changeover in the industrial structure during the interwar period posed a major challenge to rural economies, which were also supported by the development of the light industry. How did the financial systems based on popular funds respond to the difficult conditions faced in regional economies in the interwar period? This question was addressed in Part II, entitled "Share," which examined how the funds people saved for their everyday livelihood came to be used in times of economic hardships during the interwar period.

Chapter 7 examined how the massive popular funds of the Ministry of Finance's Deposit Bureau and industrial cooperatives, organizations more closely attached to regional economies, came to form partnership ties. This process represented the formation of a financial network that differed from the so-called multilayered financial structure that consisted of private-sector banks and large corporations with the Bank of Japan at its summit. The chapter showed how the Central Bank for Industrial Cooperatives, established in 1923, became an important connecting point for smoothing cooperative financial relationships between industrial cooperatives, grassroots nonprofit financial institutions, and the Ministry of Finance's Deposit Bureau, a government institution. The Deposit Bureau, though it handled a huge amount of funds, was itself a small-scale organization and did not have associated outposts in rural areas. In addition, the Deposit Bureau had inadequate clerical abilities, its loans involved cumbersome paperwork, and so it was difficult for the Deposit Bureau alone to provide funds rapidly to specific localities. In contrast, the Central Bank for Industrial Cooperatives, as the central organization controlling and uniting industrial cooperatives, grassroots nonprofit financial institutions, had the means to provide funds to individual industrial cooperatives in local areas promptly and with relative ease.

The financial crisis of 1927 pushed the general financial system to its limits and an almost simultaneous outbreak of serious frost damage in the core regions of Japan's sericulture and silk-reeling industries provided an opportunity for the network of popular funds to solidify as a system deserving the name of "another financial system." The responses to the financial crisis and frost damage set the precedent for an extraordinary supply of Deposit Bureau funds to the Central Bank for Industrial Cooperatives in times of social and economic crises. This precedent helped to create smooth flows of funds from the Deposit Bureau to the financial network known as "*keitō*" cooperative financing of industrial cooperatives. As mutual cooperation between the central institutions of postal savings and industrial cooperatives became possible, the networks of popular funds became able to pursue their own responses to subsequent rural crises in a way that differed from the ordinary financial sector.

Chapter 8 scrutinized the role that financial cooperation between Deposit Bureau funds and industrial cooperatives played in regional economies faced with depressions induced by changes in industrial structure and falling prices in agricultural products and cocoons, again taking up the case of Kano Village. It analyzed the business of the industrial cooperative of Kanō Village and clarified the role and impact that the presence of a small-amount financial institution under the cooperative union system had during the interwar depression. The case of Kanō Village showed that industrial cooperatives that provided small-amount financing by collecting savings in rural areas and returning them locally were able to salvage regional economies and local societies from crushing impoverishment by connecting them to the nationwide networks of popular funds. These connections made it possible for the individuals of local communities to receive external financial assistance through these routes in times of crisis and depression. Furthermore, the case study showed that besides financial support, community-based cooperative unions were also able to provide further support in areas such as agricultural management strategies.

In the case of Kanō Village, the industrial cooperative set out a management policy that encouraged diversification away from the monocultural specialization in sericulture that was often seen in Nagano Prefecture. It encouraged farmers to gradually shift to other cash crops, such as fruit trees. To this end, the Kanō industrial cooperative drew up a blueprint for the new mode of agricultural management and provided technical guidance and financial support to cooperative members. The cooperative also successfully embarked on the development of sales channels and product branding. These extended activities gained the support of the local community and saw the cooperative recruit a range of skilled staff, becoming a supporter and leader of the regional economy and local community. The presence of a well-functioning industrial cooperative in a community ensured adequate support was available to cooperative members through access to the network of popular funds, mitigating the effects of the economic depression.

Chapter 9 addressed the case of a community in Nagano Prefecture that was not served by an industrial cooperative, even though the industrial cooperative movement was particularly active in the region. Indeed, Seinaiji Village did not have an industrial cooperative until around 1940 and instead continued into the modern period with the inherited habits and systems of livelihood stabilization from the early modern period.

In Seinaiji Village, it was the "*Seinenkai,*" or young men's association, reorganized from "*Wakashū*" young males, and "*Kukai,*" self-governing organizations existing since the early modern period, that took proactive steps to help people through livelihood crises by using revenues based on common forest resources.

At the same time, however, the case study of Seinaiji Village showed that such methods devised in the early modern period had financial limitations. The absence of industrial cooperatives, and thus the lack of smooth connections with external financial networks, made access to relief measures by the government, such as the supply of Deposit Bureau funds in emergencies, relatively difficult compared with villages that had industrial cooperatives. As a result, Seinaiji Village became one of the largest senders of emigrants to Manchuria in Nagano Prefecture. Though there were no reports of people starving to death in the village, the mass emigration suggests that the village's social and economic foundations were no longer able to sufficiently maintain the livelihoods of its population following the interwar depression. It can be argued that the failure to form and circulate popular funds within the area and the inability to connect the village to nationwide financial networks became major destabilizing factors for regional economies that for long bore the brunt of boom-and-bust cycles linked to the global market economy.

Based on the building and development of "alternative financial systems" prior to World War II, as seen above, Chap. 10 presented a brief overview of how, and in what form, the networks of popular funds were inherited in the postwar period. The major assumption was that massive amounts of household savings were accumulated during the postwar era of high economic growth. Since the modern period, savings habits had been praised and promoted under government policies and spread by the activities of both educational institutions and regional communities. This continued in the postwar period and massive household savings were created in the Japanese economy after the war, serving as a key source of investment funds that underpinned Japan's era of high economic growth.

While the growth of deposits at banks and other ordinary financial institutions was remarkable, the expansion of the networks of popular funds was of even greater significance. The growth of postal savings and savings at "*keitō*" cooperative financial institutions was particularly impressive as they were able to make good use of their embeddedness in the regions they served. The share of funds held by the networks of popular funds continued to grow in all forms of savings and deposits, surpassing the level of deposits at private-sector banks. In other words, postal savings and savings at "*keitō*" cooperative financial institutions came to have an even greater economic role than they had in the prewar period.

What types of institutional changes did postal savings and cooperative unions go through and how were they managed in the postwar period? The short answer is that they included both elements carried over from the prewar period and new elements introduced after the war. During the war, postal savings and savings at "*keitō*" cooperative unions, popular funds built in the modern period, became suppliers of funds for the war effort. Their management policies were negated, and with respect to cooperative unions, even their management principles as democratic organizations were temporarily denied. After the war, however, it was reaffirmed that these two types of financial institution were not organizations obligated to provide funds to the government; they were democratic, nonprofit financial institutions whose principal function was social redistribution by collecting funds from, and then returning them to, the general public. In this way, both of types of financial institution were rebuilt.

In the case of postal savings, the Ministry of Finance's Deposit Bureau was renamed the Trust Fund Bureau of the Ministry of Finance under instructions from GHQ. In the process, it became impossible for the Trust Fund Bureau to lend funds to a business plan in the form of investing the total amount of the capital required, even though financial institutions associated with cooperative unions or special banks. This inconvenient institutional change deprived the Trust Fund Bureau of the previously available means for providing funds to local economic sites. Instead, the Trust Fund Bureau came to adopt a method of lending a part of the funds required for infrastructure investment and other large-scale projects, thereby exhibiting the useful signaling effect of lending by a government institution and inducing funds from private-sector financial institutions to policy-backed long-term investment.

Industrial cooperatives, most of which were located in rural areas, were reorganized into agricultural cooperatives in the postwar period. The relative weight of agriculture in the Japanese economy declined amid postwar industrial and demographic change. The average size of farms managed by rural households became smaller as a result of the occupation-era land reform, but investment funds were required to alleviate wartime damage of farmland and in order to pursue the mechanization of agriculture. Agricultural cooperatives in the postwar period, like cooperatives before the war, came to fulfill the function of small-amount financial institutions for regional economies, providing investment funds to deal with the above changes, as well as funding to meet the educational and housing expenses of cooperative members. However, an expansion of small-amount financing for purposes other than agriculture was called into question by the government during the era of high economic growth as it was seen as not fitting the agricultural cooperatives' main purpose. Unable to find enough borrowers, agricultural cooperatives saw their lending to savings ratio decline. Against this background, some financial institutions affiliated with agricultural cooperatives used part of their accumulated popular funds to extend cooperation to the ordinary financial system, providing their funds to the Bank of Japan's market operations and to ordinary securities markets.

As seen above, with postwar institutional changes, the networks of popular funds experienced an interruption of the financial cooperation between the state-run financial institution and those affiliated with cooperative unions that had been built in the prewar period. On the other hand, however, in the rapidly expanding Japanese economy, these networks of popular funds mutually sustained the performance of nonprofit financial functions under their respective management principles by accumulating further funds from people in their respective areas. Their financial positions actually gained in importance over time, expanding in both aggregate and relative terms, and they therefore provided an important foundation for the era of high economic growth of the postwar Japanese economy. What role did the development of these popular funds play in the era of moderate economic growth in the 1970s, during the bubble economy, and into the so-called lost decades? While these periods are beyond the scope of this book, the principles and functions of the financial networks of popular savings formed in the modern period still can be observed in nationwide financial institutions in the twenty-first century.

In the modern Japanese economy, the multilayered financial system led by banks and the stock markets moved large amounts of capital and undertook the distribution of funds for international trade as well as financing Japan's remarkable industrialization, including the provision of funds for the introduction of modern technologies. Almost simultaneously, however, another financial system was formed in parallel. This was a system that returned popular funds formed from personal small-amount savings which were provided as small-amount financing to support the economic activities of local areas. Behind the activities of large corporations and big banks in the financial markets, there always existed this other system, which supported livelihoods in regional communities. This other system has rarely received attention, perhaps because it appeared to have hardly anything to do with the leading sectors and companies of Japan's economic transformation. However, despite its somewhat inconspicuous existence, this other financial system was deeply rooted in local areas where it served to alleviate market fluctuations and economic risks associated with modernization. In this way, it played a vital historical role in the development of the modern Japanese economy and society. Thus, it can be concluded that this system for collecting small-amount funds from ordinary people and then recycling them to the same people was "another financial system", one that complemented the conventional market-oriented financial market and worked to reduce risks associated with market growth.

11.2 "Alternative Financial System" and the Modern Japanese Economy

The presence of this financial system helped bring about economic growth and stability in modern Japan by providing microcredit opportunities with personal funds to regional economies. However, Japan's catch-up industrialization during the era of high economic growth after World War II, underpinned by this financial system, and the era of more moderate growth in the 1970s significantly altered the social and economic environment surrounding the networks of popular funds. In this final section, therefore, I would like to make some additional remarks about the current position of this financial system.

In twenty-first century Japan the networks of popular funds, described in this book as "another financial system," have faced a barrage of criticism over their perceived inefficiency. The aging population, combined with the diminishing birthrate and the depopulation of rural areas after the era of high economic growth, posed a major problem for the efficiency of networks of popular funds as they were tasked with the revitalization and maintenance of the rural economy and its communities. One of the consequences of these criticisms was the passage of a Diet bill for the privatization of postal services under the cabinet of Prime Minister Koizumi Junichirō in 2005.

With respect to cooperative union financing, the microcredit function long performed in rural areas by this financial system lost momentum as demand for new investment in agriculture slackened. Consequently, some of these funds were diverted to supplement the ordinary financial markets during the era of high economic growth. In 2008, a former bureaucrat of the Ministry of Agriculture, Forestry and Fisheries published a highly critical article entitled, "We do not need this kind of JA [Japan Agricultural Cooperative]".[1] At essence the rising criticism directed at the management of postal savings, or the Fiscal Investment and Loan Program, emanated from the slowdown in the growth of the Japanese economy. The calls for the reform of agricultural cooperatives were also related to the stagnation experienced in rural Japan in the twenty-first century.[2]

In contrast, internationally cooperative unions are recently being reappraised as democratic institutions that undertake vital financial and distribution operations in rural communities despite their status as nonprofit organizations. Many developing countries are newly introducing the cooperative union system believing in the "strength in unity" that they entail. Additionally the activities of NGOs such as the Grameen Bank perform similar functions to the financial function of non-corporate organizations, in particular the microcredit function, and have recently drawn renewed attention. This indicates that in solving social problems such as poverty and social inequality, social enterprises are increasingly being considered in financial areas as a kind of safety net, as profit-oriented corporate organizations are deemed unsuitable in this regard.[3]

Japan's "other financial system" fulfilled its social role as a nonprofit financial network comprised of cooperative union financing in combination with the postal savings-based Fiscal Investment and Loan Program. The presence of this financial system derived from popular funds, established in the prewar period, lessened the growth in disparities in postwar Japan and thus played an important part in creating the social system that underpinned postwar Japanese society, an affluent society

---

[1] Yamashita Kazuhito, "*Konna JA wa iranai (We do not need this kind of JA)*," WEDGE, September 2008 issue, pp. 20–23.

[2] Yoo Jaesang, "*JA Inobēshon eno Chōsen—Hieiri Soshiki no Chōsen (The Challenge of JA Innovation—The Challenge of Nonprofit Organizations)*," Hakuto-Shobo Publishing, 2009.

[3] Dame Pauline Green (President, International Cooperative Alliance), "Shakai to Shōrai ni Okeru Kyōdō Kumiai no Yakuwari (The Role of Cooperative Unions in Society and in the Future), Ie-no-Hikari Association ed., "*Kyōdō Kumiai no Yakuwari to Mirai—Tomoni Ikiru Shakai wo Mezashite (The Role and the Future of Cooperative Unions—Striving toward the Society in which We Live Together)*," Ie-no-Hikari Association, 2011, pp. 4–6; OECD, translated by JTUC Research Institute for Advancement of Living Standards, "*Shakaiteki Kigyō no Shuryūka—'Atarashii Kōkyō' no Ninaite Toshite (The Mainstreaming of Social Enterprises—As Bearers of 'the New Public'*," Akashi Shoten, 2010, p. 109; Kurosaki Takashi and Yamagata Tatsufumi, "*Kaihatsu Keizaigaku—Hinkon Sakugen e no Apurōchi (Development Economics—the Approach to Poverty Reduction)*," Nippon Hyoron Sha, 2003.

characterized by relative equality and the idea that "[virtually] all Japanese self-identify as middle class".[4]

The networks of popular funds in Japan have long been involved in sustaining the household economy in rural communities. Though it was a financial system, it has been deeply involved in the stability and reproduction of the same society that was the source of its funds, instead of being geared towards economic efficiency or financial profit as ends in themselves. Regrettably the economic sciences, including economic history, have largely failed to positively evaluate this "reproductive" function treating it instead as "a given".[5] However, as this book has shown, this system was an important influence on modern Japan, initially a developing country with intense disparities, and worked to provide poverty alleviation measures that differed from government financing or NGOs. The case studies examined in this book indicate that this financial system was able to fulfill the a crucial role in Japan's social modernization by bringing greater stability to communities by helping them to grasp new business opportunities, delivering relief funds in times of crises, and controlling severe poverty through redistribution. Under these circumstances, cooperative unions in modern Japan, within JA, for instance, intended to pursue "the rebuilding of the balanced relationship between the economy and society…by reconsidering the notion that society works exclusively in pursuit of economic growth," presenting the idea of returning to the principle of social contributions to rural communities instead of pursuing economic efficiency as management entities.[6]

On the other hand, however, with respect to the reform of the Fiscal Investment and Loan Program, the program's de facto main purposes since before the war, i.e. the amelioration of disparities and relief for the socially vulnerable, are under review in recent Japanese government trend.[7] When industrial cooperatives in Japan attempted to deal with the severe economic plights across Japan in the 1930s, the phrase often

---

[4] Sakakibara Eisuke, "*Shihonshugi wo Koeta Nihon (The Japan That Has Transcended Capitalism)*," Toyo Keizai, 1990.

[5] It was not only Japan that did not take an interest in the social and economic importance of popular funds. As evidenced by the fact that neither the postal savings system nor the cooperative union financing system originated in Japan, in other countries, particularly in advanced nations, similarly massive personal small-lot savings were often accumulated in nonprofit financial institutions. Nevertheless, financial institutions handling these popular funds in these countries have seldom become the focus of research in financial history. For case studies in Germany see: Jeremy Edwards and Sheilagh Ogilvie, 'Universal banks and German industrialization: a reappraisal', in *Economic History Review*, 69: 3, 1996, p. 431. On the treatment of cooperative unions in the field of economic history see: Philip B. Whyman, 'Co-operative principles and the evolution of the "dismal science": The historical interaction between co-operative and mainstream economics', *Business History*, 54: 6, 2012, p. 833.

[6] Central Union of Agricultural Cooperatives, "Kyōdō Kumiai ga Nihon wo Kaeru (Cooperative Unions will Change Japan)," Ie-no-Hikari Association ed., "*Kyōdō Kumiai no Yakuwari to Mirai—Tomoni Ikiru Shakai wo Mezashite (The Role and the Future of Cooperative Unions—Striving toward a Society in which We Live Together)*," Ie-no-Hikari Association, 2011, pp. 4–6, p. 65.

[7] Economic Research Institute, Economic Planning Agency, "*Zaisei Tōyūshi Kaikaku heno Teigen (Proposals for the Reform of Fiscal Investment and Loan Program)*," p. 7.

used was "coexistence and coprosperity".[8] Economically helpless individuals undertake economic activities for their communities on the basis of their relationships of mutual trust. This is indeed the basic idea of the cooperative union system that has been enshrined as an intangible cultural heritage by UNESCO.[9] It had the objective of preventing disparities among people from widening so as to protect the prosperity of communities as a whole. Popular funds were collected in that way, used in that way and shared in that way. Scholars and commentators, both within Japan and internationally, have long overlooked and underestimated popular funds and their management despite the massive scale and extensiveness of these funds. The time has come, this book contends, to reevaluate them.

These networks of popular funds, such as postal savings and financial institutions affiliated with cooperative unions, have often drawn sharp criticism in Japan in recent years. However, the negative remarks in Japan are not necessarily characteristic of how popular funds are regarded throughout the world. In Germany, which like Japan has a long history of large-scale financial organizations affiliated with cooperative unions, cooperative union banks continue to see increases in their total assets and loan amounts even now, the deposited amounts far surpassing those of private-sector banks. Furthermore, the development of new types of cooperative union banks has been observed in recent years, and these banks are rated more positively than private-sector banks. For example, GLS Bank (Gemeinschaft für Leihen und Schenken, literally meaning the "Bank-Cooperative for Loaning and Giving") is a bank affiliated with cooperative unions, founded in 1974 with the idea of "undertaking social and ecological financial operations." This not-for-profit financial institution was awarded the title "Bank of the Year" in Germany for six consecutive years from 2010 onwards. Furthermore, GLS Bank, which limits the recipients of its loans to "ecological agriculture, renewable energy, social welfare/social networks and education," received the "Sustainable Bank of the Year - Europe" award, sponsored by The Financial Times and International Finance Corporation, in 2013, in recognition for the foresight of its financial products and innovative power. In 2016, it was also recognized as the bank with the best customer satisfaction, outperforming major commercial banks such as Deutsche Bank, etc.

In Europe, as represented by Germany's GLS Bank, the trend has been to recognize cooperative union banks as a financial system that supports the formation of a cutting-edge society and social infrastructure, a trend very much in line with the ideas displayed in the networks of popular funds in Japan. This book concludes with a call for more research to verify the roles, functions and importance of financial networks created by popular funds, that is the "alternative financial system", on a global scale. The presence of such funds collected from ordinary people making everyday efforts

[8] Nagano Branch, National Federation of Industrial Cooperatives, "*Dai Sanjūichi Kai Zenkoku Sangyō Kumiai Taikai Kinen (In Commemoration of the 31st National Convention of Industrial Cooperatives)*", 1935.

[9] Johannes Hansen, *Genossenschaftliches Unternehmertum :Aufgabe der Raiffeisengenossenschaften in der modernen Volkswirtschaft*, Neuwied: Raiffeisendruckerei GmbH, 1976, p. 16. Upon the application by Germany, the ideas of cooperative unions and their practices were registered as a UNESCO intangible cultural heritage in 2016.

to save, and then used in everyday settings within their region or neighborhood, has supported and sometimes saved many of our livelihoods. It is hoped that this book serves as a starting point for others to examine other cases.

11.3 Summary

This chapter appeals the summary and conclusion of this book. The networks of popular funds, so called the alternative financial network in Japan have long been involved in sustaining the household economy in rural communities, with providing low-cost micro-finance opportunities. Though it was a financial system, it has been deeply involved in the stability and reproduction of the society that was the source of its funds, instead of being geared towards economic efficiency or financial profit as ends in themselves.

Name Index

H. Tanaka, *Micro-Credit in Modern Japan*, Studies in Economic History,
https://doi.org/10.1007/978-981-97-6940-7

Subject Index

H. Tanaka, *Micro-Credit in Modern Japan*, Studies in Economic History,
https://doi.org/10.1007/978-981-97-6940-7

The manufacturer's authorised representative in the EU is Springer Nature Customer Service Centre GmbH, Europaplatz 3, 69115 Heidelberg, Germany. If you have any concerns regarding our products, please contact ProductSafety@springernature.com

Printed and bound by CPI Group (UK) Ltd, Croydon, CR0 4YY
01/10/2026
02225923-0014